Daniel Boone and His Neighbors

Writings of William S. Bryan
Illustrated with Photographs, Drawings and Sketches Picturing the
Romance and Realism of Pioneer Life
By Bryan P. Broderick and Barbara N. Broderick

Daniel Boone and His Neighbors
Anecdote, Romance, Tragedy
Heroism, Humor, Pathos, and Poetry of the Wilderness

ISBN: 978-1-09838-373-2 eBook 978-1-09838-374-9

A mirror of the daily life and Exciting experiences of Daniel Boone and his neighbors while laying the foundations of
<u>The Empire of the West</u>
Illustrated with Photographs, Drawings, and Sketches Picturing the Romance and Realism of Pioneer Life
William Smith Bryan, 1846 – 1940
Historian and Encyclopedist

Author of "Pioneer Families of Missouri", "Footprints of the World's History", "The World's Wonders", "Sea and Land", "The Story of Man", "Our Islands and Their People", "French and Spanish Exploration in the Mississippi Valley", Three volumes of Ridpath's Universal History, Associate Editor Encyclopedia America, and other Historical and Miscellaneous works.

Introduction

William Smith Bryan was my Great Grandfather. His daughter Mable Bryan Broderick was my paternal Grandmother, who I fondly remember baking me the largest sugar cookies in the whole wide world. As a child I spent much loved time with my family's Elders and absorbed their stories of times gone by.

Three years ago my sister passed, leaving me her house, spilling over with family history in the form of furniture, oil paintings, photos, letters, and decades of her beloved research regarding the Broderick Family Genealogy. Thank you Anne. Several large boxes contained various items from/about Wm. S. Bryan, whose last name is my first, in recognition of the historical American Pioneer family of America, from whom my ancestors came.

This book, consisting of 83 Episodes, typed and penciled hand corrections in 1932, "Daniel Boone and His Neighbors", was one of the most exciting finds in Anne's basement to date! This is in its essence, the long lost memoirs of Daniel Boone and his beloved wife, Rebecca Bryan Boone. It has long been said that Daniel Boone scribbled down his life's adventures, with the assistance of Uncle 'Ligy. Boone gave these papers to his son-in-law, who loaded them in his canoe and headed down the river, only to capsize just before landing, losing the Boone manuscript forever.

William S. Bryan's father, Elijah Bryan, fondly referred to as Uncle 'Ligy, in this book, lived with Daniel and Rebecca Boone at the age of 16 for about 2 years, while they treated him for a snake bite. He went on many hunts and adventures with his Uncle Daniel. Uncle 'Ligy (Elijah Bryan) was the scribe of the lost memoirs, the stories of Daniel's life were dictated to him by the old hunter himself. Years later, Uncle 'Ligy shared these stories with his son and author, WSB, who so brilliantly compiled the notes for this book.

We have made every attempt to keep the stories as he had written them. Also discovered in the basement were many photos, newspaper clippings, letters, and drawings regarding the stories, characters, places and history in his book, much of which are included here.

William S. Bryan wrote Pioneer Families of Missouri which became very popular decades after he finished publishing the work. It is a collection of stories from pioneer families that settled the Missouri frontiers. An interest in genealogy sparked his interest in the book for those seeking family histories.

American History is rich within the pages of this book telling vivid and "current" stories of the newly arriving white people, or pioneers, and the American Native Indians who had been living in America for thousands of years, and all the wildlife and forests. This book contains vivid descriptions of the lands, rivers, forests, animals, and local red people's customs and beliefs, as related by the first white folks to tread into the unknown wilderness brimming with wild animals and unknown Indian tribes. Bryan is clear in bringing forth truths about the good and the bad in the whites and the Indians. He shares much wisdom, laughter and tragedy along the trails shared by all.

A very important character in this book is Wilse, (WIL zee) a born slave around 1795. He is a hero by nature and I remember hearing stories about him at my Grandmother's cousin Arch's place in Gray Summit, MO. There were many elderly folks both black and white that remembered Wilse. It has been exciting to find so many stories in this book which I remember hearing as a child. And now it is exciting to pass these same stories and American History on to my children and you, the reader.

May the great American Hero Daniel Boone always be remembered for who he was, a philosopher, a simple, honest, thoughtful, caring leader who everyone loved, including many Indians who revered him as a great White Chief. As William S. Bryan wrote:

"If all white men had been like Uncle Daniel, and all the red ones like Black Hawk, there would have been little if any trouble between races."

-Bryan P. Broderick

William Smith Bryan

BRYAN, William Smith. Born on a farm 2 ½ miles N.E. of Augusta, St. Charles Co., Mo., <u>January 8, 1846</u>; son of Elijah and Lydia Anne (McClenny) Bryan. Educated at home under instructions of two elder sisters, who were teachers. Graduated Stewart's Commercial College, St. Louis, 1875. Married November 25, 1875, Nancy Mildred North, of Franklin Co., Mo., to whom two daughters and a son were born.

Founder, 1865, and editor until 1872, St. Charles News; editor of a lit. paper, St. Joseph, Mo., 1872-3; editor Montgomery Standard, 1873-5, and Mississippi Valley Democrat, St. Louis, 1898. Offered Democratic Nomination for Lt. Gov. of Mo., 1900, but declined. In spring of 1865 went to Council Grove, Kan., and learned to set type in printing office of elder brother James, who was conducting a small weekly paper. During brother's absence of three weeks was left in charge of paper, and changed it from Republican to Democratic, increasing the circulation about 300 copies.

During winter 1865 taught school near Council Grove, and in spring of 1866 returned to Mo. and founded the St. Charles News. Sold the News in 1873, and for a short time was editor and contributor to literary paper in St. Joseph, Mo. Editor and publisher Montgomery, Mo., Standard, 1873-5. Editor Mississippi Valley Democrat, St. Louis, 1898. Editorials were widely copied in American and foreign papers, and circulation of Democrat increased from 10,000 to 90,000 in three months.

Founded the Historical Publishing Company in St. Louis in 1880, subsequently establishing branch houses at Boston, Philadelphia, Richmond, Toronto, Chicago, and other leading cities. The branch houses failed during the panic of 1893-6, and eventually caused the parent house to discontinue business. During the life of the Company its publications reached a total sale of more than 15,000,000 copies, those of which Bryan himself was author attaining a circulation of over 6,000,000 copies.

1906 Editor United Editors Encyclopedia and assistant editor Encyclopedia Americana; compiled 10 volume series of scientific works.

<u>Author.</u> (Only a partial list of books can be given.) Pioneer Families of Missouri, 1875; Footprints of the World's History, 1893; America's War for Humanity, 1898; Our Islands and Their People, 1900; 8 volumes of a 10-vol. History of the United States, commenced by Dr. Ridpath before his death, also 3 volumes of Ridpath's Universal History, bringing that work down to date after Ridpath's death. In 1904 wrote for another author a 2-vol. History of the Explorations of the Mississippi Valley by the French and Spanish, to which the Literary Commission of the St. Louis World's Fair awarded a gold medal for excellence of Literary style.

(During the period of Bryan's greatest literary activity he was publishing books as well as writing them, and for the sake of convenience in advertising he issued his own books under other names; he also wrote several books for other authors; and these facts prevented his name from becoming familiar as an author. He is still actively engaged in literary work, and will probably not lay down the pen until he puts on the shroud.)

During one of the great floods in the Southern rivers, he was visiting his old friend, Senator Cockrell, in Washington, and suggested a plan for the control of the rivers, which so pleased the Senator that he introduced a bill making the plan obligatory in future work on the rivers. But the bill was defeated by the influence of the Government engineers, who were not willing to change their methods of work at the time. The plan has since been adopted and is now in operation in all river improvement.

Prologue

Daniel Boone's Lost Manuscript

About 1810, when the completion of the Stone house gave assurance of comfort and leisure, Uncle Daniel began to compile the leading events of his life. It was a slow and painful task, for he had kept no notes and his hand was more familiar with a rifle than a pen.

What he wrote was in the form of data, without the sequence of narrative; but four years later my father, who was fairly well educated for the times, came to live with Uncle Daniel and Aunt Rebecca, in order that the former might treat him for the lingering effects of a snakebite which had been inflicted several years previously. He remained with them nearly two years, and during this time Uncle Daniel had him copy and put in fairly good form the matter that he had written.

Boone carried this manuscript to the home of his daughter (Jemima) and son-in-law, Flanders Callaway near Marthasville, where it was seen and read by a number of persons; among others Rev. James Welch, a personal friend of the old pioneer, whom I knew very well. In later years I listened with eager interest to many of these thrilling stories as they fell from the lips of this picturesque pioneer preacher, and treasured them in my memory for future use.

During the summer of 1815 an alarming rumor spread through the settlements to the effect that more than eight hundred Indian warriors, under the leadership of the famous Black Hawk, had crossed the Mississippi from their towns in Illinois and were moving southward with the avowed purpose massacring the settlers or driving them out of the country. The rumor was unfounded, but it had the effect of causing the remote settlers to flee to Boone's Fort, which was located near the Missouri River several miles below the present town of Augusta.

Flanders Callaway sent his family overland during the night, while he personally loaded a canoe with some of their effects—among the rest his father-in-law's manuscript--- and started down the river to the Fort. He made the trip in safety, but as he was rounding-to at the landing an opposing current upset the canoe and emptied its contents into the river. Thus disappeared forever the precious manuscript!

But my father remembered much of its contents, and often repeated the incidents and adventures to me. Most of this matter, together with the stories and adventures that were related by Rev. Welch and others, are now preserved in this book, forming a new and highly interesting prelude in the romantic life of Daniel Boone.

A Western Palatinate

In 1795, when Boone entered into an agreement with the Spanish Government to locate a hundred or more American families in Upper Louisiana, or "New Spain" as it was sometimes called, it was with a view to establishing beyond the Mississippi a community of Baronial Lords of the Soil, such as had existed for years along the banks of the Hudson River in New York, and to a lesser extent in the Carolinas. The idea of such a Western Palatinate had originated with the Spaniards and was approved by Boone, who knew something of the nature of the system from his familiarity with it in North Carolina.

It was his purpose to surround himself with a hundred families or more of his personal friends and relations, each of whom should own not less than a thousand acres, over which they would rule as Barons and Patrons. Slavery appeared to be a necessary feature of the system, and nearly all the families that participated were slave owners; though always in a small way. None of the great slave lords of the South ventured beyond the Mississippi at that early date.

Boone himself owned a few slaves, though by nature and experience he hated the system. It seemed to him a permanent evil which could not be cured, and his idea was to mitigate its horrors by planting the patriarchal system in a new Canaan, making each slave-holder ruler over a great family. He believed that such a community of independent landlords, moved by liberal and humane sentiments, would be willing and able in their affluent circumstances to institute and carry out reforms better and more thoroughly and justly than could be done by the small farmers of the older States, or by the Government itself. It was an iridescent and impracticable dream, but it represented the benevolence of his disposition and the breadth of his statesmanship. If he had succeeded it would have made an interesting page in history.

But the plan was scarcely inaugurated when the second war with England intervened, and the great Indian chief and statesman arose on the banks of the Wabash and cried with impassioned eloquence, "The Sun is my Father, the Earth is my Mother, and on her bosom will I repose!" No cry of Scottish clansman ever aroused his followers to a higher pitch of enthusiasm than this inspiring utterance of Tecumseh as it rang among the Res Men of the Mississippi Valley. It was caught up in the borders of the Boone settlements by the no less distinguished chief, Black Hawk, and for a period of several years the struggle lasted intermittently that was to determine whether the West should remain a wilderness or become an abode of civilization. Though the result was in favor of the later, the circumstances and conditions that grew out of the struggle put an end to Boone's vision of a Palatinate. The growth of the country in population and resources was greater than his dream; but the population that came was mixed and heterogeneous, and could not be molded into the plans of the man who was greater than his environment.

.   .   .   .   .   .

The chief merit that I claim for this work is its truthful pictures of the life and times of those hardy men and women who came into a wilderness and in a brief space of time performed the astonishing miracle of converting it into a land of peace and plenty.

I am well aware that some of those good people had a habit of drawing upon their imaginations to a considerable extent, and that these imaginations were sometimes as prolific as the soil which their owners cultivated. But in every case where Munchausen fairy stories are woven I have cautioned the reader to be on his guard, so that there is no reason why any one should be deceived. The truth is wonderful enough to grip both mind and heart; while a flight of fancy now and then will only add spice to the pudding.

The wilder flights are samples of what the pioneers told one another around their campfires and cabin hearthstones, when each understood that the other was lying for his amusement. It was a test of skill as to which could tell the tallest yarn, and keep within sight of the distant realms of truth. I think the reader will appreciate the conditions, and enjoy himself as much in reading the stories as I have in compiling them.

The main purpose of the effort is to show the manner of life that was lived by our predecessors; to take the reader into their cabins, on their hunts, sit with them around their campfires at night, and listen to their graphic and sometimes tragic narratives. In other words, to show what kind of people they were and how they lived and conducted themselves. I shall endeavor to raise the curtain and let the reader see what was going on in our land a hundred years ago. (1832)

The Indian Chief, Black Hawk, was one of the greatest characters our country has produced; and we find him not only fighting bitterly against the white people of his age, but in peace-time associating with them on terms of the utmost amity. He and Daniel Boone were personal friends. From Black Hawk's dictated writings we learn a great deal about the domestic and warlike customs and habits of the Indians. He takes us to their homes and shows us how they lived; and strangest of all, he reveals the fact that they were a highly religious people. No romance was ever more thrilling than the personal relations of this distinguished Chieftain, as they will be found in this work.

More battles with Indians were fought in the land west of the Mississippi than in all the remainder of the country, and there were more tragic and thrilling events than elsewhere; as well as incidents of the grotesque and laughable.

Special attention is directed to a dozen or more quaint illustrations. They will be recognized at a glance. These pictures were drawn seventy years ago, (1860) with pen and ink, by a pioneer who wished to portray his memory of scenes and incidents with which he had been familiar. Their age and fidelity render them almost classic. This is the first time they were ever printed for general circulation. The artist went to his reward---whatever that might be---many years ago.

-W.S.B.

Contents

Photos, Pioneer Drawings, Original Drawings

PHOTOS

William S. Bryan Introduction

Daniel Boone's Spring *Episode 7*

WSB Standing at the Judgement Tree *Episode 7*

Old School House *Episode 25*

Jonathan Bryan's Log Home *Episode 29*

Fort Zumwalt *Episode 32*

Black Hawk *Episode 51*

Daniel Boone's Grave *Episode 83*

D. Boone home, front *Episode 83*

D. Boone home, rear view *Episode 83*

PIONEER DRAWINGS 1830s

Early Days in Missouri *Episode 10*

Going To Church *Episode 19*

Mr. Groom *Episode 60*

General Burdine Weighs His Wife *Episode 72*

Skilt and the Turkeys *Episode 76*

Suggett and the Buck *Episode 77*

Tallman of Calloway County *Episode 77*

Daniel Boone In His Casket *Episode 83*

WSB Birthplace *Episode 83*

5 ORIGINAL DRAWINGS 1930s

Daniel and Rebecca Headed Westward *Episode 1*

Uncle Billy and a Wounded Buck *Episode 23*

Wrestling a Bear *Episode 23*

A Catfish Tried to Eat a Boy *Episode 24*

Savage Murders *Episode 26*

Farewell Brother Ham *Episode 61*

AT THE BACK OF THE BOOK

Drawing of Daniel Boone *Episode 83*

Photos and Drawings of 8 Neighbors of D. B. *Episode 83*

Photo of Uncle 'Ligy and Uncle Jim *Episode 83*

Uncle 'Ligy's House *Episode 83*

Into The Wilderness

DANIEL AND REBECCA HEADED WESTWARD

The story of how Daniel Boone came to the valley of the Femme Osage is told in the records of Louisiana Territory. About 1790, weary and discouraged over the failure to secure titles to his lands in Kentucky, and burdened with debts which he could not pay, the old pioneer gave up all the acres that he had acquired by right of discovery as well as purchase, and removed with his family to the valley of the Kanawha. There, in what was the northwestern part of Virginia, but now within the limits of Mason County, W. Virginia, he located. The place was not far from Point Pleasant, where in former years he had fought the Indians.

The Northwestern Territory, as it was then called, was beginning to be occupied by white settlers, and it was believed that the valley of the Kanawha was a good place to catch the drift of trade as it flowed from the east to the west. And there Boone proposed to establish a small store and go into the mercantile business!

Imagine Daniel Boone as a country merchant! He had never tasted a drop of whisky in his life and did not believe in its utility; and he and his family were more accustomed to buckskin clothing than they were to calico or gingham. Without these essentials of the times there was nothing for the country merchant to buy or sell; but the old hunter did not consider these things. In matters of every-day life he was as simple as a child. He dreamed of empires and lived in the woods among the flowers and the birds.

We do not know what progress he made in selling calico and molasses and fiery licker, for there is no record of his experience as a country merchant. Not a line even in his "Lost Manuscript" mentions it.

But soon after the new settlement had been effected, the eldest son, Daniel Morgan Boone, himself a pioneer of growing reputation, traveled into the distant Territory of Upper Louisiana on a hunting and trapping expedition, and the fame of his father having preceded him he was most cordially welcomed by the Spanish authorities at St. Louis. Senor Zenon Trudeau, Lieutenant-Governor of the Territory, suggested that if the celebrated Colonel Boone would come with his family to Upper Louisiana the Spanish King would appreciate the act and reward him handsomely. He even intimated that the great pioneer would be appointed Commandant of a vast district north of the Missouri River and extending indefinitely westward to the fabled South Sea; and in addition would be richly rewarded with land grants that would enable him to establish in that region a Palatinate more extensive and powerful than any European Empire. The Lieutenant-Governor was profuse in building empires in the air!

When Daniel the younger returned home and told his father of these things, explaining the cordiality of the Spanish authorities, the excellence of the climate, the richness of the soil, the great rivers on whose bosoms would float the commerce of a new world, and especially the abundance of game,the imagination of the old hunter was inflamed. Without waiting to dispose of his little stock of goods, he placed his family and a few essential necessaries on pack-horses, and with himself at their head set out to become a builder of empires. Clad in buckskin, a coonskin cap on his head, and his flint-lock rifle on his shoulder, he represented the beginning of what was to be the world's greatest nation.

There were no roads through the forest, no bridges or boats to carry them across the intervening streams and rivers, and almost every step of the way was infested with wild beasts and savage men. There was not even a path or a blazed tree to intimate that some white man had traveled that way before; but at almost every step could be heard the rattle or hiss of some deadly serpent, the howl of a hungry wolf, or the ferocious shriek of the bloody-minded panther.

Through this teaming wilderness the old hunter led the way, a smile of hopefulness lighting up his face, his eyes flaming with a vision that none but he could recognize, his courage supported by the brave woman who followed and believed in him as she did her God. At night she looked after the comfort of the children and the preparation of their food, broiled the bear and buffalo steaks, and was at all times the life and soul of the party. We may admire Boone and wonder at the things he did, but back of him and serving as his inspiration was the beautiful woman who had made her life a part of his. Truly, if there had been no Rebecca there might have been no Daniel.

A Brilliant Messenger

Somewhere in the wilderness, perhaps a hundred miles east of St. Louis, they were met by a messenger carrying a letter of welcome from the Lieutenant-Governor. The letter stated that the Lt.-Governor had been informed by his runners that Colonel Boone and his family were on the way, and he was taking this method to extend his personal and official welcome; and to assure them of a cordial reception on their arrival at the Spanish capitol. Every necessary thing would be done for their comfort, and a state barge would meet them at the landing opposite the city to convey them across the great river. The communication was couched in the usual grandiloquent terms of Spanish official documents of the period, but it bore evidence of being sincere.

The messenger was suited to the occasion. He was a chief in the great Fox tribe of Illinois Indians, tall, straight, dignified. In his scalp-lock he wore an eagle's feather, to intimate that while he had taken many scalps himself his own was still in place. In his hand he carried a rifle of the most modern type, the stock ornamented with carvings and inlaid with silver, while the polished barrel flashed and glittered in the sunlight. In his belt rested a tomahawk and hunting knife, keen-edged and dangerous, and over his shoulder was carelessly folded a blanket of the finest texture, confined at the waist by his belt and giving to his stately person the dignity of a Roman Senator. Boone thought he was the finest specimen of an Indian chief that he had ever seen, and appreciating the importance of the message he did not wonder at the splendor of the messenger.

"How!" exclaimed the chief, as he strode up to the great white hunter and extended his hand in a friendly greeting.

"How!" responded Boone, grasping the proffered token. And such was the introduction of the splendid messenger and the famous white chieftain.

"Me heap plenty run!" said the red chief, by way of explaining his office; and Boone understood that he was head of a band of runners employed by the Government. It was the duty of these men to be not only familiar with the vast domains, but also fleet of foot, polished in manner, brave and alert.

The camp for the night had already been made, on the bank of a stream with water clear and cold as that of the springs by which it was fed; and when the chief had been formerly introduced to the family, a collation more ample than any to which he had been accustomed was spread before him. He ate heartily, almost greedily, for since leaving St. Louis he had tasted nothing but a little water and a few grains of parched corn, always provided in cases like this. Meanwhile Boone cut and arranged some cedar boughs for a couch, and covering them with a blanket signed to the chief that it would be his resting-place for the night. Wearied with his long run, he retired early, and slept until the break of day.

An Impolite Bear

When the chief awoke the smell of roasting meat gladdened the heart, for he was still hungry. Arising and bathing his hands and face in the stream, he came and sat by the fire and watched Rebecca as she broiled a thick buffalo steak and baked some corn bread in the hot ashes. It was the grateful odor of the steaming food which had awakened him.

"Plenty good!" he exclaimed, by way of complement, sniffing up the fragrant air and smiling in anticipation of the good things that were to come.

"We also have honey," said Rebecca, exhibiting a large comb which Daniel had just brought in from the woods; "and some fish."

The chief was delighted. It was to be a grand feast, and he longed to be at it.

"Heap plenty good!" he cried.

But the words were scarcely out of his mouth when a huge black bear ambled into the midst, and overturning the frying-pan helped himself to the hot steak.

With a yell of anger the chief sprang upon his back, and began beating him about the head with his fists; whereupon the bear dropped the meat and fled into the woods roaring with terror. The chief wound the fingers of his left hand in the thick fur of the beast and grimly held on as they raced through the forest, yelling at each jump and pounding the bear with his right hand. Boone tried to draw a bead on the fleeing animal, but its movements were so rapid and irregular that he dared not fire lest he might wound the chief.

Over logs and across ravines, brushing against trees and tearing through canebreaks, dashed the terror-stricken bear; but all to no purpose. The yelling warrior could not be unseated, and all the while his blows were coming heavier and more telling. Boone expected the bear to roll over and crush his rider or brush him off; but the beast was so tremendously frightened that the expedient did not seem to occur to him.

At length he dashed up to the stream and plunged headlong into a pool of water, but this proved to be his undoing; for the chief, letting go his hold in the fur, seized the bear by both ears and held his head under water until he was drowned.

Then he swam ashore, dragging the carcass with him, and Boone helped him make a landing.

"Woof!" he grunted, shaking the water from his person, "heap plenty fun!"

He did not seem to realize that his performance was anything extra-ordinary, but Boone complemented him with expressions of "Heap great hunter! Bold warrior!" And led the way to the fire, where the chief dried his buckskin leggings while Rebecca broiled another steak.

Episode Number Two

Old St. Louis

When breakfast was over, the messenger announced his return. He would go and make heap good for the pale faces. Boone urged him to stay another day and rest, but he was not tired. "Plenty run! No give out!" was his reply.

Then Rebecca made him a nice hot sandwich, a thick pone of cornbread, with a juicy steak of the bear he had conquered in the middle.

"Umph!" he said, with a smile; "heap eat, no can run quick!"

But he took the sandwich and tied it in a corner of his blanket. It was better than parched corn.

Then he told Boone that he would mark the best path, by blazing a tree every quarter of a mile, so they could "come to big village plenty quick".

Whereupon he shouldered his gun, adjusted his blanket, and stalked away into the wilderness with much dignity. He faithfully kept his word by blazing trees on the way every little while so that in following him they had no difficulty in finding the best route.

. . . . . .

On arriving at the slough which then formed an island opposite St. Louis, they found a large raft moored to the shore for their convenience; and in a little while they crossed over and came to the great river, where they were met by a state barge that carried them to the western bank. They landed at the foot of Walnut Street, near the old Cathedral, which was then only a large log cabin. Here they were met by officials in brilliant uniforms, with guard of honor lined up on either side; and preceded by the Spanish and American colors and the beating of drums, were conducted to the Governor's house.

Their welcome was as cordial as it was hearty and sincere. Spain was seeking a place in the heart of the great new Republic side by side with the one which France had gained by material help in the hour of great necessity; and Boone was recognized as America's representative. Nothing was left undone to make the wanderers feel that they were in the midst of friends.

The official ceremonies occupied several days, during which the honored visitors were assigned to a house for themselves, and supplied with all the necessaries of food and furniture.

At that time St. Louis was more French than Spanish, for the place had been settled by colonists from the former country. There were barely enough Spaniards to give the city an official setting; but the two populations were equally cordial toward the new arrivals.

The future great city was a straggling village, spread out for half a mile or more along the summit of the bluff overlooking the river. It's inhabitants were composed of hunters, trappers, Indian traders, gamblers, and the usual floating elements of towns in embryo. Those who had anything in the nature of permanent homes lived in log-cabins of single rooms, or huts formed by setting posts in the ground at intervals of a foot or more apart and filling the spaces with a plaster of mud and grass. Some of these habitations had been whitewashed, and thereby assumed an aspect of special neatness. A wooden chimney at one end, also plastered with mud and grass, gave passage to the smoke from the fire on the hearth, where cooking was done and around which the family gathered for warmth and sociability. The floor was composed of tramped or beaten earth, swept clean with brooms of the buckey bush. A few of the more affluent had erected stone huts, also of single rooms, and a stone chimney in place of the common wooden one. In other respects they were the same as the log-cabins. The stones were built into the walls just as they came out of the quarry, with no touch of chisel or hammer.

Others made their homes in caves, or under shelving ledges of limestone in the bluff, where they had an expansive view of the river as it rolled along out of one wilderness of mystery into another. These people who lived in the face of the bluff were in many respects the same as the ancient Cliff or Cave Dwellers; for all its interminable stages of civilization Nature has been about the same.

As there were no shingles to be had, most of the roofs of the houses were composed of primitive clapboards, held in place by wooden pins or "weight poles" laid on transversely. There were no nails in the Territory, except a few which had been hammered out by blacksmiths and were too expensive for the pioneers. Some of the roofs consisted of wide strips of bark peeled from the "slippery elm" in springtime, when the sap was "rising", and laid with the rough side upward so the sun would not warp them.

There were not many dishes or cooking vessels. A few of the well-to-do had an oven or a pot of iron and their owners were regarded with some degree of envy. Venison and bear and buffalo steaks were broiled before the fire on forked sticks, or boiled in pots of clay or bark by dropping red-hot stones into the water. Soup was thickened with potatoes, onions and garlic, and seasoned with red peppers to the tenth-degree. It was essential to swallow quickly in order to avoid throat constrictions. Some of the inhabitants had a family dish or bowl made of wood, into which the steaming mess was poured and allowed to cool; but as there were not many of these the population in general drank their soup out of the pot. All service was by hand. Pieces of bark and broad splinters were substituted for cutlery. Knives and forks and metal spoons were seen only in the governor's house, and limited to state occasions. They were brought forth in honor of the Boones, but Uncle Daniel, not understanding them, utilized his hunting-knife and drank his soup out of the plate, much to the discomfort of Aunt Rebecca, who knew better.

As a rule each family had a wooden spoon, sometimes two, which served the family in turn. Meat and the more solid vegetables were lifted with the fingers, which were licked clean when the meal was over. The pot of clay or bark was set in the middle of the circle, on a block of wood or a stump which had been left to serve as a table; and each member of the family helped himself as he had occasion. The little fellows were served by mother, who as everywhere else in all the world, denied herself for their comfort.

The village was surrounded by forests of oak, walnut, and pecan trees, and in the fall great stores of nuts were gathered by the children, to be eaten as dessert by the winter fireside. On the boarders of the sinkholes were hazel bushes and thicket of blackberries, and many a blackberry found its way into a pie with cornmeal crust. Hazelnuts were delicacies of an especially fine flavor, reserved for Sunday evenings and holiday occasions, when heavier nuts, such as walnuts and hickory nuts, did not set well on stomachs already well-laden with meats and stews. Lovers sat in the most distant corners of the cabins and ate philopenas, a kiss for each double nut, and two kisses when each lover found two kernels at the same time. Hazelnuts were convenient for courting purposes and many of the first-families would have no difficulty in tracing their lineage back to this humble condiment. Those who did not provide themselves with plenty of nuts were regarded as shiftless, and sympathy was not wasted upon them.

The muddy water of the river was looked upon with suspicion, and but little of it was used by the inhabitants. A number of springs and a few public wells supplied the average demand. The outlets to some of the sink-holes had also become clogged, until rainwater collected and formed small lakes, out of which many drew their supplies for domestic purposes. In summertime the lakes were utilized as bathing places, which agitated the water and was supposed to keep it pure. None bathed in winter or when the weather was cold; and there was no bathtub in the Mississippi valley until fifty years afterward. The inhabitants, being students of nature, observed that no animal bathed except when the weather was hot.

Owing to suspicion about water, there was much consumption of a stronger liquid, either straight or in the form of grog, mixed with rain water. In warm weather mosquitoes and flies abounded, and the licker was taken to prevent reoccurring fevers. If one escaped the fever, he took the cure to insure safety.

Bear skins and buffalo hides tanned with the hair on, were used as sleeping rugs. They were warm, required no washing, and modified the labor of housekeeping.

No system or regularity had been observed in placing the houses of the inhabitants. A single street was beginning to take form along the levee, where a few years later palatial steamboats chugged and snorted and pushed their noses into the landing. There came a time when St. Louis regarded herself as the greatest city in the Mississippi Valley, and expected always to remain such.

When the Boones came a log building, a little larger than the others, was occupied by the Territorial offices, secluded from the curious by a rail fence with armed guards behind it. This was the capitol of the Territory, and the only courthouse that St. Louis had until 1823, when the stately old building on Broadway was erected. It still stands, a splendid example of the public spirit and good taste of the period---a classic of "Old St. Louis".

Such was St. Louis in 1795, and some of the first families could easily trace their origin back to similar beginnings. At the end of the line they might find a pretty Indian squaw, who preferred freedom with a white hunter to slavery in the wigwams of her own people. There were priests to see that these unions conformed to the ritual of the church, but the parties themselves did not bother their heads with such minor details.

Another village and trading post had been established at Carondelet, twelve miles below the "big village"; but its prospects were so uninviting that the aristocrats of the larger town mentioned it with contempt as "Vide Poche", or "Empty Pocket", a designation which clung to it until the mother city reached out her arms and took the orphan to her bosom.

A third French settlement had been effected at St. Charles, on the Missouri River eighteen miles above St. Louis, which bore the poetic title of "Les Petit Cotes", or "The Little Hills", from a series of smooth round-topped mounds a short distance from the village. These mounds are known as the "Mamelles", from their fancied resemblance to the breasts of a woman, from which little French children derive their pet name for "Mother".

The "oldest inhabitants" of St. Charles formerly wagged their heads and claimed for their town a more ancient beginning than St. Louis; and by such means succeeded in having it chosen as the first capital of the great State of Missouri.

Again the Star of Empire Moves Westward

On a beautiful morning in September, accompanied by his faithful hound dog Cuff, Boone again turned his face westward, with the purpose of locating the thousand arpents of land which the Spanish government had granted him. Rebecca and the children were left in St. Louis as guests of the city, to await his return.

Pursuing a course due westward toward a point on the south bank of the Missouri river, he knew that within about thirty miles it would bring him opposite the mouth of Femme Osage Creek, near the place where his land-grant was to be located. The region over which his course lay was covered with the same primeval forest that nature had created. No human habitation was there, and he was probably the first white man who had ever trod the path. The region was inhabited only by wild beasts, hunted occasionally by red warriors more savage than the beasts themselves. Boone knew, therefore, that it was a dangerous land, and that it would be well for him to be well on his guard.

His accoutrement was light and suited to the nature of his journey. In his hand he carried his flint-lock rifle, and fastened to his shoulders in the form of a knapsack was a package containing a deerskin robe, tanned with the hair on, light and warm. When the rain fell the robe served as a water-proof cloak, and at night it was his only covering. In the belt around his waist hung a tomahawk and a long hunting-knife, two essentials to every man having the hardihood to venture into the wilderness.

His dress consisted of buckskin pants and a hunting jacket of the same material, with moccasins also of buckskin on his feet, and a coonskin cap on his head. Under his hunting jacket he wore a gray flannel shirt, and folded in the pack on his shoulders was a second garment of the same kind; together with extra supplies of bullets for his rifle and a handful of parched corn to serve as food in case of necessity. His powder was contained in a polished horn, swung by a cord over his left shoulder and reaching to his waist on the right side. He carried no compass, being accustomed to finding direction and distance by the sun, the stars, and the moss that grew on the north side of the trees.

For food he depended upon the game which his rifle would supply, and by way of dessert he ate wild grapes, pawpaws and persimmons, or yellow and purple plums that hung in tempting clusters.

By the end of the first day he came to a point near the present site of the Court House of the city of Clayton, and camped there for the night. On the way he had shot off the heads of a couple of quails, and these broiled over a fire of sticks, supplied him with a bountiful supper. Cuff had attended to his own wants by catching a fat young rabbit, which he ate with pleasure and profit to himself; after which the two turned in and slept through the night.

A Narrow Escape

At daylight the next morning they were again on their way, but had proceeded only a short distance when an incident occurred which came near costing Boone his life. While approaching a ravine bordered on either side with a thick growth of cane, there suddenly flashed out of the ambuscade a puff of smoke, followed by the crash of a musket, and a bullet whizzed so close by his side that he could feel its impact as it glanced from his powder-horn. Realizing that his hidden enemy was now at his mercy, Boone drew his tomahawk and ran to the thicket; but Cuff had preceded him. When his master came he found the dog hanging grimly to the ankle of a frightened Indian, who was struggling and vociferating in bad English for the animal to be called off.

"Me good Indian!" he yelled; "Me not shoot on purpose! Gun go off himself!"

Boone knew of course that the savage was lying, but preferring his friendship to his enmity, he ordered Cuff to let go ; and advancing with his hand outstretched, he said in a conciliatory tone;

"How!"

"How!" responded the savage, with a sincerity that was evident; for he was at the mercy of the white man and had no desire to make an immediate journey to his happy hunting ground.

The two men looked into each other's eyes, and each realizing the sincerity of the other they were from that moment ever after good friends.

"Why shoot?" inquired Boone.

The savage hung his head and replied hesitatingly:

"Gun go off himself." It was the only explanation he could make, and the white hunter knew it was best to pretend a belief he did not feel.

"Name?" he inquired, for the Indian prides himself upon his personality and the title by which he is distinguished.

In reply he muttered a long compound word, signifying "Man-who-fell-off-his-horse," by which Boone understood that he belonged to the "foot" Indians, who are not accustomed to riding; and wishing to ascertain his tribe, he inquired:

"Fox?"

The savage nodded assent, and it transpired that he was in fact a member of the Fox tribe, whose towns lay in the Rock River region of Illinois.

"Name too long", said Boone. "I call you Poncho".

"Me, Poncho!" cried the savage, with evident satisfaction, striking himself on the breast with his open palm. "Heap good name! Me like um!"

It transpired that Poncho was out on a scalp-hunting expedition, with a view of winning glory and at the same time wreaking vengeance on the Osages of the west, who had been trespassing on the hunting preserves claimed by the Sacs and Foxes.

Poncho Demonstrates His Sincerity

Boone now directed the Indian to reload his gun and follow him, with which command he cheerfully complied. Presently they came to a spring, and having satisfied their thirst sat down to rest. Poncho observed his companion inquiringly, and with considerable degree of respect; for he felt instinctively that he was in the presence of a man above the common level. At length he inquired:

"Name?"

"Boone" replied the white man, without looking up.

Poncho was electrified! The great chief was known and honored by the Indians as well as among his own race; and now to be his friend and companion was a greater honor than Poncho could ever have dreamed.

"Boone!" he cried, in a tone implying something close to adoration. "Boone, him plenty great warrior! Me like um!"

The two men of divergent races now felt more closely allied than ever. There was no longer room for suspicion on the part of either. Boone knew that he could trust Poncho to the limit, and the Indian soon gave evidence that he would die for so great a friend.

As the men rose to continue their journey, they were startled by the warning buzz of a rattlesnake, followed by the launching of the hideous body in a deadly strike toward Boone; but at that instant Poncho threw out his right leg and caught the sting just above the ankle. Boone saw the movement, and realizing that his companion had offered his own life as a sacrifice for him, he mashed the serpents head with the butt of his gun. Then turning to render aid to Poncho, he saw the Indian vanishing in a thicket of cane and underbrush. A moment later he returned, chewing an herb and smiling to intimate that he was in no danger.

"Poncho plenty good!" he exclaimed; but observing Boone's anxiety, he continued, in broken sentences: "Snake no hurt Poncho! Kill um bite with weed!"

In fact he knew an infallible antedote for the poison of serpents, if taken before it had time to circulate through the system; but he kept the secret in his own bosom. When importuned to reveal it he would reply, "Bimeby", until eventually, in his old age he disappeared and was never seen again. It was supposed that some reptile may have stung him when he was not within reach of his precious "weed".

In the evening of the third day they came to the river where there was a large island in the middle of the stream; and Boone knew by the directions he had received that this was the place where they must cross. It was necessary therefore to build a raft, and as this would require several days, they made a permanent camp. But Boone was in no hurry. A few days more or less would make no difference in the founding of the Palatinate. The land would not run away; and so the September days glided along. A little hunting in the morning, a little work on the raft in the afternoon, until gradually it assumed proportions and was almost ready to be launched.

A Tragedy In the Wilderness

Then one morning Cuff came dashing into camp from one of his daily rambles in quest of rabbits, in the state of mind bordering on the hysterical. He barked and circled around his master, pulled his hunting coat with his teeth, ran into the brush and back again, and with other evidences of supreme excitement made it known, as plainly as he could in dog language, that he had discovered something which demanded investigation.

So Boone took his gun and followed him into the woods, keeping the weapon ready for use in case of surprise. The dog led the way a quarter of a mile, through underbrush and canebrake, until he came to a thicket where a bed had been contrived of peavines, upon which lay an Osage woman in the agonies of death. Tugging at her breast was a newly-born baby boy, to which she pointed appealingly. Her meaning could not be misinterpreted. She knew she was dying and she wanted some one to care for her baby.

Boone's heart was touched. By signs and a few words to emphasize his meaning, he made her understand that he would comply with her wish. A look of gratitude lighted up her face with the glory of human trust, for she knew by his noble presence that the white chief would not fail her. Then closing her eyes she chanted the death-dirge of her people, and so passed into the unknown.

Boone inferred that she had been cast away by some brutal husband in a fit of intoxication, and that she had wandered into the wilderness to give a new life and yield up her own. There was no vessel of water or sign of food. The woman had made her bed near a seeping spring, into which she could dip her hand; and there, alone and broken hearted, she paid the last debt of humanity.

The old hunter now turned his attention to saving the life of the infant. In a bundle by the mother's side he found several clothes, and a little blanket in which the child could be wrapt. Tenderly tucking it in the blanket he made his way back to camp, where food could be prepared. But here he met with furious opposition from Poncho. The Osages were his deadly enemies, and he could not be expected to show compassion for one of their offspring. Seizing his hatchet he made a motion as if to brain the little one, but Boone caught his hand and wrenched the weapon from him.

"Osage heap bad Injun!" snarled Poncho; and again he attempted to carry out his murderous purpose by plunging his knife into the body of the child. But Boone caught the descending weapon, and wrenching it from the infuriated savage sent it clanging into the brush. Then his commanding glance upon the Indian, he made him understand that any further such attempts on his part would be accepted as a challenge to the death.

Poncho cowered beneath the stern gaze, and after a moment's hesitation went sullenly to their stores of meat, and cutting a thick slice laid it in the palm of the child. It was a surrender and offer of peace. The hand of the little one grasped the meat, and with the promptings of nature put it in its mouth and sucked out the nourishment.

In a few minutes the baby was asleep, when Boone, lying it tenderly on a bed of peavines, motioned to Poncho to follow him. Leading the way to the dead woman's body, he and the Indian dug a shallow grave with sharpened sticks, and lifting the insenate form into it covered it with earth. It was the last rites of a life which perhaps had been a failure.

Rebecca Mothers an Indian Baby

Several days passed, and the little brown baby slept and grew and chuckled. Even Poncho became fond of it. At least so far had his civilization progressed that he no longer cared to tomahawk the little Osage. So Boone decided to send the baby to his wife in St. Louis, and Poncho was to be the messenger. At first he rebelled! While he cared for the little mite of humanity in his own savage way, it was too much to ask a great warrior to carry a baby into the "big village". But Boone overcame his repugnance by representing that he could enter the city by night, when no one would see him or become aware of his degradation; and so at last he agreed to perform the service.

"Tell my squaw", said Boone, "that papoose's name is Paul".

"Humph!" grunted Poncho, "plenty good name for heap bad Injun!"

But he made the trip, found the white squaw, and laid the little one in her arms.

"Boone say his name Paul", he exclaimed and with no other word stalked out into the darkness and disappeared.

But Aunt Rebecca understood! Her Daniel had found an orphaned Indian baby, and like the Egyptian princess in the story, she took it to her heart.

Episode Number Four

Poncho Finds Fire-Water

Having fulfilled his mission for Boone by placing the little papoose in the arms of the motherly Rebecca, Poncho set out to find a place where fire-waters were dispensed. In his savage mind some consolation must be had for his wounded manhood in serving as a nurse for a baby, and nothing could fill the place so well as the strong waters of the pale faces, which yielded both hilarity and forgetfulness.

Knowing where to find what he wanted, he bent his steps along a path which led to a cabin on the edge of the bluff overlooking the river, a beacon of light for searchers and a convenient place from which to toss cadavers that might otherwise be in the way. For it was also a gambling resort, where the red men not only made their souls glad with the hot water, but sometimes pledged their bodies as forfeits in the game that fascinates beyond the limits of reason. A cemetery for dead Indians would not be pleasant adjoining a place of carousal, so it was the custom when one of them paid the forfeit, to toss his body over the brow of the cliff and let the river take care of the funeral exercises. It was merely another dead Indian gone to the happy hunting ground, where all Indians are good. No account of the tragedy would appear in the morning paper, or be inquired into by the accommodating government.

Toward this place Poncho now directed his steps. He had been there before and knew the way. The proprietor also knew Poncho and trusted him for future payments when his pelts or wampum were exhausted; for he had never failed to return with fresh wampum or another pack of furs and honestly balance his budget. Poncho being a good Indian, could fill himself with fire-water on credit. The account was obligingly entered, with "overage" for luck or chance, and full assurance that it would be "squared" at no distant date; unless some wary Osage got his scalp in the meantime. In that event the overage would take care of the profit and loss.

Food was extra. The proprietor did not keep a restaurant; he dealt only in liquids, the customer himself looking after food and lodging. Very little of the former was required, strong-water being both food and drink, while lodging could be free outside the cabin on the bosom of Mother Earth.

"How!" amiably grunted Poncho, as he set his gun down in a corner and called for "heap plenty fire-water".

The hard-featured Frenchman behind the unplanned board counter looked his customer over to make sure of his identity, and having satisfied himself on that point, held out his hand and spoke his greetings:

"How! Man-who-fell-off-his-horse!-----Good cheer to you!"

But Poncho was not pleased, and he replied with some show of asperity:

"Me no fall off horse!" he retorted with wounded dignity. "Boone, great white hunter, call me 'Poncho'!" and he slapped his breast with his open palm to indicate that he had been promoted.

"Oh, si!---oui, oui," responded the Frenchman with urbane hospitality; "Poncho, or Man-who-fell-off-his-horse, all the same with me. Poncho may have what he wants."

Poncho accepted the apology and proceeded to explain the conditions.

"Me got no wampum---no skins", he said.

"It matters not---you will get some bime-by".

Whereupon he pushed a gourdful of whiskey across the counter to the savage, who, grasping it eagerly, sat down on the earthen floor with his back to the wall of the cabin, and swallowed the contents with satisfaction.

Sweet Revenge

All that night and the next day Poncho reveled in the glories of intoxication, with now and then a yell or a war whoop to indicate his character as a great warrior, when new supplies were required. Meanwhile other warriors came and were served, until the floor and portions of the yard outside were occupied by revelers, some in the yelling stage and others in that condition of silence and for-getfulness which brings only visions of war and glory.

These drunken warriors owed allegiance to different tribes and nations; some came from the distant west, others from the Illinois region, and a few from the rich hunting grounds of the southern Cherokees. If they had met in any other place they would have been deadly enemies, but this miser-able cabin and its immediate vicinity were neutral grounds where no battles were to be fought. Only quiet assassinations were legitimate.

As evening approached, Poncho realized that it was time for him to return to Boone, who would be anxious to know the results of his journey. So he nerved himself against the urge for more pota-tions of fire-water, and started inquest of nature's milder quencher of thirst.

On his way to the spring he stumbled over a warrior stretched at length on the ground enjoy-ing the bliss of complete intoxication. Observing him carefully, he saw that he belonged to the tribe of the hated Osages, with whom his people were at war; and attached to his belt was a fresh scalp but recently torn from the head of a Fox Indian. Hot indignation leaped into Poncho's bosom, and he would have brained his enemy on the spot except for the strict rules forbidding assaults on the neutral ground. He was therefore obliged to play a shrewder game, and perhaps in the end acquire a sweeter revenge.

Poncho's first step was to get himself thoroughly sober, which he did with large draughts of cold water; after which he satisfied his hunger from his frugal supply of dried venison. Then he sat down grimly to watch the Osage until the latter recovered consciousness---when he would play him a game for life or death! Meanwhile he kept his eyes fastened upon the bloody scalp, which he easily recognized, by certain peculiarities in the trimming of the hair as having belonged to a member of his own tribe.

He had not long to wait. The Osage, having slept off the effects of his potations, arose and reeled into the cabin for fresh supplies. As he came out Poncho met him at the door, and the two war-riors faced each other, deadly hate blazing from opposing eyes. Although Poncho was now entirely sober, he feigned partial intoxication, and by pretense of friendliness led the Osage on to boast of his prowess. How he had waylaid and shot his victim in the tall grass, scalping him before life had left the body; then plunging his knife into the heart had left the carcass for the wolves. For he was a "heap big warrior", and would treat all Foxes the same way. He was barely sober enough to realize that he was addressing a warrior of the nation that he was denouncing, which only incited him to broader insults.

Poncho could scarcely restrain his eagerness for vengeance. At each fresh provocation his rage became more intense; but he must play a shrewd game or lose his opportunity. He dared not toma-hawk the Osage openly, as he would have rejoiced to do; so he led him on to heavier drinking and louder boasting. The Osage was afraid of no Fox! Indeed he held them all in such contempt that he was planning to invade their country and fill his belt with the scalps of that tribe of squaws. Intense drunkenness and the ferocity of his savage nature made him an ideal boaster. In his own mind he was greater than the famous Black Hawk, whom he longed to meet in personal combat!

To all this Poncho listened in grim silence. His time was coming! Not only would he wreak hot vengeance, but he would take two scalps, one that dangled at the belt of the boaster, and the other that was ornamented with feathers on the top of his head. So he plied him more and more fire-water, until as the sun sank lower behind the western hills and the gloom of darkness came on, the savage beast sank into a dreamland of complete drunkenness.

Then Poncho drew his knife, leaned over his unconscious enemy, and with a smile of profound satisfaction drove the glittering blade into his side until the point penetrated the heart. Another red warrior had become a good Indian. Tearing off the scalp, he placed it in his belt side by side with the one that the Osage had captured from his countryman, and silently glided away into the darkness. Two scalps were a double trophy which would advance him to the rank of a great warrior among his people, and he smiled with savage ferocity as he contemplated the glory that was his.

Poncho Has Misgivings

Obtaining his bearings by the stars that were shining over his head, he took a straight course for the place where he had left Boone, knowing well that he would have nothing to fear from pursuit. The affair would be regarded by the authorities as only a brawl between two drunken Indians, and no consequence to them. The dead savage would be thrown into the river, and there would be one less red skin to bother about.

But it might be different with the great white chief, and as Poncho hastened on his way he pondered with some apprehension as to what his reception might be, with two gory scalps in his belt. It was no sense of shame that disturbed his conscience; for it was a feeling of proud satisfaction that he considered the trophies of war; but he dreaded the probable resentment of the white chief, whose friendship he prized, and who was noted even among his enemies for his sentiments of humanity.

It was twilight the next morning when Poncho reached the camp, Boone had already prepared breakfast for two, in anticipation of the return of his messenger. When Poncho came and reported the success of his expedition, Boone complimented him in terms that were dear to his savage heart, but he said nothing about the scalps that he could not fail to see attached to his belt. His silence, therefore, meant disapproval.

It was no part of Boone's nature to condemn the acts of others, especially in a case like this, where such trophies were regarded not only as evidence of courage but also partook of the nature of a religious rite. He did not feel that it was his duty to argue with the Indian about his ideas of war or the ceremonies of his religion; but he showed his disgust of the barbarous custom by paying no attention to Poncho's highly prized relics.

The savage ate his breakfast in silence, wondering at the curious ideas and customs that prevailed among different kinds of men. He and his people gloried in scalps as mementoes of valor in battle, while the pale faces hugged their bosoms the folds of a stripped flag, or pinned on their breasts a little silver star, to indicate that they had been bold in war. Therefore let each consider the ways that pleased him best, according to the nature of his tribe. Or, as the famous Black Hawk had expressed it: "Why did not the pale faces remain on their own island, and leave the island of the Indians free to them?"

Game in Abundance

Poncho took a day off and lay around on the grass to rest and recuperate from the effects of his dissipation. Nor did Boone manifest any haste. It is the little people of earth that are always in a hurry, trying to do the many things that seem essential and accomplishing nothing; while the great ones leisurely contemplate and plan, and when the time is ripe strike and the thing is done. So it was with Poncho and his beloved white friend.

While Poncho lay dreaming of the glory that he had won, Boone took his rifle and, following the faithful Cuff, noiselessly proceeded to a place on the river bank near where he heard the grabbling and honking of a large flock of wild geese. Beyond a line of thick bushes he could see glimpses of water, where a shallow lake of considerable dimensions spread over the landscape; and this he knew to be the habitat of wild fowl.

Concealed by the bushes, his moccasined feet making no responsive sound in the soft earth, he came up to the very edge of the water, where he witnessed a scene which made the instincts of the hunter swell within his bosom. Spread out before him was a lake of half a mile or more in circumference, whose surface was almost black with great throngs of ducks and wild geese, hilarious with the feast of tender roots and bulbs and fresh fish which they were enjoying. It was a great resort for these splendid birds, and he stood silent for several minutes enjoying the wonderful spectacle.

At length he selected for his aim a proud old gander who seemed to have charge of a detachment of several hundred hens, and was about to touch the fatal trigger when a mink rose out of the water and with savage ferocity cut the throat of the gander. Clenching his prey by the neck the mink pulled the dead bird under the water and started to swim away to his den, when Boone, with quick and unerring aim, sent a bullet crashing through its head. Instantly Cuff sprang into the water and towed both prizes to the bank, laying them at the feet of his master as he shook the water from his shaggy sides. So unaccustomed were the fowls to the sound of a gun that only those nearest the danger-point paid any attention to it, and these quickly resumed their search for food after a few quacks and honks, evidently supposing it to be merely a crash of thunder.

Boone removed the pelt of the mink, which would bring him money in the St. Louis market, and shouldering it along with the goose made his way back to camp. That day they were to have roast goose for dinner, and no one knew better than the old hunter how to barbecue the game to a perfect tenderness. Digging a trench in the earth, he kindled a fire of brush and limbs at the bottom, and while it leaped into flame and then smoldered into hot coals he dressed the bird ready for cooking. When the sweet odor of the roasting flesh began to spread abroad, Poncho sniffed and came and sat by the side of his companion.

"Heap good bird", he said; "me like um!"

"You are a wise hunter", replied Boone, conveying a compliment to his good taste as well as his skill; whereupon Poncho demonstrated his appreciation by swelling with pride. A compliment from so great a man was well worth considering.

When the goose was ready to serve, done to a turn and so tender that no carving knife would be required to separate the choice bits from the main roast, the old hunter spread it on a broad piece of bark and invited his red companion to help himself. Poncho was not slow in responding to the invitation. First he devoured a leg, then he attacked the tender breast, and filled himself so full of goose that when he was through he was scarcely able to waddle back to his bed of grass, where he slept until the sun shone in his face the following morning.

By this time the white hunter had warmed over the remainders of the feast, and the two men had a second repast. Truly, thought Poncho, such a life had its rewards and was worth the living. Congratulating himself upon having fallen into such pleasant lines, he returned to his bed and again fell asleep and dreamed of roast goose, and scalps, and the glory of war. Scalps and glory never departed out of his mind, even when his belly was full of meat and his soul wandered in dreamland. This central thought, constantly active in his brain, gave him great satisfaction with himself and nerved his arm for future encounters with Osage warriors. But while Poncho dreamed of scalps and glory he judiciously said nothing about it to his white master.

During the absence of his messenger on the mission to St. Louis, Boone had done a little work on the raft, but he had been in no hurry. A little more work would be necessary before the craft was launched. One of the outer logs needed stouter splicing to the others with withes in order to make it a firm part of the whole. But there was plenty of time. A paddle and a pole must also be provided, and when all this could be done the boat could be shoved into the water with assurance that it would float and obey the direction of the pole and the paddle. But this could be done tomorrow as well as today; even if it delayed until next week it would make no particular difference.

So Boone took his gun and Cuff, and while Poncho snored in the bliss of imaginary glory, slipped away into the silent forest. Presently the crack of his rifle announced results, and he soon reappeared carrying a turkey as fat as the goose of the previous day. Truly, it was an elysianic paradise for hunters! A second feast followed, with another night of rest and dreaming, and once more Poncho slept until the sun awakened him.

Poncho's Adventure with a "Cat"

But that day the success of his great white master encouraged Poncho to try his own skill as a hunter, and in the middle of the forenoon he shouldered his musket and turned his face toward the dark woods.

"Be careful", said Boone, with real apprehension. "Yesterday I saw signs of the big cat."

He knew Poncho would understand better than if he said "painter", the term by which the dread panther was known to pioneers. This beast was one of the most cunning and ferocious with which the hunter had to deal, and it was well to be on guard when there were signs of the prowler in the vicinity. Large as a young lion, fierce as the leopard, with a tread as soft and sly as that of the cat, the immediate presence of the animal often was not suspected until its fangs were fastened in the victim's flesh. Then it was too late! The panther generally announced its coming into a locality by loud screams, resembling the sound of a modern steam whistle, or quite as often the agonized cry of a terrified child, and inexperienced persons had been known to meet a dreadful fate by running to the assistance of supposedly helpless innocence. The cry indicated also that there were two of the animals not far distant, for it was the male's call to his female mate.

But Poncho was not afraid! "Me heap big hunter", he replied to the friendly caution of his master. "Me no 'fraid of cat—me shoot!"

So he took his departure, while Boone examined his rifle to see that it was in condition for an emergency.

Half an hour later the silence was broken by the loud crash of Poncho's musket a few hundred yards from the camp, followed by loud yells for help, rapidly approaching nearer.

Instantly Boone was on his feet, gun in hand, running to meet the ominous calls, but with a caution which he felt to be necessary under the circumstances. Soon he observed the Indian, bounding forward at full speed and yelling lustily as he ran, while close behind him came—not the panther, as Boone had feared—but a large, good natured black bear, grinning as he ambled along. He might easily have overtaken Poncho, but this was evidently not his purpose. It was fun that he wanted, more than food or a fight. In his terror the Indian had lost his gun, and was doing his best to keep beyond range of a personal combat, while the bear kept close enough to be just out of actual contact.

Boone knew by experience and the nature of the animal that his "grin" might have a sinister purpose behind it, and throwing his rifle forward he sent a leaden ball into the heart of the beast. Its momentum was so great that the falling body struck Poncho and threw him to the ground, where he yelled louder than ever with the dead bear on top. The scene was so ludicrous that Boone felt obliged to laugh, but he quickly extricated the savage from his uncomfortable position and raised him to his feet.

"Umph!" snorted Poncho, shaking himself to see if his machinery was in working order, "Umph! Heap big bear!"

"Sure enough!" replied Boone, "but why didn't you shoot him?"

Poncho explained in broken English that he had shot "the cat" and the bear had come upon him before he had time to reload. This proved to be the true story of the adventure. He had been stalking a deer as it fed in the forest, and the bear and the cat were probably also on the same quest; when, in passing under a tree, he heard a rustling of the leaves overhead, and looking up was horrified to see the panther about to spring upon him. Having no time to take aim, he threw his gun upward and fired, the charge fortunately breaking the forelegs of the beast, which fell to the ground in helpless rage. Then the bear appeared, and Poncho remembered an engagement which he had at the camp and struck out with results as already stated.

At Boon's suggestion he led the way to the wounded panther, which though unable to use its claws was none the less enraged at the approach of foes. Growling and floundering about on the ground it was still a foe to be dreaded, and keeping well out of range of its fangs Boone drew his tomahawk and hurled it with such unerring aim that its keen blade sank into the panther's brain and put an end to the adventure.

They now proceeded to skin both of the dead animals, removing a liberal supply of spareribs from the side of the bear; and then returned to the camp for rest and another feast. Meanwhile, with peace and plenty food, Poncho became reminiscent over the results of his adventure. "Me heap big hunter!" he mused, as he gnawed the tender meat from a bone. "Me kill um cat and bear!"

Boone smiled, but said nothing. He had no heart to disillusion the savage, and nothing was to be gained by arguing with a boaster. Let Poncho think as well of himself as he pleased, it might nerve him to greater exploits in some future battle.

A few weeks later, when a settlement had been effected, the hides of the bear and panther were tanned, and the latter, with the help of Rebecca's shears and needle, was wrought into a handsome hunting jacket for Poncho, which he wore with much dignity and pride whenever he appeared in public throughout the remainder of his life. And no softer bed than the hide of the bear could have been found for the red warrior as he lay upon it for many years in his cave near the home of his white friends.

Episode Number Six

Crossing the Great River

It was time now for action! The raft must be finished and the great adventure of crossing the river entered upon. During the day everything was made ready, the pole and the paddle were completed, but without assistance from Poncho, who slept the sleep of innocence except for the hour devoted to the noonday luncheon.

Early the following morning the boat was launched, and in announcement that everything was ready, Cuff ran up and down the outer log barking loudly. The skins of the panther and the bear were brought on board, and the guns placed in a dry position out of reach of the splash of the water. Then Poncho took the pole and Boone the paddle, and they pushed the prow of the raft into the current. It was an auspicious moment! Westward the star of empire was taking its way. The explorers were submitting themselves to the good fortune which they believed awaited them. They were entering upon the conquest of a wilderness which was soon to teem with life and energy and echo to the peaceful sounds of civilization.

It would be out of place, however, to suppose that any such thoughts entered the mind of Poncho. He did not trouble about conquering the wilderness, or the progress of civilization. What interested him was the getting of food to fill his inner vacuum, and finding a place where he could slumber in comfort.

At this season of the year the river was low and the channel narrow so that no great time elapsed after the current caught the prow of the boat until it chugged into the soft sand that formed the bank of the island which lay in midstream. It was then no great effort to propel the raft forward around the head of the island and into the opposite channel. Poncho doing his part with the pole while Boone guided the course of the vessel and added to its momentum with vigorous strokes of the paddle. In a few minutes they rounded the headland and struck out across the lesser channel for the open mouth of a creek, which Boone recognized as the Femme Osage, soon to become famous in history by association with his name and deeds. After him came streams of eager pioneers, lured by the stories that he sent back of the richness of the soil and the beauty of the land; and following these, eight years later, came the famous expedition of Lewis and Clark, all landing in the mouth of this same renowned stream. Nearly the whole of the early population of Missouri made this their point of debarkation.

A Hunter's Paradise

On ascending the gray shore the explorers found themselves in the midst of a wide, flat bottom, resting on a foundation of sand, over which was spread a top-dressing of rich alluvial clay and leaf mold, forming the most fertile soil in the world. The entire area supported a forest of enormous trees, whose thick interlocking branches shielded the rays of the sun from the earth to such an extent that there was scarcely any underbrush. It resembled a great park kept for the pleasure of man. In whatever direction they looked the vision was met by ranks of huge cottonwoods, hackberries, syc-amores, elms, walnuts, and great oaks and hickories, whose branches were so thickly intermingled that even the September sun could scarcely be seen through the blanket of foliage. Some of the oaks were six feet in diameter, straight as arrows from the ground to the first limbs fifty feet above. These gigantic members of the forest were known as burroaks, and later when the axmen came they found that the great logs could be split into rails almost without the intervention of maul and wedge, so straight and clear was the grain. A single "cut" would make a hundred fence rails.

The nut of the burr oak is much larger than that of any of the other species, and so sweet that it formed a favorite repast for bears and other wild animals; and when civilization came it fattened thousands of hogs whose flesh was prized above measure for its rich, nutty flavor.

The absence of underbrush left the vision clear, so that in every direction were avenues and vistas, resembling the well-kept lawns of colleges and public buildings. Here and there were cane-breaks located on the borders of lakes or sloughs, where briars grew and thick clusters of wild fruits season. Boone's experience as a hunter told him that in the cane he would find bears, while in the clear waters beyond he could hear the quacking and gabbling of thousands of ducks and wild geese, reveling in undisturbed security as they fattened on the fish in the water and the fruits whose clusters hung along the banks. It was a scene of wonderful activity in the midst of nature's primeval silence.

Observing these things, Boone began to feel that what he had lost in the green uplands of Kentucky was about to be compensated to him in this new land of promise; and here he resolved to lay out and establish his thousand arpents as an everlasting estate. Soon afterward he did locate and cause to be surveyed a tract of the same kind of land a few miles below his landing place, but neglected to have his grant properly recorded at New Orleans, and so lost his title. Meanwhile the river threw its current against that particular point and washed away all of the original survey except about two hundred acres, which he sold to a nephew for a trifle; with the result that at his death he did not own land enough in which to bury his aged body.

But these are sad reflections, aside from our present purpose and fruitless to be mentioned except as an indication of the too-common fate of mankind.

Two Bears and a Nest of Yellow Jackets

Presently as they made their way through this elysian scene, Boone discovered two bears high up among the branches of a leaning sycamore tree where they had climbed for the purpose of rob-bing a bee's nest. The bear is a clumsy climber, and these could not have made their way up the trunk of so large and smooth a tree except for the fact that it inclined at such an angle as to afford them safe foothold. They were now perched out over the top of a smaller oak, which in case of need would afford a comparatively safe means of descent.

The discovery was mutual on both sides, whereupon the larger of the bears let go his hold and came lumbering down through the branches of the oak, checking the rapidity of his descent by clinging to the limbs as he came. No sooner did he touch the ground than Boone shot him dead, while at the same instant Poncho blazed away with his musket at the bear in the tree, and missed it: whereupon it came down through the branches of the oak as the first one had done. It landed within a few feet of where the Indian stood, and immediately gave its attention to him. But Poncho, having an empty gun in his hands and no desire for a personal tussel, made off as fast as he could, the bear following close upon his heels with fierce growls and other intimations of an unpleasant disposition. Within a few yards the doughty warrior came to a large fallen and partially decayed tree, over which he leapt with the agility of a deer. But in doing so one of his moccasins disturbed a nest of yellow jackets, whereupon the infuriated insects swarmed out and attacked both him and the bear. When a yellow jacket stings it does not let go and fly away, as most other venomous insects do; it clings close and continues the fight. The only way to get rid of it is to brush it off.

A scene now occurred which excited Boone to laughter. On the side of the tree next to him was the bear, snorting and slapping at the busy insects; while on the opposite side was Poncho engaged in similar gymnastics, punctuated with much swearing in bad English.

"Heap dam' bugs!" yelled the savage, vigorously slapping himself and rolling on the ground in vain efforts to escape the torture of the stings.

Meanwhile Boone, according to his custom, had reloaded his gun and soon relieved the bear of further annoyance by shooting it in the head. Then quickly cutting a branch of cedar to serve as a brush, he ran to the relief of his companion and drove the insects away.

"Umph!" growled the Indian, shaking himself free of any remaining tormentors; "heap dam' bugs! Much bite!"

Poncho Loses a Treasure

When he began to inspect the results of the combat a look of consternation spread over his features; for he had lost one of his precious scalps. It was the very one which he had taken from the head of the Osage warrior, and therefore prized above all his other possessions. In spite of his most painstaking efforts he could not locate the relic. In his struggles it had been torn from his belt and doubtless thrown into the matted peavine or ground into the soft earth. Now that it was gone his glory had departed! He dared not ask his venerated master to assist in the search, knowing well that Boone would regard the loss of the scalp as a fortunate circumstance; as indeed he did, for he saw and understood what it was that had brought sorrow to the bold warrior. But he made no sign. It was just as well to let some things alone.

As for Poncho, he would rather have been stung a thousand times than lose the trophy he prized so highly. The pain of the stings was temporary, but he might never again have an opportunity to scalp another Osage. He had counted on it as a certain means of great advancement, but now his hopes were blasted.

He knew that his people would make light of any claim he might set up to having scalped an Osage warrior single-handed with no evidence to show for it, and he himself be regarded as a boaster and unworthy of respect. If he had been alone he would have indulged in larger volumes of profanity, but he had observed that Boone, unlike other white hunters whom he had met, and from whom he had acquired the small amount and poor quality of his English, never used an oath or expressed his feelings in any but quiet and measured terms. The dignity of the great white chief so awed him that he felt obliged to endure his loss in silence, but resolved mightily within his suffering bosom to seek out and scalp another Osage as soon as circumstances would permit.

For half an hour the poison of the yellow jackets made Poncho sick, and acting on Boone's advice he lay down on the grass and rubbed his sore spots. Meanwhile the old hunter cut a mess of spareribs from the side of the larger bear and had it broiled crisp by the time his companion recovered his appetite. The spareribs and a liberal portion of half a peck of ripe plums which Boone gathered, restored the warrior to his natural state and caused him to announce his readiness for any new adventure that might happen along. Instead of returning to his own people and being promoted to a chieftaincy, as he had fondly dreamed, Poncho now decided to remain in the country of the pale faces, and live in solitude and sorrow until chance or some happy incident might throw another Osage in his way, when he would repair the loss and proceed on the road to glory.

Episode Number Seven

Boone's Dream

Having skinned the two bears and stretched their hides on limbs beyond the reach of ravenous animals, to be tanned later into sleeping rugs, the two men resumed their way over the bottom lands in a northeasterly direction, until they came to a limestone ridge which rose a hundred feet above the level of the valley. Here, as Boone expected, he found a large spring flowing from under a ledge of rock, and throwing himself upon the ground he drank gratefully from its refreshing waters.

"Heap good drink", remarked Poncho, as he followed the example of his master.

Then after kindling a fire Boone broiled some of the bear steaks which they had brought with them, and as they sat on the grass and ate meat and drank water out of the spring Poncho filled himself so full that he felt obliged to spend the remainder of the day in restful slumber.

DANIEL BOONE'S SPRING.

The little boy looking so intently into the spring, from which he has just been drinking, is a third grandnephew of Rebecca (Bryan) Boone.

Special photograph for sketch entitled, DANIEL BOONE IN MISSOURI. Release Sunday, August 4, 1901.

Olivares Syndicate, 204 N. 3d St., St. Louis, Mo.

Close by the side of the spring stood a great elm whose branching limbs spread out over a considerable area of the sward, and was destined soon to become famous as "Boone's Judgement Tree", a title which the fragment yet remaining still remains. After his appointment as Alcalde of the Femme Osage District—an office carrying both civil and military authority—he established his court under the shade of the tree by the side of the spring; and as the country grew with rapid settlements of the good and bad, culprits were brought to him and he decided in a patriarchal way how many lashes were due each offender in proportion to the nature of his crime.

DANIEL BOONE'S "JUDGMENT TREE."

At present, while Poncho slept, Boone lounged upon the grass and gloried in the new acquisition, longing to gladden the heart of Rebecca with the story of later land of promise which lay just beyond the great river. But first a shelter must be provided for her and the family, and the following morning, with such help that Poncho could render, he began the erection of a temporary cabin. It was located about fifty feet northwest of the spring and composed of small, straight logs and poles, notched at the same time form a solid structure. The roof was composed of strips of bark held in place by weight-poles, and at one end there was a wooden chimney, plastered with clay to accommodate the smoke that would arise from the fire on the hearth. Here also would come the fragrance of roasting meats and baking bread to indicate the hospitality which lay beneath. On the grass, between the cabin and the spring happy children would romp and play, and make excursions into the adjacent woods to bring bouquets of wild flowers and armsful of luscious fruits.

When the cabin was finished and ready for occupation, Boone returned to the city for the family, while Poncho sought and found a habitation for himself. When located it was neither a palace nor a hovel, but an open space under a shelving rock extending back far enough to form a small but comfortable cave. Here Poncho lived and dreamed and absorbed as much whisky as his system would accommodate, until in his old age he mysteriously disappeared and was never seen again by white man. But he will reappear at intervals during time progress of these Episodes, and render his need of entertainment to the public.

On returning to St. Louis, so eager was Boone to get himself and family domiciled in their new home that he scarcely took time to call on the Lieutenant-Governor, and wholly neglected the formalities necessary to make sure of his title, as stated previously. With the implicit trust of a child he had faith in all men, and supposing that the occupancy of the land would be sufficient evidence of his ownership, he departed with the family to found a new home in the wilderness.

The "Palatinate" Takes Form

As soon as they were at home in the cabin Boone and his son, Daniel Morgan, Jr., located and surveyed the thousand arpents that had been granted to him in the bottom bordering on the river, and on the bank of the latter they built a cabin and began to found a town, which they named Missouriton. They also erected a small mill and brought the necessary machinery from St. Louis; and in time several newly arrived immigrants chose locations and built houses near the mill. Thus Missouriton became a place of great expectations, even later coming to be regarded as the future capital of a new state; and Boone's vision of affluence and a great landed estate seemed on the way to realization.

But following the purchase of Louisiana by the United States, no record was found of the Boone grant and his claim was held to be void, his land reverting to the domain. Subsequently our government ceded him a thousand acres, partly embracing the tract which he had derived from Spain; whereupon the river formed an eddy and pushed its muddy waters into the space occupied by Boone's land. Only a small plot of 181 acres escaped the greed of the river, and in 1815 the old pioneer sold this to his nephew, William Coshow (Uncle Billy), for the sum of $315. Thus again, the founder of two empires became landless, without even the narrow four-by-six feet necessary for each individual's last resting place.

The Washington of the West

By commission dated on the 11th of June, 1800, Boone was appointed Commandant of Femme Osage District, and on the transference of the territory to the United States our government continued him in the duties of the office until the close of the war with Black Hawk and his warriors in 1816. His commission made him commander-in-chief of all the military forces in the District, and on several occasions he assembled an army as large as Washington's and fully as effective in fighting quality. It is not inappropriate therefore to recognize the title which has been conferred upon him as the "Washington of the West."

In civil affairs Boone's decisions were final, with the exception of disputes over land titles, which had to be referred to the crown or its local representatives, or to the higher courts after the territory came under the jurisdiction of the United States. In all respects Boone was as much an emperor in the domain over which he ruled as Napoleon of France, but he never exercised his authority with similar despotic assertion.

Punishment for crimes and misdemeanors of the lessor sort was summary and quickly inflicted. No juries were impaneled, but the accused, if he confessed or was proven guilty, was bound to a sapling that stood near the Judgement Tree and whipped with a hickory withe, the number of lashes being proportioned to the gravity of the offense. That is to say, the punishment was made to fit the crime, and it met the requirements of the age. No thief or lawbreaker was ever known to resent the judgement of Daniel Boone. Dressed in buckskin and seated at the roots of the ancient elm, he dispensed justice to his neighbors in a manner that never failed to win their approval. The confessed or proven thief who had shot or placed his mark on the shoat of a neighbor, was promptly "whipped and cleared" and sent about his business without further annoyance or loss of caste. It was not an unusual thing after an offender had paid the penalty of his wrong doing, for Boone to bathe the welts on his back with cold water out of the spring, and then invite him to the house to partake of one of Aunt Rebecca's famous dinners.

It was only the minor classes of criminals who were brought to trial before the patriarch. The offences were mainly hog-stealing, or gouging of eyes; or possibly an occasional shooting without justifiable cause. But there were not many of the latter. It was generally conceded that in cases of this kind justice was on the side of the quickest trigger. The slow-trigger man, having passed beyond earthly jurisdiction without leaving any evidence in his behalf, was regarded as having taken an appeal to a higher authority, and there was no use to worry about him.

All kinds of stock were free to run on the "range", and if the hunting was poor, or the family provider too lazy to go after the game and his children were crying for food, it was not deemed a serious misdemeanor for the possessor of an easy conscience to go into the woods and shoot another man's fat shoat. There were plenty of fat shoats in the timber, and what difference did it make about their ownership? Moreover, when a pig was in the pot with his ears containing the legal mark removed, no witness could testify whether it belonged to Tom Jones or Pete Bryan; and an accommodating conscience could readily fit itself to the conditions. So it was the rule to bring home the bacon, and take the chance of a whipping under Daniel Boone's Judgement Tree.

Lest some may imagine that Uncle Daniel did the whipping himself, I take this occasion to say, very emphatically, that he did not. He passed judgement and the penalty was inflicted by the sheriff, or in the absence of that official, by a constable especially appointed for the occasion. The heart of the old patriarch was too tender to admit of his punishing a culprit. In fact he had serious doubts if there were any such people, and therefore it was as much as could be expected of him to pass sentence and let somebody else render the punishment. And so it happened that lovers of pork, with elastic consciences, found it convenient to risk the judgement of "Uncle Daniel" rather than suffer the pangs of an empty stomach or hear the children cry for meat.

Pete Bryan's Coon-Skin Cap

Among those who were most frequently up for trial on the charge of pig-stealing, was Pete Bryan. He was comparatively a regular attendant at the Judgement Tree, and he raised the art of acquiring pork that did not belong to him almost to the height of a learned profession.

Pete was a distant relative of our family, but the connection was so shadowy and dim that we made no effort to trace it home. His reputation was not the kind that one cares to court. He was one of those free-and-easy philosophers who believe that a living is due every soul born into the world, whether the soul is worthy of a living or not; and if the living does not come freely it is his duty to go after it. Therefore Pete did not worry. When deer and bear were scarce, there were usually plenty of pigs in the forest; and if your gun happened to go off by accident and kill one of them, it was not a mortal sin. At least that was the way Pete looked at it.

He wore a cap by which he was distinguished all over Femme Osage District, and he was never known to plead an alibi when the cap was found where he might have been. It was perhaps the most peculiar cap that ever graced a human head, in the fact that it was made of tanned coonskin with a red fox's tail depending from the rear. There were other coonskin caps in the country, but they were adorned with the tails of the animals which had formerly worn them. Uncle Daniel himself had a cap of this kind, which he wore whenever he went hunting; but if it had been found in the woods, or near the smoke-house of Grandfather Jonathan, no amount of evidence would have convinced a jury that it belonged to Pete Bryan. That gentleman's headgear was the only coonskin cap in the District that had a red fox's tail. The tails of other caps had been attached by nature, but Pete's was fastened with a buckskin string.

Episode Number Eight

Horse Thieves and Counterfeiters

No sooner did it become generally known in Kentucky and the Carolinas that Daniel Boone ("Uncle Daniel" as he was familiarly known) had removed with his family to the wilderness beyond the Mississippi, than other pioneers began to turn their steps in that direction; and while the country did not settle with the amazing rapidity that characterized the more recent occupation of Oklahoma, it did acquire a regular and consistently increasing stream of immigrants. Black Hawk and his people became alarmed at the rapid growth of the white population, which at the beginning of the Indian war, about 1813, numbered several thousand. It is impossible to give anything approximating an exact enumeration; but the settlements extended from St. Charles on the east westward along the Missouri River to a point opposite where Jefferson City is now located, and thence back in a wide circle northward and eastward, through the present counties of Callaway, Montgomery, and Lincoln, a space large enough for an empire in the more hampered regions of Europe.

Most of this influx of population was composed of honest pioneers seeking land on which to build homes for themselves and their families; but following in their wake came also reckless and desperate characters, gamblers, horse thieves, counterfeiters, desperadoes, and murderers. Under such conditions it was only natural that Boone's duties as head of the only court in this vast region should increase to a very large extent and except for the necessarily summary character of the proceedings no one man could have disposed of a tenth part of the cases that came before him. Many of the people took the law in their own hands and quickly disposed of the worst characters, but hundreds of the smaller offenders were brought before Boone. Pete Bryan, with his peccadilloes was a fair representative of this class, and as we have just been introduced to him it may be interesting to extend the acquaintance.

Pete Bryan Pleads His Own Cause

On a certain occasion Pete was brought before Uncle Daniel on the usual charge of pig-stealing, and he elected to plead his own cause. He admitted killing the pig that did not belong to him, but claimed that it was an accident. He said he was cleaning his gun and getting ready to go after a big fat bear that was hibernating near his cabin, when the blamed old shootin' iron went off unbeknownst to him and without malice prepence and hit the pig squar' in the head. Under such circumstances it was the most natural thing in the world for the pig to die, and bein' a man of good intentions he did not like to let it lie thar and spile, 'specially with the children hungerin' after meat. So he took it in and dressed it and the little folks e't it.

"Now, Uncle Dan'l" he pleaded, "if you do something ag'in the law without meanin' to do it hit ain't no crime, 'specially if hit helps to feed the children at the same time."

The appeal to Uncle Daniel's love of children was irresistible, and he admitted that there were extenuating circumstances in the present instance. He therefore adjudged ten lashes for Pete instead of the scriptural thirty and nine; and when the punishment had been duly inflicted and the welts bathed in cold spring water, he invited Pete to dinner, and Aunt Rebecca baked him several platesful of her fragrant hoecakes. Smoothed with home-made butter and sweetened with honey fresh from the hive, Pete ate all that was set before him and asked no questions. Indeed he was so overcome by the kindness of the family and the delicacy and abundance of the repast that he shed tears, and vowed on a stack of Bibles a mile high that he would never shoot another pig that did not belong to his own herd. But he was on hand again at the next meeting of court for his regular whipping.

"Whipped and Cleared"

Several years previous to this incident my grandfather had settled on a tract of land adjoining the Boone plantation on the west, and the public road followed the rail fence that bordered the yard in front of the house. Observing Pete approaching, Grandfather went out and leaned on the fence for the purpose of getting news concerning the trial and its results.

"Well, Pete," he said, as that worthy came shambling by, "how did you come out?"

"Eh gad," replied Pete, with a triumphant smile, "whipped and cleared in the reg'lar way!"

Pete Loses His Cap

Grandfather was so pleased with the outcome of the affair that he invited Pete into the house, and gave him a pewter mugful of his best corn whisky; whereupon he resumed his way homeward in high spirits but his gun went off by accident and killed another stray pig before he arrived.

Grandfather kept his bear bacon and smoked venison in the smoke-house that stood in the back yard, and Pete was fond of that kind of meat. One night after the family had retired there was trouble in the smoke-house, and the dogs turned out and raised a row. A general rumpus, with some swearing and a good deal of yelling followed, but grandfather did not worry. He told mother Mary that he thought the dogs would attend to the case, and rolled over and went back to sleep. He had a broad suspicion as to the cause of the trouble, but did not wish to catch the culprit red handed. Next morning Pete Bryan's coonskin cap with the red fox's tail was found in the yard, and grandfather sent him word to come and get it.

Pete came, and was profoundly grateful. He said he had lent his cap to a "trifling feller" who had promised to bring it back, and he wouldn't have lost it for a thousand dollars. The casual manner in which he referred to large sums of money might have indicated affluence on Pete's part, but the most he was ever known to carry at one time was a counterfeit two-bits that he kept as a pocket-piece. In the present instance he was powerful glad Uncle Jonathan had found his cap, as it was the only one he had, and if he lived to be as old as Methuselah he never expected to get another like it. Grandfather apologized for having caused him any trouble in the matter, and gave him a haunch of venison to carry home to the children. Pete did not forget the kindness, but returned the following week and stole the ham of a bear.

German Justice

On a certain occasion Boone was visited by a distinguished German jurist who had come to America to look the country over. "We are very strict mit 'em in Yarmany" he confided to the old pioneer. "We don't allow no foolishness," he amplified. "We make 'em come right up unt dake the medicine."

So Boone invited him to a seat on the grass by his side, and suggested that he try some of the cases. Among others, of course, was Pete Bryan, the old stand-by, who kept the court from getting rusty. The German regarded him fiercely, and put the usual question of guilty or not guilty.

"Not guilty," responded Pete.

The German regarded him with augmented fierceness.

"If you are not guilty," he said, "vhat are you doing here, taking up the time of the court? You think ve got nodings to do! If you are not guilty, begone mit you, or I vill mineself gif you the best licking you ever had!"

Then turning to Boone he continued, "That's the vay we do 'em in the oldt country. Ve don't stand for no foolishness. If a feller says he ain't guilty ve send him aboudt his peesness mighty qvick."

Boone admitted that it was a new way of administering justice, and undoubtedly saved time and expense. It was probably suited to an older country, where the population was greater and cases were more numerous; but he had his doubts about its corrective influence on such characters as Pete Bryan.

Some years later, after the German immigration had brought a considerable population from that country to Femme Osage District, an intelligent German named Mueller was elected Justice of the Peace, and in due course of time pete Bryan was brought before him for adjudication.

The judge regarded him with composure.

"Vell, Mr. Prisoner," he said, "are you guilty or not guilty?"

In this instance the evidence was so clear that Pete decided it would be wise to plead guilty and throw himself on the mercy of the court; so he responded,

"Guilty, your Honor."

The justice regarded him with stern judicial dignity.

"Vell, Mr. Prisoner," he snorted, "you say you are guilty, but you don't come no such shenanigan over this court. Py tam', if you are guilty you shall prove it, or git a tam' goot vipping!"

Pete had no difficulty in proving his guilt, and was assigned to the whipping-post as usual.

Horse-Stealings and Shootings

The most serious offense that ever got as far as Boone's court was horse-stealing, but not many cases of that kind ever lived long enough to travel far. The culprits usually died of heart-failure or shortness of breath on the way.

If a man was found riding a horse whose name he could not call, it was the custom to send him west by means of a rope, a noose and a friendly limb. Horse-stealing was a crime that Boone's fellow-citizens preferred to handle in their own way, for it was well known that the old hunter could barely stick to the back of a horse himself, having spent most of his life on foot, and he was therefore not qualified to appreciate a horse or render judgement in a case of this kind. For this reason very few of those free-and-easy gentlemen who rode other people's animals ever came to judgement under the tree where Boone presided.

But a different view was taken of shootings. The pioneers felt that under certain conditions it was absolutely necessary that they should shoot an offending neighbor, and throw themselves upon the mercy of the community. As no one knew when his turn might come, none were disposed to regard the crime with severity. If a man got shot it was partly his own fault, in not being as expert with a gun as he should have been. They did not care to execute sentence against a fellow-citizen, when it might soon be necessary for them to appeal for mercy in a similar emergency. Therefore the man who shot first was generally assumed to have been innocent, unless there were adverse circumstances to the contrary which event he was hung to a limb and the case dismissed.

Boone, therefore, was never required to try a single murder case, and only one of that class ever came before him. In this instance he declared his incapacity, and signed the man's bond to appear before the court in St. Charles, where he was tried and acquitted. If he had run away and left the country it might be interesting to estimate the worth of the old hunter's bond. He evidently believed the man was innocent.

Episode Number Nine

A Wealthy Pioneer

For some reason which I never was quite able to understand, my grandfather Jonathan was a man of considerable means. That is to say, he might, in case of a pinch, have raised as much as three or four thousand dollars over and above his immediate necessities, and that was more than any other member of the family could have done at the time. The rule with the Bryans was---and is---to make a little money while they are young, and lose it and die poor when they are older.

On the other hand, the Boones never made money at any time in their lives. I never heard of one of them who had more than the law allowed. If a member of the family had found a pot of gold at the end of a rainbow, and a fresh bear trail at the other end, he would have disregarded the gold and gone after the bear. This was a never-failing Boone characteristic.

When Grandfather Jonathan came west to be near Uncle Daniel and Aunt Rebecca, he had several thousand dollars ahead and was esteemed a rich young man for those times. This was in 1800. He not only kept what he had then, but added other thousands to it; so that at the end of his life he was what might even now be termed a man of affluence. How he managed it I never could understand, for no other member of the family has ever manifested that kind of talent. Several have been money-makers, but they invariably contrived to lose all they had before "passing on", and depended on their more fortunate relatives for decent burial. Three representatives of the generations that followed Grandfather Jonathan became millionaires, but before dying made good the family record by losing their last dollar and depending on sorrowing friend to send them heavenward in a decent sort of way—assuming, of course, that heaven was their destination. (Some doubt has been expressed on this point.)

Jonathan Bryan made money and bought lands and transmitted them to his heirs. What the heirs did with them is another thing, as King George IV. would have said if the matter had been submitted to him.

When Jonathan became an elderly man—no Bryan ever gets old—it was his custom to ride about the country in a carriage drawn by two blooded horse and driven by a negro servant in livery—and this was more than a hundred years ago, in the wilderness of Missouri! But in spite of all this show and glitter he was unpretentious. He never "put on a style". What he sought was decent respectability and comfort, and these he had in degree large enough to satisfy him and those who knew him.

Traveling by Keel-Boat

On Christmas day of the year 1800, Jonathan Bryan and his family landed at the mouth of Femme Osage Creek, having made the trip in style, according to his custom, in a keel-boat from a point on the Ohio River where the city of Maysville is now located. A keel-boat was a long, slender vessel with a keel in the center to assist in steering and do its part in preventing the craft from turning over; for it was so uncertain in its floating capacity that a slight displacement of cargo might upset it. Or, in modern terms, if a buxom Lu-Lu had walked across the deck from starboard to larboard, or the contrary way she probably would have capsized the "floating palace" and produced a Johnstown flood. The gunwales were protected by heavy boards of oak set on edge to a height of about three feet, for the purpose of catching leaden bullets that were occasionally fired by playful savages dancing among the shores. At the stern there was a more or less protected shack in which the mother of the family did the cooking and washing, spanked the babies, read her Bible (when she could read anything), went to bed at sundown, and felt she was leading an exemplar life.

The family and the crew were supplied with an abundance of fresh fish caught in the river, buffalo and venison steaks and choice spareribs of bears' meat, obtained by right of superior marksmanship. If any objected to such rich fare he was regarded as effeminate and unworthy to travel in a palatial keel-boat. They had also "pone" corn bread and hominy beaten in a wooden mortar, with plenty of wild honey for sweetening. They lived so high that the men were generally sorry when the voyage ended. For the women, it made no difference, one place being the same to them as another. The main thing was to be good, read a chapter in the Bible every day, smoke a cob pipe of tobacco at bedtime, and be always prepared for the worst.

The boats were held together with wooden pins in place of iron nails, of which there were few. Such as they had were wrought out by blacksmiths, and any old anvil will reveal the hammering-place. Hence the title "Wrought-nails". They were soft and easily bent, but when driven into the head they would "stay put" until the end of time. But such nails were regarded with suspicion by those who had souls to save.

In traveling by keel-boat, you floated in grandeur down the rivers whose currents happened to run in your direction, but on coming to upstream tributaries you were expected to "cordelle", or row with an oar, or push with a pole, according to your condition and circumstances in life. It was in this way that you paid your passage. Such mode of traveling was regarded by some as good for the health, and they claimed to adopt it for that reason.

The term "cordelle" was derived from a man of that name, who was fond of the exercise and followed it as a profession. All one had to do was to get out on the bank, among the Indians, bears, and snakes, and help pull or cordelle the boat by means of a rope, or grapevine when no rope was to be had. On coming to a fallen tree you jumped over, or on arriving at a briar patch you ducked your head and plunged through, regardless whether you ran into a bear or panther, or possibly disturbed a family of rattlesnakes summering on the bank of the river. If you happened to plunge into a nest of yellow jackets or hornets, they put life into your movements and helped you on the way. Such traveling was a never-ending source of variety, and was regarded as highly beneficial to those suffering from weak lungs or eccentric digestion. Cordelling a keel-boat was easy to learn, and there were no workmen's unions to discourage the profession.

As soon as Jonathan rounded-to and cabled his boat in the mouth of Femme Osage, he changed his every-day suit for raiment of tanned and fringed buckskin, and wended his way through the peavines, cane brakes, and hibernating bears to the home of Aunt Rebecca and Uncle Daniel, where he spent the night .It will be remembered—or at any rate it is a fact—that Rebecca, a sister of James Bryan, married Daniel Boone, who thereupon became "Uncle Daniel" in the family. Although it was a brevet promotion he always seemed like a real uncle, and evidently felt that way himself.

(James Bryan was my great grandfather, a Colonel in the Continental Army, and for a season served on Washington's staff as treasurer.)

They were mighty glad to see nephew Jonathan, for he brought the first news they had had from the folks at home for five long years; and besides, Jonathan was a favorite nephew. They were now well fixed in the cabin of 12 x 16 feet, and if one felt crowded for room there were vast open spaces on the outside, where he could slumber in peace and comfort. That night they did little but commune and converse, and went to bed so late that Uncle Daniel suggested it was hardly worth while to get up, as they would pretty soon have to go to bed again.

After breakfast of hoecake, bear's bacon and eggs, sweet potatoes roasted in hot ashes, butter cold and sweet from the spring-house, and a great wooden bowl of honey in the comb, Uncle Daniel and the boys accompanied Jonathan to a very desirable location for a home. (By "the boys" I mean Daniel M. and Nathan, each of whom afterward became almost as famous as their father.)The place was about a mile west of the Boone cabin, beyond a murmuring brook, where from the top of a knoll there was a fine view of Femme Osage valley. A spring of water bubbled at the foot of the knoll, and Uncle Daniel admitted that it was almost as fine a spring as his own; a considerable admission for him to make! Taking everything into consideration he declared his opinion that there was not a finer location for a home anywhere else in the District, and Jonathan being of the same mind lost no time in coming to a decision. There he planted his staff and said he would abide; and so well did he keep his word that both he and Grandmother Mary still lie side-by-side only two hundred yards away. There also lies James Bryan, brother of Rebecca Boone, a colonel of the line in the year of the Revolution and a member of Washington's staff. I was there not long since and witnessed the dedication of a monument to him by the ladies of the D. A. R.

Curious Freak of a Turkey

While they stood by the spring and drank of the cold water and admired the beauty of the surrounding scenery, a flock of wild turkeys came out of the woods to drink and bathe in the brook nearby. They afforded a tempting mark, but neither of the boys had brought a gun, and Uncle Daniel had only "old Checlicker", whose ball was big enough to tear a turkey to pieces. It was a fine gun for Indians, bears, and buffaloes, but the only way to make it effective in turkey hunting was to shoot the birds through the head. He could easily have done this in the present instance, but preferred to try a little sporting rifle which Jonathan had brought with him. It carried a ball about the size of a goose-shot, and Jonathan used it exclusively in hunting squirrels, quails, and other small game. Uncle Daniel took up the little piece and shot one of the turkeys through the body. It flew straight up, as straight as a bullet goes, and kept on until it became a mere speck in the sky. Then it closed its wings and came down, down, with tremendous sweep until it struck the earth within twenty feet of where it started. The fall was so great and the turkey so fat and tender that it burst open and was not worthy carrying home. Meanwhile the rest of the flock had flown away as soon as the shot was fired, and that day they had no turkey for dinner.

But they were not to go without fresh meat, for on the way back to the house Jonathan shot off the heads of six quails with his little rifle and Uncle Daniel did the same for a fine fat grouse that was drumming in a plum thicket. Then to cap the climax, Cuff sprang into a pool in the creek and brought out a ten-inch trout, thus adding fresh fish to the flesh and fowl which had already been secured. There was no need to go hungry in a country that abounded in all kinds of game, and a bee's nest on every acre.

Episode Number Ten

Building A Home In the Wilderness

The day following the incidents previously related, Jonathan undertook the building of a residence for his family, and with the help of the Boones and the colored people they "raised" and roofed in a cabin on the knoll above the spring. An opening was left for a window, and a door was hung by leather straps; whereupon the abode was ready for the coming of the family. In place of beds, soft and warm bear skins and buffalo hides were provided, and nothing could have been more comfortable or inviting.

Then came the removal from the boat, a matter of only a few hours with so many willing hands to help. Last of all the family arrived, walking and carrying their household goods, and by night they were installed in the new home by the spring. I never heard what became of Jonathan's keel-boat. It was a valuable asset in his possessions, and he was too keen a trader to allow it to become a dead loss. I imagine that he sold it to some St. Louis trader, and it may have been the boat that Lewis and Clark embarked in when they started on their famous voyage to the Pacific Ocean; but I do not state this as a fact. It is true, however, that they used a boat of this kind, and when they came up the river they landed at the mouth of Femme Osage and came out and camped in Jonathan's yard about ten days, for the purpose of consulting him and Uncle Daniel about the western country, and what course to pursue in maintaining friendly relations with the wild Indians. This incident will be more fully presented in a future Episode.

A House-Warming

The night following the completion of the cabin and the removal of the family, the Boones came over, and with a few other neighbors who had heard of the new arrivals they had an old-time house-warming that was worthy of the name. A white-haired darky scraped a fiddle and beat time, while the guests danced in the yard, for there was not room enough in the house.

As frolic went on Uncle Daniel and Jonathan watched the others enjoy themselves, for neither of them ever learned to dance; and Uncle Daniel remarked with some degree of sadness that he did not know there were so many people in the District. The population was becoming congested, and he might have to go west again to get a little fresh air.

Trail of the Boone's Lick Road

He did go west a few days later, accompanied by Jonathan, into the distant wilds of what is now Howard County, where some Indians had told him there were "heap plenty" salt springs and much game that came to lick the salt. They found the springs and the game, as the Indians had represented, and planned to develop the place for supplies of salt for the settlements. Transportation could be had by pack animals overland, or "dug-outs" and canoes in the river, all of which were subsequently employed. Out of this came the great "Boone's Lick Road", which remains to this day (1930) the chief artery of travel east and west across that part of the state.

At first most of the salt was brought down the river, a dangerous and uncertain mode of transportation, as Uncle Danial himself discovered. On a certain occasion, having loaded a large dug-out with salt, he made the trip in safety up to the very last moment, when on rounding-to at his own landing place in Darst Bottom, a whirlpool caught the craft and overturning it dumped the salt into the river. It was a serious and provoking loss, and afterward most of the salt was carried on the backs of horses over the trail which Boone and Jonathan had blazed. The trail soon became a recognized road, when carts and wagons were substituted. With the coming of the salt problem solved itself, but previous to that time "salt was salt" among the settlers, and was regarded as one of the most precious of their domestic requirements. Only a few days ago a friend asked me what the hunters did for salt when they were in the wilderness; did they eat their meat "raw"? By no means! It was the custom for every hunter to carry a small pouch of salt with him, and when this got low or gave out, he traded for a fresh supply with some Indian or fellow-hunter; or found a salt spring and made salt himself. And how did they do it? They boiled the water in a bark pot, by inserting red-hot stones, until it evaporated into pure salt.

The First Steamboat

The first steamboat that came to St. Louis was the "General Pike", in 1817, only three years before Boone's death; and it is probable that he never saw the vessel or any other of the kind. The "General Pike" has been described as a flat boat with a small steam engine on deck and a paddle-wheel on each side. It was not much of a boat, but it floated and could make its way upstream (when the current was not too swift), and it was a great advance over anything which had been seen before.

It was a long time before the era of "floating palaces" arrived, followed by railroads; and now we have automobiles and airplanes. The next thing will be for each individual to have wings of his own, and fly to the kingdom whenever he feels like it.

During the winter Grandfather Jonathan and his black slaves cleared a field in the bottom, and raised the first crop the following summer. He also obtained some blooded horses and cattle from Kentucky, and turning them loose on the range they increased so rapidly that in a year or two they more than doubled his fortune. Peavine and grass were so abundant and nutritious that the stock remained in good condition all the year round, and were only kept from going wild by regular "saltings" at home.

A Barrelful of Silver Dollars

St. Louis was the market to which the cattle and horses were driven, and the price returned in Spanish milled dollars, as they were called. As there was no use for money, it was stored in a barrel in the loft, where it accumulated until in a few years the barrel was full.

The year following his location in the Boone settlement Jonathan began the enlargement of his habitation; and having been told that a house of walnut logs would never be infested by any of the "creeping and crawling things" that seem to have been made by mistake on the sixth day, he hewed enough logs of that species to build a double-cabin, with a passage between. This passage was boarded up and had a door at each side so that there were three good-sized rooms in the house. Overhead was a loft that could be utilized as a place for storing silver dollars or sleeping when company overran the space, as it frequently did. The house stood at the top of the knoll fronting south, with a fine view of the valley and field. Back of it was the garden, and still back of that the cow-lot where the cows were milked if they could be persuaded to stand still long enough. The loft was reached by means of a stationary ladder pinned to the wall of the west room; and if you went to bed there, not duly sober at the time, you might lose your footing and land on your head at the starting place. Or, seeing a barrelful of silver dollars you might imagine you had found one of Captain Kid's places of deposit, and become so excited that you could not sleep.

(I have been particular in describing the house and its surroundings, because tragedy was enacted there a few years later in which Grandmother Mary and Aunt Jemima the cook slew two Indian warriors and saved the family from being massacred; and an understanding of the surroundings will afford a better comprehension of the incident when it is related.)

In those days practically all commercial dealings and trading were carried on by barter, or swapping, and as there was but little use for money it had very little value. No pioneer would be so foolish as to load himself down with silver dollars and assume the risk of being chased through the woods by a rampant bear or a painted savage armed with a tomahawk and a razor-edged scalping knife; therefore Jonathan never had any cause to worry about his barrel of dollars.

The new house was finished in time for a Christmas celebration at the end of the year 1803, and it remained on its original foundations for about a hundred and twenty years; when a German farmer, learning that it had historical associations, removed it to his own adjoining farm, where it still stands, an interesting relic of a past age.

Jonathan's house had no locks or bars. When it became necessary to fasten the front door—which did not often occur—the buckskin string which was attached to the wooden latch on the inside, was withdrawn and the door was locked as completely and firmly as though iron bars had been driven home. The latch string generally hung on the outside, day and night, and it was the custom for visitors to enter without knocking.

One of the first things Jonathan did after getting the family settled was to build a small stone house over the spring. It was about 10 x 12 feet in size with a flat rock extending over the bottom, and barely high enough for a six-foot man to stand straight under the roof. The rock was so arranged that the water stood at a level of about three inches in depth, and was maintained at that stage by the outflow into the brook. In this house they stored the "crocks" of milk, barrels of butter and honey, baskets of fresh eggs and game, and other articles of food that were to be kept in good condition for the table.

Honey Sandwiches

They had an abundance of wild honey, or if the supply happened to run low they had merely to go into the woods and cut a fresh bee-tree. The honey was strained before being stored in the spring-house, and there were never less than two or three barrels at a time. If the supply had been reduced to one barrel the children would have thought they were about "out of honey", and might have spread only one thickness over their bread instead of two or three. After standing a while the honey "candied" or congealed, when it was cut out in slices with a knife; and two or three of these slices between two slices of bread made a healthy sandwich. First a slice of bread well buttered, then whatever amount of honey the bread would hold, with another slice of bread on top, also well buttered. Such a sandwich was worth considering. Jonathan used to say that he did not suppose old King George the Third ever ate anything like it, and I am of the same opinion.

If you hungered after something more substantial at the breakfast table, you could help yourself to a hunk of fried ham and red gravy, backed by a tender bear or buffalo steak, or a slice of venison, and as many fresh eggs as you could accommodate on your pewter plate; and if you still suffered with the pangs of hunger you could take a run down the hill to the brook and get a jack salmon or a speckled trout to help out. There were also hominy and corn bread, and all the fresh milk and butter that heart and stomach could desire. If anyone went hungry under such conditions it was his own fault, and he was regarded with suspicion by the rest of the family.

Episode Number Eleven Missing

Poncho Raids the Hen-House

We now come to an adventure in which Cuff and our old friend Poncho were the principal actors, and it is difficult to determine which got the best of it in the end, the warrior or the dog. It happened only a few days after Cuff's celebrated fight with the two bears, in which, as we have already seen, he was easily the victor.

Early one morning the whole family were aroused by loud calls for help in the vicinity of the hen-house, accompanied by numerous imprecations in disreputable English. The sounds could not be mistaken; they were issuing from Poncho, and he was in trouble. There were several inches of snow on the ground and the weather was cold, but Jonathan had not the heart to leave his old friend in distress. So, hastily throwing a buffalo robe around his shoulders and seizing a loaded gun, he ran into the yard to ascertain what was going on.

There in close proximity to the hen-house, too close to be entirely clear of suspicion, he found Poncho and Cuff, the latter having caught the warrior by one of his ankles and stubbornly refusing to let go. Under average circumstances the two were the best of friends, but in this particular instance the dog knew the Indian was out of place and he wanted to know the reason why. Poncho kicked and yelled and swore in the worst kind of English, but it did him no good. Cuff held on grimly, and every little while gave a vicious shake, which made the warrior yell all the louder.

It soon became clear that he had come on a chicken raiding expedition, which was altogether unnecessary, because he was well liked by all the family and could have had every chicken in the house for the mere asking. But Poncho was a great warrior (in his own estimation), much too proud to beg, and he thought nobody would miss a single fat pullet where there were so many. If he had asked Grandmother Mary she no doubt would have given him a dozen, and dressed them besides; for there was no harm in Poncho, they all liked him very much, and on several occasions he had given warning of threatened Indian raids which made everyone have a kindly feeling for him. Now his vanity had gotten him into trouble and excited enmity between him and Cuff, who had been the best of friends. The dog had no evil intentions in his mind; he was merely entertaining the early visitor in his own way and keeping him out of harm until assistance came. As soon as Jonathan appeared Cuff let go, turning the intruder over to him. Jonathan led the trembling warrior into the house, where he administered a hot toddy to warm his interior. Then he dressed his wounds, and as soon as breakfast was ready sat him down at the table and urged him to eat. Poncho was not backward in complying with the invitation, but did full justice to the abundance spread out in profusion before him. Meanwhile Grandmother Mary had killed and dressed a fat hen, and rolling it in the warrior's blanket he stalked away with dignity and circumstance to his home in the cliff. As evidence of the superiority of dogs and savages over civilized men, it may be mentioned that this incident made no difference in the relations of Cuff and Poncho. They were as good friends afterward as before; but the warrior never tried to steal a chicken when he knew Cuff was guarding the hen-house.

Poncho as a Rain-Maker

In his old age, when his mind began to fail, Poncho imagined that he talked with the Spirits of his ancestors, and even with the Great Spirit himself; and that with their help he could work miracles. One day when he came to Jonathan's for his thrice-a-week remedy for snakebite, the weather was very warm, and a drought had prevailed so long that there was no water in Femme Osage Creek. Jonathan had heard of Poncho's claims in the miracle line, and asked him if he could make it rain.

"Heap plenty rain," responded the old Indian; "me make um rain same like Noah." The missionaries had taught him a little sacred lore.

Thereupon Jonathan arranged with Poncho to bring on a flood the next day and put an end to the dry spell. The old warrior was willing enough to make a display of his powers, with a fair outlook for an extra drink or two. But he said he would require some preparation in the way of suitable clothing in which to appear before the Great Spirit, or otherwise no rain would fall. The Great Spirit would turn a deaf ear to his appeals if he wore nothing more conspicuous than his loincloth and blanket.

Jonathan assured him he would attend to that, and to be on hand promptly when the sun was halfway to noon. Then he applied to Grandmother Mary for suitable raiment in which to bedeck the warrior on such an auspicious occasion, and between them they selected what seemed essential.

Uncle Daniel and his family were invited to witness the ceremonies, and a number of the neighbors, hearing of the impending miracle, assembled early next morning until the yard was filled with people of all ages and sexes. Pete Bryan was there clad in his best and wearing the celebrated coonskin cap with the red fox's tail. As the sun rose higher and higher and grew hotter and hotter, the crowd began to show signs of impatience, but Jonathan assured them that Poncho would appear on time; he was in the house at that very moment arranging his ecclesiastical robes.

Precisely at ten o'clock the chief issued from the front door, arrayed in one of Grandmother Mary's old petticoats, a "poke" bonnet such as was worn by ladies of fashion a hundred and fifty years ago, and a couple of dry sticks in his hands with which to keep time while he danced in the presence of the Great Spirit. Before commencing the exercises he paraded down to the creek and painted his face in stripes of mud, which gave his countenance a most bewildering appearance under the gaily decorated bonnet. It would be difficult to imagine a more striking picture than Poncho presented; but this was not all. The crowd had commented upon a mysteriously painted red and black striped coffee-pot, resting on a stump in the front yard, and wondered what its purpose might be. Their curiosity was now to be satisfied. Approaching the vessel with numerous bows and twistings of his body, and muttering words in an unknown tongue, Poncho removed the lid and drew forth a buffalo horn containing a mysterious brown powder. He explained to Jonathan that the powder was composed of dried mud from the bottom of a pig wallow, and that many Spirits had taken refuge in it. Some of these Spirits were bad, having come from the pigs, and it would be necessary to propitiate them before any rain would be permitted to fall. But there were other spirits of bears and antelopes in the powder, and as the ceremonies progressed these would fight the bad ones and overcome them, and "heap much rain" would result.

Then Poncho drew out of the pot a small gourdful of snake bones, and another containing the bones of frogs, which he said would bind the clouds together and hold them tight while the good spirits squeezed the water out. Afterward the snake bones would eat the bones of the frogs, and in five hours the rain would pour down. All these things were necessary in producing a full-grown flood, such as was needed at the present time.

Everything having been arranged, Poncho entered a circle which had been marked off in the yard, and began slowly dancing round and round, keeping his face raised toward the sky. As he danced he rattled the sticks and shook them toward the sun, increasing his pace until in a few minutes he was literally flying around in the circle, shouting and shaking his head and uttering inarticulate sounds. After ten or fifteen minutes of this violent exercise he fell to the ground insensible, and Jonathan was obliged to revive him with a stiff horn of corn licker.

Having thus acquired renewed energy, Poncho sprang to his feet and seizing a pewter wash-basin that lay near he beat upon it with his sticks, howled and jumped and turned hand-springs, and otherwise conducted himself in a manner pleasing to the makers of rain.

The ceremonies lasted more than half an hour, when Poncho reeled outside the circle and fell to the ground exhausted. Again Jonathan administered a "horn", and laid him in the shade to sleep off the effects of his potations and hysterical excitements.

Thereupon most of the crowd dispersed, but it could be seen that many of them were strongly impressed. One woman had a fit of the "jerks", and shrieked and bounded around in imitation of the savage chief, until her long hair came loose from its buckskin fastenings and switching back and forth cracked like a whiplash. This incident affected the crowd even more than the performance of the chief, and some remained to shout and pray during the remainder of the afternoon.

But the most impressive feature of the whole performance was, that before sunset distant thunder was heard, dark clouds came sweeping up, and a tornado of rain poured down upon the earth. It was a veritable cloud-burst. Femme Osage Creek, from a dry bed of gravel, rose into a raging flood and washed away the fences around the bottom fields. It was truly an impressive incident, and became the nucleus of an extensive revival of religion under the leadership of the local preacher. Even Pete Bryan was converted and became a licensed exhorter; but before the next quarter his gun went off by accident and killed a neighbor's pig, and Pete was whipped and cleared as usual.

The revival was in fact an outcome of a remark by Uncle Daniel. He came over to consult Jonathan the morning after the storm, and said it was a good thing Poncho had exercised restraint in his ceremonies, or he might have drowned the whole country and produced a real Noah's flood, He admitted that such an exhibition would convince almost any crowd, and he thought it ought to be taken advantage of by the preachers, in order that the community might be saved from its increasing wickedness.

But Uncle Daniel was not much impressed himself as he viewed the wreckage of his own and Jonathan's fences, and he wondered why, if Providence was so easily moved by Poncho's petitions, the rain had not been distributed more evenly over the surface of the ground.

"Poncho's Flood", as it was called, remained in the memories of the people for many years; but it was his last public performance. The irrational excitement and his heavy potations doubtless affected his health, and he mysteriously disappeared without leaving a trace. Grandfather Jonathan believed that he had been bitten by a serpent, and in his enfeebled old age he could not find his infallible remedy in time to save his life. He had probably wondered into the depths of the forest in quest of the herb, and being overcome by the poison of the serpent died and left his body where it was never found. And such was the end of Poncho the warrior.

Into the Wilderness with Boone

In 1815 when my father was sixteen years old, he was invited by Uncle Daniel to accompany him on an exploring expedition into what is now known as the Ozark region of Southwest Missouri. At that time this section was entirely unknown to white men; there was not a single road or trail leading into it, and no one had the least idea of the grandeur of the scenery or the extent and number of the water courses. It was therefore precisely the kind of country to excite Boone's imagination, and he resolved to penetrate its mysteries and see what he could find.

There was a settlement of Indians belonging to the Sac family in what is now the southwest corner of Franklin County, and a delegation from these people had visited Boone and told him that there were "heap plenty black rocks" in that region, which could be melted into bullets; and knowing this to be lead ore he was desirous of locating the deposits for the future uses of this valuable mineral.

The Indians had also told him that there were many buffalos in the same vicinity, and that they were very fat and sleek from feeding on the rich prairie grasses and peavine; the kind of buffalos that not only produced good meat, but yielded the softest and finest robes. It would be impossible to determine which of these inducements interested the old hunter most, but his imagination was fired and he made up his mind to penetrate this new land of wonders and lift the veil from its mysteries.

Of course my father joyfully accepted the invitation, for what could be more inspiring to a healthy and vigorous youth than to become the intimate companion of the most famous explorer in the world, and a man whom he knew and loved as though he had been his own father? Boone's negro boy Dan, who was a little older than my father, was to accompany them and look after the camps and do the cooking; though it was known that these duties would occupy so little of his time that he would be as free as the others to sport with his rifle and demonstrate his prowess as a hunter.

They were to travel with but little baggage, each having a robe of light-weight deerskin for sleeping purposes, a rifle, a tomahawk, and a hunting knife. In addition to these, Dan carried a small frying pan in which to cook their meals, and it may be taken for granted that for this reason he regarded himself as the most important member of the expedition.

They set out on a Sunday morning in the early part of September, and crossing the river in a canoe at the famous mouth of Femme Osage, they landed in what is now the northeastern corner of Franklin County, whence they started on their long tramp into the unknown.

Boone's Personal Appearance and Characteristics

Boone was now in his 81st year, and although time had frosted his long locks into the whiteness of the virgin snow, there seemed to be no letdown in the vigor of his movements. He led the way during the trip, manifesting the activity and spirit of his younger days; amusing himself by turning occasionally to ask "the boys" how they liked it. Of course they were delighted. They would have cheerfully walked their legs off for the glory of the adventure.

My father's recollection of Boone at that time would make him about six feet in height, rather stoutly built, though not to the extent of interfering with is movements or producing fatigue. He was slightly bowlegged, probably from the excessive use to which he had subjected those members; and he had a habit of walking with his feet in a straight line, after the Indian fashion. There was no outward turning of his toes, and an experienced hunter coming unexpectedly upon his trail would at once have pronounced it that of Boone or an Indian. His form was as erect as it ever had been, no drooping of the shoulders to indicate age, he could easily passed for a man of fifty except for the blanching of his once brown hair. His forehead was unusually high and broad, his nose of the pure Roman type, and his mouth square-cut and firm, while the moderate fullness of the lips indicated the geniality of his disposition. His chin was prominent, sloping gracefully to a rounded point, where there was a faint dimple. His eyes were a brownish gray, large and wide apart and twinkling with the good-humor for which he was famous. At no time in his life had he ever worn a beard. No matter under what conditions he might be placed he never failed to shave at least once a week. This was done when in the woods with the fine steel blade of his hunting-knife, which would cut the beard as smoothly as the best of razors.

Such was Daniel Boone at the age of eighty-one, a man to be loved and trusted by all who knew him. The face was that of a strong, determined character, yet so gentle and benevolent as to excite universal confidence. Women and children loved him as if by natural instinct.

He had spent so much of his life alone in the woods that he had become a "silent man", but he was never a morose or disagreeable one. He smiled more frequently than he frowned, and the store of clean jokes which he had acquired during his long life enlivened the camp at night. On this trip he manifested great geniality toward "the boys", amusing himself and them by playing occasional tricks on them, which they returned with interest as opportunity offered. No matter how much a joke might go against himself he never showed annoyance or resentment, but laughed as heartily as though he had been an uninterested party. His voice was low and musical, resembling a woman's more than that of a man, though it was keenly penetrating and could be heard for a long distance when released. Such was the picture that Boone created in my father's mind as they tramped through the wilderness.

An Indian Thanksgiving

Directing their course toward the southwest, and traveling by easy stages, they came at the end of the fourth day to an Indian town near where Franklin County corners with Gasconade. This was the place where his Indian friends lived who had told him about the "black rocks" and the "heap plenty buffaloes "and they were now prepared to entertain the travelers with their great annual Dog Feast. Their approach had been announced by runners, and as they drew near a grand welcome was extended to them. The following day was to be a holiday similar to our Thanksgiving, when all the people gathered to return thanks to the Great Spirit for his bounties and gifts. The Indians were a very religious people, as will be explained in subsequent relations by Black Hawk, and many of their ceremonies were similar to those of the whites.

On this occasion of public thanksgiving the principal dish was to be barbecued dog, garnished with beans, sweet potatoes, corn on the cob, wild lettuce—of which the Indians were very fond—and other dishes peculiar to the children of the forest. The dog was eaten in the belief that they would absorb with its flesh a certain portion of the faithfulness of the devoted animal, and especially its genius as a hunter. In their estimation it was a compliment to the dog to be eaten, because by means of his death his spirit was transmitted to the happy hunting grounds, where he could lie down upon the earth and witness the absorption of his physical parts by noble warriors who would transmit his fame and valor to future generations. The sentiment was so natural and poetic as to make it seem as though either dog or man ought to be willing to die for the renown it would bring him; but in either case if the victim himself had been consulted he probably would have preferred to remain among his friends whom he knew than venture into a land of strangers in quest of theoretical glory.

A Great Indian Arsenal

This village, or town, was the focus of an extensive arsenal where bows, arrows, flint hatches, and spears were manufactured and sold to other tribes in exchange for wampum, the universal currency of the red man.

The Indians who lived there were a branch of the great Sac tribe and had become wealthy as a result of their manufacturing industry; and as they did not engage in war themselves they were regarded as a people set apart for a special purpose and were never disturbed by other tribes or warriors. For a similar reason they had always remained friendly with the whites.

The origin of the arsenal grew out of the fact that in the immediate locality there were large deposits of a peculiarly hard and tough flint rock, separated into seams which rendered it flakey and easy to split. The flakes were broken into sizes convenient for the purpose intended, and ground into arrow-tips, hatchets, and spear-heads with edges almost as sharp as steel. Remains of the excavations and scattered particles of flint are still to be seen at this place of ancient industry, which disappeared after firearms had been generally introduced among the tribes.

A Ceremonious Reception

As Boone and the boys approached the village they were met by a large concourse of warriors, painted and decorated in gorgeous array, and headed by the principal chief bearing the calumet. This was a pipe with a long stem, ornamented with brilliant feathers and painted with red and blue ochre, and regarded by the red men as one of their most sacred emblems. The pleasure and geniality engendered by the smoke of the tobacco represented hospitality, while the smoke itself was regarded as the spirit of the weed, rising into the higher realms to mingle and rejoice with other spirits which had preceded it; for the Indians believed that everything had a spirit.

When the procession drew near the warriors separated into two files, which advancing on either side, danced and intoned their welcome to the strangers. Coming together in the rear they formed a circle, whereupon the head chief advanced with the calumet in his hand, and having first put it to his own lips, passed it in turn to Boone and his companions. No difference was made on account of Dan's color, in which respect the Indians knew no distinction.

This ceremony of smoking the calumet was a sign of perpetual peace, which could not be broken without treachery to the Great Spirit, or by a formal declaration of war sent in advance of hostilities. This was done by the tribe wishing to engage in war delivering a bundle of arrows wrapped in the skin of a snake to the chiefs of the opposing tribe, and the return of a similar declaration by the latter. Then both sides were free to burn the villages and kill and scalp the others, or be killed and scalped themselves, according to the fortunes of war. A more appropriate beginning of hostilities could hardly be imagined, when we consider the hideous results that usually follow struggles between nations.

No people were ever more formal and ceremonious in their intercourse with others than the red men of America, and in several respects they had a better civilization when Columbus came than the Europeans themselves.

A Dog-Feast

Following the exercises came a feast, which had been prepared in advance. Food of several varieties and in lavish abundance was pressed upon the visitors. There were barbecued roasts of venison and buffalo, fish of several kinds, muscles baked in the shell, like oysters, corn, beans, and potatoes, with hominy in lieu of bread. The Indians had not yet acquired the art of making bread. The feast began and ended with speeches of welcome by the chiefs and dances by the braves, ceremonies in which the women did not participate.

When the festivities had ended and the visitors were rolling themselves in their deerskins for the night, Dan whispered solemnly to my father:

"Say, Marse "Ligy, I got de stummick ake."

"Well, sleep it off, "was the response.

A minute later Dan appealed again:

"Say, Marse "Ligy, is you gwine ter eat dawg t'morry?"

Father laughed and said he would be obliged to, or the Indians would think he was impolite. But this did not satisfy Dan.

"I dunno 'bout dat," he said. "Hit may be perlite ter eat dawg, but I doan' believe I can git him down."

Another pause insued, which was broken with a third request for information from Dan:

"Marse 'Ligy," he said, plaintively, "will Marse Dan'l eat dawg too?"

"Certainly," replied my father; "I have heard him say that he had eaten it on several occasions, and he gave me the impression that he rather liked it."

"Umph!" grunted Dan, "he mus' 'a bin laik de man whut eat de crow. But Marse Dan'l 'll eat mos' anything."

Nothing further was heard from Dan during the night, but in the morning he was up early and very hungry.

It was a beautiful day and the festivities were already under way. Two large wolf-dogs had been especially fattened and were already being barbecued over a pit in the center of the village. The aroma of the roasting meat was sweet to the smell of a hungry man, and Dan sniffed the savor with approval.

"Marse 'Liggy," he inquired, "am dat de way a dawg smells whin he's gittin' cooked?"

"I suppose so," replied my father. "I never smelled one before, but I think it must be dog that I smell now."

Dan was silent for a little while, pondering over some great philosophical subject. Then he broke out with:

"Marse 'Ligy, did yo' ever think how good de Lawd was to us all whin he created us? He made us so dat any kin' o' meat smells good whin we's hungry: an' he even made us so dat we likes ter smell ou'selbs, else'n some ob us couldn't stan' hit."

Social and Religious Customs Among the Indians

By this time the ceremonies were beginning, and Father suggested that they had better repair to the place where food was to be served.

The warriors were assembled in a circle around the pit where the dogs had been roasted, with the guests and chiefs in the center. Outside and beyond were the women and children, for they too were to partake of the good things which the Great Spirit had provided. The guests were served first, with liberal portions of roast dog and vegetables and delicacies similar to those they had eaten the night before: then came the chiefs and warriors, and last of all the women and children.

The food was eaten in silence; no conversation of any kind was indulged, for it was a religious function. Each one was absorbing his share of the good qualities of the faithful dogs, and silently giving thanks for it. Moreover, the Indians in their natural state always regarded the act of eating as a ceremony, not to be disturbed by conversation or laughter. Neither did they wish to be observed by outsiders. Idle spectators were regarded with disfavor, and made to understand that their absence would be more agreeable than their presence. So there was neither talking nor hilarity while the feast lasted. Even the little boys and girls ate in silence; but when the feast was over the merriment began.

They had music and dancing, there were shouts of laughter and other indications of good-will, similar to what we witness at our own merrymakings. But there was not the same freedom between the sexes. The warriors danced by themselves and the women followed their example. Many of the exercises of the former were dramatic representations of scenes of war and the chase, on which of course no woman could participate.

But in general the rules prevailing between the sexes were not any more peculiar or strict than they were at the same time period among their white neighbors. At church in my youth the women occupied pews on one side of the house and the men and boys on the other. There was no mingling of the sexes. Girls and their gallants separated at the door, and did not rejoin one another until the services were over. No young man was permitted to sit in church with his mother, sister, or sweetheart; if they had attempted to exercise such a privilege they would have been tabooed. Even husbands and wives were separated, and little boys sat with their fathers and little girls with their mothers. Conditions may not have been so strict in some other localities, but they were that way where I lived and grew to manhood.

In the matter of dances, the Indians were more liberal than the white people, probably because dancing was a religious ceremony with them. In my youth I was never allowed to attend a dance, but I was told that at such places the girls sat on one side of the room and the boys on the other, entirely separate. No doubt many sly glances crossed the intervening space, but there was no opportunity to whisper sweet nothings into pretty ears. When they danced there was no intimacy further than the holding of hands; if a young swain had been so imprudent as to put his arm around the waist of his partner he would have been ostracized. No other girl would have danced with him. For similar reasons all waltzes were denounced as immoral. Yet the morals of the young people of that period were no better, if as good, as they are now. It is possible to go too far even in being good.

Dan Becomes Fond of Roast-Dog

At the feast Dan ate as heartily as any of the others. In fact he was so pleased with the taste and flavor of "roas' dawg" that he confided to "Marse 'Ligy" his purpose to raise a few fine specimens and devote them to festival occasions, such as Christmas and Thanksgiving; and especially the Fourth of July. He thought nothing could be more appropriate than to celebrate the "Glorious Fourth" with tender "roas' dawg an' sweet taters." He went so far as to declare that he liked dog better than turkey, whereupon my father brought him to time. He said he was not willing to go so far. He liked roast dog well enough in its place, but there were other kinds of meat that he would prefer as a regular diet. Such for instance as quail on toast, broiled young squirrel, nice tender duck, bear steaks, roast buffalo, and especially possum and sweet potatoes. The latter with a wink at Dan.

"Hol' on dar!" roared Dan; "whin yo' say possum an' sweet taters yo' make my mouf watah so's I doan' keer fer nuthin' else, not even roas' dawg. Possun and sweet taters am de queen's own dish, made 'speshully fer her own se'f an' not to be menshun'd 'ceptin' in de bes' society."

In the morning when they were ready to resume their journey, there was more pow-wowing and stately ceremony, and the head chief and a number of warriors accompanied them several miles. This was the same chief who had visited Boone at his home and told him about the black rocks and the buffaloes, and he now emphasized his former information by spreading his hands out to embrace the whole country as he repeated and added to what he had said before. Buffaloes were there in great herds, and black rocks could be found everywhere. As to the first of these assurances they soon had a thrilling confirmation of the fact, and on their way back they gathered quite a load of the black rocks. The chief could speak a few words of English very well, and he was as proud of them as the college professor is of his Greek and Latin.

When it came to the parting there was more ceremony, and pow-wowing, and lofty metaphor whereupon the chief turned and stalked back home at the head of his warriors, while Boone and the boys pursued their westward course.

The Englishman and the Green Persimmons

At noon they stopped to rest and eat their lunch in a grove of persimmon trees, laden with ripe and ripening fruit; and they all set to work gathering and eating the ripe ones, at the same time brushing away the bees and yellow jackets that were disposed to resent their intrusion.

"I greatly admire the wisdom of the possum," remarked Boone. "He knows a good thing when he sees it, and there is nothing that delights him more than ripe persimmons. There are wild grapes and black haws, which he also relishes, thus adding to his reputation for wisdom; but he gives the preference to the persimmon. He is an animal of rare culture and good taste. Any animal that feeds himself as daintily as the possum does is entitled to consideration. And when he is nicely roasted with sweet potatoes-------"

"Now hol' on dar Marse Dan'l !" interjected Dan, "yo' jes tryin' ter maik me jealous."

Boone observed the interruption, but proceeded with his story.

"The possum is a wise animal," he resumed. "I knew an Englishman in Kentucky who didn't know as much as the average possum. He had heard about the excellence of the ripe persimmon, and one day he filled his belly with green ones. As he labored to get the pucker out of his mouth, he said it was no wonder the Americans were classed as barbarians, when they would eat such fruit and pretend they liked it. I have seen many possums, and eaten several of them, but I have never heard of one that didn't know more than that Englishman. You couldn't make a possum eat green persimmons unless you passed them off on him for "Paulk's Pink Purgative Pills', and then they would have to be sugar coated."

The point of the joke was, that these pills were known all over the country for their drastic effect, so much so that some of the pioneers declared their belief that a dose of them would cure a mule of diabetes or a disposition to kick. The possum swallows the seed of the persimmon along with the meat, and Boone thought if he were less wise he might be persuaded to take Paulk's Pills as a relief, though the results might be surprising.

But Boone had not finished the story about the Englishman when an incident occurred which came near putting a tragic end to their further progress.

A Buffalo Stampede

As Boone was about to proceed with some additional remarks about the Englishman who ate the green persimmons, their attention was attracted by an ominous sound coming out of the thick wood that lay on the opposite side of a small prairie in which they were resting. The boys caste startled glances toward their leader to ascertain if there was any answer to the approaching danger. Boone's face was set and anxious, but he said nothing.

The prairie was merely a narrow break in the forest, only a few hundred yards wide, and they had advanced a short distance out of the woods to reach the persimmon grove. The sound, which was now assuming alarming proportions, seemed like the coming of a storm, yet the day was cloudless and the sun shone brilliantly. Boone was clearly alarmed. He turned and looked back toward the timber out of which they had come, as if there might be safety in that quarter; but shook his head and seemed to gather himself together as if to meet a dire emergency. Whatever the mysterious roar might be, he and the boys were too far advanced to seek safety by running back to the cover of the timber. Some other means of safety must be provided.

The sounds were approaching rapidly and becoming louder and more ominous. None of them had ever witnessed the outburst of a cyclone, now were the conditions such as always precede this fear-inspiring phenomenon. They could feel the earth tremble with the weight and vibration of the hidden mystery, when suddenly there burst out from the thick timber a herd of stampeding buffaloes, like a rolling sea of black devastation. In front was a long line of cows and calves, running at the limit of their speed and so compacted together that if one should fall, those behind must inevitably trample it to death. In the rear of these, and in the same dense formation, came a line of bulls whose duty appeared to be to urge on the weaker members of the herd regardless of what might lie in front of them.

In the lead of all was a lordly bull, king of the herd and master of ceremonies, directing the course of the others. They were coming in a direct line toward the spot where the men were standing, and now so close that escape seemed impossible. Horrified at the prospect of being trampled to death by the charging beasts, my father looked keenly into the face of Boone, hoping there to find some sign of safety. But the old hunter's countenance was impassive. No indication of what was passing in his mind appeared on his face; but my father was reassured by the fact that he showed no evidence of fear. Certainly there must be some way out of the awful danger, or Boone would not be so calm. He held his gun ready for instant action, but had not yet brought it to his shoulder.

Poor Dan was completely overcome with devastating fear, and dropping on his knees he shouted:

"Oh, Lawd, let me off jes' dis time an' I'll nevah do hit ag'in!

What it was that Dan had in his mind concerning some particular wickedness none but himself knew, but he evidently meant his appeal to embrace all past sins with a promise to be good ever after. Boone turned his head and smiled. There must be some way of escape, or the old hunter would not be so cool. Or was it possible that he had become dazed in the presence of such awful peril?

The rushing herd was now within fifty feet of the men, and the infatuated animals showed no sign of lessening their speed or changing their course. In another moment death beneath their grinding hooves would be the portion of the helpless men, and my father nerved himself for the frightful shock.

They had come so close that the big leader ducked his head in order to bring his horns to a proper level, while the fires of hate and fear blazed from his bulging eyes. At that moment Boone brought his gun to his shoulder, there was a flash, an explosion, and the great bull, propelled by his own velocity, turned heels over head and fell a quivering mass almost at their very feet. The huge carcass made a barrier around which the rolling sea divided, leaving an open space and safety where the men stood. As the frightened animals roared by on either side they bellowed their terror, but made no effort to harm the hunters, seeming to accept the fate of their leader as a warning which they could not comprehend.

When they were gone and hidden in the enveloping timber, Dan arose and brushed the dust from his knees.

"Mighty close shave, Marse Dan'l" he said. "Effen't hadn't bin fer me an' de Lawd A'mi'ty no tel-lin' whut mout 'er happened."

Boone smiled. "It's a good thing," he remarked, "to put your trust in Providence, but when a herd of crazy buffaloes are coming at you it does no harm to help Providence by using your gun."

He then explained to the boys that the animals were changing pasture, and having selected their new location in advance they were rushing toward it under a crazy impulse of hunger which overcame all sense of reason or fear. Under such conditions they would plunge in a solid mass into a stream of water and half the herd be drowned, or over a cliff and be crushed to death. So far as he knew they were the only animals dominated by such an insane frenzy.

"Gosh!" cried Dan, his eyes still bulging with horror over the narrow escape, "dey hain't got no 'casion ter run ober us—plenty ob room ter go to pasture on de outside."

Boone looked the trembling boy over and smiled, as much at his ease as if nothing had happened; but it was quite different with my father. In after years when he recited the adventure to me, he said that he was as badly frightened as Dan, and would probably have tried to run away except for the confidence he had in Uncle Daniel. The horror of such a frightful death clung to him throughout life, and he never mentioned the incident except with reluctance.

They camped for the night a short distance beyond the scene of their adventure, where they found a spring and an abundance of grass for a soft bed. The boys were so nervous and unstrung by their dreadful experience that they had no desire for further adventured that day, and were glad of the opportunity to rest. Boone had cut a good-sized roast from the big buffaloes hump, which he now proceeded to broil for supper; for Dan was in no condition to resume his duties as cook. His appetite, however, was not impaired, and after a bountiful meal and a night of slumber he arose the next morning declaring that he was himself again. He "wan't feared o' no buffaloes," and if a nice fat bear "come lopin' erlong" he would skin him for breakfast.

Uncle Daniel remarked that he would not object to a little bear steak himself, but that it had always been his custom to see that the bear was dead before he skinned it.

"Ob cou'se," admitted Dan, "but I'm feelin' so fine dis mo'nin dat effen a good fat one cum hoppin' erlong I mont lay holt an' skin him alibe."

Uncle Daniel replied that he had never tried to skin a bear alive, and he imagined it would be a rather exciting performance. He would prefer to try old Checlicker on him first.

Dan's vitality being now fully restored, he said he "wan't feared o' no b'ar nor buffalo," and such animals had better keep out's his way. Boone expressed admiration for his courage, but said he had too much respect for wild animals to attack them single-handed without a gun; and especially he would not care to undertake the task of skinning them alive.

Dan is Interviewed by a Mother Bear

But Dan took a different view of the matter, and was feeling so exuberant that he said he would go back to the persimmon grove and get some fruit for breakfast.

"Better take your gun," suggested Uncle Daniel. "Bears are as fond of persimmons as possums, and you might find one or two when you get there."

But Dan said he wanted plenty of fruit, and his gun would be in his way; so he left that useful instrument behind. The old hero smiled, but said nothing; but father noticed that he put fresh priming in the pan of his gunlock.

"Just in case of accident," he said, noting the look of inquiry.

When Dan came to the grove he found a cub bear in one of the trees, helping himself to the fruit. He was such a cute, fat little creature, and apparently so good natured and sensible, that the boy decided to capture and take him home for a pet. So he shook the cub down and tied him with a bark string, while he filled the pockets of his hunting jacket with ripe persimmons. The little bear whined and growled and pulled at the string, but could not get loose; and just as Dan was about ready to start back to camp he heard fearful crashing and growling on a hillside near him.

Looking in that direction he saw the old mother bear coming down, her mouth wide open and her white tusks gleaming in the sunlight. The spectacle was fear imposing, and reminded the boy that he had a pressing engagement in camp. Forgetting all about the little bear, he left it tied to the tree and set out for camp by the shortest and quickest route. The old bear followed, growling ferociously and gaining on him so fast that the outlook was discouraging. It was a free race between the two, Dan hoping to reach a place of safety and the bear just as determined to catch him. It was his first marathon, and in order to improve his running capacity he tore off his hunting jacket, the pockets filled with ripe persimmons, and threw it back over his shoulder at the bear. Seizing the garment, and evidently supposing it to be part of her antagonist's anatomy, she stopped and rent it into strips, and then resumed the race with greater vigor than ever.

Closer and closer came the raging mother bear, until Dan imagined he could feel her hot breath on the back of his neck, then he began to yell for help.

"Marse Dan'l," he shouted, "please shoot dis ole b'ar—I cayn't git away frum her—fer de lub o' heaven shoot her!"

Uncle Daniel heard the call, as he had expected, and with old Checlicker in his had started on a dead run for the scene of disturbance. He had not far to go. The boy was putting in his best licks and doing himself proud as a runner, and despite the old bear's most desperate efforts she could not quite reach her victim. The climax, however, was about to be reached when Boone came in sight, just as the bear made her final spring. With a tremendous bound she landed on Dan's back—with a bullet in her brain; for, as usual, old Checlicker had done its work well.

A Talented Cub Bear

The bear having fallen upon Dan with her whole weight, he was knocked over and rolled on the ground, shouting with all his might for "Marse Dan'ls" help; and he was a truly thankful darkey when he found that the trouble was over, and he was still all in one piece.

"Neber ag'in!" he said, as he got up and shook the dust from his clothes. "Oncst is 'nuff fer me!"

"I thought you might find a bear" said Uncle Daniel coolly, "and if you hadn't been as big a fool as the Englishman you would have taken your gun with you."

He and Dan returned to the grove, where they found the cub still fast to the tree and whining for something to eat. They filled him up with ripe persimmons and led him back to camp, where he was installed as a permanent member of the expedition. Meanwhile my father had cut some steaks from the haunch of the old bear, and had them nicely browned and ready for breakfast. After all, no harm had come of Dan's exciting adventure.

They named the little bear "Cub", and he proved to be an interesting addition to the party. His hunger was insatiable. He had been born hungry and remained so all his life. Nor was his taste in any respect delicate. He would eat anything that came within reach, with equal avidity and impartial satisfaction.

They shared their fruit with him, and when at last his stomach seemed partly filled he appeared to consider himself the chief personage of the expedition. He danced and frolicked and was playful as a kitten, without showing the least worry over the death of his mother.

For several days Dan kept him in leash as a precaution against accidents, until he became so tame and attached to his new friends that he probably could not have been driven away. He was as devoted to Dan as a pet dog would have been, and Dan was excessively proud of the relationship. Cub's principal object in life seemed to be to find something to eat and when his hunger was satisfied, or partly so, to entertain the company in the performance of several simple tricks that Dan taught him. He was a wonderfully cleaver beast and an apt scholar. When he came to fallen logs he would scratch under them in quest of bugs and worms, which he swallowed with a relish that was amazing. In crossing streams he kept a sharp outlook for fish, and showed by his dexterity in catching them that he was an expert. It made no difference to him what kind of fish they were; a mud cat satisfied him as well as a speckled trout. Bulk was what he was after. When the supply of fish was low he filed himself on tadpoles and frogs. His tastes were shameful.

One day just before camping, they found a hive of bees in the hollow trunk of trees, and Cub was first to avail himself of the opportunity. In fact he was the discoverer of the treasure; and swallowed nearly half of it, along with the bees, before the rest knew what he had found. He did not mind the stings, so long as he could fill his belly with the sweets.

Boone gathered some large laurel leaves, and wrapping as much of the honey in them as he could carry, they resumed their journey; assured that if they missed getting game for supper they would at least have something to eat. But in a little while they were startled by the flight of a flock of turkeys out of the grass close by their path, and father brought down a fat gobbler. So, with the turkey, the honey, and plenty of cold water they had a feast where a famine had seemed impending.

Dan was so pleased with their experiences in general that he hoped their explorations would continue indefinitely, he liked it better than staying at home. Each night at bedtime Cub would come whining and begging to sleep with him, a privilege which the boy was not backward in granting, and thus the two became the best of friends. After their return home Cub rose to the dignity of one of the most famous citizens of the community, winning a wide reputation as the only bear that ever learned to talk. It will afford me pleasure a little further along to give some account of his remarkable progress in civilization, and especially to relate how on his final disappearance he acted in so disreputable a manner as to convince the Rev. Daniel Sherman that he had seen the devil, all of which will be the truth and nothing but the truth, remarkable as it may seem.

An Amazing Flood of Waters

The second afternoon after the acquirement of Cub, they came to a brook flowing out of an opening or cavern at the foot of a hill, and the water was so shallow that they crossed over by stepping from stone to stone without wetting the soles of their moccasins. On ascending the bank they found a convenient place for camping, and made their arrangements for the night. Before retiring the whole party, including the little bear, took a bath in a pool which had formed in the channel of the brook. Cub enjoyed the sport immensely, splashing around in the cold water and looking for fish to satisfy his aching void. He even regarded it as legitimate sport when Dan gave him a dunking, but his main object was to find something to eat, and failing in his quest he retired in disgust.

At supper they feasted on roast squirrel and pheasant that my father had shot on the way, but before retiring they were startled by a loud roaring and rushing of water in the direction of the brook. It sounded as if a waterfall or cataract had burst into sudden action, and running down to the brook to ascertain the cause of so remarkable a phenomenon, they beheld a scene which had in it the elements of terror as well as beauty and grandeur. The little stream which they had so recently crossed dryshod was now a roaring torrent, fifty feet or more wide and waist deep to a man. Out of the cavern in the hillside a great flood was pouring and rushing down the winding course of the brook in a volume and with a velocity that were awe inspiring.

The scene was amazing as well as alarming. If the water continued to rise it would soon flood the adjacent valleys, and no one could estimate the final result. None of the party, not even Boone himself, had ever seen the ocean or witnessed the ebbing and flowing of its tides, and if they had been ever so familiar with these displays of the mysteries of Nature they could not have accounted for the present alarming manifestation.

Even Boone, accustomed as he was to danger in its numerous aspects, was at a loss to account for the amazing spectacle, and he felt an apprehension which he could not conceal. It seemed to him as if some great fountain in the interior of the hill had suddenly been released and was now pouring out through the opening. In his philosophical way he began to wonder if the interior of the earth might be composed of water, which would account for the numerous springs that he had found everywhere in his wanderings; and if such were the case was there not danger of this protecting hill being washed away and the whole country drowned in the flood? Though not a religious man, he was familiar with the stories of the Bible, and he remembered that at the beginning of Noah's flood "all the fountains of the great deep were broken up." Was not the scene now before him a repetition of that mighty catastrophe? The same language would fit the present as well as the past. It seemed as if the hill must soon give way under the awful strain and leave them no place to set their feet.

But fear did not possess him. It was generally believed by those who knew him that he did not know the sense of fear. He could not understand the mighty works of nature, but he was not afraid. There must be some explanation for such a tremendous spectacle.

For more than an hour the men stood and watched and wondered. Gradually the devastating fear of the boys died away under the steadying influence of their leader, and in its place came a wonder and amazement. They were encouraged by the fact that the volume of the flood did not increase. Presently it began to recede, and by the time they were willing to leave the scene and retire to their camp the stream had sunk to its former dimensions and resumed the proportions of a spring branch.

So amazed were they over the phenomenon that they remained in the same place several days, and by their observations discovered that the brook overflowed in the same manner twice every twenty-four hours. In this way they conceived the idea that the fountain within the heart of the hill might have some connection with the ocean, and that they were witnessing the operations of the tides more than a thousand miles from the nearest contact with the sea. As already stated, neither of the men had ever seen the ocean, or had any personal information about its tides, but Boone and my father had a general understanding of their nature. They knew that the rising and falling of the waters of the sea were due to the attraction of the moon, and they came to the conclusion that the internal reservoir from which the spring drew its supplies was controlled by the same influence. They could not believe that there was an aperture or open passage under the surface of the ground through which the ocean flowed back and forth as it rose and fell, but it was reasonable to suppose that the mighty power which could lift the sea an appreciable distance into the air might also produce the amazing scene which they had just witnessed. Whether this was the correct solution of the matter or not, no one can tell but it was the only one they could think of, and it satisfied them.

Dan said simply that he didn't know, and he would not bother himself about something which he could not understand or explain; and this is probably the attitude of men in general. So long as they are permitted to live in comfort they will continue to enjoy the good things of life and let others study its mysteries.

When Dan was an old gray-headed man I talked about this wonderful ebbing and flowing spring, and he confirmed my father's recollections, at the same time adding some speculations of his own. He believed it was a special manifestation of Providence, and spoke of it with that sense of religious awe. He suggested that this was probably one of the "fountains of the deep" which God had utilized in producing Noah's flood, and that he had allowed it to remain as a warning to the wicked generations that have followed. But as this is a subject for theology rather than science or philosophy, I shall pass on to other theories, which, however, are necessarily based largely upon speculation.

Episode Number Seventeen

Wonders of the Ozark Regions

In the meantime what has become of the wonderful ebbing and flowing spring? Has it ceased its manifestations, or is it hidden in some secluded place where no one has happened to stumble upon it? But this theory would hardly be possible. The great volume of water pouring out twice daily would require an outlet large enough to point the way to the fountainhead. I am inclined to believe that some internal convulsion has so altered the conditions that the spring no longer flows, or if it is still there its volume is not great enough to attract attention.

Since the time that Boone and his youthful companions stood upon the bank and viewed the marvel, other ebbing and flowing springs have been discovered in the Ozarks, all apparently influenced by the same power, and giving that locality an interest possessed by no other region in the world. True, there are geysers and spouting springs in other localities, but with one or two exceptions they do not act with the regularity of the ocean's tides. In this respect the Ozarks are ahead of the rest of the world.

The men could give no definite location of the place, because they kept no record of their route, but it seems that it should long since have been found and given a position on the maps. Why should so great a wonder of Nature remain concealed? Although I have made inquiries of a number of persons familiar with that part of the state, I have only two or three who ever heard of the ebbing and flowing spring.

Some years ago I suggested the matter to my friend, the late Prof. Garland Broadhead, who at the time was state geologist, but he never heard of the spring and of course could give no information concerning it.

I know the great fountain was there in 1815, just as my father described it, but what has become of it? Has it dried up in mist and left only a crooked branch as a memory of an ancient mystery?

Recently I obtained some information from the researches of my little granddaughter Mary. She had been studying a publication issued by the State Geological Bureau, and learned that there are fifteen ebbing and flowing springs in various parts of the world, and that five or six of them are located in the Missouri Ozarks. One in Shannon County seems to be better known than any of the others, but if it is the same that was discovered by Boone and the two boys in 1815, its characteristics have been greatly modified. It is still one of the wonders of nature, but it does not compare with what it was when they stood upon the banks and viewed its tremendous agitation.

Meanwhile numerous legends have grown up around the place. Some say that the Indians knew of the fountain and came there to worship the Great Spirit, and it is claimed that the exploring

Spaniards poured treasures of gold into its waters as an offering to the divinity of their conception. But the greatest treasures that have been found in that locality were grown in the rich soil of the adjacent farms. He who looks for gold in the springs of the Ozarks will find it only in renewed health and strength and vigor of thought and purpose.

A later state geologist and others learned in such matters, attribute the movements of the fountain to symphonic action. They claim that a "large subterranean chamber has been eroded in the limestone formation, which fills faster than the smaller outlet that carries away the normal flow. After reaching a certain stage a second outlet is encountered, which once started, sets up a symphonic action which finally drains the chamber. This explanation is as clear as the mud in the bottom of the spring, and was no doubt written by a man who had never been there, but felt obliged to say something. He does not account for the extraordinary regularity of the ebb and flow, and therefore his explanation comes in the list of those that do not explain. My little granddaughter quite naively inquires, "What becomes of the water in the big chamber, for as long as the flow into it is uninterrupted, why should there be any flux in the stream as it comes out?"

It does not seem probable that the large subterranean reservoir would overflow twice every day without variation, or that it would produce the same volume every time. There are dry and wet spells in nature as well as in politics. In very dry weather the syphon would not work at all, and in wet seasons the fountain would display its most remarkable characteristics. You may set a syphon in a vessel so it will work whenever the liquid reaches a certain stage, but in order to make it flow at regular intervals, with the accuracy of the sun, you must see that the supply is also regular.

However, in this connection the geologist gives us an interesting piece of news. He says the famous fountain of Bethesda, near Jerusalem, is an ebbing and flowing spring, which after having been "troubled" by an angle, gave health to those who bathed in its waters. The same may be true regarding this Ozark marvel. I have seen people in my time who might have been benefitted by bathing in its waters either before or after they had been "troubled".

A River Under a Hill

Several days after leaving the ebbing and flowing spring, the travelers came upon another natural wonder which excited their curiosity to a considerable degree. They had been following a small river for some distance, when suddenly it disappeared under the ground at the foot of a ridge. On pursuing its course over the hill, they found it issuing on the other side in line with the point where it disappeared, with slightly increased volume. It burst out like a great fountain and swiftly pursued its way to the sea. They made no effort to follow the river on its course under the ground, fearing subterranean falls or whirlpools, but the passage has since been made. Prof. Broadhead informed me that he had gone all the way under the ridge in a skiff, coming out in perfect safety on the opposite side. But strange to say, he could not give me the location of the mysterious river, and I have not found any one else who could. It remains as much a mystery as it was the day Boone and his companions discovered it. There are two "Lost Creeks" in Missouri, one in DeKalb County, in the northwest corner of the state, and the other in the opposite corner in Wayne County; but neither of these fits the case, either as to location or size. There is no "Lost River" on the map, but some day it will find its place there, and add another wonder to the great Ozark country.

The travelers followed a different route on their return home, more to the eastward, and were rewarded by finding a number of rich specimens of lead ore. These were the "black rocks" which the chief had mentioned, and they found the ore so pure and soft that they could melt it into bullets by their camp fires. One of the specimens I remember as occupying a prominent place in my father's workshop in my early boyhood, and I often viewed its glittering surface and wondered at the riches which lay concealed in its bosom.

I was not the only one who was fascinated by the results of this trip. The news which Boone brought back about the splendor of the scenery and the numerous rivers and streams stocked with the finest fish, turned a hegira of emigration into that region, and settlements sprang up in many sections. Great deposits of lead and zinc were discovered and their treasures brought to light, and cities were built where previously there had been only desolate wilderness and the howl of the wolf.

Where Buffaloes Roamed

There were also thousands of buffaloes there when Boone and the boys penetrated the mysteries, as they found almost at the cost of their lives. Buffaloes did not always change location by stampeding, as in the incident described, but they had orderly methods of moving from place to place, with trails as plainly marked as our modern highways. Traces of these trails can be seen yet, where the farmer's plow has not obliterated them. The buffalo needed water and grass, and where these existed he was always to be found. Those who imagine that this curious animal was confined to the vast prairies and ranges of the distant west, would be surprised to know that Missouri and Kentucky, and even western portions of Virginia and the great spaces of Ohio and Illinois, were as familiar to him as the open prairies that now form the states of Kansas and Nebraska. He had been driven from his chosen habitat into his "last roundup" when Buffalo Bill and other hunters of his generation assisted in his extermination. The Indians were proud to claim the buffaloes as their "cattle", and they pointed to the vast herds grazing on the hills and in the valleys as evidence of wealth surpassing even that of the pale faces.

For ages preceding the coming of the white pioneers the buffalo had been allowed to live and increase in comparative peace, the red people killing only what they needed for meat and skins to cover their habitations and the warm robes which supplied their beds. There were in consequence immense herds of these "wild cattle", and when impelled by some unknown reason to go on stampede, death lay in their path, for themselves as well as any other living thing that came in their way. No impediment stopped or turned their course. They swam rivers, and plunged in untold millions over cliffs, where after the coming of civilization their bones were dug up and ground into fertilizers. It hardly seems possible that so numerous a species could have been annihilated in so brief a space of time, but there is not known a single wild herd in existence. The only place to see the buffalo is in the zoo, or on some specialized farm where he is raised for the excellence of his "beef". He was not as useful as the plodding ox or the timid cow, and was oblige under the laws of nature to give way to them.

At the time of this famous trip into the Ozarks there were also elk and deer there, the latter by thousands, and they have persisted better than any of the other original animals. The elk was a moose-deer, probably out of his region of snow and frozen moss, and he soon disappeared. Two generations have come and gone since a wild elk was seen in the Ozarks. The wolf is still there, but his glory has departed. He is seen now only in remote or waste places, and always howling for meat. But he does not haunt the door of the industrious farmer.

Episode Number Eighteen

Educating a Cub Bear

The cub bear that Dan brought back from the southwest proved to be one of the most disreputable rascals that ever visited the Boone settlements. He had no moral sentiments and was a thief and a drunkard by nature, and as he fattened and increased in size his native wickedness grew in proportion. Yet he was so good natured and amusing that no one except grandfather Jonathan had the heart to whip him. He would steal anything in the shape of food that he could lay his paws on, and then dance and perform tricks like a spoiled child. No matter what kind of sinfulness Cub might engage in, he never failed to raise a laugh at the end.

Finally he became so bad that Dan lost control of him, and gave him to father, and he and my uncles, Ab and Jim, proceeded to teach him new tricks and polish off his education in general. In matters of this kind Uncle Jim was a professor of high standing, and what he trained that bear to do was remarkable. Whenever there was the least hint of a new line of fun Uncle Jim was there to teach it to Cub, and he was no backward pupil.

He taught Cub to stand on his head and forepaws and wag his hind feet in the air and say "Whoopee!" He would also dance in circles, grin like a boy with a red apple, and repeat "whoopee" at each turn. It was admitted by all who became acquainted with him that Cub was the only bear in that part of the country that had ever learned to speak the English language, and seeming to understand the encomiums that were passed upon him he continued the repetition of his only part of speech until it became almost a monotonous whine.

The boys also taught him to suck eggs and climb trees, but these accomplishments were not difficult. They seemed to come to him by the inspiration of nature. He became so great an expert in sucking eggs that grandmother Mary never knew whether her "settings" would develop into chicks or find a resting place in the stomach of Cub. As a rule he swallowed the edible parts and left the shells. Sometimes he swallowed the shells.

His capacity for food had no limit. Daily he fished in the brook for minnows and perch, and when these were scarce he filled the vacancy with frogs and mussels. He did not even neglect tadpoles when they were fat and juicy, and his tastes were so degraded that he had even been known to eat snakes when his hunger was raging.

When fishing in the brook was not satisfactory, he watched the cook as she prepared breakfast, and when her back was turned he would snatch the hot fish out of the frying pan and swallow it before she could wallop him with the poker. On one occasion he tried to steal a ham that was boiling for dinner, but turned the kettle over and put out the fire. Then Aunt Jemima expressed her opinion of bears in general and of Cub in particular. She said "dat Cub was worser 'n old Sat-in, 'kase Sat-in wouldn't eat pork an' Cub would, even when hit was b'ilin' hot." It was the custom in those times to call the old gentleman who ruled the lower regions "Sat-in," and Aunt Jemima knew the correct pronunciation.

Cub was fond of pork in any of its forms as he was of venison or fish. He had no religious scruples in the matter of his diet. So he devoured pork, and bacon, and ham and sausage with the same avidity that he devoted to the more delicate varieties of meats. Space-filling qualities were all that he considered.

Aside from his other disreputable habits Cub became a common drunkard. On "still days" he observed Jonathan testing the "proof" of the liquor with a spoon, and he soon learned to imitate the trick. He was never able to fathom the mystery of a spoon, but he licked the fiery liquid with his tongue as it trickled from the spout, and soon became as expert in "sousing" himself as if he had been a civilized white person. Then he would stand on his head, dance a round or two, growl "whoopee" and lie down on a bed of leaves to sleep off the effects. In this way he became the most degraded sot in all the settlements, and would undoubtedly have come to judgement in Uncle Daniel's court if he had been a human being instead of a worthless bear.

Being a bear, he was naturally fond of honey, and it was this overwhelming appetite that at last got him into trouble. Jonathan's bee gums were never safe except during the brief intervals that it took the bees to fill them. As soon as this was done Cub overturned the gums and swallowed the honey. This went on until the old gentleman could stand it no longer, and one day, under the influence of an especially aggravating case, he cut a stout hickory and advanced upon Cub. But the bear knew perfectly well what was in the wind, and he made his escape up the tall sugar tree that shaded the front yard, and there, resting on a comfortable limb, demurely sucking his paws. Jonathan tried to coax him down with offers of sugar and fresh fish, but Cub had more regard for the hickory than he had for the proffered delicacies. So he continued licking his paws while he watched the proceedings from his safe and lofty perch.

At length Jonathan got out of patience and called to Wilse to bring his gun and shoot "that infernal bear". He was not going to stand for any more of his tricks. But Cub understood enough of the English language to comprehend what was coming, and he made a rush for the ground, skidding along the trunk of the tree and bounding from limb to limb. Then he whined and circled around Jonathan, and stood on his head and said "whoopee" until the old gentleman's ire was mollified, and he told Wilse to put his gun away.

The Rev. Sherman is Tempted of the Devil

But the threat to shoot made an impression on Cub's mind, and the next morning he was missing. He had evidently concluded that the wildwoods was safer for his kind, and he accordingly took to the tall timber. He was next heard of fifteen miles away, in Teuque Prairie, where he had an encounter with Brother Sherman which made a lasting impression on the mind of that good man. Brother Sherman had been converted and received a "call to preach," and was peddling windmills while preparing for his profession. Business having been good, he had sold out his stock and was on his way to St. Louis for a new supply of mills, when he had the memorable meeting with Cub. He was in fine spirits as he drove along the road seated in the front end of his long wagon-frame. Another load or two would meet all the requirements, and enable him to ascend the pulpit, where, by inspiration, he beheld crowds of sinners listening to the drippings of the gospel as they fell from his lips. Releasing the lines, he let the horses pick their way, nipping grass from the side of the road as they progressed, while he hummed a stanza of a Wesleyan hymn and repeated some lines from his forthcoming sermon, which he had memorized.

Suddenly the team snorted and looked back, and then started on a run down the road. But he succeeded to pull them up just in time to avoid a dangerous gully, and looking back beheld a sight which he never forgot during the whole term of his ministry. A big black bear had taken possession of the long frame of his wagon, and was standing on his head waving his hind legs in the air and growling "whoopee." Having given what he regarded as a sufficiency of this part of his performance, the bear reversed himself to his natural position and danced in circles on the boards of the frame, never ceasing his croon of "whoopee!" This was the first time brother Sherman had ever seen a bear act that way, and he honestly believed he was being tempted of the devil. Again the team got loose and tore down the road, and the jolting of the wagon threw the bear to the ground, whereupon he ambled away into the woods growling his shibboleth of "whoopee" until he was out of sight and hearing.

This was the last time that any civilized white person ever saw Cub for it was none other than he. Some believed that he found a secluded place in the wilderness, to which his reputation had not extended, and there finding himself a wife and entered upon the process of raising a family of young bears. Others declared among them brother Sherman himself, that what he had seen and heard was not a bear at all, but an impersonation of Old Nick, who had assumed this disguise for the purpose of deceiving him. When he fell off the wagon the shock broke the spell, and he made his way back to the place of his natural residence. But I am disposed to accept the first solution. I believe Cub reformed, quit drink, and having raised a family of respectable bears moved to Arkansas, where they prefer bears to monkeys.

Uncle Jim was very fond of Cub, and would not listen to anything that had a tendency to blacken his reputation. He said if the bear had not been frightened by the bringing of the gun he might have reformed and become an exemplary citizen, and there is ground for this belief in the fact that no one ever heard of his going on a spree after he ran away. If he had been utterly immoral and bad he would have visited the first still house he could find and filled himself to repletion. But it seems that when he disappeared he reformed and became as good as any other bear. This was Uncle Jim's theory. He claimed that Cub was not bad by nature, but on the contrary he had as good a disposition as any bear he ever knew. He would not allow any theory of "original sin" to smirch the fame of his pet, but attributed the evil that was in him to unfortunate associations. For instance, he would not have been a drunkard except for the temptations of grandfather Jonathan's still house, and he never would have harmed the bee hives if they had been kept out of his reach. This line of reasoning appears to be convincing, and as I never knew Cub personally I am disposed to believe that he might have been an angle if he had not been a little devil. At any rate, his character was better than that of some white people who lived in the same region, and I think the ladies of the D.A.R. ought to erect a monument to his memory. An appropriate epitaph might run something like this:

Here lies Cub,
A Bear who Was Born Without Sin,
But He Fell Into Temptation,
And Became a Worthless Drunkard,
And Died Without Salvation.
Take Warning by His Fate,
And Drink Nothing But 3.2 Beer.

A Bear That Said His Prayers

Whatever might have been the cause that led to the ruin of Dan's cub bear, it must be admitted that the American Black Bear is an animal of good sense and correct morals, as bears go. He is by nature a sociable animal, and is rarely ugly except when hungry or obliged to defend himself. If you see him at the zoo, where he is well fed and retains a memory of the nuts and sweets given him by the children, you will notice that he has a pleasant countenance and seems to be always smiling, and his face is a fair indication of his character.

I shall now relate an adventure that Uncle Davey Darst, of Darst Bottom, had with a bear whose character appears to have been very much like that of Cub, though less brilliant in mental capacity, for he never learned to talk. (Some of the things that Uncle Davy said about his bear may be considered with reserve. W.S.B. hand written and crossed out)

When I knew Uncle Davy he was a perfectly truthful old gentleman, a good citizen and a kind neighbor; and I have not the least doubt that the main facts that he related to me about his bear are correct. His love for the best may have led him to extenuate some of his faults and over-emphasize his virtues, but in a general way I am sure the bear was almost as good as Uncle Davy pictured him. I shall therefore proceed with the story and let the reader decide for himself.

One cold morning about Christmas-time Uncle Davy went out to feed his hogs, and had taken only a few steps from the house when he saw a large black bear standing on his haunches in the path and evidently waiting for him. The bear had his arms crossed on his breast and was smiling in a very satisfied way, as though there were neither guile nor malice in him, and at first glance Uncle Davy believed that his intensions were good. But he had seen bears before, and he knew it was not always safe to trust them. Sometimes they were not as good as they looked, which may also be said of some people.

So he ran back into the house and got his gun, and when he returned there was the bear still in the path with his arms folded and smiling. He had not changed his position, and seemed to think his neighbor had gone to bring him something to eat. But regardless of what his thoughts might be Uncle Davy was resolved to stay on the safe side; so he leveled his gun and pulled the trigger. But the powder flashed in the pan and the piece was not discharged. The bear, evidently supposing this was some sort of entertainment being staged for him, smiled broader than ever, and if he could have spoken the language he probably would have thanked his friend for his consideration. Meanwhile Uncle Davy reprimed his rifle, the bear watching the operation with interest, doubtless wondering what kind of food his host was preparing for him.

Again the gun flashed, and the bear winked his right eye as if to assure his friend that he was pleased with the exercises as far as they had gone. Indeed he was so much encouraged that he got down on his all-fours and began to amble toward the host, a movement which Uncle Davy did not approve, and so retreated into the house. Thereupon the bear sat down on the porch and wondered what was the matter.

Uncle Davy had never seen a bear act that way before, and his curiosity was aroused. Obtaining a piece of fresh meat he stuck it on the end of his ramrod and pushed it through the partly open door as a peace offering. The bear swallowed the meat in a single gulp, and would have swallowed the ramrod too if Uncle Davy had not quickly pulled it in.

By this time he was so much impressed with the friendly intentions of his visitor that he opened the door and invited him to come in. The invitation was no sooner given than accepted. The bear came in and seated himself in the chimney corner, where he rubbed his paws and enjoyed the warmth of the fore. He also smiled and nodded to Aunt Hannah, who was preparing breakfast; and as soon as the meal was ready he took a seat at the table and helped himself bountifully.

From that time on the bear became a member of the family, though he would never sleep in the house. He preferred to bundle in with the pigs in the pen, who appreciated the warmth of his great furry hide and relished him as a bedfellow. In all other respects the bear acted like a pet house dog, and lived with the family for more than a year. He went hunting with Uncle Davy, and had several fights with male animals of his own species. In one of these he lost an eye, and might have been killed if Uncle Davy had not shot his opponent in time to save his life. The bear understood and appreciated the friendly service, and the two became more devoted to each other than ever. Uncle Davy said he believed the bear would have died for him, and I really think he would if an opportunity had arisen; for his devotion was something very lovely.

It was Uncle Davy's custom to hold family prayers night and morning, and the bear became a regular and very devout attendant. He would sit silently on his haunches while the chapter was being read, then keel reverently and growl in low tones while the prayer was said. But Uncle Davy never could teach him to say "amen". As soon as the prayer was over he would get up and go about his business, seemingly indifferent as to the formal ending.

At length the bear disappeared one night and was never seen again, but side-by-side with his tracks in the snow were those of a smaller bear, which led Uncle Davy and some of his neighbors to believe that he had been led astray by a female of the species and had departed with her to raise a family of young bears. My father used to mention this incident in support of his contention that bears were naturally of a domestic and religious turn of mind, and he believed they might have been civilized if missionaries had been sent among them. But this is a matter of speculation, and as my father was different from all the other men I ever knew I would prefer not to accept his conclusions as final. The missionaries might also have something to say about it.

In conclusion I wish to caution the reader that Uncle Davy in his enthusiastic devotion to his pet may have painted some of the incidents in brighter colors than they deserved; but I have endeavored to give the story as he told it, and the reader may "believe it or not" as he prefers. My personal opinion is that it would be safe to adopt a medium course.

Uncle Davy Darst and His Ways

If any interest has been aroused in Uncle Davy's story of his pious bear it may be as well to say something about Uncle Davy himself. In 1798 he left Woodford County, Ky., and following the magnetic name of Daniel Boone came west and settled in the bottoms of the Missouri River, near the historic mouth of the Femme Osage. At intervals he purchased several considerable tracts of land, and the region became known as Darst's Bottom; a name that it will probably retain for the remainder of time.

One of Uncle Davy's sons, whose name was Isaac, married my aunt Phoebe, and she gave her name to a line of noble women which remains unbroken to the present day. My cousins descending from her and bearing the name of Phoebe have never failed to maintain her reputation for beauty and good sense.

Uncle Davy was a man of method and decision. He kept the first diary that was ever written in English west of the Mississippi; and though much of it was lost in the years that followed, these pages are indebted to what was left for several interesting items.

His domain lay between the river and the upland on which we lived, the distance being about two and a half miles; and this space was covered with an immense growth of timber, through which Daniel Boone and Poncho had walked. It was so tall and dense as to completely hide the view of the river from our place on the hills, and when steamboats began to run it was a real deprivation. In those days it was a wonderful thing to see a steamboat go by, with its painted cabins and tall smokestacks; and Uncle Davy, realizing this fact, had a swath a hundred feet wide cut through that timber from the foot of the bluff to the bank of the river. Therefore we could see every boat as it passed up or down, and though the view was for only a moment as the vessels dashed by, it was a very sweet pleasure to know that we could really see the steamboats. I mention this incident as evidence of the generous kindness of Uncle Davy's heart, demonstrating the manner of man that he was.

When I was quite a small boy my mother took me with her on a visit to Uncle Davy's house, and among other remarkable things that I saw there was an immense old-fashioned sword in its scabbard, resting on a couple of wooden pins over the mantel in the sitting room. The weapon so fascinated my childish imagination that I gazed and wondered. I thought what a hero Uncle Davy must be to have carried a sword like that, and finally when no one was listening I asked my mother about it. She said it was the sword Uncle Davy had used in the Indian war, when he was captain of a company and led his men in furious assault on the lines of the enemy. After that I never wondered why Black Hawk surrendered and quit fighting. That sword was so prodigious and awe-inspiring that when it flashed in the sunlight I imagined the very thunders rolled and crashed in the heavens, and it was prudent and wise for the great red chief to come in and beg for terms. I said to myself that I would have done it if I had been in his place.

The "Blind Staggers"

Uncle Davy was a breeder of hogs, and as an abundant "mast" grew on the tall trees it came into his mind to let the pigs root for themselves. He could not understand why he should raise corn to feed them, by a little extra effort on their part they might fatten themselves on the thousands of bushels of nuts that lay on the ground. So one winter he decided to let them "root hog or die," and quite a number of them took him at his word. They got along very well until the heavy snows came, when the pigs declined the effort required to do their own feeding; and most of them died and passed on. Uncle Davy noted in his diary that no sooner had he finished training them to live without feeding than they turned up their toes and gave up the ghost; and in a footnote he remarked that nobody could say in advance just what a pig would do under any given conditions.

There was another trouble which he experienced with his hogs, and it led him to remark that the Lord knew what he was doing when he forbade the chosen people to eat the flesh of that stubborn and silly beast. In the rich soil of the bottoms there grew a plant known as "cow weed", because it was the first green thing to appear in the spring, and the cows devoured it greedily. It did them no harm, merely increasing their fat and output of milk and butter; but it was death to the hogs. They dug into the ground with their sharp snouts and ate the root of the plant, which made them stagger as if they were drunk. They would get "funny", like men who absorb too much alcohol, and dance around and play with one another until they became blind and fell down and died in a stupor. For this reason the disease was called the "blind staggers", and it seems rather remarkable that the modern bootlegger has not discovered the intoxicating qualities of "cow weed" and used it in his business.

Episode Number Twenty

(The General, crossed out)
Uncle Davy's Versatility

Uncle Davy Darst had an inquiring mind and was addicted to scientific experiments. Teaching his hogs to fatten themselves was not the only new thing that he tried. Some one had told him that the cocklebur contained a large amount of humus and was therefore a good fertilizer; and while his own virgin acres required no artificial help, he decided to lose no opportunity to render them still more productive. So he ordered a bushel of burs from Kentucky and scattered them over his fields. When spring came and the seeds sprouted he would not allow the plants to be disturbed, but cultivated them with the same care that he devoted to his other crops. The yield was satisfactory. In a single season he raised enough cockleburs to supply the whole community; and from that day until the present time that prolific pest had never ceased troubling the farmers of that region. No doubt the cocklebur was created for some good purpose, but so far its uses have not been determined.

A Pioneer Custom

In those times it was not an unusual thing for people of various degrees of consanguinity to arrive from Virginia or Kentucky on a visit to relatives and remain as members of the family for indefinite periods. Some of them made themselves useful by helping with the work on the farm or about the house, and were welcome to stay as long as they pleased.

Uncle Davy had a relative of this kind who was known as the "General". Whether he acquired the title in gallant action with the enemy, or whether it attached itself to him as a spontaneous production of Nature, I never knew. He was a neat, dapper little old bachelor, ranging in age from a hundred to a thousand years; and he had the appearance of being kept in a glass case. He always wore the same suit of clothes, composed of blue-black broadcloth, the coat cut sharply away on both sides at the waist and ending in a long, pointed, split tail. It came to be known as a "jaybird coat". The rolling collar was upholstered and stiff and elevated to a level with the back of his head. In front and rear the garment was decorated with brilliantly polished brass buttons, and when he walked his red bandana swayed back and forth from an invisible pocket in one of the split tails. The vest and trousers were of the same material as the upper garment. On his head he wore a tall beaver hat of the President Jackson type; and his small feet were encased in a pair of boots in whose perpetual gloss the rampant rooster might have found his sworn enemy. Regardless of the dust or mud in the roads, this dainty figure would make his way along them without the least tarnishing effect on the leather of his boots. He was of a social disposition, and paid many visits to the neighbors of Daniel Boone, but not one of them ever saw a speck of clay or a blemish of dust on the General's footwear. How he contrived it was a mystery that no one ever solved. Some claimed that he had wings by means of which he carried himself through the air, and several of his lady admirers were heard to declare that he was sweet enough to have almost anything.

This immaculate creature came one day on a visit to our house, and the family was marshalled for his inspection. Brother John and I were lined up as special examples of what we should not be, mainly to exhibit what we knew about literature. John recited the "Boy Who Stood on the Burning Deck" as an original effort, and the General said it was wonderful, as indeed it was. Anybody who tried to round up or head off Brother John had to get up very early in the morning and strike a light as soon as he got out of bed.

What became of the General I am not prepared to say, but it is to be inferred that he died in the regular course of nature and buried somewhere in the Darst Bottom, with his boots on. Probably their gloss might reveal his location if research were made.

First Families

Practically all the first settlers of Missouri came from Virginia, the Carolinas, Kentucky, and the older parts of Tennessee; and the people of each locality brought with them the peculiarities of their local customs and ideas. Especially was this true of their provincial accents, by which a stranger could determine the place of their origin by the mere formality of an introduction. The Virginians were justly proud of their state, for the reputation it had won in the Revolution and the great men and women it had produced. Of course everybody was bound to admit that there could be no greater man than George Washington, who always spoke of his native state as "Virginny", and referred with respect to the animal that supplied the milk for his eggnog as a "keow". He was a Virginian of the first water, a man to be admired and emulated, regardless of the fact that he spoke the language of the Restoration. Then there was Thomas Jefferson, the greatest statesman of this or any other age; and Patrick Henry who out-talked old King George and brought on a revolution. Why should not Virginia be proud of her sons?

No Virginian was backward in admitting that he came from the First Families, and if all their claims had been true it might easily have been inferred that all the First Families had abandoned their homesteads and gone West, moved by the magic in the name of Daniel Boone. He was the one great man who could not trace his descent back to Virginia, and it was quite certain that he had never worn a broadcloth coat ornamented with brass buttons and a peaked collar to push the coonskin cap off his head. For these and other reasons some of the First Families questioned his right to the imperial highness which his fame had attained.

Overcoming Difficulties

Most of the people who came west traveled overland, on foot and by pack-horses; for at that time Fulton was only beginning to dream of steamboats; and if any man had mentioned railroads with an amazing speed of twenty miles per hour he would have been denounced as a blasphemer---as actually happened in Ohio not many years later.

Nearly all Boone's neighbors were intensely religious, each in his own way; and every one believed that all who did not belong to his church were in the broad way that leads to destruction. But this made no difference in their loyalty to one another. A Baptist would fight for his Methodist neighbor, and the Methodist would go the limit for his Baptist friend, each sincerely believing that the other was destined to land in the smokehouse.

How these people managed to cross the mountains and rivers and creeks that lay between the Atlantic coast and the center of the Mississippi Valley is one of the mysteries that no man has been able to solve. But they did it, by hook or by crook, and seemed to enjoy the doing of what we in our time would call impossible.

Only the rich, or those who chose to so regard themselves, could afford the expense of a keelboat passage down the Ohio and up the Mississippi; and as many of the early arrivals were adventures, without so much as a picayune in their pockets, such palatial voyages were beyond the range of their imaginations, unless they came as cable-pullers and snake-fighters, as many did.

It was not only Nature that rose up with seemingly impenetrable barriers, but there were stampeding herds of buffaloes without respect for man; myriads of bears and hungry wolves; screaming "painters" whose ferocious cries froze the marrow in the bones; hideous reptiles of the poisonous species. From the slimy water moccasin to the insidious copperhead, and the imperial rattler whose sting generally meant death; and above all, roving bands of painted savages with gun and tomahawk, the gauntlet and the stake for the men and death or degraded slavery for the women. What a glorious people were those brave old neighbors of Daniel Boone, and how great was the fascination of his name! If it had not been for him and them Missouri and the Great West would not now be inhabited by the most lordly race that the sun ever shone upon!

The Custom of "Not Speaking"

A number of singular customs prevailed among those fine old spirits, some of which I cannot refrain to mention; for great people in all ages have been peculiar. When two neighbors had a misunderstanding they either settled it with fists or guns or "quit speaking". Cousin Willis Bryan and my father had acquired this habit, due to the fact that one was a Baptist and the other a Methodist; and they kept it up for years. They lived less than a half a mile apart, and often met in the road or in the woods and passed each other without speaking or recognition. Not to speak was a direct and cutting insult and those old pioneers knew how to apply it. Finally one night our house burned down, and Cousin Willis, who was an early riser, saw the light and came over to see what was the matter. When he came to the creek that separated his land from ours, he saw that the house was gone, and hearing no sound and seeing no person, he was seized with the awful apprehension that the whole family had perished in the flames. Calling at the top of his voice, he rushed through the water and climbed the hill-to find that we were all alive! Then he and father shook hands and embraced like brothers, just as if nothing had ever been wrong between them. It took a tragedy to make these men understand that they had been acting foolishly.

The whole family went over to Cousin Willis', and were entertained and cared for until they could find a lodging place; and never again did those two old men do so foolish thing as not to speak when they met. It was their determined characters and absolute conviction that each was right which had made them irreconcilable enemies, until that one touch of nature came and showed them all men are of one blood, regardless of the church they belonged to.

One of the most singular cases of the "non-speaking" habit that occurred in the Boone neighborhood was that of Uncle Billy and Aunt Nancy Logan, and I do not believe that a merciful God in his goodness ever created a better man or woman. They lived happily together long enough to rear a large family of intelligent children, and then quarreled about some trivial thing and "quit speaking". They continued to live in the same room, though occupying opposite corners of the fireplace, slept in the same bed and ate at the same table; but when it became necessary for either to address the other the communication went through the medium of the children. They were the stations through which the messages flashed. If Uncle Billy wanted another biscuit at breakfast, or fresh cup of coffee, the request was sent to the head of the table by way of the sons and daughters; and if Aunt Nancy was feeling badly and wanted to communicate the fact to her husband, she pursued a similar course. Neither would have spoken to the other if the heavens had been suddenly rent. And yet they loved as tenderly as they had ever done. It was the stern stuff of which the pioneers were made that caused them to act as they did, and supported them in their determination to build an empire in the heart of the wilderness.

I must refer other incidents along the same line to the next episode.

Episode Number Twenty-One

Uncle Billy and Aunt Nancy

The following incident will afford a fairly good idea of the extent to which Uncle Billy and Aunt Nancy Logan carried their domestic warfare. My father met the old couple one day coming out of the woods with a large basket of walnuts between them. They had gathered the nuts and were now carrying them home, one on either side of the basket, without a word having passed between them. Father accompanied them home and had dinner and spent most of a pleasant afternoon, without a word from either to the other. During the dinner Uncle Billy felt that he would appreciate another piece of pumpkin pie, but as none of the children were there to carry the message he spoke it into the air and it reached Aunt Nancy over the wireless.

They never resumed speaking terms during the remainder of their earthly lives, and I am not competent to state what happened afterward. Uncle Billy died first, and was buried with Masonic honors at Marthasville, where his tombstone still stands to commemorate his many virtues; but whether he said goodbye to Aunt Nancy or not is beyond my ability to fathom. A word or two may have passed between them at the last moment, but the probability is that Uncle Billy merely pointed upward as an indication of the place to which he was going; and the expression of a hope that Aunt Nancy would follow him there. If any spoken message passed between them it is not recorded.

During Uncle Billy's lifetime the public highway passed in front of his double-log cabin and along the side of his largest field, and he conceived the idea of building a permanent fence there. So he plowed a furrow and planted a row of walnuts in it, only two or three inches apart. He made no allowance of room for the trees to grow, but inferred that they would be able to take care of themselves. It seemed as if every one of the nuts sprouted, and when the trees grew to some size they were jammed so close together that a weasel could not have made its way between them. Indeed it may be doubted if a healthy grasshopper could have hopped into a field. The only way the trees could accommodate themselves in space was to spread sidewise, and the last time I saw that fence it reminded me of an effort to grow paddles for a stern-wheel steamboat. Many years have past since then, and I can only imagine what sort of a freak the fence assumed. Probably the trees were cut down and made into gun stocks during the great war with the German Kaiser.

A Ghostly Experience

Sometime after Uncle Billy's death, father sent me with a message of some kind to Aunt Nancy. The distance was fifteen miles and I made the trip in an ox-wagon, which I think was doing pretty well considering that a two hundred foot bluff had to be climbed on the way. I arrived at sunset, and of course remained over night in order to make the return trip the next day. I was only eight years old, and not robust; so Aunt Nancy, in the kindness of her heart, took a fancy to me and entertained me until midnight with ghost stories. Then she put me to bed by myself in the room across the passage, where I spent the remainder of the night interviewing ghosts. I saw and communed with each separate and particular one that she had mentioned, and no boy was ever more rejoiced to see the sun when it rose than I was. To this day, if I had the time and cared for that sort of amusement, I could repeat every story she told me; especially the one about the man whose head the Indians cut off, and who came back after he was dead and scalped the whole tribe. Or the man who died and went to the wrong place, and came back and entered his body again and lived another and better life. Aunt Nancy's ghost stories were all of a highly moral character, and I inferred at the time that she told them to me with a view of improving my condition, for my reputation was not above reproach, even at that early age.

Talt Goe

Uncle Billy and Aunt Nancy were not the only people in the Boone community who had peculiarities. In early days there came into that part of the country a man named Goe, with the accent on the second letter. According to my father's account of him, derived mostly from Uncle Daniel's "lost manuscript", he was more disposed to come than to go; but being a genial and inoffensive sort of creature most of the neighbors were glad to have him around. His first name was Tarleton, which indicated Tory origin; and this was probably one reason why Uncle Daniel did not like him. He came from the Carolinas, where the British General Tarleton operated during the Revolution; and that was the explanation of the front part of the name. Uncle Daniel said it was bad enough to be a Tory, or a descendant of one; but there was absolutely no excuse for perpetuating the infamy by naming a boy for a bloody-minded Britisher. For this and other reasons Mr. Goe's first name was shortened to "Talt," and he must go down to fame as Talt Goe.

In some distant and unknown way he was related to the Boones, but Uncle Daniel had no use for him. How or by what means he arrived in the Femme Osage settlements is not known; but he came and never went away. The common expression was that Talt came but did not go.

Talt had no place of habitation, but traveled at will over the country, housing himself and horse wherever night or his own pleasure overtook him. When he came to a place where it was his intention to stop, it was his custom first to look after the comfort of his horse, a fat and lazy sorrel, by rubbing him down and feeding him the best hay and corn that the barn afforded. He was never accused of neglecting the comfort either of his horse or himself. When the old sorrel had been attended to, Talt took up his saddlebags and came to the house and made himself at home.

Most of the women were glad to see him, for he did their little chores and made himself generally useful; though he scorned everything in the nature of hard work. He would bring water from the spring, wipe the dishes, make up his own bed, look after the children and keep them out of danger, and make whistles and plait bark whips for them. Therefore the little ones loved him, and their mothers regarded him as a household treasure.

But back in Kentucky there had been a misunderstanding between Talt and Uncle Daniel, and the Boone home was one that he did not include in his itinerary. The secret of the mutual dislike was explained in this way: While Talt was living with his relatives in Kentucky, they were rearing a little orphan boy---they were always looking after somebody who needed care and sympathy---and one day while Uncle Daniel was away Talt took it upon himself to discipline the little orphan by giving him a severe whipping. When Boone returned and discovered what had been done he was furious. It was one of those rare occasions when his anger flamed into passion, for he could not bear to have a child punished corporally. So he decided to give Talt a dose of his own medicine, which might do him good in after life; and with his own hands he administered a tanning that the recipient never forgot. It was a good thing for Talt. He never afterward whipped a child; on the contrary, he became a universal favorite with the little people; but he never liked Uncle Daniel from that day to the end of his life. The state of mind between the two was mutual, and Talt never put his horse in the Boone stable or sought shelter at the Boone house.

A Pioneer Philosopher

But he was a philosopher of the first water and had ideas about creation that would have puzzled a doctor of divinity. He came to our house a few days after my father had been bitten by a rattlesnake, and when supper was over he descanted on snakes in general. He said God never made serpents or poisonous insects and ferocious animals; it would not have been in accordance with his reputation for benevolence to have done so. But all such bad and wicked creatures were the result of evil thoughts of men. Thoughts were things, he said, and when they were turned loose and set in motion they filled the earth with creatures like themselves. Therefore when Uncle Daniel thrashed him he punished the wrong man; he should have gone after the fellow who whipped the first child. This would have been more comfortable for Talt, and the idea may have influenced the trench of his philosophy.

When Grandfather Jonathan asked him what kind of thoughts produced rattlesnakes, he replied the worst that any man could possibly think. Such thoughts, for instance, as a bad man has when he is drunk; and tigers and "painters", and wild cats, and all that kind of animals came from the thoughts of men who went out to murder their fellow-beings. A single murder might produce a thousand wild cats, which explained why there were so many of that kind of animals in the country. It was the Indians who made them, because they were always killing somebody.

Mosquitoes, and flies, and bed bugs, and that sort of pestiferous creatures were domestic in their habits, and came from the bad thoughts of women. This explained why they infested houses and disturbed people when they were trying to sleep. Talt said he knew a woman in Kentucky who "thought" so many bed bugs that no man could sleep in her house, and for that reason he quit visiting there.

He knew a man also in Kentucky who "thought" his horse-pond so full of mosquitoes that they poisoned his horses until they died or ran away into the woods and became wild, and as the man was engaged in the horse and mule business it nearly broke him up. At last he took Talt's advice and quit swearing and using bad language (near his pond), and the mosquitoes died or flew away. Then the horses and mules came back and were perfectly healthy and contented, and the last Talt heard of the man he was getting rich.

He said he knew a man who formerly lived near Bryan's Station in Kentucky, who used to go into the woods and swear just for amusement; and he kept it up until Simon Girty marched in with an army of five hundred Indians and they would have murdered every soul in the station if it hadn't been for the women who didn't swear.

It was dangerous to swear or think bad thoughts, because they produced red Indians as well as wild cats and "painters". If you went into the woods and swore loud enough you were just as liable to bring out a full blooded Indian as a catamount or a rattlesnake.

After the trouble at Bryan's Station the inhabitants wouldn't allow that man to live in Kentucky, so he went back to Virginia, and the last that Talt heard of him he had been employed to swear the devils out of whiskey. But when the devils left, snakes came in their place, and the people were obliged to quit drinking liquor because it made them see snakes . This so discouraged the owner of the distillery that he discharged the man; but he was still swearing somewhere in the Valley of Virginia, and wherever he went snakes became so numerous that the people had to move away. Most of them came to Missouri, which accounted for the rapid settlement of Femme Osage District.

House-Raisings and Log-Rollings

Whatever there may have been in Talt Goe's peculiar philosophy, there was no disputing the fact that Missouri was getting population. The Femme Osage District was beginning to have the appearance of an old-settled country, and Uncle Daniel complained a good deal about the pressure of his lungs for the want of fresh air.

House-raisings and log-rollings were of frequent occurrence, and they were mileposts in the lives of the people. Men and women would travel ten to twenty, and even thirty miles to these gatherings, the women carrying the babies and the men shouldering their rifles and looking after the game. The dogs and the little boys and girls walked the same as their elders. When they came to the place where the house was to be raised, a camp was formed and a frolic entered upon that lasted until the work was done. Indeed the frolic was generally the main thing. While the men raised the house or rolled the logs and shot the game, the women cooked the dinners of wild turkeys, venison, and bear meat, balanced and apportioned with sweet potatoes, corn bread, and wild honey. There seemed never an end of these essentials and delicacies; wherever the traveler went he found them in abundance.

Commodity Currency

There was little use for money. The time for hoarding had not come, and the speculative era in lands had almost ceased. Exchanges were effected with furs and peltries, or by plain swapping. When trading was done by contract it was based on the value of peltries at the time. It was a "commodity" currency. If values went up or down before the completion of the contract, more or less furs were delivered. Lead and gunpowder also passed current, and liquor would have done likewise if there had been any means of transportation other than by internal combustion.

Spanish milled dollars were the standard, and a few were beginning to find their way into the settlements. For the sake of change these dollars were cut into "bits", running from eight "bits" to ten to the dollar. An expert might cut as many as twelve "bits" out of a single dollar, according to his moral status. This was the origin of the terms "two bits", "four bits", "six bits", etc. A "bit" was valued at 12 ½ cents, and there was a smaller coin called a "picayune", which was worth half a bit, or 6 ¼ cents. This was the smallest coin that circulated among the pioneers, and a great newspaper in New Orleans has preserved the name to the present time. As there could be only eight legitimate "bits" in a dollar, and but few pioneers were ever known to have more than a dollar at a time, if one were found with ten or more "bits" in his possession he was regarded with aversion. The suspicion was liable to develop into trouble, and occasionally a shooting-match. It was permissible to own and carry all the "bits" you pleased, provided eight of them would fit a dollar; but too many "bits" in one pocket were dangerous. As already intimated, an expert would sometimes cut a dollar into five quarters, and these divided into halves made ten "bits", which were called "sharp shiners". These were the coins that sometimes got people into trouble. The possession of ten "sharp shiners" was regarded as a polite invitation to go west and it was better to emigrate than take a chance of being shot.

Counterfeiting as an Industry

As population increased and the need of a circulating medium became imperative, counterfeiters undertook to accommodate the public. Greasy, bad-smelling dollars began to make their appearance, and for a while they circulated almost as well as the genuine ones. They were roughly cast out of the basest kind of metal and should not have deceived any one; but the pioneers were of a trusting disposition and less acute in such matters than they might have been. Companies were organized to manufacture the slick dollars, and they sent their agents out among the people to circulate them. As the men were generally in the woods it was the women who received the money, and many an admiring housewife was fooled by a smooth-tongued rascal into exchanging eight good bits for a slick dollar. But when these found their way to St. Louis and were refused by the merchants in exchange for goods, the pioneers became suspicious to such an extent that several smooth agents had heart-failure and met with sudden death.

So much spurious money found its way into circulation that there was hardly a family that did not have one or more samples. My father had an old pocket-piece of sterling pewter which he carried to the day of his death, as evidence of the fact that he was greener than the man who passed it on to him. The worthless piece was as slick as if it had been oiled, and when it emitted a vile copperish odor from metal which had been employed to stiffen the pewter.

Trade Centers and Peddlers

The only trade centers were St. Louis and New Orleans. The latter was reached by flatboats, keelboats, or large dugouts called pirogues, and only dealers of considerable resources could afford to but produce in sufficient quantities to load such vessels and float them to the distant market. Commerce of this kind was uncertain, for having no market reports, the boatmen might find on reaching their destination that they could not sell their goods for as much as they had paid. But they protected themselves as well as they could by paying prices low enough to "cover accidents", and produce was so abundant that the people were glad to accept any price that might be afforded.

Trips to St. Louis were quicker and more certain, and for this reason most of the trade went there. Transportation was effected by pack animals and covered wagons, the latter of the old sway-back Virginia type. There were wagoners who made monthly trips with loads of turkeys and other wild meats, returning with such goods as the people ordered in exchange. For many years there were no local stores in the settlements. Even St. Charles had but two small dealers whose entire stocks might have been carried on the back of a mule. At a later date peddlers began to make their appearance, staggering under great packs, and they were a boon to the settlers. The coming of the peddler was an event to be remembered and talked about. Of course they charged enormous profits, but they dealt in little conveniences that every housewife needed, and the prices did not seem out of the way when distributed over a number of small articles. The peddler was the predecessor of the five and ten cent stores. He was also a news messenger and kept the backwoodsmen informed about affairs in the great outside world, the victories of Napoleon and the tottering of empires.

Most of these men subsequently established country stores, or went into business in St. Louis or New Orleans; and their knowledge of conditions enabled them to prosper in large measure. Many of the great mercantile houses of the cities originated in this way.

The Trader's Wagon

The coming of the trader's wagon into the community was always an event of interest. Families flocked from all quarters to receive the goods they had ordered, to hear the latest news, and exchange local gossip. Little children stood expectant with their fingers in their mouths, hoping the wagoner had not forgotten them in the matter of cheap toys or beautiful sticks of striped candy. Others brought new supplies, either to trade with the wagoner or have him sell for them on his return trip; and the pleasure and excitement of the occasion were visible in all the eager faces. The St. Louis wagoner was a great man! It was supposed that he knew almost everything, and that he had seen the greater part of the world. One of his tribe named Ulfries, a sensible and progressive German, lived on a farm adjoining ours, and when I was in his presence I felt that he was by all odds almost as great as Napoleon.

At these monthly meetings if a man had nothing to barter, he took his rifle and went into the woods, returning soon with wild turkeys or venison haunches, and so did his part in extending the avenues of commerce. So great and wise a man as the wagoner could find a market for anything in the mysterious and wonderful city to and from which he drove his sway-backed vehicle.

The scarcity of money reduced values to low levels. Corn was worth ten cents a bushel, in furs or peltry; wheat sold for thirty cents a bushel, when a buyer could be found, and bacon brought a cent and a half a pound. No respectable householder would eat bacon, when venison or bear meat was so plentiful; so the bacon was shipped to St. Louis and consumed by the people who knew no better.

A Terrified Jew

There were Jews in St. Louis then as now; and indeed where will you go in the wide world without finding members of this enterprising race? On a certain occasion my father was in the city on an errand for Grandfather Jonathan, and he went into a restaurant and ordered a luncheon. A moment afterward a Jewish merchant came in, and seating himself at the same table, ordered a pork chop. A storm had been threatening, and just as the waiter put the chop on the table there was a brilliant flash of lightning, green electricity sizzled and cracked through the room, followed by a crash of thunder that shook the building to its foundation. "Holy Moses!" shrieked the Jew, sliding under the table for safety, "I didn't think the Lord would make such a fuss over a little pork chop!"

Fifty Arpents for a Horse

On this trip my father had brought a drove of horses to market, which he sold at a record price of $25.00 a head, and carried the money home in silver dollars deposited in hempen sacks. The dollars were poured into the barrel in the loft with the others, and grandfather thought so little of their value that he did not take the trouble to count them.

At that time my father owned and rode a beautiful bay filly, with flowing black mane and tail. She was a beauty to look at and a treasure to ride, for she had a gait as easy as a rocking cradle and almost as fast as an ordinary horse could run. A French merchant took a fancy to the filly and offered three times the price that the other horses had brought; but father did not care to part with his riding animal. Then the Frenchman proposed to trade him fifty arpents of land in what is now the heart of the business district of St. Louis, and it seemed so favorable a proposition that father took it under consideration. But on inspecting the property he found so many sinkholes that he did not think he could plow the land, and so turned the offer down. At the present time that piece of land is worth more than a billion of dollars, and if father had made the trade and held on to the property he would have been the richest man in America a long time before he died.

They tell a similar story about a man in Chicago. He was offered fifty acres in what is now the famous "Loop District" of that city for a pair of boots. When expostulated with by a friend for not grabbing so splendid an offer, he replied that he didn't have the boots, and the fellow didn't own the land. The Dutchman who bought Manhattan Island for as much as the hide of a cow would measure, was wiser than either the man from Chicago or my father. He had the hide, and cutting it into strips surrounded and took in nearly the whole island for the price of five shillings. It is probable that this story and its relations have done duty in every large city in the world; but in my case it was literally true. When I was nineteen years old I was offered a block of ground in what is now the business district of Kansas City, for a little black pony that I had bought from an Indian for $13. But I thought the pony was worth more than the land, and so put him up at auction and sold him for $35.00. It seemed to me that Kansas City was not worth the price of a pony because it had so many hills.

Uncle Billy Coshow and the Wounded Buck

Grandmother Mary was a widow when she married Jonathan, her first husband, a Captain Cashow, having been killed by the Indians in the battle of Point Pleasant. She had a son name William who was destined to become one of my favorite uncles.

When "Uncle Billy" reached maturity he stood six-feet-six in his moccasins, weighed two hundred and fifty pounds, and was as active as a wild cat. I mention these otherwise nonessentials because they made it possible for him to do the things that fell to his lot, and do them well. In addition to his size and strength Uncle Billy had a voice that rumbled like distant thunder and could be heard far away, as he demonstrated on a certain memorable occasion.

One morning he went hunting and forgot his knife, and a hunter in the midst of wild animals without such a weapon is a misfit. When he was about two miles from home he shot and wounded a large buck, whose branching antlers stood out on both sides of his head like thirsty bayonets. The animal having fallen to the ground from the shock of the bullet, Uncle Billy dropped his gun and ran in to finish the fight with his knife. This was a thing which no experienced hunter would not have done, and Uncle Daniel told him so in unequivocal terms. A hunter should always reload his gun before making a rush upon a wounded animal, for he never can tell what the beast will do, especially when he is smarting with the pain of his wound and fighting for life.

At the critical moment Uncle Billy discovered that the knife was not in its scabbard, and at the same instant the deer rose to its feet and made a lunge at him. On came the deer with poised horns and blazing eyes, and Uncle Billy realized that a single thrust of one of those wide-spreading antlers would be his finish. So, bracing himself for the encounter, he caught the deer by the horns on both sides of its head, and by a sharp twist of the neck threw it to the ground. But it was up in an instant and ready for the second round. Again Uncle Billy caught the deer by the antlers, as he had done before, but this time led it to a sapling against which he held it firmly. The animal showed no signs of weakening, but raged and snorted, his eyes blazing with hate. And there they stood, their faces within a few inches of each other and neither able to defend himself.

The boy thought he could hold the animal for any reasonable time, until it would be so weakened by loss of blood that he could manage it; but it seemed a ludicrous thing to stand there in the woods looking into the eyes of a mad buck. So he called to Wilse for help. "Bring me a knife!" he yelled. "I've caught a deer and can't let go".

Introducing a Black Hero

Wilse was a black boy of about his own age, and they had been playfellows most of their lives. Either would have fought a dozen panthers to help the other in case of peril; but Wilse was two miles away, and the buck was on the spot. The black boy could plainly hear and understand the call of his chum, and realizing the need of hast, he seized a knife and set out on a run through the woods and over the hills.

"Wait fer me, Marse Billy!" he shouted; "I'm a-comin'!" and every little while as he drew nearer he renewed his call of assurance. "Hold on to him, Marse Billy, I'm a-comin'!"

At length he arrived at the scene of action, but the situation was so ludicrous that he burst out laughing.

"Stop your laughing!" snorted Billy, "and come here and kill this buck---or I'll lick you!"

"Lick nothin'!" retorted Wilse; "yo' know yo' cayn't do hit—an' 'sides, dat ole buck gibin' yo' all de lickin' yo' can handle right now!"

But it was no time for argument, and Wilse closed in. It was his intention to stab the deer in the heart, but the animal gave a quick twist of his haunches and kicked the knife out of his hand, making it rattle and clang against a rock several feet away.

"You're a great hunter!" roared Billy, "to let a deer kick you that way!"

"An' you's anoder!" retorted Wilse, "standin' dar in de woods holdin' a buck by de horns an' lookin' him in de eye! Why doan' yo' twiss' his neck?"

"You black rascal!" roared Billy, "come here and kill this buck and quit your foolishness, or I'll twist your neck so your nose will look backwards."

"Dat is effen yo' could!" responded Wilse. "Sayin' yo's gwyn' ter twist somebody's neck am one thing, but an' doin' it 's anoder."

But it was time for action! The deer was getting stronger, and Billy was growing weaker. This time Wilse advanced on Billy's side of the tree, and reaching around with his knife soon put an end to the combat.

Removing the entrails, the boys tied the feet of the carcass together and carried it home between them on a pole, each declaring on the way that the other was "no hunter," and that he "could lick him with both hands tied." But no blood was shed, and for many years Uncle Billy's "Battle with the Buck" was regarded as a good joke.

Uncle Billy and the Black Wolf

On another occasion Uncle Billy had an adventure with a black wolf, which was even more exciting than the one just related. The black wolf was a fierce beast that the pioneers especially dreaded, and Billy's encounter gave him renown all over that part of the country, even winning the warm encomiums of so famous a hunter as Uncle Daniel.

He tracked the wolf through the snow to its den and kindled a fire to smoke it out. The heat and smoke soon drove the animal to the front, where with furious snarls and growls it began to tear the blazing embers. It was one of the biggest and blackest of its species, a tiger of the forest, and Billy knew if it made its escape he would have but little chance for his life. So he fell into a panic and ran away, firing his gun from his shoulder as he ran. But the shock of the exploding rifle restored his senses, and realizing what a ridiculous figure he would cut among the neighbors, he turned and ran back to the den as fast as he had come, reloading his gun on the way. By this time the wolf had retreated from the heat and smoke into the invisible depths of its den; whereupon Billy renewed the fire and kept it blazing until he thought the beast must be dead. Then taking his knife between his teeth he crawled into the darkness, but had advanced only a few feet when an angry growl warned him that his enemy was still alive and ready for a fight.

Then followed a combat which probably never has been surpassed in the annals of hunting. In the darkness of a cavern, where the gloom was so dense that he could see only the fiery eyes of his antagonist, he was to meet and overcome one of the most dreaded beasts of the forest or be himself torn to pieces. Not many boys would have the nerve to meet such a crisis as Billy did.

The vault of the cave was so low that he could not stand on his feet, but was obliged to meet the onslaught kneeling. He could see nothing but the two glittering eyes of the wolf, and realized that the fatal spring was about to be made. Settling himself firmly and bracing his knife well in front, he awaited the onset, which came with a suddenness of a flash of lightning. But the wolf, instead of fixing his claws in the flesh of his expected victim, rushed upon the keen blade of his knife, which penetrated the heart laid him dead at the feet of the victor.

Dragging the carcass to the light outside, Billy removed the hide and returned home in triumph. The story of Putnam's combat with a wolf was familiar to all the pioneers, but every one admitted that Billy's adventure surpassed that of the famous Revolutionary hero; and it was the proudest moment of his life when Uncle Daniel confirmed the claim.

Holding a Bear by the Tongue

But Uncle Billy was to add other laurels to his fame. His next adventure resembled that of Sampson of old, in the fact that he overcame a bear in personal combat very much in the same way that the prophet is said to have done. And it was not a young bear, either, but a fierce full grown one that measured seven feet from snout to tail.

Billy went bear hunting and found what he was looking for. It was near the end of the hibernating season, when bear meat was at its best, and it was Billy's idea to make a killing without using his gun or wasting his powder. If he could find one in a comatose state he would bear it in its den and depend upon the knife alone. In due time he came upon a trail leading into a dense canebrake, and knew a bear was there because there were no outgoing tracks. He estimated that it was a big one too, for the tracks were enormous.

Leaning his gun against a tree Billy drew his knife and began carefully threading his way into the thicket; when suddenly he found himself face to face with a rampant bear standing on his hind legs and at least a foot taller than he was. Now he regretted not having brought his gun, for the beast seemed as big as a mule and fierce as a lion, with an aspect that was terrifying. He was not comatose by any means, nor was he disposed to lie still and invite an attack. Under the circumstances Billy might have justified in running away, but he knew that his first motion to retreat would be followed by a rush in which the great weight of the bear would crush him to the earth. So he stood his ground, and instead of giving the bear the benefit of the first rush, he himself sprang forward with his knife in hand. But with a single sweep of his right paw the bear sent the knife ringing against a stone ten feet away. It was now man against bear, each armed only with the weapons that nature had provided, with no advantage to either except human reason against brutish instinct.

Ducking his head in order to avoid the deadly "hug", Billy leaped upon the bear, and thrusting his hand into its open mouth seized the tongue near the roots and held on in a life-and-death struggle. The boy's quick movement disconcerted the bear, while the grip on his tongue made him sick and groggy. It was now the bear's turn to wonder what he should do! Grimly pressing his advantage, Billy slowly pushed the staggering beast toward the point where the knife lay, and in a moment his moccasin touched the handle of the weapon. Seizing it with his free hand he plunged the blade into the heart of the beast, and so ended the combat. The bear trembled and sank down, and with a lurch fell at full length on the ground, where it lay like a great log. It was Billy's most desperate struggle with a wild beast, and he knew he had won his greatest battle.

Episode Number Twenty-Four

Remarkable Adventures with Lions

The incidents connected with Uncle Billy's battle with the bear were so extraordinary and out of the usual course of things, that I feared they would not be accepted as true, and for that reason I had decided to eliminate the account from the manuscripts. But no sooner had I reached this conclusion than the daily papers published two incidents of almost precisely the same character, of recent occurrence and even more remarkable in some of the details. The stories were to this effect:

The first stated that a lion had escaped from a circus while it was giving exhibitions in an Alabama town, and fled to a wilderness nearby. As soon as the fact became known the men of the place organized themselves into several companies and went on an impromptu lion hunt. None of the men had ever previously engaged in the "royal sport", some had never seen a lion; and of course they were not prepared for so dangerous an adventure.

Two of the men, hunting together in the midst of some thick brush, were suddenly rushed by the lion before they had time to use their guns; and the nearest one received the impact of the charge, was thrown to the ground with the beast on top of him. Acting on the impulse of the moment, he thrust his right hand into the lion's mouth and seized the roots of its tongue, just as Uncle Billy had done with the bear, and with the same result. The lion grew sick and dizzy and struggled to release itself from the strangle-hold; and meanwhile the other hunter shot it dead. It seemed so exact parallel of Uncle Billy's adventure that I decided to retain and use both incidents.

In the second place, two Americans were hunting lions near Tanganyika, in Africa, when one of the men shot a large lion and supposed he had killed it. But it was only wounded and temporarily shocked. The other man ran up to photograph what he supposed to be a dead or dying lion, when it suddenly rose and charged the one from whom it had received the shot. He was borne helplessly to the ground, where a desperate struggle ensued. The hunter thrust both hands into the open mouth of the beast in an effort to prevent a fatal bite, while at the same time his companion shot and killed it. But the wounded man was so badly hurt that he died of his injuries several days later. In this case it does not appear that the hunter tried to grasp the lion's tongue, or even thought of doing so, but merely endeavored to keep the beast from biting him; thereby losing the advantage of the dizziness which always accompanies pressure on the roots of the tongue.

A Catfish Tries to Swallow a Negro Boy

The fall following the incident which gave fame to Uncle Billy as a bear fighter, was destined to add new luster to his reputation. He and one of the negro boys were bathing in the Missouri River, which formed the south boundary of the farm; when suddenly the boy screamed and sank out of sight. A moment later he reappeared on the surface of the water, shouting lustily for help; but immediately disappeared the second time. Uncle Billy was too far away to render assistance, but he swam rapidly to the spot, and when the boy rose the third time he grasped him by the wool and with a desperate effort freed him from what proved to be an immense catfish. In its efforts to swallow the boy the fish had caught him by one of his legs, while the other, swinging and kicking on the outside, prevented the accomplishment of its purpose. The fish was so large that it could easily have swallowed the boy if it had caught him by both legs, or taken him head-first. During the struggle they were drawn into shallow water, where the fish was out of its element and could not compete with Uncle Billy, who soon disposed of it. It weighed a little over seven hundred pounds, and my father who saw it a few hours later as it lay on the bank of the river, declared that it seemed to him as large as a mule. The incident confirmed his faith in the story of Jonah and the whale, about which he had previously entertained some doubt; for he said, "If a Missouri River catfish can swallow a negro boy, why should not a whale swallow a prophet?"

I remember only one other story about Uncle Billy that seems worthy of repetition. It happened in this way:

Battle with a Panther

Three panthers had invaded the neighborhood in quest of lambs and pigs, announcing their presence not only by the slaughter of the victims, but also by their blood-curdling shrieks. All the men and boys of proper age shouldered their guns and went into the woods in quest of the marauders, among them of course Uncle Billy.

In order to prevent the escape of the animals they formed a wide circle and stalked the woods singly, advancing cautiously toward a common center. It was a dangerous maneuver, for it left each individual exposed all to the combined attack of the three beasts. But it was regarded as the surest way to relieve the community of its dangerous invaders, and none of the hunters hesitate to incur the risk.

Uncle Billy was weaving his way through some thick underbrush, when he was startled by an ominous noise almost directly over his head. On looking upward into the overhanging branches he saw a panther in the act of launching its body upon him, and having no time to bring his gun into action, he sprang behind a large sapling. His quick movement was all that saved his life, for the panther had already made its deadly spring; but missing its aim, struck the side of the sapling opposite to Uncle Billy with a blow that stunned it temporarily. Availing himself of the opportunity, the boy caught the long tail of the beast and wound it round the sapling, at the same moment drawing his knife and striking out with the intention of piercing its heart. But in the excitement and hurry he severed its tail instead, whereupon the frantic beast ran howling into the thicket. In an instant Uncle Billy was ready with his rifle, and firing more by the instinct of the hunter than with accuracy of aim, the bullet struck the panther in the rear and ranging through the body buried itself in the brain. The impact was so terrific that the beast turned a somersault, emitting a shriek that informed the other hunters as to its fate. With shouts and cries they came running from all sides, and loudly proclaimed Uncle Billy the hero of the day.

The incident was so remarkable and out of the usual course that it gained a wide circulation, being repeated even in foreign countries; and when travelers came from abroad they never failed to seek an introduction to the youthful hero.

Two Panthers at One Shot

Almost at the same instant that the sound of Uncle Billy's rifle proclaimed the death of one of the panthers, Grandfather Jonathan performed a feat which excited almost equal wonder. He was stalking the woods only a short distance away, and hearing the discharge of Billy's gun and the expiring cry of the panther, was about to turn in that direction when he was startled by a noise overhead. Looking upward he saw a panther crouching on a limb and about to spring upon him. But the death scream of its mate caused a moment's hesitation, and gave Jonathan the chance that saved his life. Taking quick aim he shot the beast squarely between the eyes, and its tawny body crashed to the earth.

At the same instant, and very much to his amazement, another panther fell out of the opposite side of the tree, having been hit by the same bullet that killed its mate. The two animals, though separated by the width of the tree, happened to be in a direct line with each other, and thus became victims of a single discharge. The incident was regarded as one of the most remarkable in the history of hunting, and became widely circulated.

Many years afterward the reputation of the gun as a double-shooter was to be still further enhanced, but in a much less dangerous adventure. My younger brother Robert, while hunting squirrels with the ancient piece took aim at a squirrel that was gnawing a hickory nut on the side of a tree next to him, and at the flash of the gun two squirrels fell. As in the case of the panthers, they were on opposite sides of the tree but in direct line of the bullet. My brother was as much surprised in bagging two squirrels at one shot as Grandfather Jonathan had been at bringing down a couple of panthers with the same gun.

A Boy and a Black Wolf

At the time of the panther hunt my father was only twelve years old, but already a good marksman, with permission to go hunting alone provided he did not wander too far from home. In the present instance he was out with the "rest of the men", proudly shouldering the rifle that he was permitted to carry. It was early fall and there had been a heavy frost, until the foliage had assumed its annual splendor so dear to the heart of every lover of nature. My father, being of a poetic disposition, was attracted to the woods as much by his love of the beautiful as from any desire he might have to kill a panther. The latter, however, was at present the exciting motive, so he shouldered his rifle and marched forth as boldly as if he had slain a hundred panthers.

Presently he found himself approaching a large white oak tree which had been blown down while in full leaf, and its colors, now wearing the hues of gold and crimson, so concentrated his attention that he did not observe, or even suspect, the presence of a full sized black wolf concealed in the midst. As the boy approached, the wolf became alarmed, and abandoned the seclusion of the leaves ran into the open on the opposite side of the tree, where it stopped and growled and snapped its teeth.

Greatly excited by the unexpected appearance of so dreaded an enemy, the boy threw his gun over in line with the body of the beast and pulled the trigger, but the lock snapped. The wolf ran a little further and again stopped and snapped its teeth; and once more the gun also snapped. Then the wolf, considering the old aphorism about discretion and valor, especially when a half-grown boy was around snapping a gun at him, took to his heels and was soon out of sight.

When the wolf was gone and the danger over, my father tried his gun at a mark on a tree, and it fired as clearly as it ever had done. Being Methodist by birth as well as conversation, he always afterward contended that his encounter with the wolf and the failure of his gun, were manifestations of Providence in his behalf. If the gun had fired instead of snapping while the wolf was near him, he probably would have missed or merely wounded it, and been torn to pieces by the enraged animal. His faith afforded him so much comfort that I never had the heart to question its relevancy, though I could not understand the intimate sympathy of Providence with the eccentric operations of the old flint-lock rifle.

Aunt Ann Hays's Adventure with a Panther

While I was still a small boy an event occurred in our vicinity which became indelibly impressed upon my mind. Aunt Ann Hays, a distant relative of the Boone family, was a devout Methodist and firm believer in special Providences; and the tragedy which came into her life confirmed her faith. Her home was two miles beyond where we lived, and a dark and dismal wood lay between, through which there was only a bridle-path. In returning from church at Marthasville on Sundays it was her custom to stop and take dinner with us, and in the afternoon she and father would sit in the shade of the sugar-maple tree that stood in the yard and discuss their religious experiences.

On the occasion which we are now considering Aunt Ann lingered longer than usual, so that it was almost dark when she set out to ride home. She had proceeded more than half-way when the scream of a panther a short distance to the right of the path sent a thrill of horror through her veins. The horse was so frightened that it reared and threw its rider, and ran home leaving her helpless on the ground with a fractured leg. The remainder of the story I heard her relate to my mother a few weeks later, as we sat by her bedside.

When she was thrown and left alone in the woods Aunt Ann believed that her time had come, but having faith that whatever happened would be for the best, even to being eaten by a panther, she resigned her soul into the care of Providence. However, she continued to pray and call for help as long as consciousness remained; after which she knew nothing until she came-to in her own bed at home, with her leg encased in splints and bandages.

The place where she had fallen was near a field that belonged to the Lemme family, and my cousin Arch Bryan, who lived there with his widowed mother, hearing the screams of the panther got his gun and calling the dogs went into the woods to find the intruder. He had proceeded only a short distance when he heard Aunt Ann's appeals for help; at the same time the dogs caught the scent of the panther, and with loud calls rushed into the woods after it. This diverted the attention of the beast from its intended victim, and Arch hurried to her rescue. On the way he caught sight of the glare of the animal's eyes in a tree where it had taken refuge, and fired a shot which brought it to the earth. There whatever life still remained in its body was quickly dispatched by the dogs.

On reaching Aunt Ann he found her unconscious, but the firing of the gun, the screams of the panther, and the barking of the dogs had aroused the neighborhood, and in a little while a number of men arrived on the scene. Aunt Ann was still unconscious and they supposed she was dead; but among the men was a young doctor, who after a preliminary examination announced that there was nothing more serious than her broken limb and nervous reaction to the pain and fright.

She was tenderly lifted and carried home on an improvised litter of cedar boughs, and in due course of time recovered. For the remainder of her life her chief sources of thankfulness were her gratitude for not having been eaten by the "varmint" and her pleasure in relating her adventure with the "painter".

Wilse, the Black Hero

Having made some mention of Wilse the black boy, in connection with an adventure of Uncle Billy Coshow, I shall now relate some of his own exploits, which won him the admiration of all who knew him, white as well as black.

Wilse lived to be a very old man, bringing him well within my memory and forming a connecting link between Uncle Daniel Boone and myself. Many of the incidents which I am relating were obtained in personal conversations with Wilse, whose mind and memory remained clear and distinct to the end of his life. Like many other slaves, he did not know who his parents were or how old he was, though he must have been at least a hundred when he passed to a reward which he had won like a hero.

I remember him as erect, tall and dark, but not the dusky black of the Central African. He was more than six feet in height, straight as the proverbial Indian, and built like an athlete. His strength must have been very great. I remember when his hair was gray, and later in life when it was white as snow and it made a truly venerable background for his shinning and intelligent face.

He never married or made any effort to have a family of his own, being always devoted to my father and mother and their children. In his sturdy affections we were also his children, and he loved us as if we had in fact been his own. We knew better than to disobey Wilse's orders, for he was a strict disciplinarian, though by no means a believer in the rod that smites. If any attempt had been made to discipline one of us in his presence, he would have resented it with vigor. He had a great big heart that loved with the tenderness of a woman, and we children satisfied any personal longing he may have had for a family.

Many a handsome mulatto girl would have given her head for a union with Wilse, especially after he became one of the recognized heroes of the community; but his fancy did not run that way. He used to say that when he was young and might have married, the girls he preferred would not notice him; and after he had become a hero the devil himself would not have those who cast eyes at him.

Wilse Breaks a Wolf's Neck with His Hands

In wintertime he wore a coat made of the skin of a black wolf, fastened from the waist to chin with brass buttons that shimmered in the sunlight; and his reputation as a hunter lost none of its flavor by his manner of telling how he acquired the coat. Chief in his own mind was the adventure by means of which he won his famous coat and the applause of no less a personage than Daniel Boone himself. It happened in this way:

One moonlight night as he lay asleep on his bearskin rug, he was aroused by a commotion among the sheep, and taking his gun down from the rack he ran to the lot to see what was the matter. In his path he found the carcasses of several dead sheep killed by wolves, for the wolf loves blood more than he does flesh. It is his habit to sever the jugular vein with his sharp tusks, lap a little of the spurting fluid, and hasten on to another victim. In this way a single wolf will destroy a dozen or more sheep in the course of a few minutes; and if given time he will kill the whole flock. The same tactics are practiced by the "sheep-killing dog" which inherits its bloodlust from its wolfish ancestors; hence the expression among the pioneers, "Mean as a sheep-killing dog".

In the dim light of the moon Wilse could see two large black wolves dashing hither and thither among the white sheep, leaving a line of dead bodies on the ground as they ran. He brought one of them down with a shot from his rifle, when the other, a ferocious male, turned on him. Crouching an instant, the wolf sprang directly at his throat, intending to destroy him as it had done to the sheep; but as it came Wilse caught it by the throat and with a tremendous twist broke its neck. This ended the combat with Wilse the victor; though if any part of his strength or vision had been lacking the beast would have cut his throat at a single lunge with the facility of a practiced swordsman.

Next morning when Uncle Daniel came over and was informed of Wilse's feat, he declared it to be one of the most daring adventures he had ever known; and at his suggestion the skins of the wolves were tanned and made into a coat that was both warm and ornamental. In cold weather Wilse never failed to adorn his person with his famous coat, to which he added a cap made of the skin of a wildcat, which he also slew with his own hands. Thus attired he made a splendid figure, and no one stood higher in the estimation of those pioneers than the handsome black hero.

Breaking the Neck of a Wounded Buck

When Wilse was a boy of only twelve he had an encounter with a stag that gave him a good deal of reputation. He shot and wounded a large buck and not being the experienced hunter that he afterward became, he rushed forward with his knife to finish the fight. But the deer rose to its feet and made a lunge at him, striking an antler under the hem of his buckskin breeches and ripping the leg to the waistband. The skin was broken in several places, and when it healed it left a white scar from his ankle to his waist. In after years when he went bathing with white boys it was his custom to exhibit this scar as his right to claim lineage with "white fo'ks".

The weakness of the deer from loss of blood was all that saved Wilse. Watching his opportunity he laid hold of the animal by the horns and with a twist of his brawny arms put an end to the combat. It was this that he meant when he advised "Marse Billy" to "twis' his neck" while the latter was holding a mad buck against a sapling.

The School Teacher "Catches a Cat"

Having made reference to Wilse's wild cat cap, I will now explain how he obtained the trophy. Soon after his combat with the deer he was sent on an errand to a neighbor's house, and the path led by the school house. It was too early for the school to open, but as he drew near he was startled by a great commotion in the house, snarling and growling of a wild cat and cries for help from a man. Pushing through the open door, he found the school master in deadly struggle with a wild cat, which he was endeavoring to overcome by pressing it against a desk with his own body, the cat resisting with claws and teeth. It had already lacerated his person frightfully, and would soon have killed him if Wilse had not come at the critical moment.

THE OLD SCHOOL-HOUSE ~~NEAR THE BOONE CEMETERY~~.

"Help!" shouted the teacher; "I've caught a cat!"

He had indeed caught a cat, and needed all the help he could get, and without delay.

Wilse took in the situation at a glance, and running up within reach he seized the cat by the neck and with a single mighty twist crushed the spinal cord. Then quickly giving the teacher such attention as he could, he hurried away for Uncle Daniel, the only doctor in the community who knew how to treat wounds. The teacher was so badly hurt that it was several weeks before he was able to resume his duties, and afterwards when he went to school early in the morning he was careful to see that no wild cat had preceded him.

Out of the hide of the cat Wilse made the jaunty cap with which it was his custom ever after to decorate his head on all public occasions; and his wild cat cap became as well known in the community as Pete Bryan's coonskin cap with a fox's tail, but with a nobler significance.

Wilse Trails Two Indians

It seems to me that Wilse's greatest adventure was the time he trailed two Indians through the woods alone, and spent a sleepless night a short distance from them without either party being aware of the proximity of the other. He was at the time about twenty years old, but already the admitted black hero of the Boone settlements.

It was during the summer of 1815, on the occasion of the massacre of the Ramsay family near Marthasville by a band of Indians under the leadership of Black Hawk. As will be related elsewhere, the murders were committed early in the morning, and the dreadful news flew so rapidly that by sunrise a number of armed men were on the ground ready to trail the savages; and half an hour later Boone himself appeared to direct the movements. By nine o'clock every man and boy who was able to use a gun was on the way to the point of assembly, leaving only the women and children at home.

There were six Indians in the band, but in order to hide their trails and confuse the pursuers they separated into parties of two, with an agreement to meet at a designated place that night. (The details were obtained from Black Hawk himself after his surrender.) Two of the most bloodthirsty savages in the band made their way directly toward the heart of the Boone settlement, intending, as was afterward ascertained, to kill and scalp the great white chief himself. But their purpose would have failed, even if they had not themselves met with a deserved fate, for Boone was on the ground and directing the pursuit before they had covered a tenth part of the distance.

My father and Aleck McKinney hurried to the scene of the tragedy on horseback, but Wilse having no horse, set out on foot. The distance was about sixteen miles, but he was a rapid walker and hoped to arrive in time to be of service; and as it turned out he was the only one who came into actual contact with the Indians that day.

About noon he struck the trail of the two who were making their way in the direction of his home, and believing he could be of better service watching them, he turned and followed. It may seem an easy task for one man to trail two, but in those days it was a dangerous experiment. One of the best known tricks of the savages was to make a plain path for some distance, thus inviting pursuit; then double back on their own trail and ambush their pursuers. But Wilse was no novice in Indian warfare, and he was shrewd enough to avoid their wiles.

In their progress eastward the two warriors came to the headwaters of the Femme Osage, high up in the hills near the sharp bend of the stream. Here they resorted to one of their familiar stratagems, for breaking their trail, by wading upstream until they came to the bend, where they emerged on a rocky point opposite the side from which they had entered. Then crossing the narrow peninsula they forded the creek again and were once more on the same side as at the start. Evidently they had not yet discovered that they were being pursued, but resorted to the deception as a matter of safety in case they should be.

A Night of Anxiety

Here Wilse lost valuable time in looking for the confused trail, and when at last he found it darkness had come and it was impossible for him to proceed. He knew by their course that the savages were making for the Boone home, which would include his own, thus placing the lives of those he loved in deadly peril. But he also knew that it was their invariable custom to make their attacks early in the morning, when their victims were less on guard than at any other time; and that these two savages having come a long distance since the early massacre, were tired and would probably rest during the night. In any event it was impossible for him to follow their trail in the dark, or if he attempted to do so he would probably stumble into their camp and himself become a victim of their ferocity. He decided therefore to remain where he was until just before daylight, when he would hurry home in time to meet the anticipated onslaught.

It was a lonely and anxious vigil. He had no idea how near he might be to the savages; perhaps they were separated by only a few rods, so close that any indiscretion on his part might bring them upon him. So no sleep.

But he was up even before the first gray streaks of dawn and feeling his way forward. It was no longer necessary to lose time by following the trail, his main object now being to reach home ahead of the savages. He therefore pushed on through canebrake and peavine, over ravines and rocks, and at last across the little stream that separated the Boone and Bryan farms.

A Dead Indian in the Yard

He was now in sight of the house, and stopped a moment to listen for any sounds of the enemy. At that instant he heard the sharp crack of a rifle, which he knew by location and distance had been fired at the house. Then all was still. There were no whoop or yells such as always followed attacks by Indians; neither was it the sound of an Indian's gun, the dull crash of a musket; it was the clean, clear crack of a rifle. Some white finger had pressed that trigger; and there was a mystery, for there were no men at home! And why had every sound so suddenly ceased? Wilse could think of no reasonable explanation, but he felt assured that some white person had shot an Indian, and victory was on his side!

Holding his gun ready for quick action, he pushed his way through the grass and cane, winding his course around obstructions with the sinuous motions of a serpent, and he soon came in sight of the house. There he beheld another mystery more difficult to solve than any that had preceded it. Out of the chimney of the kitchen came the blue smoke of breakfast in preparation, indicating that all was well. But prone upon the grass in front of the house lay an Indian, his tomahawk and gun on the ground where he had dropped them in falling. Weather the savage was dead or alive Wilse could not determine, but the indications were that he had fallen a victim to the mysterious shot which had so startled him a minute before. On the other hand it might be a trick, and it was well enough to be sure before going further. A dead Indian would be safe, but a live one might make trouble.

Moreover, there had been two Indians, while now he saw but one. What had become of the other? There had been no mysterious rifle shot to account for him. Was this lone one on the ground waiting for his companion to open the attack on the other side of the house, and if so why had he dropped his weapons? These were mysteries which Wilse could not fathom, for they surpassed anything he had ever seen before.

Unable longer to control his feelings, he brought his rifle to bear on the recumbent savage, and in his great roaring voice called out:

"Miss Mary! Miss Mary! It's Wilse! What's the matter?"

In response to his call the door opened and "Miss Mary" appeared and waved her hand to indicate that all was well.

A Couple of Women Slay Two Warriors

With a yell of joy Wilse came bounding forward, through the grass and cane like a lumbering black bear. The story was brief and soon told. At daylight Aunt Jemima, one of the colored women, had gone into the lot to milk the cows, while "Miss Mary" was in the adjoining garden looking after her flowers. Suddenly the cows began to snort and shake their heads and tramp the ground and bellow, as they always did when Indians were near, their keen scent warning them of the presence of danger. At the same moment a little black boy ran around the corner of the house, his eyes bulging with terror, and yelled:

"Injuns! Injuns!"

Close behind the boy came a tall savage, his musket trailed in his left hand, while in his right he grasped his upraised tomahawk. He feared to use his gun because of its alarming sound, but was depending on the silent though equally effective hatchet. He paid no attention to the boy; he was too small and too badly scared to be in the way; and moreover the Indians regarded the negroes as a people more or less akin to themselves, and were lenient with them. A scalp of wool excited their contempt.

The women, acting on a single impulse, ran to the open door of the house. Aunt Jemima, being fat, brought up the rear, the warrior treading close upon he heels. But she reached the door first, and pushed her way through just as "Miss Mary" slammed it to. In his efforts to prevent the closing of the door, the Indian inserted his arm in the aperture, and it was caught between the door and the facing, with his tomahawk in his hand. Holding the door fast against his arm, Grandmother Mary directed Aunt Jemima to brain the warrior with his own weapon, which she was not slow in doing. A single blow sent him "across the way" to his happy hunting ground.

Then again came the little black boy screaming that there was another Indian on the south side of the house. On this side over the door there always hung a loaded rifle. Seizing the weapon, Grandmother Mary threw the door open, and there within ten feet of the house also with his tomahawk ready for action came running another Indian. But he never reached the door. A click of the lock and a flash of the gun sent him reeling to the earth. The women of those times could shoot almost as well as the men. This was the mysterious shot that had puzzled Wilse, and it accounted for the savage that he had seen lying in the front yard.

A Savage Murderer Meets His Fate.

A grave was dug by the side of a big rock north of the house, and the bodies of the two warriors were dragged there and buried in it; and to this day it is known as "The Rock of the Strangers".

But the event became sealed in the records of the family. Grandmother Mary could not bear to have the subject mentioned in her presence, and it might have passed out of memory except for the justifiable pride of Aunt Jemima, who never missed an opportunity to relate to her own people how she and "Miss Mary had slewed a pack ob red skins".

Aunt Jemima and "Miss Mary" have long slept close together in the little cemetery on the hill, where no warwhoop or sound of hostile gun disturbs their rest.

Wilse Finds Little Lost Jane

The event that endeared Wilse to our family more than anything else was his rescue of my little sister Jane when she was lost in the woods. She was some years my senior, and the tragedy occurred before I was born; but frequent repetitions of the details impressed them indelibly upon my mind.

She was only three years old at the time, but although the weather was cold and light snow fell she wandered alone three nights and two days, without food or care and without serious harm.

Near our house was the home of a little girl with whom Jane had been visiting with an older sister, and as the dusk of evening began to fall she bade her little playmate goodbye and started home. She was not seen again until the morning of the third day afterward.

News of the tragedy literally flew on wings of the wind, from neighbor to neighbor and house to house; and by morning more than two hundred men had assembled to assist in the search. At that time a lost child meant a great deal more than it does now, harrowing as such cases are; because the woods were haunted by wolves and other ravenous animals, and the imagination could not do otherwise than picture the most horrible results. Rough frontiersmen brushed the tears from their eyes as they saw the agony of the family, for they had little ones of their own at home, and it was easy to reverse the picture and imagine themselves the stricken ones.

All day and into the gloom of night the search was continued, without a trace being found; not so much as a torn piece of garment or the print of a little foot. During the night another hundred men arrived from more distant places, forming a force of three hundred active and experienced woodsmen; but their efforts of the second day were as fruitless as those of the first had been.

At the beginning of the second night, when it was too dark to continue the search and the men went to camp, not one of them believed that little Jane was alive. If found at all it would be merely her frozen or mangled body; but among all those men there was not one who even hinted at giving up the search. Nor did they whisper the dreadful thought which lay uppermost in every bosom. They remembered their own little ones at home and put themselves in the place of the stricken parents. As they lay sleepless upon their robes of bear or buffalo skins, each pondered over some feasible means of ending the awful suspense. That night snow fell to a depth of two inches, and the little one, lost in the woods, had no covering but her own thin garments. How gladly would every man in that great company have shared with her, the warmth of his own comfortable robe!

"She Is Alive! She Is Alive!"

As soon as it was light enough to see, on the morning of the third day, it was agreed that if little Jane should be found, or any trace of her discovered, a signal should be given by the firing of a gun. As none expected her to be found alive, no signal was provided for that event. All that they could expect was her little frozen and mangled body, or some remnant of her clothing—for it was the common belief of all that she had been destroyed by wolves. The howlings of these wretched animals had been heard each night of the search, and especially on the night just past, when the cold and snow sent the shivering sounds to the very marrow of the bones. Every one felt that this was the end, but not one spoke the fear that lay so heavy on each individual's heart.

That last day, as on the previous ones, Wilse was left at the camp to keep up the fires and prepare food for the men; and having some time to spare, and as keenly anxious as any one in that great assemblage, he took his gun and followed a ravine a hundred yards or so to where the falling water had formed a shelving cavity in the clay; and there, crouching and shivering like a frightened animal, he found little Jane!

His first act was to fire his gun as the agreed signal of discovery, but more joyous than all was his stentorian shout,

"She's alive! She's alive!"

The child was so frightened and dazed by the dreadful experiences through which she had passed, that she shrank from Wilse and would have fled again into the woods, except for the restraining banks of earth. But he spoke to her tenderly, lovingly, as though he had been her own father:

"Honey, don't you know me? It's Wilse! Come honey, let's go home to mother."

And so by his gentle manner and loving words she overcame her terror and she permitted him to lift her in his arms. Removing his warm wolf skin coat he wrapped her tiny form in it and carried her quickly to the camp, shouting all the way,

"She's alive! She's alive!"

The cry was taken up by the men, and from all quarters they came running toward the common center shouting the joyous refrain.

It was a spontaneous outpouring of relieved and happy hearts. The men wept like little children and embraced one another in their transports of joy. Perhaps in the whole history of humanity there never was another scene like it, and no man who was there ever forgot it. And Wilse was the hero above all others, because he had found the little one who had been lost.

My sister lived to be ninety-one years old, though she was blind in one eye and helpless during the last few years of her life, but not as a result of the tragedy of her infancy. In her youth and middle-life she was a teacher and exercised a wide influence for good. Later she became a nurse, and is remembered with love and gratitude by many to whom she brought comfort in their time of need. Everywhere she was known as "Aunt Jane", and it may be reasonably doubted if the passing of any one ever left a larger blank in a community.

Sold as a Slave

And after all this it will be shocking to know that father sold Wilse for a price, as a slave. But before condemning, let us consider the conditions.

Boone and my grandfather each owned a few slaves, as did most of their neighbors. They were brought from the older states, and were regarded as members of the family as much as the white children—for among the better classes the slaves were looked upon as children and treated as such. There was a genuine sentiment of family affection and pride between the races. The black children took their masters' names, and the boys associated together on almost equal terms. The negroes had their own quarters and cabins and ate their meals separately; but all had the same food, cooked in the same vessels, and wore the same kind of clothes.

If Boone and his neighbors had known what to do with their slaves they would have set them free, but in addition to the affection which existed between them there was a large responsibility on the part of the masters. At that time the negroes would have been helpless if free, because no master had means enough to set them up for themselves, and without such assistance they would have been helpless wanderers, dependent upon public charity. For these and other reasons the hated and hateful system had to remain until a better time.

Wilse was the only slave that my father ever owned, and he received him as a gift from his father. They had grown up together as boys and young men, but Wilse being a few years the senior had as much to do with the management of the farm as father himself. He was as free as his boyhood master, and always addressed him by his first name, omitting the usual "master" or "marse".

When Wilse was past his prime and his head beginning to get white, my father's affairs became involved, and there was danger that his property might be sold under execution. At the same time there was an English doctor named Paulk, living and practicing in Franklin County on the opposite side of the river from our farm. His success as a practitioner had established his reputation on both sides of the river to such an extent that it was impossible for him to visit all his patience in person, so it was his custom when coming into our neighborhood to stop at my father's house and blow a trumpet, and the sick would flock to him for treatment and advice.

In this way he became acquainted with Wilse, and said he would like to have him drive his buggy and look after the horses. When Wilse was told of the doctor's proposition he was delighted. It was just such a place as he would like. He was getting old and work on the farm was hard; and Wilse also had another idea. He thought to himself that if he could drive around with Dr. Paulk he would have many opportunities to relate his adventures to wandering crowds, and he begged father to sell him to the doctor. But father dismissed the idea with scorn; he said he would as soon sell his own brother.

At last however, the matter was compromised by "leasing" Wilse to Paulk for a year. The term sounds strange in our time, leasing a human being; but it was common then. Good reliable slaves were "leased" but the unreliable ones were hired or sold.

Thus Wilse passed temporarily from our family to the English doctor, and drove around the country in great style. When they came to our house it was difficult to determine "which was which", except that one was white and the other black. The old wild cat cap was discarded for a cast-off "plug" of the doctor's, and Wilse never failed to remark with dignity about the large practice "we" were doing. The coming of the two doctors was an event of the greatest joy, for it revived memories of old times and gave Wilse opportunities to tell us what was going on in the great outside world.

At the end of the term of the lease father's affairs were worse than ever, and there was real danger in Wilse remaining an item in the scheduled of his property. He might be levied upon and sold to some uncongenial master, and he therefore told "Ligy" quite authoritatively that it was time for him to be sold to Dr. Paulk.

And so the deal was consummated, and much to Wilse's pride he brought a good price. In spite of his advancing age his reputation had much to do with his value, and when he spoke of the matter in future conversations, as he frequently did, he never failed to mention that he was still worth a good deal more than any "common young nigger".

Wilse outlived father by a number of years, and was always an honored guest when he came to our house. He visited my father in his last illness, and attended the funeral with the "rest of the family". In conclusion, I can only say, "God bless Wilse, the black hero of the Boone neighborhood."

Extraordinary Adventure of Jim Davis

One of the most interesting characters among the neighbors of Daniel Boone was an old hunter and Indian scout named Davis—"Jim Davis," as he was familiarly called by friends and associates. The story that I am about to relate concerning him seems almost incredible, and I would hardly venture to repeat it except for the fact that my father, from whom I obtained the particulars, assured me that every word was true. I therefore feel justified in staking my reputation—such as I have—on the assurance that each incident happened just as it is described. I have not attempted to make the relation more exciting by the use of dramatic terms; it is my wish to unfold the story in language so simple and plain that he who runs may read and understand.

Jim Davis had no fixed habitation, but "lived around", spending his nights and days wherever he happened to be at the setting or the rising of the sun. Later he married and reared a family in a log cabin, and among his descendants were some of the best people in the state. One of them, a nephew of mine, who was a young physician in charge of a yellow fever hospital at the time, discovered what he believed to be the germ of that dreaded malady, and while he himself died in serving the afflicted, he left a paper outlining the theory that a certain species of mosquito was the carrier of the germ. This led to an investigation by the government and a demonstration of the truth of the theory, whereby many millions of lives have been saved, and countless millions of others will be saved by the devotion of a single individual.

Late in the fall of 1808, Davis went alone on a hunting expedition to the salt licks in Howard County, where Uncle Daniel subsequently had a romantic adventure in saving the life of an Indian woman. The distance from the settlements is a little more than a hundred miles on an airline, but there are numerous streams intervening which hindered Davis in his progress. When they were too long to walk around and not large enough for the navigation of a raft, he waded or swam them, without regard to the state of the weather, drying his clothes afterward as he walked. He followed a path which Daniel Boone had already blazed, and knew he could not go astray while pursuing the footsteps of the famous leader.

Arriving at last at the licks, he had a successful hunt and was on the point of returning with his pack, when a winter storm arose and the weather became suddenly very cold. A deep snow also fell, adding materially to the difficulties of travel; but the disturbances of nature did not dismay the hunter.

Stripped and Turned Loose in the Snow

Binding his peltries into a compact bundle, he was about to start on his long tramp homeward, when he was surrounded and captured by a band of Fox Indians under the leadership of Black Hawk.

The Indians were also on a hunting expedition, and rejoiced to avail themselves of what had already been acquired by the white man. Their first idea was to have a winter evening's entertainment by burning their prisoner alive, but they were diverted from their sport by the objections of their leader. Black Hawk himself was of humane disposition, and having spent much time among the whites he revolted at the idea of burning an associate of his old friends at the stake. The young men of the party then decided to strip their prisoner of his clothing, and turn him loose to freeze or starve in the chilling blasts. To this mode of punishment Black Hawk did not object, and the preliminaries were accordingly entered upon. Having removed all his clothing, even to his moccasins and cap, they gave him an old flint-lock musket, with a single charge of powder and ball, and advised him to move on.

It was a dreary outlook, with a hundred and thirty miles of snow and ice between him and comfort, and not a stitch of clothing. Game for food was plentiful, but a single charge in an uncertain gun was not a hopeful outlook to hungry stomach. Besides, he had no knife with which to prepare the game or sharpen the implements for making fire. It seemed there was not much to be considered in a situation of that kind; but Davis faced it rather than trust his fate to further association with his facetious friends. Nothing is ever quite hopeless so long as there are life and breath in the body.

After walking a few miles over the glistening surface of the frozen snow, Davis came upon the trail of a bear leading into a canebrake, and by long experience he knew that the animal was hibernating and probably comatose. At any rate he could do nothing better than take the risk. So following the trail into the thicket he came upon the bear in the deep stupor of its winter sleep, and placing the muzzle of the gun against its head he quickly disposed of that feature of his troubles.

But there were other difficulties yet to be overcome. The approach of darkness and the benumbing of his limbs by the desperate cold warned him that he would freeze unless he contrived some way of producing artificial heat. Therefore, removing the flint from the lock of the gun, he cut a groove in the side of a dry stick with its sharp edge, and trimmed another stick to fit the groove. It was now a question of only time and friction when he would have a blaze. Collecting some dry leaves and brush under the side of a log, he began a rapid movement with the grooved and sharpened sticks, and in a little while was encouraged to see the rising smoke. A little more rubbing and the smoke burst into flame, and the hunter felt that once more the world was his. What a comfort there is in a little fire, and how thankful we should be to the man who first utilized it!

A Bear Skin Suit

The blaze caught the leaves and brush, and communicating with the log he soon had a comfortable campfire. Then he undertook the slow and painful task of skinning the bear with the sharp edge of the flint, and with grim endurance accomplished the task in a little more than an hour. He was an expert and knew how to go about the job, which would have seemed impossible to one who had not been there before. It is easier to skin your hundredth bear than the ninety and nine.

He removed the skin as a whole piece, arms, legs, feet, bulk and all and drawing it warm and out over his person he had a comfortable suit of fur! He even retained the head-piece to protect his face, and felt that in all the world there could not be any one better conditioned than he. What the bear had lost the hunter had gained, and there was no discrepancy in the provisions of nature.

Meanwhile he had cut a juicy steak from the rump of the bear, and put it before the fire to broil, and when he was ready for supper he had a meal good enough for a king. All that was lacking was a little seasoning of salt and pepper, but hunger supplied these, and nothing was lacking.

When he retired to sleep that night by the side of his warm fire, he envied the discomfort of his late captors, who had no bear skins to keep them warm and no bear meat to satisfy their hunger; and he wondered if he were not the happiest and most fortunate of men.

After a night of refreshing slumber, the hunter arose and prepared and ate a hearty breakfast, and then cutting off enough bear meat to last him through his journey he set out in high spirits for the distant settlements. Life had assumed new and brighter lines, and if he had had a voice attuned to music he would have sung; but having no such accomplishment he merely whistled. At night he slept in caves or hollow logs, and varied the monotony of his meat diet with a dessert of nuts and sweet persimmons which were yet clinging to the bushes. He was lord of all he surveyed, and required nothing more to complete his satisfaction with himself and nature.

The Devil in the Cabin

At the end of the tenth day he came in sight of Grandfather Jonathan's house, and quickening his pace he was soon at the front door and pulling the latchstring. In the room to the left a bright fire was burning, and before it sat Donald McPheeters, the school teacher, enjoying the warmth and lost in profound meditation over the difference between the hypothenuse and the vernacular. On such occasions Donald was liable to stray off into the realms of unconsciousness and forget everything except the subject which was finding solution in his ample brain. On this occasion he heard a noise at the door, and looking in that direction beheld an object the like of which had never before crossed his vision, and which he sincerely believed to be the devil. The strange and gruesome object, or being, was standing in the doorway, and as there was no other means of egress except through the window or up the chimney, Donald chose yelling with all his might that the devil was in the house!

Then everything was in an uproar, and everybody came running to see what was the matter. Grandfather Jonathan brought his gun and went in pursuit of McPheeters, who was doing his best licks along the road toward the home of Uncle Daniel. Jonathan had not yet seen the strange object in the west room, and he imagined that the school teacher had gone crazy and might drown himself in the creek. Unable to catch in a straight race, he was on the point of tweaking his leg with a shot from the rifle, when Uncle Daniel's Cuff came racing along eager to ascertain the cause of the rumpus, and laying hold of Donald pulled him to the ground and held him until Jonathan came up.

"What's the matter?" he cried pushing the dog away and lifted the teacher to his feet. "Have you gone crazy?"

"No! No!" whimpered Donald; "I'm not crazy---the devil's in the house and things are not safe."

Jonathan laughed and led him trembling back home, where his fears were modified on seeing Jim Davis in his bearskin suit sitting before the fire and rubbing his hands in the general warmth. But it took him a long time to recover from the effects of his fright, and he always declared afterward that if the devil looked any worse than Jim Davis he had no desire to make his acquaintance.

The bear skin had frozen and dried on Davis's body until it could not be removed by hand, but Jonathan trimmed it off with his hunting knife. Then having warmed the old hunter inwardly and outwardly he dressed him in a comfortable buckskin suit of his own, and leading him to the kitchen filled him up with a bountiful supper.

But McPherson was so nervous that he could not sleep in the same house, and Wilse guarded him over to Uncle Daniel's, where he spent the remainder of his assignment.

Episode Number Twenty-Nine

Playing a Trick on the Professor

Donald McPherson, a Scotchman, as the name indicates, represented a class of teachers that prevailed in early pioneer times. Some of them were preachers as well as teachers, but Donald did not combine the two professions. He was a teacher and a professor of languages, and nothing more. It was taken for granted by the uneducated woodsmen that a man who could talk Latin like the Romans, and probably understood Greek better than the Greeks themselves, ought to be qualified to teach the youth of the land. Some of those early teachers also understood bottles as well as they did Greek and Latin, but again Donald was not in this class. He was almost fanatically temperate, which adds to the mystery of his conduct when Jim Davis appeared in his bearskin suit.

It was the custom of the teachers to "board around" among the neighbors, a week at a time at each place; which accounts for Donald's presence at the home of Grandfather Jonathan on the memorable night in question. The homes of Uncle Daniel and Johnathan being carefully located, it happened that during the school term there was nearly always a teacher at one place or the other.

Donald McPheeters was a little old dried-up man, whose mind was larger than his body and of a roving disposition. It was absent as often as present, and frequently unable to account for itself anywhere. He was therefore a true representative of the "absent minded" professor.

Between Uncle Daniel's and Jonathan's homes there was ---and still is--- a small creek, over which the road passed by means of a ford. It is now spanned by a rustic bridge.

One Sunday morning when the teacher was preparing to take his departure for a week's hospitality at the Boone home, father and Uncle Abner decided to use this brook for their own pleasure, and incidentally the discomfort of old Donald McPheeters. They were boys of nine and seven respectively, and possessed of the usual mischief which attend youth of that interesting age. Accordingly, they took special pains in preparing teacher's horse for the journey. They curried and rubbed and slicked him up—and put the saddle on backward!

McPheeters mounted and rode away without observing the trick, his mind being in such a maze at the time that one end of the saddle was the same to him as the other. On coming to the brook, which was swollen by recent rains, the horse ducked its head to drink, and the teacher, holding fast to the bridle, was pulled into the water and nearly drowned before he could crawl out. He arrived at the Boone home in a dripping condition and an unfavorable state of mind, and rather discourteously declined the horn of hot toddy that Aunt Rebecca offered him. She did not tender it to Uncle Daniel, because she knew he never indulged; and in order to save the liquor she drank it herself. This was not one of Aunt Rebecca's regular habits, but the weather was cold, she had a touch of rheumatism, and she applied the rejected toddy where she thought it might do some good. McPheeters soon forgot his irritation in the warm hospitality extended him, and went off into a speculation concerning the formation of the universe and the probable conditions of life on the planet Mars.

Two Scouts Captured by Indians

The following winter Davis went on another hunting expedition into the unexplored regions now constituting the northwestern part of Missouri, undeterred by his previous experience with Black Hawk and his red warriors. This time he was accompanied by Lewis Jones, another character even more adventurous than himself, and the two imagined that no matter what might happen they would be able to work out their destiny. They were going into a region which had never seen a white face or been trodden by a white man's foot, and the novelty of the adventure appealed to them in a peculiar manner. The difference in conditions then and now is emphasized by the fact that the locality of their romantic adventure is now embraced within the limits of the populous county of Platte, almost opposite the point where Fort Leavenworth was subsequently established. It is true that five years previously Lewis and Clark had passed that way, but they confined their course mainly to the channel of the river, without venturing into the wilderness on shore.

In the 16th century the expedition of Coronado reached the west bank of the Missouri River about opposite the point visited by the American hunters nearly three hundred years later, but there is no record of any Spaniard having crossed to the east side. The expedition broke its force on the west bank of the great river, and flowed back into the unknown regions of the setting sun.

Thus the two white civilizations did not come together, and during all the intervening years the forest remained primeval. But the red men knew there was plenty of game there, and the Sioux and the Fox fought and scalped one another in their struggle for its possession. Now the American hunters were to discover that they were regarded as poachers, and must pay the price accordingly.

They selected a place for their permanent camp on Platte River, about where Platte City now stands; and soon found themselves in the midst of an abundance of game. Beavers especially were there in numbers large enough to satisfy their most ambitious expectations, and as the fur of this animal surpassed all others in value at that time, they went busily to work acquiring as much as they could carry to market. They hunted and trapped successfully for a week or more, when one morning they were captured by Black Hawk and a band of his painted warriors.

"I told you not to come again," said the red chieftain to Davis. "But you must be a great warrior, or you would not have reached home alive last winter."

He demanded that Davis tell him his experiences on the former occasion, and having listened attentively to the end, he replied:

"Now you are more than twice as far from home as you were then. The weather is cold and the snow is deep. I shall give you one more chance, but if ever you come into this land again my warriors will kill and scalp you or burn you at the stake."

As in the previous instance, the young men of the party demanded that the prisoner be burnt, but the chief drew his tomahawk and threatened to brain any warrior who dared molest them. The truth is, that while Black Hawk fought the white settlers bitterly through a long period of years, he had many friends among them, and had but recently spent a winter as a guest of one of the Zumwalt families in the Boone neighborhood, where he had been entertained as a distinguished visitor. Among others whom he met was the great white chief himself, and these two men, so different in character and race, ever after remained friends. It is said that Black Hawk danced with the Zumwalt girls, who were known for their beauty and vivacity, and that he complimented them by saying they were "almost as handsome" as the women of his own tribe.

Now, therefore, he was willing to give Davis and his companion their lives under circumstances which seemed to render the gift worthless; but it was better than being bound to a stake and roasted alive. While he furiously forbade their torture, his own terms seemed almost equally cruel. He directed that they be stripped of their clothing, as Davis had been the winter before, that they be given an old musket, barely in condition for use, with six charges of ammunition, and turned loose in the snow and freezing cold. It was the dead of winter, with no probability of any moderation in the weather, and they were more than three hundred miles from home. The outlook was so desperate that the chief had no idea they could make a trip; but he would give them the chance, such as it was.

A Friendly Squaw

Bidding them farewell, he motioned them into the cover of the woods, fully persuaded that he would see them again. They were barely out of sight of the camp when they observed that they were being followed by an Indian woman, who, for a little while, accommodated her pace to theirs. It was evidently her purpose not to overtake them while there was any danger of being seen by her own people.

"Watch the squaw!" said Davis to Jones.

As long as they were within hearing of the hunting party the woman maintained the same relative distance, but as soon as they were well out of sound and sight, she quickened her pace and came up with them. Then brushing against Jones, she said gruffly:

"Steal um blanket!"

They now understood her purpose. Thrown loosely over her shoulders was a thick red blanket, and Jones was not slow in obeying her injunction to "steal" it.

Perhaps she was moved by the compassion which is inherent in her sex, and could not bear to see even the enemies of her people sent into the wilderness to perish; but the men believed it was a stratagem of Black Hawk to give them such comfort as he could without arousing the animosity of his warriors. In a general way it was characteristic of him.

Having now a blanket between them, the men were able to share its comfort by walking close together, and so in a measure shield themselves from the biting cold. But something better was in store for them. They soon came to an abandoned Indian camp and found a large panther asleep in the warm ashes. One of their six loads was expended on it; and removing the skin, as Davis had done with the bear the previous year, they had one first-class suit of clothes. Being too small for Davis, it fell to the lot of Jones, who soon found himself comfortably clad from head to feet. But Davis was still barefooted, although he had full possession of the blanket; and the frozen surface of the snow was not comfortable skating for naked feet. Jones suggested that he had no use for the tail of the panther, so they cut it off and skinned it and contrived a pair of moccasins for Davis.

Things were now becoming cheerful, and they proceeded on their way like a couple of boys out for a lark. Late in the evening they found a shelving rock in the side of a cliff and decided to retire for the night, first cooking an ample supper from some steaks they had cut out of the panther's rump. But the steaks were so tough that they had to pound them with a rock before they were palatable; and the sound of the pounding and the scent of cooking meat soon brought a visitor in the form of a red fox. It seems that the cavern was the fox's home, and he objected to the presence of visitors: whereupon they disposed of him and added some fox steaks to their bill of fare. The improvement, however, was noticeable only in quantity, the flavor of fox steaks being no better than those of the panther. But the next morning they killed a turkey with one of the remaining charges, and now they had a menu good enough for anybody. Those who did not prefer panther or fox might have turkey. They began to argue that they were living too high and might get the gout. But more was to come.

Davis treed a possum in the persimmon bush and Jones shot a fat squirrel with another charge of the old musket; and when to all this layout they added a quart of ripe persimmons and half a gallon of luscious black haws, there was nothing more to be desired.

The hunters arrived at Grandfather Jonathan's hospitable home in good time, and received a cordial welcome. But the school master was absent, and escaped seeing two devils instead of one

The Grizzly Bear and the Man Who was Not Afraid

Lewis Jones was a Virginian by birth, but ran away from home at the age of sixteen and made his way to the Boone settlements. There, in due course of time, he fell in love with pretty Suzanna Hays, a granddaughter of Daniel Boone and Aunt Rebecca, and they were married and reared a considerable family. I am told that this event had something to do with the large number of Joneses in that part of the country.

Lewis became famous as a woodsman and hunter, and went on several expeditions even as far as the Rocky Mountains, as scout and guide for Indian traders. During one of these trips he bought a beautiful little snow white pony from a chief, and became much attached to the gentle animal. The pony was as affectionate as a pet kitten, and being extremely fond of its new master, a mutual attachment grew up between them.

But one day while grazing on the prairie the pony was killed and eaten by a grizzly bear, and Jones vowed deadly vengeance. He would either kill the bear or die in the effort.

In those times they had no such guns as modern hunters use, and going after a grizzly bear with a single-shot flint-lock rifle meant something of an adventure. If the bear came after you, the only certain assurance of salvation was to shoot it in the brain, and owing to the toughness of its skin there was no way to reach that organ except through an eye. In order to hit a bear in the eye while it was running toward you with no friendly purpose, required a steady nerve and quick sight, as well as confidence in your gun. If the hunter missed the mark and wounded the beast, it added much to the latter's fury, and it would be a rare thing if the man with the gun lived to tell the story. The grizzly bear was about as ferocious a beast as nature ever produced, and so though that it took a real bullet to kill him.

Being aware of these things, and hearing that Jones was going after the bear, one of the traders volunteered to accompany him in the capacity of friend and protector. But the hunter warned him of the danger, and advised him to remain in camp unless he had a good nerve to take along with him. The trader replied that he had plenty of nerve and was familiar with bears, and was not afraid of anything that ever walked on four legs; and if Jones was not careful he would get the first shot and rob him of the glory of the adventure. The man bragged so much that the scout imagined there must be something in him, and consented to let him go, though with apprehension.

Repairing to the place where the pony had been killed, they began a search for the trail of the bear, and that gentleman soon put in his personal appearance. He was as anxious to meet the hunters as they were to find his trail, and the meeting was therefore a case of mutual pleasure. The bear had digested the pony and was hungry, and not being a delicate feeder evidently believed that a man would fill his desires as well as a small horse. So he advanced upon the hunters at full run, with his mouth open to show the purpose of his call.

Jones stationed himself in front of his companion, with instructions that if he missed, the trader was to lose no time in making the second shot; "and be sure to hit him in the eye!" warned Jones. The trader replied that he understood his business, and that particular bear would never live to return to his family.

As soon as the bear came within range Jones fired and killed it, but on turning to his companion was surprised to see him fifty yards away, running for his life.

"Hello!" yelled the hunter, "What's the matter? Are you afraid of a dead bear?"

The man came back meekly. He said he was not afraid of any kind of bear, dead or alive; but when he saw that grizzly loping toward them with his mouth open he lost his nerve and ran in spite of himself. He begged the scout not to tell on him at the camp, and promised never to be so cowardly again.

"I have heard of "buck ager", retorted Jones, "but this is the first case of 'bear ager' that I ever ran up against."

He promised not to tell, but the story leaked out and the man's feelings were so badly hurt that he sold his interest in the outfit and returned home.

Combat with a Grizzly Bear

The name of the trader was Amos Kronk, and he was a man of standing in the community. The story of his running away from a dead bear soon got into circulation, and it mortified him so that life became a burden. He therefore resolved to redeem his reputation, even at the hazard of extreme peril. Normally he was not afraid of anything in particular, especially of live bears, having shot many of them; and there was no reason in the world why he should have run away from a dead one. So he prepared himself for a desperate adventure.

He bought two of the best bear dogs in the country and trained them in the profession. Then he had his rifle and hunting knife put in first class order; and in loading his camp equipage on the back of a pony set out alone for the distant Rockies. One of his neighbors, to whom he had revealed his purpose, advised him to take a negro along to bury him; but Kronk said no, he was going to kill a grizzly bear if it was the last act of his life, and he would bring the skin back as evidence. It was the bear that would need burying, not Kronk. So he went to the mountains in search of a bear that needed killing, as most of them do.

On arriving at his destination, he pitched his camp on the site of his former adventure and lost no time in finding the object of his search. He was not kept in suspense. Scarcely had he stretched his small tent when he was visited by an extra-large grizzly. It may have been a brother of the one that Jones had shot, for he seemed fond of Kronk's pony, a talent which may have run in the family.

But the dogs disputed his presence, and barked and snapped until he ran away, the hounds yelping close behind. Meanwhile the bear had not been still long enough for Kronk to get a good shot, and he did not dare take the chance of firing at random. But in the midst of the excitement he was proud of himself in observing that his nerves were steady and he had no sense of fear.

He set out after the quarry and had no trouble in keeping in sight and hearing, for every little while the bear would stop and have a tussel with the dogs. Finally, in one of these battles, the bear fell into a crevice between two rocks, barely wide enough to crowd its body in. When Kronk came up the beast was standing upright at the opening of the crevice, facing the dogs and having a fierce fight with them; and the dogs were charging around so fiercely that he was afraid to shoot lest he might kill or wound one of them.

Unable to accomplish anything in front, he went around behind the bear and entered the cleft from that side; but there was a sharp turn in the opening which hid the beast from view. As he could not use his gun, he decided upon an expedient so desperate that no experienced grizzly bear hunter would have ventured upon it. Laying aside his rifle he drew his knife and felt his way along the narrow opening until he came within reach of the fur on the bear's back. But he hesitated to stab it in that position lest he should miss a vital part and fall a victim to the rage of the beast. In the meanwhile the dogs kept the bear engaged in front, until it struck one of them a dreadful blow and put it out of the fight, for that time at least.

This gave the bear a moment of respite in front, which it employed in pushing backward against Kronk, whereby his body became so tightly pressed against the walls that he could not move. He imagined now that his time had come, for another backward lunge of the beast would crush the breath out of him. But his right hand was free, with the knife still grasped in it; and striking out at random and with the desperation of a last hope, he happened to pierce the heart of the beast, and the bear sank down limp on the bottom of the crevice. The battle was over.

Kronk now crawled out over the hairy body and gave his first attention to the wounded dog. Its right foreleg was broken and it had received a number of bruises and scratches; but with careful nursing its hurts were all healed in the course of a week or ten days.

One day while waiting for the recovery of his dog, Kronk was visited by a chief, who came in such a state, riding a little white pony the counterpart of the one to which Jones had been so much attached; and on inquiry he learned that the ponies were brothers. The chief had bred and raised them both; and he now offered to sell the remaining one to Kronk for five dollars. The offer was accepted, and the white man became the owner of the little white pony. Then the chief begged for the carcass of the bear, saying it was "heap good meat", and Kronk hitched his team of ponies to it and dragged it to the chief's wigwam, a mile away. There his two wives and all the family came out and cut it into suitable pieces for baking, whereupon there was much rejoicing at the chief's home.

His reputation having been reestablished, the hunter returned home, carrying the bear's skin with him as evidence of the truth of his claims; but never again did he go hunting for grizzly bears.

Kronk's Eloquent Prayer

Kronk was a staunch Methodist, and had a prayer which he repeated on all legitimate occasions, for the guidance of the Almighty and his own pleasure. He repeated it so often and with such emphasis and unction that he excited the envy of some of the other brethren, among them my father. The presiding elder had appointed father exhorter, and it was his duty to urge outsiders to join the church and save their souls, and he was expected to pray in a style that would arouse sinners to a sense of their condition. But he would not compete with brother Kronk. So he appealed to the throne of grace for help, requesting especially that he might be inspired to pray as Kronk did; and soon afterward, at the weekly prayer meeting, he poured for Kronk's prayer verbatim, with all the accents and inflections that characterized the original. The brethren and sisters were amazed, and peeked through their fingers to see who was praying, Kronk or brother 'Ligy.

When father was through he did not wait for a response, but sneaked out of church and went home, mightily resolved that never again would he ask the Lord to let him pray like some other man.

The Family Musket

My first independent hunting adventure was a clandestine affair, and though it occurred eighty-one years ago it has never passed out of my memory.

The pioneers had a custom of attending public sales, where they met the neighbors and bought a lot of stuff they didn't need or want. This was one of my father's failings, and if you could have seen the varied assortment of junk that he accumulated you would have felt like advising him to stay at home. He couldn't bear to see something offered for sale and nobody bid, so it was his custom in such cases to make a bid "just to give it a start", and nine times out of ten he got the relic, because nobody else would have it.

Among other things which he acquired was an old Queen Anne musket, built so it would kick both ways. It was a fearful weapon to fall into the hands of an innocent boy who had no experience with firearms, as I discovered very much to my amazement. It was known in the family as "the musket", and its main duty was to stand in the corner of the attic until Christmas or the Fourth of July when it was brought down with ceremony and some innocent specimen of the race into firing it off.

The reason for manufacturing the weapon so it would kick "two ways on Sunday", was to give the soldier in battle notice that his piece had been discharged and it was time to reload; and there is no record that any soldier ever made a mistake. When the gun went off the person behind it became aware of the fact.

In this connection a curious incident happened at the battle of New Orleans. Most of the soldiers in that memorable affair were armed with rifles, but one man had come to camp without a gun, and they gave him a musket like my father's. He fought all through the battle, loading and reloading; but not until the British came up in their last charge did the first load ignite and go off, exploding all the others at the same time for the soldier had not fired a shot during the whole engagement. The results were disastrous in front and rear. How many casualties it produced in the British ranks no one knew. But most of those on the American side were due to the explosion of that old gun.

During the Revolution most of the British soldiers were armed with muskets of this kind, and the officers trained the men to fire from the hip, so the guns would have room to kick back into the surrounding landscape without fracturing the shoulders of the rank and file. This amounted to the same thing as shooting at random, and explains why the American riflemen always whipped the British in a fair stand-up fight. The British soldiers were as brave as the Americans, but our riflemen took aim and fired as though they were hunting buffaloes, while the Britisher held his musket down by his hip and "let her fly". The charge was bound to hit something, generally the earth at the limit of the range. If it happened to hit an American rebel by accident, it was the last of that particular rebel.

He was no longer fit for any kind of service; for those old muskets carried a ball almost as big as your fist, and behind it several buckshot that went hunting on their own account. Therefore, when a few Continentals happened to be in the way and got hit, Washington was obliged to appeal to Congress for another.

I understand this to be a digression, but perhaps the information it contains about our national history is worth the detour.

So father bid a picayune for the old musket to give it a start, and acquired the gun. It was put carefully away and we boys forbidden to hunt with it, because father did not want a family of the halt and lame on his place. But brother Jim, being older than John and me, destined for the ministry, was permitted now and then to take the gun into the woods and give her a little exercise, just to keep her in mind of the fact that she was a gun. One day she went off too soon and broke Jim's nose, which explains why that organ was crooked ever after.

A Rabbit Gets a Surprise

When I reached the mature age of seven, I decided to slip off and take a hunt all by myself, and I selected the old musket as my fowling piece. Father instructed me that in loading a rifle I should lay the bullet on my open palm and cover it with powder. This was the correct charge for a rifle, but an old Queen Anne musket was something else. After slipping around through the tall timber until I was out of sight, I boldly sallied forth to clean up the game in that part of the country. I remember even now how brave and reckless I felt! I crawled through the bars that opened into the "woods pasture", and a big rabbit came hopping along and squatted down to see what sort of a person he had to deal with. It did not take him long to find out. I blew the head off that rabbit clean up to its shoulders, but did not discover the fact until an hour afterward. When I came to, the rabbit was there waiting for me, and I concluded that if I had held the butt of the gun against my head, instead of my shoulder, the results in front and rear would have been about the same.

Stephen Patton and His Riding Ox

As already intimated, nearly every family had a Revolutionary relic in the shape of an old musket, which was reserved for special occasions, such as came to Stephen Patton, for instance.

John Crockett and his sister Lucy, who lived on Loutre Island, were crack shots with a rifle, and could bring down the game at almost any distance. But they were short of riding animals, and their neighbor Stephen Patton, having been informed of the fact, came over to see them, mounted on his riding ox. He explained that an ox was much better than a horse or mule. He was more sure-footed, and had a soft, rolling gait that made riding a pleasure and if you got hungry you could eat him. In summer the flies and other biting and stinging insects did not worry the ox; and in the winter when the ground was covered with ice he was not so liable to slip and fall. Indeed, Stephen dwelt so eloquently on the merits of his ox that he sold him to Jim for twenty-five dollars, when he would have been glad to get ten. He returned home well satisfied with his day's work, for he had the money in his pocket in the shape of big silver dollars, which he jungled now and then for the pleasure of hearing the sound.

When Patton was gone, John mounted his ox and rode into the woods to round up some game; but the animal, not being accustomed to the ways of his new master, ran away and taking his course through a thicket of crab apple bushes tore his clothes into tatters and came near killing him. Then he threw John into a creek and loped off for the home of his former owner.

When John got home and his sister saw his condition, they put their heads together and decided to get even; though they agreed to keep perfectly still until the opportunity came. So John recovered his ox and led him back home with a rope, and everything seemed to be serene and satisfactory.

Not long afterward, when John was away and sister Lucy happened to be at home, neighbor Patton called to borrow a gun. He said he had tracked a deer to a copse of wood, and wanted to slip back and get him, and would Miss Lucy please lend him a gun. He was afraid if he went back home for one the deer might run away. Miss Lucy was delighted with the opportunity to accommodate him. She would not only lend him the best gun they had, but would load it for him. So she brought out the old family relic, charged it in a way that she thought would be satisfactory and handed it to him with a smile that was captivating.

Patton immediately set out for the place where he had seen the deer, and as he approached he heard a noise like the sound of wild animals in combat. Slipping up to ascertain the cause, he found the deer fighting the panther, and the encounter so fascinated him that he stopped to look and listen. The panther would leap at the throat of the deer, only to be caught on its horns and tossed into the air, shrieking with rage and pain. Again and again the charge was repeated, each time meeting with similar results; until at last the panther was gored almost to insensibility and was about to give up the combat. Just as he was making his last spring Patton fired and brought down both the animals; but the gun also did something to him! It cropped one of his ears, bruised and blackened an eye, knocked him flat of his back and reduced him to a total wreck. Then according to Patton's own statement, the old gun had the audacity to stand on its breech and dance round and whoop and yell like an Indian. That's what Patton said the gun did.

By this time John had returned, and hearing the racket in the woods, and suspecting that something might have happened, he and his sister hurried away to ascertain what was the trouble. They found Patton and brought him home and patched him up as well as they could; and Miss Lucy especially was very much put out because of the disgraceful conduct of the old musket. She said it never had cut up that way with her, which was very true because she had never given it a chance.

But Patton declared it was just the gun he wanted, and he asked what they would take for it. He was willing to pay anything reasonable for a gun that would kill a deer and a panther at a single shot, and then dance and whoop like an Indian warrior.

So John and sister Lucy consulted, and they decided to ask Patton the same price for the musket that he had charge for the ox. They would gladly have accepted a picayune from anyone else, but it seemed that Providence had come their way and it would be sinful to let the opportunity pass. So they descanted on the value of the old fuse, its remarkable accuracy, and especially its historical associations. John said it had fought in the Revolution and killed forty Hessians at the battle of Trenton, and Miss Lucy added a touch by saying that the battle of Saratoga, when one of Burgoyne's Indians had taken refuge behind a tree, her grandfather shot the tree down and killed the savage with a single shot of the famous old gun.

"Never mind what it did to the Hessians and Indians," interrupted Patton; "it did a-plenty to me and the buck and the panther, and any gun that will act that way is a good thing to have in the family".

He pressed the twenty-five dollars on them, which they finally accepted with reluctance; and Patton shouldered the musket and wended his way homeward while John and his sister felt that they had evened up a score.

The old musket was still in the Patton family when I last heard of it, but as the Indians had all become civilized it no longer danced and whooped like a painted brave.

A Pretty Girl and Her Split Bonnet

The original Jacob Zumwalt was a German, who came to America soon after the close of the Revolution, and settled on a tract of land adjoining the town of York, Pa. He had an incurable disease, and by the advice of his doctor removed to Virginia, where the climate was milder and his sufferings would be modified. He bought a tract of land on the east bank of the Potomac River, not far from the future town of Georgetown.

Instead of getting better his complaint grew worse, and he died a year or two afterward. I have mentioned him in particular because his name was Jacob, and a number of his descendants honored his memory by adopting the same name with characteristic adjuncts to distinguish one from the other.

Meanwhile the deed to his land in Pennsylvania was lost, and his heirs were deprived of what would have been a princely fortune; for the town grew and expanded until it embraced the farm. The deed vanished in a singular manner, which may be regarded as emblematic of the uncertainties of life. The Zumwalt girls were noted for their beauty, and like all pretty women they took commendable pride in appearing well to those with whom they associated.

One of the girls had made herself a new sun-bonnet, sometimes called a "split bonnet", because the crown was stiffened with splits of the inner bark of an elm tree, which was light and substantial. Such bonnets were in style among the pioneers for many years, and were popular with ladies because they shaded their fair faces and kept the sun from burning them. They also had another advantage; the face of the wearer being hidden in the cavernous depths of her bonnet, her sweetheart could not see her blush when he proposed, and by this means she kept him in suspense as to whether she would say "yes" or "no". The sun-bonnet had so many advantages that it may come into style again sometime or other.

Miss Zumwalt having made her new sun-bonnet, looked around for splits with which to finish the crown; but it was not the season for peeling the elm and there were no splits in sight. So while rummaging in various drawers and receptacles she came upon the deed to the land on which they were then living, and as it was written on parchment it was substantial enough to make the crown of a sun-bonnet stand out straight. Like many other pretty girls of that period, Miss Zumwalt could not read, and therefore had not the least idea of the value of the old piece of paper. With the aid of her shears she soon reduced it to splits, which went into the bonnet; and when the bonnet had run its course it was thrown away and the deed went with it.

Afterward a long suit was maintained by the family in the courts in their efforts to prove their title to the land, which had come to be worth a great sum of money. But the deed had not been recorded, and no one supposed that the splits in Miss Zumwalt's bonnet had anything to do with the title; so the property passed to others. The better part of the city of York stands on the old Zumwalt farm.

An Old House with a History

The first Jacob Zumwalt had a son also named Jacob, who came to the Boone neighborhood in 1796, only a short time after Uncle Daniel himself had arrived. He settled on Peruque Creek, not far from the present town and railroad station of O'Fallon. Two years later he built a two-story hewed log house, which is still standing, and has been immortalized by the ladies of the D.A.R. as the first house of that kind erected north of the Missouri River. Many tourists pass that way daily along the great state highway that follows the old Boone's Lick Road, and they all stop to view and comment upon this curious relic of ancient days.

The old house has a number of claims to historic and romantic associations. It was here that Major Heald brought his bride after their capture and thrilling escape from the Indians at the massacre of Fort Dearborn, and where they subsequently entertained the chief and his son who had aided them in making their escape. This is one of the most thrilling captures in the history of the west, to be embraced in a future Episode.

The great Black Hawk also visited the Zumwalts in this house and spent most of a winter with them, meanwhile complimenting the young ladies of the family by saying they were almost as handsome as Indian girls. Black Hawk was a gallant warrior who possessed several of the accomplishments of polite society, among them the art of dancing and complimenting a pretty girl.

During the Indian war, which came after Black Hawk's visit, the old house was utilized as a fort, and the marks of the port-holes are still to be seen in its walls. At one time as many as ten families were crowded into its limited space, but no attack was made and no Indians or white people were slain there. While the old house often rang with the laughter of happy young people, no laden bullet was ever fired into its hospitable walls.

The first Methodist sacrament north of the Missouri River was administered in this house in 1807, by Rev. Jesse Walker, one of the old-timers who believed that he would not die until his time came, in spite of anything the devil might do to the contrary. The wine for the ceremony was made by Mrs. Zumwalt and Mrs. David Bailey, by straining the juices of ripe poke-berries through a linen cloth and sweetening the outcome with maple sugar.

In 1797 another member of the Zumwalt family came to Missouri and settled near the site of the present town of Flint Hill, which has maintained its dignity by remaining "about the same" throughout all these years. This Zumwalt was named Adam, and he seems to have possessed a good deal of the world's wealth, for it is recorded that he brought with him from Virginia in a keelboat eight hundred dollars worth of merchandise, thirty head of cattle, twelve horses, and eleven sheep; all this and these in addition to his family and their effects.

FORT ZUMWALT, *Near O'Fallon, Mo.*

Blackhawk passed a winter here. Maintained in original condition by W.B. Daughtery 8/1812.

Selling Frozen Whiskey to Indian Warriors

Adam built two still houses on his place and made whiskey for the Indians. His product became noted among them to such an extent that they often camped at the spring which supplied the water for the liquor, and bought and consumed as much as two hundred dollars worth of fire-water in a single day. Black Hawk was opposed to the traffic, but could not control the thirst of his warriors. They loved the fiery liquid better than the glory of war, and it rumored at the time that the great chief entered upon the conflict with the white settlers as much to save his people from the degradation of intemperance as for anything he expected to gain on the war-path. Yet it is also claimed that he often absorbed enough of Zumwalt's fire-water to make himself "very drunk", though never to such an extent as to forget that he was a chief and a gentleman.

The liquor contained so much water that in very cold weather it would freeze into solid ice, which Zumwalt cut into blocks and chunks and sold to his red customers in that form, and they satisfied their thirst by sucking the ice. A chunk of ice had as much intoxication in it as a horn of pure liquor.

When the war broke out, Adam sent his family to his brother's house on Peruque Creek, only he and his son Jonathan had learned to use a gun when he was only five years old, and became a noted marksman; so much so that no hostile red man cared to come within range of the boy's rifle. But his facility as a marksman did not prevent him having a severe spell of "buck ager" on a certain memorable occasion. When he was six years old he shot a large buck, which plunged about so much in its death agony that Jonathan ran home and lost his gun on the way. It was never found, but was supposed to have been picked up by some savage warrior and used in shooting pale faces.

On one occasion during the war, Black Hawk led a large party of warriors across the Mississippi River on the ice, and murdered a family of twelve persons who lived near the Zumwalt place. As soon as the Indians were gone Adam and Jonathan wrapped the bodies in quilts and buried them in a cellar under the house; but the savages returned not long after and burnt the house, and the dead were consumed in the flames. Such was Indian warfare in the Boone neighborhood.

At another time, during a skirmish with Indians at Adam's house, a chief was wounded, and as soon as it was safe to venture out he and Jonathan carried the chief into the house and dressed his wounds. But he died a few days later, and at his request his body was burned near the wall, with a loaf of bread in one hand and his hunting knife in the other. Also by the chief's special request, they shot his dog and buried it at his feet, in order that he might be prepared to make a start in the happy hunting-ground.

Five Jacobs in One Family

All the Zumwalts were Methodists, and their homes were meeting places for the services of that denomination. The names of the children were also selected from the Bible. Each generation had a Jacob, and at one time there were five Jacob Zumwalts living close together in the Boone settlements. In order to distinguish one from the other they were called "Big Jake", "Little Jake", "Calico Jake", "St. Charles Jake", and "Lying Jake". Now, I am quite sure that the latter never told any more lies than the average Boone settler, and how he acquired his title is therefore a mystery. I made exhaustive inquiry concerning the matter, but never succeeded in reaching a satisfactory explanation. It was suggested that perhaps he was the only Zumwalt who ever told a lie, and the fact attached itself to him in his sub-title. But what did he lie about? It must have been while he was quite young, when he probably deviated from the truth in order to avoid a switching. This seems the most plausible explanation, because I know by my personal experience that it was a common practice among pioneers. If all the lies that I told to avoid whippings are recorded against me, my chances in the future will be very slim.

Adam Zumwalt had three daughters who broke over the traces and abandoned Methodism for the Baptist faith, whereupon he was profoundly worried but their mother said she was glad of it. Why, she did not explain, for she remained a faithful Methodist. But her sympathy for the deserters only added fresh fuel to the old gentleman's disorder. He said he had serious doubts about any Baptist going to the "right place", but now that his family was divided he hoped some of them would find it and be saved, as he did not wish to spend eternity alone. So far as can be ascertained all the Zumwalts went to the "right place", and have evidently been content to remain there, since no complaints have been returned. I am doing my best to meet them, in spite of my early propensity to stray away from the example of the great G.W.; and I think I deserve some consideration in the fact that I have quit lying, while George never knew how.

Episode Number Thirty-Three

Adventures of Major Heald and His Wife

One of the most romantic and thrilling incidents of our entire national history was that of Major Nathaniel Heald and his beautiful and accomplished wife. A short time before the outbreak of the war with the Indians, resulting from our last conflict with England, Captain Heald was placed in command of a small garrison at Fort Dearborn, which occupied a place on the site of the present city of Chicago. He had received a military education and entered the army as lieutenant, but was soon promoted for gallantry to the rank of Captain.

Soon after being placed in command at Fort Dearborn he was visited by Major William Wells, on an inspection tour, and the Major was accompanied by his niece, Miss Rebecca Wells of Louisville, Ky. Her father also was an officer in the army, and her descent from a line of soldiers gave her an inheritance of courage and presence of mind in danger that was truly remarkable.

Love at first sight resulted from the meeting of Captain Heald and the brilliant young lady, and they were married in the city of Louisville soon after her return home, the wedding occurring on the 23rd of May, 1811. The young bride accompanied her husband back to his post on the great lake, but in August of the same year the conduct of the adjacent Indian tribes became so threatening and the garrison was so small, that the government decided to abandon the place. But the decision had been delayed too long. Scarcely had the garrison marched out of the fort when it was surrounded by an army of painted and yelling hostiles, and nearly all the officers and men were killed. Among the few saved were the Captain and his young wife, both of them severely wounded. The Captain was shot through the hips, and so disabled that he could scarcely move, while his wife was shot through the body and both arms; but fortunately her wounds were of the flesh and not serious. This left her freedom of action to help her husband, who otherwise would have fallen a victim to the fury of the savages.

The massacre was accompanied by the usual revolting atrocities, some of them too shocking to admit of publication. Mrs. Heald's uncle was killed and scalped in her presence, under details so horrifying that she never could speak of them without tears.

While these things were being enacted, a squaw approached the prisoner and tried to snatch a beautiful white-and-red-striped blanket which she had folded on her saddle, when, driven to desperation by what she had witnessed, she slashed the woman across her shoulders and face with her riding whip, until she fled out of reach. The warriors applauded the act of the white woman, and would not allow the squaw to approach any of the other prisoners. This incident had much to do with the subsequent safety of the brave little woman and her husband, for it won the admiration of the warriors who witnessed it.

But their good-will did not extend to the horse and its equipment. These were taken from her, and she was also robbed of all her jewelry and most of her clothing, and in spite of her painful wounds, obliged to walk in the march which immediately ensued. Her jewelry consisted mainly of presents from her father and husband, and was greatly prized on account of the associations; but it was all restored to her eventually in quite a remarkable manner. One of the savages who had participated in the massacre, acquired the jewelry as his shore of the loot, and carrying it to St. Louis exchange it for trinkets more in accord with his untutored tastes. The trader recognized the name engraved on the separate pieces, and returned all of them to the fair owner as soon as he could get her address. His name was O'Fallon, and it was in his honor that the railroad station near the future home of the Healds received its title. A street in St. Louis is also named for him.

Mrs. Heald and her husband were separated and taken as hostages by different tribes living on the borders of the lakes; but a chief named Shandary, to whose charge the Captain had been assigned, took a fancy to the wounded officer and demonstrated the sincerity of his friendship by buying his wife and restoring her to him. For this service he asked and received in payment an army mule and a bottle of whisky. The husband and wife were profoundly grateful to the chief for his humanity, and a lifelong friendship arose out of the incident.

A Young Indian Hero

Throughout all their experiences, including their journey to their place of imprisonment, Captain Heald had three hundred dollars in gold concealed in his underclothing, and part of his money eventually secured freedom for himself and wife. Having let Shandary onto the secret, the chief induced a young warrior named Robinson to secretly convey the white prisoners by canoe in making the journey along the shores of Lake Michigan, traveling only at night and sleeping in the woods during the daytime. Shandary had also restored to Captain Heald a highly prized little single-barreled shotgun, which he had used for shooting ducks while stationed at the fort; and the gun now became the means of supplying them with food, through the good marksmanship of their Indian guide. The Captain himself was too badly wounded to hunt, but Robinson brought in fresh ducks every day, which he and Mrs. Heald prepared for their meals.

In seeking out-of-the-way places of safety during the day, the water was frequently so shallow that the canoe would not float, and they had to wade ashore and drag it after them. In these undertakings Mrs. Heald supported her husband, who was on crutches and too lame to walk, and they jokingly referred to the trip as their "wedding tour".

On arriving at Mackinaw, the Captain paid Robinson a hundred gold dollars for his services, which seemed like a fortune to the grateful Indian and indeed it proved to be such. Investing it in land at the new city of Chicago, it increased so rapidly in value that in a few years Robinson and his family became wealthy. He also begged for the little shotgun, to which he had become much attached; but the Captain told him kindly that he could not part with it, and he did not persist.

The prisoners were delivered to the British commander at Mackinaw, who did all in his power to make them comfortable. Their wounds were dressed and attended to by the garrison surgeon, and the commander promised to send them to Detroit as soon as they were able to travel, where they would be exchanged and allowed to return home.

But soon afterward their original captors appeared on the scene and demanded the restoration of their hostages, whom they wished to use in acquiring bounty for their release. Under the terms existing between the British and the Indians the officer would be obliged to submit to their demands;

but he secretly conveyed the prisoners to a British vessel in the harbor and ordered it to sail to Detroit. There they were exchanged and returned to Louisville; where, in the midst of their rejoicings, Captain Heald was informed of his promotion to major in the regular army, the advancement having been made during his captivity in recognition of his gallantry. He continued in the service with distinction until the end of the war, when he removed with his family to the Boone settlements in Missouri, where he bought the Zumwalt place and remained there for the rest of his life.

Major Heald and his wife became widely known in that part of the country, and now they rest in the little cemetery near their home. In my youth it was my pleasure to count them among my friends, and to realize that it was such as they who laid the foundations of our national greatness.

A Rich Indian Chief

In the meantime Robinson, the young warrior who had so bravely rescued them at the time of their greatest need, had married a girl of his own race; and as their children came on they were educated in American schools until, when they were grown, they could be recognized as Indians only by their physical characteristics. But Robinson himself always remained an Indian. He built a handsome residence for his wife and children out of his rapidly multiplying fortune, but he lived alone in a teepee in the yard. Unable to speak English, his daughters acted as interpreters; and by their loving ministrations assured his comfort and happiness.

Many years afterward, when Robinson had become a stately white-haired chief, he was visited by Mr. D. Heald, a son of the Major and his wife, who took this method of thanking him for his kindness to his parents. He found the chief in his wigwam, surrounded by bear and buffalo robes and skins of the deer that he had slain, living as his fathers had done for centuries before. Not understanding the object of Mr. Heald's visit, and unable to connect him with the adventure of his youth, he at first regarded him with suspicion and ill-will; but when one of his daughters made him understand who his visitor was, his attitude changed entirely and he became friendly to the full extent of his Indian hospitality. Speaking through his daughter, he gave Mr. Heald to understand how grateful he was to his father for his liberality to him in his youth, which had enabled him to obtain a home and wealth for himself and family.

The chief in turn was greatly moved by the praise which his visitor bestowed upon him for his kindness to his parents, in saving their lives and restoring them to liberty, even at the risk of his own life. In the exuberance of his hospitality the chief tapped a keg of whisky which he declared was twenty years old, and pressed his friend to drink liberally with him. But the visitor was obliged to decline on account of his temperance pledges and principles; whereupon the chief was amazed to learn that any one could be so bound by a pledge as to refuse what was to him the greatest of all physical blessings and he did what he could to supply his guest's deficiencies by absorbing extra potations himself.

Then he took down a strip of dried buffalo meat that hung to the supporting timbers of the wigwam, and handing one end to Heald carefully divided it in the middle with his knife, to make sure that each would have the same share; and as they continued their conference they chewed the tough meat and wished each other long life and happiness. When the first strip was consumed another was provided, and the process was repeated until Heald afterward declared he never could look a buffalo in the face again.

When the time came there were evidences of emotion on both sides, showing that friendship is not a matter of race or color; and this proved to be their last and only meeting. The white man sleeps by the side of his parents, and the red man has joined his fathers in the happy hunting grounds.

Samuel Howell and the Friendly Chief

When peace was restored after the wars with Black Hawk and his people, the Indians seemed more desirous to resume friendly relations than the whites themselves; but they were diffident in their way of going about it. This was due to the varying customs of the two races, as well as their difficulty in making themselves clearly understood in our language. The following incidents will throw some light on the subject.

Samuel Howell settled in Lincoln County near Wood's Fort, and being devoted to the sport of hunting, he had supplied himself with as fine a rifle as could be made in those days. It was profusely ornamented with gold and silver trimmings and inlaid woodwork, and was handsome enough to excite the admiration of any hunter, white or red.

One day Howell and several of his friends visited the Mississippi bottoms to look for deer, and the first day he secured a fine one as it ran along the bank of the river. On the opposite side there was an encampment of Indians, hidden in a growth of willows, so that the hunters did not observe it. But the red people had seen Howell when he shot the deer, as he learned the following day.

The next morning he went alone to the same place, hoping for a renewal of his good fortune. Presently he saw a handsome warrior step into a canoe on the other side of the river and start paddling in his direction and being in doubt as to his intentions Howell deemed it wise to be on his guard. The camp of the hunters was a short distance below where he stood, and as the warrior drew near he turned the prow of his canoe in that direction. It now occurred to Howell that he might be intending to raid the camp, and as his companions were absent he hastened to the place himself.

As soon as the canoe touched the bank the warrior sprang out and came forward, his hand outstretched and his face beaming, and grasping Howell's hand exclaimed:

"How!"

The salutation was cordially returned, but while the white hunter thought he was about the handsomest specimen of a red man that he had ever seen, he was suspicious of his motives and watched him closely.

The Indian reached over and took his gun, a maneuver which Howell did not appreciate, but as every movement and act revealed a friendly purpose he made no objection. The warrior carefully inspected the weapon, with many smiles and grunts of approval; and having satisfied his curiosity brought the gun to his shoulder and taking aim at an imaginary object, made a sound with his lips to indicate the discharge of a rifle; whereupon he handed the gun back to its owner with expressions of approval.

"Heap good gun!" he exclaimed.

He then pointed to the spot where Howell had shot the deer the day before, and by signs informed him that he had observed the incident from his wigwam on the opposite side of the river.

"Heap good <u>bang</u>!" he cried, again imitating the sound of a gun as a compliment to the white hunter on his marksmanship.

Howell then took him to the camp, which he inspected with evident approval; whereupon he once more extended his hand and uttering the friendly "How!" stepped into his canoe and paddled back home. So ended the interview. The warrior felt a friendly interest in the white hunters and their success, and had taken this ceremonious method of expressing his good will.

Howell and the Pretty Squaw

A few days later as Howell was riding in the woods near the mouth of the Cuivre (pronounced Qwiver) River, he came upon an Indian teepee. In the door sat an ancient chief smoking his pipe, and inside was a hideously ugly old squaw boiling some meat over a fire of sticks. The odor of the meat was not inviting, but on the floor sat a wondrously beautiful Indian girl, who became the inducement for the hunter to seek a more intimate acquaintance with the family. She was really very handsome, with regular features and deep dark eyes, from which flashed a gleam of hatred as the hunter came into view. She left no doubt as to her sentiment concerning him, neither did she show any pretense of coquetry, or make a gesture inviting familiarity, but pretended to be seriously offended at his admiring glances. Tossing her pretty head, she veiled her face behind a deerskin and remained covered during the rest of the interview. Meanwhile Howell conversed in familiar terms with the old chief, but nothing could induce the haughty beauty to uncover her face or pay the least attention to him.

"Young squaw heap big fool!" explained the chief.

But she shook her shoulders in angry disapproval, and said nothing.

Jerked Venison

The old squaw now came forward and offered the visitor a piece of jerked venison, at the same time pouring a little salt in his palm with which to season it. The meat did not appear to be especially clean, and it had an odor which was far from agreeable; but for the sake of hospitality he tried to eat it. He thought perhaps his acquiescence in their customs might mollify the feelings of the pretty girl; but she ignored him as completely as before, and gave him to understand that the space he occupied would be more agreeable to her if left blank.

In addition to its disagreeable odor, the meat was so tough that the longer he chewed it the larger the morsel seemed to get, and the tainted taste made him sick at stomach. He was enduring absolute torture for the sake of hospitality. At length, fearing if he chewed the meat any longer, it would choke him, he slipped it into his hand and thence into his pocket. But the girl observed his embarrassment and smiled; his sufferings were a pleasure to her.

The chief explained that they caught many deer by driving them into the overflowing bottoms, where they were drowned; and so many were trapped in this way that it frequently required many days to skin the carcasses and dress the meat. Howell concluded that the deer whose flesh had been tendered him must have been drowned several weeks before it received attention.

The Indian claimed that it is custom and habit that regulate our taste for food. The buzzard, for instance, having been brought up on bad meat, prefers it to any other kind; while the eagle must have his meat fresh and warm. When I was a boy something happened to one of my father's shoats, and it lay dead in the pen. In a day or two the pig emitted an odor that was not affable, and father told brother John to bury it. But John had something else on his mind at the time and neglected the order. A day or so later an Indian warrior came along and begged the shoat, which had not reduced its fragrance in the meantime. With the greatest pleasure father complied with the warrior's request, and the whole family thanked the red man for his goodness. He rolled the pig in his blanket and carried it away, and he and his family doubtless had a feast that night. They did not object to the smell, because they had been brought up that way.

Howell said he would have eaten the chief's venison if it had choked him, if by doing so he could have won a smile from the pretty squaw, but he sincerely believed she would have rejoiced at his death agonies.

"Ripening" Wild Game

Many of the early Germans who came to the Boone neighborhood belonged to the peasantry class, and they also had some peculiar customs concerning their diet. In many cases the men were good hunters, and kept their families well supplied with wild game; but they did not consider it good to eat until it had been properly "ripened". The process consisted in hanging the game by the necks in the attic, or some unoccupied room until it was "ripe" enough to fall to the floor, when it was supposed to be in good condition for the table. It was the same as ripe fruit covered with green, and the argument seemed good to those who felt that way.

I knew a German tailor in Marthasville who was a noted hunter, and his "yager" supplied all the game his family could consume. There was rarely a time when there were not several ducks, or wild geese or turkeys, hanging by the neck in the tailor's loft, "ripening" for the table. But my education in the matter of a well-ripened wild goose had been neglected. The tailor was a jolly good fellow, but I sometimes imagined that he smelled like his meat.

Five Wild Geese at One Shot

The reference to wild goose reminds me of a little adventure that happened to me and my brothers John and Robert on a cold winter night. We had gone "coon hunting", but failing to catch either a coon or a possum, we were returning home about midnight; when our attention was centered on the loud gabbling of a flock of geese in an adjoining field by the sound of their gabbling. It was an opportunity for a great adventure. John was carrying the old flint-lock rifle of Revolutionary fame, and I a little single-barreled shotgun, the bore of which was no larger than my middle finger. Robert, being the youngest, had no arms of any kind, but was expected to carry the game.

We slipped along the opposite side of a fence until within about thirty yards of the flock, when John turned his gun loose. But the flint failed to ignite the powder and the rifle was not discharged. The noise however frightened the birds and they rose to fly. Just as they spread their wings I fired into the mass without taking aim, and certainly with no expectation of the results that followed. By the merest accident I killed and wounded five of those big wild geese, all of which we captured and carried home. John and Robert each carried two, but I being the victor and having a bad reputation, was left off with one.

We baked and ate those birds until brother John felt oblige to change his diet for fear he might gabble like a goose, as he expressed it. That flock must have numbered at least a thousand birds, and it was not an unusual one at the time. But what became of all those wild geese and ducks? Somebody must have eaten them, which may account for the gabbling that we hear at political conventions and ladies' teas. Some competent person ought to investigate the subject and write his opinion in a book.

Pioneer Fashions

In those early pioneer days the women and girls did the work, while the boys and men attended to the fishing and hunting and fighting and other essential occupations. The men also discussed politics and religion, and decided who was the best fighter or "gouger" in the community. After all these essentials were attended to there was no time for regular work; and what was the use, any way, when the feminine section of the family was glad to do it? There was plenty of cooking, and washing, and weaving, and knitting, but this was not man's work. The women also did the milking and the dressing of the butter, after some male of the species had rounded up the half-wild cows out of the woods. And of course the women looked after the babies, when they had any looking after.

Women's dresses were made of cotton or lindsey, the latter a woolen fabric for winter wear; and they spun the yarn, wove the cloth, and cut and sewed the garments with their own hands. They also raised the cotton and carded and spun the wool. They had very little to do except work. What were women for, any way, argued some of the pioneers, unless they made themselves useful? Those were the "good old days" to which we sometimes hear elderly people refer; and they were pretty good for the men.

The skirts of the women's dresses were short and narrow, though considerably longer than those worn by some of our modern beauties. If any man had seen a woman's calves in those days she would have blushed the rest of her life. The skirts were so long and narrow that they bore some resemblance to gun barrels, but there was room enough in them for the free exercise of feet and legs in hopping out of the way of coiled and vicious rattlers. (The reference to "legs" is metaphorical; pioneer women had no legs; they had "limbs". It was a deadly insult to say "legs" in the presence of the gentle beings---except the kind that belonged to men and tables and other animals.

The women displayed a good deal of art in coloring the yarn for their clothes, and weaving it into striped cloth. Some of the dresses had as many colors as Joseph's coat, and the brighter they were the better the girls liked them. The colors were produced by decoctions of barks and roots, with a little copperas now and then when it could be had. Copperas produces a brilliant greenish yellow. A more subdued and popular yellow was obtained by boiling the bark of the butternut, or white walnut. This was called by the name of the tree, and "butternut" was the uniform of some regiments in the Confederacy during the "late unpleasantness".

When buckskin began to go out of style for men's clothing, the women wove jeans to take its place, coloring it to suit the fancy of the wearer. A deep blue was the most popular color, obtained from an infusion of the indigo plant, which was grown extensively for the purpose. A blue coat, ornamented with brass buttons, was the certain mark of a dandy. For this reason Uncle Willis Bryan always wore butternut, in order to avoid the vanities and temptations of the world.

In warm weather the men and boys wore white cotton or linen suits, but they were so dressy and conspicuous that Cousin Willis and some of the other elderly men frowned upon them as worldly and unbesemming. I have a similar impression, due to the fact that they show dirt with so little provocation. It makes no difference how dirty you are, provided you do not deceive and mislead your fellow men by making an exhibition of it.

Little Boys and Girls in Summertime

The summer attire of little boys and girls, until they were seven or eight years old, was a plain white cotton shirt, reaching a little below the knees—just the shirt and nothing else. Little girls' shirts were generally an inch or two longer than those affected by little boys; but otherwise there was no difference in the sex of the garment. In cases of emergency boys and girls might have exchange garments without inconvenience. Owing to the extra length of their shirts, little girls couldn't run as fast as the boys, or turn somersaults, which quite naturally sent them to the rear in the matter of sports.

It happened sometimes that little boys' shirts got soiled and had to be washed, and during the process they were turned loose to shift for themselves; as they generally did with excellent satisfaction. Some little boys had two shirts, but they were regarded as among the wealthy and worldly and destined for future punishment. John and Robert and I had but one shirt each, and the days when they went to wash were occasions of frolic and freedom. We did not mind if the weather was moderate. I shall never forget the pleasurable emotions aroused in our bosoms when mother told us that our shirts needed washing. The announcement infused a feeling of liberty such as I have never known since. It was then that I understood the sense of freedom that swelled in the bosom of every little Indian boy. No Indian boy ever had a shirt to worry him, and perhaps that was one reason for the perpetual animosity that existed between the races. The white boys envied the freedom of the shirt-less red boys, and fought them (in our brilliant imaginations) until we slew them by the thousands.

We, John, Robert and I were armed with crooked sticks for guns and long slender rods of cane for spears, and the yells we emitted when we charged the enemy filled our souls with enthusiasm. Brother John, being the elder, was by seniority and nature our leader. With a rooster's feather in his hair he pointed the way to the battle's front as with yells we rushed to glory. Robert's yell was an infantile treble, but it struck terror into the hearts of the enemy. Our battle front was on the red-clay hill east of the house, and there we slaughtered savages by the millions. Some day their bones may be exhumed by antiquarians and exhibited as the relics of a prehistoric race. A public road---such as public roads of that date were---lay at the bottom of the hill, and occasional travelers passed that way; but our garb (or lack of it) and warlike demonstrations did not appear to disturb them. They had boys of their own at home.

When cold weather came, little boys put away their shirts and donned jeans pants and "round-abouts", and little girls put on their lindsey dresses; but life went on as usual. Little girls were never popular with the boys, because they could not participate in our exercises. We climbed trees, and turned handsprings, and stood on our heads, while little girls could only look on and wonder at our dexterity. These inequalities relegated them to a lower order. It is a great thing to be a boy, and I advise all my friends of the future who contemplate getting themselves born, to insist upon being members of that sex. Why be a girl anyway?

"I Wouldn't Choose Any More"

When company came we were careful to be on our manners, especially at table when the preacher was there. If we were handed anything after being fully surfeited, it was the very flower of politeness to say, "No, thank you, I wouldn't choose any more". It took long practice and sedulous training to master this expression; and now having been thoroughly drilled in it, if I should be asked to serve as President I would decline in the same masterful way. There is nothing like training a boy in the way he should go, or bending a limber twig when you think he needs it. Under ordinary circumstances it was customary when a boy was too full for expression, and the honey dish was passed for the fourth time, to decline with a grunt; for the polite expression, "I wouldn't choose any more", being reserved for the circuit rider and occasions when you didn't care to be President.

The circuit rider exercised a tremendous influence on the minds and characters of the pioneers. They were not considered as other men are, but were surrounded by divinity as having been set aside for the service of the Lord. Young people, especially regarded them with awe, and their coming was an occasion for the display of righteousness. During the interval of the circuit rider's presence bad little boys became good, and little girls were transformed into miniature divinities. My sister Malinda was a bright, beautiful, fun-loving girl, but she came early under the influence, and at the age of seventeen wrote the following in her diary:

"July 25th, 1847. We are to have class-meeting here this evening, if the Lord be willing, I hope that we may meet, and that the Lord will not withhold his grace from us. O Lord, revive us; revive thy work in our heart, revive it in this neighborhood; revive it all around the circuit; bless preacher and people."

It will be observed that she was unconsciously quoting one of the preacher's frequent petitions into her diary, preparing herself for the joys of the class-meeting that was to be held at our house in the evening. So intense was the religious spirit that it affected not only the elderly people, but also the good little girls and the bad little boys. They imitated the preacher in his sermons and prayers without being conscious of the act. There was tremendous earnestness in whatever they did and thought. Yet this very sister who kept the ancient diary clandestinely learned to dance in the intervals when the preacher was away, and was a universal favorite at the gatherings of the young people of her age. It was the presence of the preacher which diffused the halo of righteousness over the community. He came as a messenger from on high, and while he was in sight and hearing all the people were good.

But after all, healthy young people will be natural, in spite of preachers and every other restraining influence. Two days before the above entry my sister had written in her diary as follows:

"Now or never! Why tomorrow?

If the deed be good today,
There may lurk an age of sorrow,
In one hour that is thrown away;
For the future who may see?
And delay may lead to ruin—
Now or never, let it be!"

The state of mind revealed by my sister prevailed all over the Boone settlements, and was probably universal in the country at large. It is not a reflection of the thought and conduct of the people themselves, but it shows the manner and influence of the old-style preacher of a hundred years ago. My sister quotes what she had heard the preacher say, but does not manifest her own sentiments. These came to the surface after the preacher was gone, at the neighborhood dance, the corn-shucking frolic, the log-rolling, or the house-raising, when young and old became again what nature had made them. Between the coming and the going of the circuit rider there were numerous "back-slidings", which had to be atoned for by reconversion at the next quarterly meeting. It was this swinging of the pendulum between extra-religious outpourings and reversion to nature that produced the amazing manifestations at camp meetings and other religious gatherings of the period, which are scarcely believable in our time.

Brother John and the Circuit Rider

Our family was large and required a little more room than the average log-cabin, for which reason it became a stopping place for the circuit rider and for the holding of religious services.

My brother John did not appear to come so fully under the pastoral influence as some of our sisters did, so that I have occasional doubts concerning the evidence of his redemption, and wonder if I shall meet him in the other sphere. Several of the preachers showed an interest in his progress through this life and the place to which some of them seemed to fear he was destined, Father Barnett especially being among the number. He rode our circuit for several years and was a frequent visitor at our house where he had opportunities to observe the sinful levity that occasionally became manifest in the bosom of my elder brother. So he begged permission of my father to preach a special sermon for the benefit of John Daniel, a wish that was granted almost before it was expressed. Father said he had never experienced much difficulty in taming young colts, but John Daniel was a little beyond the orbit of his influence; and if Brother Barnett could modify his ways it would be a source of boundless pleasure to him.

When the time came for the sermon came the weather happened to be excessively cold, and the circuit rider appeared on foot with his saddlebags strapped to his shoulders. His horse had died of measles or some other complaint induced by faith in promised food, faith being, as we all know, the substance of things hoped for. The good man was clad in a great blanket overcoat, buffalo over-shoes on his feet, and leather leggings on his legs; but his heart was warm in consideration of the place that he was prepared to talk about.

A fire of hickory logs had been built in the fireplace, and by the time the services began they had burnt to a tremendously hot bed of coals. Father Barnett could not have asked for a better illustration of his subject. He selected as his text Deut. 32:22; and we are bound to admit that it was a warm one. Launching forth with Brother John and the bed of coals as his objective, he shouted:

"Look at that fire! See its red-hot embers! Do you think you could hold your hand in that tremendous heat for a single instant? No! No! You would scream with pain! You would howl with anguish! You would shout for rescue and relief! Your human nature could not endure it!"

"Ah, then, my dear young friend, think what it will be in the world to come! Imagine the fires of hell! They do not burn for merely an hour or a day, but forever!—and they get hotter and hotter all the time! They are ten thousand times hotter than those coals! And your heavenly Father has provided this for you—for you, my dear young friend!--unless you mend your ways and learn to love him with all your mind and heart and soul! This puny fire will expire and relief come, but the fires of hell will go on forever! And each minute they will get hotter!—and hotter!—and HOTTER! until the imagination is appalled at the awful torture! And this, my young friend, will continue throughout the ages of eternity—forever and forever! It proceeds without intermission! It has no end! You imagine that by tomorrow it may not be so hot, but when tomorrow comes it will be a thousand times hotter than it was the day before! The Lord will blow the breath of his anger upon it, and the white heat of his rage will wither and blast your soul!"

"Such is the punishment which he inflicts upon those who disregard his will by sinning in the flesh and rejecting the salvation which he so freely offers! O, my young brother, turn in time! Wait not until it is eternally too late! Cease to do evil and learn to do good! Come unto the Lord in the days of thy youth, and he will not withhold his blessings!"

As the sermon progressed I could see that brother John was moved. He turned his gaze from the preacher to the fire, and back again to the preacher; but made no outward manifestation of his inner state. When we retired to our trundle-bed a little later he said nothing, but I noticed that he had provided himself with two switches for cats instead of one, as was his custom. If any black cat had come that night it would have met a reception as hot as the place described by Father Barnett.

The next day passed without special incident or adventure, until the gathering of the forces for the slaughter of the savages. Then John manifested the emotions that were swelling in his bosom.

"Friends and fellow citizens!" he cried, as he stood in front of the series ranks. He raised the old conch shell for a blast, Robert held firmly to the tin pan, while to me was assigned the duty of thumping the pewter pot. "My countrymen!" continued John; "we are about to engage the enemy! This day America expects every man to do his duty! And let it be said, when the sinking sun has set, that we have met the enemy and he is ours!"

The conch shell sounded, the tin pan rattled, and the pewter pot thumped! The battle was on! That day we slew of the enemy a hundred and twenty thousand men. It was not safe to arouse brother John too much!

Tickling the Parson's Feet

But he had not settled in full with Father Barnett. When the next appointment came around the season had changed and the weather was warm. Father Barnett appeared in light clothing and a pair of brogan shoes without socks. Complaining that his shoes hurt his feet, he took them off and went barefooted. When it came time for his sermon he was still minus his shoes, and John saw an open way to victory. A chapter was read and a hymn sung, and I observed that brother John had disappeared. As Father Barnett knelt his feet spread out toward the fireplace, which had been filled with green asparagus bushes that afforded a screen for what was about to take place. No sooner had he reached the first eloquent urge in his petition than a long, slender fishing-rod glided through the hole in the back of the chimney where father had started some work and left it unfinished, and tickled the soles of the petitioner. Supposing it was mosquitoes, he slapped at them viciously, but without neglecting his prayer. Again came the tickling, with another slap and a fervent "Confound them skeeters!" For the third time mosquitoes got busy, and this time Father Barnett caught the fishing-rod!

Rising in righteous wrath he rushed out of the house carrying the rod with him but brother John was not to be found. He had remembered something that needed his attention in a distant part of the farm, and disappeared in the darkness. After half an hour's unsuccessful search Father Barnett returned, footsore, angry and perspiring. He said that John Daniel was the sorest affliction that had ever been visited upon him, and as soon as he could catch him he proposed to tan his hide to the consistency of buckskin.

Brother John spent the night in the loft of the barn, and did not show up for breakfast. In fact he made no appearance until Father Barnett was far on his way to his next appointment, and when asked to explain the cause of his absence he replied, with perfect innocence, that he had no idea it was so late.

Mother said she thought John Daniel ought to be disciplined, but father said the joke was on Father Barnett. If he felt like thrashing John Daniel he was at liberty to do it—but he must catch him first.

Miss Louise Nevitt and the Cat Story

Domestic cats were the only things that brother John was afraid of, which explains why he always took a switch to bed with him. The cats would slip into our trundle-bed on cold nights and snuggle down between us to get warm, whereupon John would wield his switch in a way that made them warmer than they expected. Nearly every night we had the excitement of a cat-fight, with a vigorous accompaniment of yowls and squalid. John especially feared a large black cat which had come to the house as an orphan, and evidently with a bad record. When the sound of that animal was heard he always took two switches to bed; for the coming of the black cat was an omen of ill.

The superstition grew out of a story that Miss Louise Nevitt told us one night when she was staying with "the boys" while the family went to early candle light preaching at a neighbor's house. She said black cats were not the real human kind, but they were possessed of witches and devils and everything mean. Sometimes they would get in bed with little children and suck their breath while they slept. This generally happened when the children had not been good the day before, and as John was never sure on that point he took no chance. On such occasions two switches were better than one. It may be inferred that Miss Nevitt was having trouble with us about going to sleep, so she told the story about the black cats for the sake of quiet. She was a maiden lady who had quit counting her birthdays, and of course she was well trained in the art of raising children.

Afterward she married one of Uncle Daniel's neighbors, and moved with him further into the wilderness; whence reports came back that she had reared fourteen children, mostly boys and girls, and that they all grew up to be good citizens. From which we understood that there were no black cats where she lived, and perhaps none of any kind except the wild ones.

I never knew the origin of the black cat superstition, but it prevailed all over the Boone settlements. If a black cat reached maturity there it was a miracle, or the cat had lives to spare. Miss Levitt did not fabricate the story out of whole cloth; she merely assisted in giving it circulation. The result was that I do not remember ever to have seen a black cat on our place except when it was doing its best to get out of the way of the clubs and stones that brother John was encouraging to fly in its direction. He urged that it was absurd to propagate black cats, when it was just as easy to raise speckled and stripped ones.

Josie Van Bibber did a good deal to popularize and circulate the black cat theory. He said that when the devil told him never to wear a hat, the message came through a cat of that kind; but he paid no attention to it, because he didn't think there was much harm in cats in general. But that night when he sat down to supper a black cat came and sat on the opposite side of the table, and ate potlicker with a hair-pin. He knew then there must be something in the cat story, and he never again wore a hat as long as he lived. But there was another reason for Josie's hallucination, a pathetic and romantic one, as I shall reveal on another occasion.

Episode Number Thirty-Seven

"Aunt Katy"

In those pioneer days there were several curious characters in the Boone neighborhood, who live alone and friendless with no one to look after or care for them; and others who ought to have been in jail. But there were no public institutions in which the unfortunates of either class could be housed, so they ran at large and seemed about as happy as other people.

One of these characters of the first class I am never able to think of except with emotion. I mean Aunt Katy. I never knew what her other name was until years after, when I was told that it was Smith—Aunt Katy Smith. But as children we knew her only as Aunt Katy. We also stood in awe of her, because she was "queer". That is, she was not like other people and she may have thought the rest of us were queer, because we differed from her.

She lived alone in a cabin in the woods, not far from our house. The cabin had no floor but earth, but her bed and chair and the little things the neighbors had given her were all very neat and clean. She was at liberty to burn all the wood she pleased to cook her food and keep herself warm; but she was not wasteful of the wood or anything else. She kept a little fire of dry sticks in the fireplace, and suffered for nothing that was needful.

She had a tiny garden of flowers by the side of the cabin, and also raised a few potatoes and other vegetables. There was no reason why she should raise anything to eat, for the neighbors kept her well supplied; but she preferred her own. She said the potatoes were fresher and perhaps a little more mealy and sweeter when she pulled them out of the ground herself.

Like nearly all the elderly women of her time, Aunt Katy smoked her pipe—a cob pipe—and she raised her own tobacco in her little garden. I heard her say once that tobacco kept the bugs away. But I do not think she ever combed her hair. It came only to her shoulders and hung in straggling gray ringlets about her head and face, giving her a haggard and rather wild look. Frequently she would gaze away into the distance at something nobody else could see, and talk to the unseen object; or to herself as we thought. If she had lived a few centuries earlier they would have drowned or burnt her as a witch; but the world had become so much better in her time that every one treated her with kindness and respect. They said that in her girlhood she had been beautiful, but when I knew her all her comeliness was gone. She was almost passionately fond of little children, and they were devoted to her; though sometimes a little afraid and backward about coming near, because she was so different from other people.

Aunt Katy had been married in her early womanhood and had a son named Riley, to whose memory she was much devoted. Her son and her husband were both taken from her about the same time—she said they passed out of one room into another, and she was going to see and live with them again before long. The neighbors thought this affliction was the cause of her dementia, and on that account they were sympathetic. Although the husband and son slept side-by-side in the lonely little burying ground on the hill were the briars grew, Aunt Katy said they were always with her, "just in the next room," where she could see and hear them any time. This was especially true with Riley, because he was her son and closer to her than a husband could be. During the day she spent most of the time in the woods hunting wild flowers and talking with Riley and the other children who she said came with him to see her. They were very real to her, and in my childish way I wondered why I could not see and talk with them too.

One night in the chill of autumn her fire went out, and she came to our house for some live coals to rekindle it. There were no matches then. Mother wrapped several large coals in a rag to keep air away, and sent my sister Jane and me with Aunt Katy to carry it for her. Mother said she might set her clothes on fire. She led the way along the path through the woods, crossing the brook on stepping-stones. It was a quarter of a mile to her cabin, and on the way she talked with Riley and the other children. Two or three times Riley strayed off into the woods, as boys do, and she called to him shrilly to come back. To the other children she spoke softly, because she said they were afraid of her, and told them they were beautiful and good. My sister and I heard all she said, but we could not hear the replies of the children. When some of them wanted to kiss Jane, Aunt Katy said tenderly, "No, not now; she can't see you and wouldn't know if you did kiss her; but you may smooth her hair and pat her cheeks if you wish." And Jane said she believed they did, for she thought she could feel them.

Dear Aunt Katy! Those groups of merry, dancing children were very real to her. We moved away to another farm before she died, and I do not know where they laid her to rest; but I am sure it was by the side of her husband and son, in the graveyard on the hill, where the briars are all gone and the green grass grows and wildflowers bloom.

Josie Van Bibber, the Man Who Wore No Hat

There was another singular character among Uncle Daniel's neighbors, whom we all called Old Josie Van Bibber. He seemed old to us because he had such peculiar ways. He wandered about the country and the hillsides talking to the birds, and they seemed to understand him as well as he did them. The confidence and admiration were mutual; no bird was ever afraid of Josie.

He never wore a hat, because on a very memorable occasion the devil snatched the one he had from his head and warned him if he ever wore another he would take his head the next time. The devil sent the message by a black cat that could eat potlicker with a hairpin, and that was why Josie knew it was so. He took the warning in good stead and never wore a hat again, because he did not care to lose his head. I have known several people who did not wear hats for similar reason; they were afraid they might lose their heads.

Neither did Josie Van Bibber wear any shoes on his feet. He said they made his feet so warm that he was apt to catch cold. Even when there was snow on the ground and the snow was frozen into ice, it made no difference to Josie. He said the snow and ice were quite warm, and he knew it was so because the roots of the flowers down in the ground said the same thing.

For clothing he had only an old battered and frayed pair of trousers and a cotton shirt. When anything else was given him he threw it away, because he could not stand the heat. While other people shivered in woolens, Josie was comfortable in his cotton shirt and trousers. He said it was merely a matter of opinion. If you believed that a cotton shirt and trousers were warm, that was sufficient. It was lack of faith that made some people cold. Besides, if cotton clothes would keep out the heat in summer, why should they not keep out the cold in winter? His philosophy was very convincing; to himself at least. The truth was, his heart was so warm and his love for the birds so great that his body never got cold.

When I was a child I thought Josie was as old as the hills; in fact I supposed he had always been there even before the hills; but I never knew what became of him. Some people said he dried up and blew away; but others assert that he is still in the same old neighborhood, talking to the birds as he did in the woods long ago.

Josie Van Bibber and His Sweetheart

There was a story that when Josie was a young man he was very handsome, and loved, and was beloved in return, by the most wonderfully beautiful girl in the whole country; but she sickened and after a long illness died. During her illness Josie was with her nearly all the time, telling her what the birds were saying—for they were both very fond of the songsters of the air. She said when spring came they would go out together and watch them build their nests. But spring never came for her any more, except the glorious spring that never ends; and Josie wandered over the hills alone, and talked with the birds, and they told him how much more beautiful she was than when he knew her. But he said that could not be possible, and so he and the birds argued the matter back and forth; which explains why he was always talking to them. Then the devil sent the black cat to warn him not to wear a hat, and Josie's mind flew away with the birds.

Borrowing a Hen

Quite naturally, in a community that was just starting, there was a good deal of borrowing and lending. One day a little girl came to our house and asked mother if she would please lend her mother a dozen eggs, which she wanted to set and raise some chickens for herself. Mother was glad to accommodate the lady, and gave the eggs to the little girl.

"But your mother has no hen to set them under," she said, intending to lend her a hen also.

"Oh, yessum, she has," replied the little one. "That is, we ain't got no hen of our very own, but Misses Alkire's goin' to lend my mother one to set on the eggs till they hatches."

Mother was so moved with admiration for the enterprise of her neighbor that she sent her three extra eggs, to take the place of any that might get broken or fail to hatch. Three weeks later the little girl called again, radiant with the consciousness of success.

"Oh, Aunt Liddy!" she cried, "all our eggs hatched but one, and now we have fourteen little chicks; and mother says our next preacher's day she's goin' to have fried chicken, and won't you and Uncle 'Ligy come over?"

Mother was so delighted with the outcome of her neighbor's industry that she promised to be there with Uncle "Ligy next preacher's day; and it turned out that they had two fried chickens for dinner, and the lady still had an even dozen for a start in business.

Little Dick and the Borrowed Cloak

My mother had so large a family of her own that she accumulated a good supply of infantile wear; and this being well known it was not unusual for neighbor women to borrow from her when a little stranger was expected. One cold winter day a lady borrowed a little cloak for her newly arrived son, promising to return it as soon as she could get time to make another to take its place. She did not return the cloak that winter, and when mother visited her at the turn of the season the following year, and hinted that she might need the garment, the lady replied that she never was so much obliged for anything in her life; but she had just sewed little Dick up in the cloak for the winter, and could not possibly spare it now; but she would sure return it in the spring. Mother did not press the matter, but in her great kindness of heart and love for babies hoped that little Dick would be comfortable. She never mentioned the cloak again, and the lady also forgot to say anything about it. But little Dick was comfortable, and that was the main issue.

Episode Number Thirty-Eight

Some Tall Stories

I am now going to tell some things about pioneers whom I knew that may seem to class amongst the marvelous, but I vouch for their literal truth in every particular. They were neighbors and friends of Uncle Daniel, and that ought to be sufficient recommendation.

Among the first of my old friends I place Uncle Frank Skinner and his brother Hugh and their families. They were natives of Culpeper County, Va., and therefore scions of the first families. Their ancestry ran back to Scotland, and when I first knew Uncle Frank he was a hale and hearty old gentleman of more than eighty, with a burr in his voice that made me think I was talking to some ancient hero of Sir Walter Scott just stepped out of the "Heelands" of his native heath.

I was visiting at his house on the occasion to which I now refer, and saw him do a thing which few men of his age would even consider. He had a young blooded horse of which he was justly proud, and in order to give an idea of his style of riding, he saddled the animal and brought him out in the bluegrass pasture adjoining the stables. He first invited me to take a ride, an invitation which my extreme modesty obliged me to decline. The horse looked to me as if he would as soon run away and kick me out of the saddle as try to amuse himself in any other way. He belonged to the breed that champs the bit and kicks up at both ends.

Uncle Frank threw his hat on the ground, then mounted and careered around in a circle; and when he came back to where his hat lay he swung himself down by the side of the horse and picked it up without in the least reducing his speed. After a second ride he dismounted and insisted that I perform the trick; but again my modesty intervened. And though I was much younger than he, and imagined I was something of a horseman myself, I had no hankering after that sort of glory. I would not have tried to ride that beast for the present of a dozen like him.

A Romantic Wedding Tour

Uncle Frank and his brother Hugh were married about the same time, and their wives were sisters, daughters of Mr. Robert Jasper; so they decided to move west and grow up with the country. But that was a long time before Horace Greeley gave popularity to the expression. They made most of the trip on foot, camping at night where the day ended, depending for food on wild fruits and the game they killed. If they missed the game they went hungry, feasting in their dreams on visions of plenty the next day. But this did not often happen, for the brothers knew how to shoot and there were bears and deer a-plenty, besides wild turkeys, and coons and possums, and other miscellaneous beasts too numerous to mention.

When they came to a river flowing the way they were going, they cut logs with their tomahawks and made rafts, and traveled in style as long as the river ran the right way. In those voyages by water they had plenty of fish to season their bear meat and venison, and thus avoided a monotony of diet. They had variety in other ways too, looking out for rattlesnakes and red Indians. They were young, very much in love with one another, and they enjoyed the journey with great zest that was never forgotten. It was a romantic wedding tour, but I imagine there are not many young ladies of Virginia at the present time who would be willing to undertake such a trip for the sake of getting husbands. Or perhaps husbands were more valuable then than they are now.

An Old Mare in Place of a Steam Engine

On coming at last to St. Louis they crossed the river on a ferryboat propelled by horse-power—one horse, or rather an old mare, that had been trained to that sort of life and seemed to like it. The craft was an ordinary flatboat, over a part of the deck of which a roof had been built to protect passengers from rain, snow, or hot sunshine, as the case might be. On a level with the roof was an endless-chain platform, where the old mare presided and munched her oats while contributing power to the wheel in the middle of the vessel. If she got tired, or stopped to grab an extra mouthful of food, her weight carried the endless-chain right along, obliging her either to eat while she walked or have her legs broken. The contraption was regarded as the very ultimate of intellectual activity, there being no other process whereby an old mare could travel without getting anywhere and chew her oats at the same time. The tread-wheel was connected by a band with a paddle-wheel that dipped into the water by a slot in the middle of the vessel; and the turning of this wheel propelled the boat at a speed which the travelers were assured would get them to the opposite side of the river if they had patience enough.

Through the exercise of this virtue, combined with the energy and perseverance of the old mare, they were eventually landed on the west bank of the great river, near where the Eads Bridge was subsequently built. As there was no hotel in the city at the time, they climbed the bluff and camped in a grove where the Broadway market was established some years later. The place was then covered with a forest of oak, hickory, and walnut trees, and had been reserved as a camping-ground for Indians when they visited the city on trading expeditions. About a hundred Indians were camped there at the time, and as it was their first experience of the red men the young travelers spent half the night watching them and observing their ways and manners.

Trouble with Indians

But in the morning they came near getting into trouble, with no thought of wrong-doing or violation of hospitality on their part. When the white travelers drew near and sat down on the grass, the Indians were seated at a long table eating their breakfast, waited on by their squaws. As soon as they observed the white people they began to growl and grumble, and several of the warriors rose to their feet and made threatening gestures toward the intruders; whereupon a native approached and warned them that the Indians objected to their presence while they were eating. They especially objected to the white women, and the native advised them to move away or the warriors might attack them. Of course they heeded the advice, for they were not looking for trouble. At the same time they begged their courteous friend to interpret their apologies to the noble red men.

After several days spent in viewing the sights of St. Louis, the young travelers moved on toward St. Charles, where they came just in time to meet the "June rise" in the river; and it was so filled with drift-wood and had so many whirlpools that they were afraid to venture on its muddy surface. Having been accustomed all their lives to the clear waters of Virginia, the stream of mud that they now saw floating past, was an amazing spectacle. The name of "Big Muddy" seemed to fit it exactly. When they saw natives drinking the mixture they were horrified. The natives not only drank it, but said they liked it and thought it was healthy, the mud having a therapeutic quality which cleansed the blood. The old ferryman said it "cleaned you out", like scouring a pewter pan. He even went further, and claimed that the water was food as well as drink; "catfish soup", he called it, a name which has adhered to the waters of the Missouri ever since.

The ferryboat had no horse-power, like the one at St. Louis, but was propelled by paddles wielded by the ferryman and his assistant. This still further excited the apprehension of the travelers. They were afraid they might get out into the river and stick fast in the mud, and perhaps form an island and trees would grow up over them. There was in fact some reason for the fear, for the ferryman told them that the island a short distance above had been formed by accretions of mud and sand, as all the other islands in the river were. Some obstruction would lodge in the stream, and immediately the sand would begin to form, on top of which willows sprang up, to be followed by giant cottonwoods and oaks, so that in a few years there would be solid ground and fertile soil where within the memory of men still living there had been a rapidly flowing stream of mud. It was all very wonderful to the young Virginians, who had no desire to be formed into an island and have corn and wheat planted in them.

Their fears were still further excited by the appearance of the boat, which seemed entirely too frail to stem the swift current of the muddy water. It was composed of two canoes lashed together and floored over like a cat-a-maran, with apparently only enough space for half a dozen passengers; but the boatman said he had safely ferried two wagons across only the week before. The most encouraging information he gave them was a statement that Uncle Daniel Boone had ferried his whole family across the river a few years before with nothing better than a raft, and as they had themselves traveled on rafts of their own construction, they began to gather courage, and after two or three days concluded to submit themselves to the care of Providence and take the chances. If Uncle Daniel and his family had made the trip in safety on a raft, why should not they succeed with a ferryboat? So at length, with much trembling and fear, they made the desperate adventure, and the ferryman and his assistant landed them safely on the opposite shore.

But the river was so forbidding in every aspect that they departed from it as quickly as possible, and none of them ever came back for a second view.

Uncle Daniel at Home

Twenty miles west of St. Charles they came to the Boone home, and spent several days with the famous old hunter and his family. Uncle Daniel was quite feeble at the time, and died not long afterward; but there was no lack of hospitality on his part or that of the young people who formed his household. He told the travelers it would be wise for them to go further west, as the country had become over-populated and there was no longer any room for new settlers. He declared that if he were a younger man he would go west himself, as he preferred plenty of room and good fresh air. He thought these desirable qualities could be found in Montgomery County, and he especially recommended that region. They acted upon his advice, and never had any occasion to regret their decision. On coming to a place which subsequently became known as Camp Branch, from the camp-meetings that were held there, they concluded it had a good home-like appearance, and they liked it so well that they remained there the rest of their lives.

These young Virginians were then the most western of all the pioneers except the French settlement at Cote-sans-dessein in what is now Callaway County, where the famous "Battle of the Petticoats" had been fought a few years before; and as may be inferred, they had some pretty lively adventures with bears, wolves, and other wild animals, to be recorded in subsequent Episodes.

A Thrilling Bear Hunt

The first winter after their settlement at Camp Branch was a severe one, and hunting was good, a fact which the young people appreciated. Wheat was scarce! Wolves infested that part of the country, and there were also many bears and deer.

On a bright November day Uncle Frank and a neighbor went into the woods in quest of fresh venison; but finding no deer, and having struck the trail of a bear, they set out in pursuit of it. The bear was hungry, and had ventured from his hibernation cave in quest of food, whereby he got himself in trouble. It was his first experience with white hunters, and being unfamiliar with that breed of animals he ran away as fast as he could waddle. The dogs took up the trail, barking and yelping and creating a din so frightful that the bear came to bay at the edge of a small prairie. As soon as the dogs saw that the bear was ready to fight they all tucked their tails and ran away, yelping louder than ever; except one sturdy old hound which ran in on the bear and snapped him first on one side and then on the other, being careful to keep out of reach of his great paws. It was a desperate fight that ensued between the two, racing around over a considerable space, and breaking down the cane and brush; but neither obtaining any decided advantage. The racket could be plainly heard by the hunters, and knowing that the bear was "treed," they ran forward to succor the hound.

As they came near the bear left the brush and raced off into the prairie, followed by the dog nipping at his heels. Just as he was getting well into the open space, where he seemed to imagine he would be safe, Uncle Frank blazed away and brought him down. Then all the other dogs rushed in, as though they were the victors, and their rumpus with one another made more noise than the pursuit had done. The dogs were young and not having been trained were not yet the bold and steady hunters that they soon became.

The bear was a fine one, weighing four hundred pounds net with four inches of fat on his ribs, and supplying plenty of bear bacon for the approaching Thanksgiving. How thankful the bear may have been is another matter.

A Bear that Laughed

A few weeks later Uncle Frank and two of his neighbors went bear hunting in the hills of Loutre, where it was reported they were numerous. By this time the dogs were better trained and proved to be not only fine hunters but dependable and courageous; and the adventure that ensued was one of the most remarkable in several respects ever known in that part of the country.

They had scarcely arranged their camp when the dogs sounded their notes of a hot trail, and on coming up with them the hunters found the tracks of a bear measuring seven inches in width. This indicated a monster, and they knew that the game was worthy of their best metal. The dogs pursued with great enthusiasm and were closely followed by the hunters on horseback. The trail led along the foot of a cliff, and they had gone but a short distance when they discovered the bear sitting on top of the cliff laughing at them! Whether he was laughing as men do when they think they have outwitted their enemies, the hunters could not say; but Uncle Frank assured me that if ever any animal laughed that bear did. It was no hyena-like laugh, but a genuine broad grin and cackle like a human being. He was enjoying himself wonderfully as he sat there above them and watched the discomfiture of the men and dogs.

They soon found the ravine by means of which the bear had made the ascent of the cliff, and spurring their horses along it they reached the top. But the bear was gone! He had observed their movements and set out on a run for a safer place. He was not only a fun loving bear, but he also knew a thing or two about taking care of his own skin.

Again the dogs caught the trail, and brought the bear to bay about a half mile further along the ridge. Now it was a battle to the finish. Bruin realized that he no longer had any hope of escape, so he quit laughing and went to fighting in his most desperate fashion. He wounded one of the dogs so badly with a vicious slap that it was put out of the fight for time being; but the others closed in and battled with a fury that was inspiring. Again the bear broke away, and mounting a log that lay slantingly up a steep hill did his best to climb into safety; but Uncle Frank fired and wounded him desperately. Then the dogs closed in and the combat renewed. One of them received a slap from the bear's paw, and being badly hurt started to run; when one of the hunters fired accidently and killed the dog. At the same time the bear made another effort to climb the log, but being weak from loss of blood he slipped and fell over and gave up the ghost.

He was an extraordinary prize, weighing five hundred pounds net and as fat as a bear could be. It has been claimed that fat people are nearly always good-humored, and perhaps the rule applies also to bears. It certainly held good in this case.

Going Into a Cave After a Bear

The following February the same party went again into the Loutre hills on a hunt. There had been an early thaw which they knew would bring the bear out of hibernation; and the sugar-makers were also boiling the sap of the maple trees into syrup and sugar. This was an occasion never overlooked by bruin, who had a "sweet tooth" and was in the habit of visiting the camps in the night and overturning the kettles in his search for the nectar of delight.

The hunters soon came upon a huge bear sitting on his haunches and watching them from the opposite side of a small stream. As he sat there he seemed almost as intelligent as a human being, and by the exercise of this talents he soon became satisfied that he was not in the presence of persons lunches he cared to associate with. So he arose and departed into the brush and cane before the hunters had time to fire at him. The dogs took up the trail and led a noisy race through the woods, barking and yelping to show the way. The chase continued for nearly five miles, glimpses of the bear appearing now and then through the glades and openings in the woods. At length he came to his den and plunged headlong into it, followed by one of the boldest of the dogs. But it was a desperate undertaking, and after a brief but furious fight the dog fell victim to the stronger beast. The hunters then built a fire at the mouth of the cave, and piling logs upon it left the heat and smoke to do their work while they sought lodgings for the night at a near-by sugar-camp.

In the morning when they returned the fire had burnt out and the ashes were cold, but there was no sign of the bear. It was still in the den, but whether dead or alive no one could determine. When it was proposed that some one go in and see, there were no volunteers. It required a tremendous display of courage to venture into the black darkness of a cave to look for a bear that might be alive; yet none were willing to go away and leave the matter undetermined. That would be as rank cowardice as the other was foolhardy bravado. Even the dogs could not be persuaded to go in and test the matter.

At length it was decided to draw lots, with a solemn pledge that the one who drew the short stick should visit the bear. So the die was cast, and the task fell to Uncle Frank Skinner. He said afterward that when he realized what was before him he wished with all his heart he had never learned to hunt bears. If the beast should happen to be alive, as there were good reasons for believing, it was more than probable that this would be the hunter's last adventure; and he shrank from the encounter. The idea of fighting a bear which he knew to be one of the largest species, in the closed confinement of a cavern whose roof was so low that he could not even stand on his knees, was simply appalling. He would not have cared so much out in the open, with light and room, but the proposition that lay before him was desperate in every respect.

For a moment he felt that his companions ought to object, and thus afford him a chance to back out; but they said nothing, which implied that they expected him to go after the bear. He wondered what either of them would do in his place; but as he could not read their minds, and being a man who had never shirked a responsibility, he grimly prepared to do what he regarded as a desperately foolish thing.

Looking to his gun to see that it was ready for an emergency, he bade his comrades farewell and crawled into the mouth of the cave. As he advanced the gloom became so dense that he could see nothing ahead of him; he was obliged to literally feel his way.

There was no sound to indicate the presence of any living creature, nothing but a ghostly, weird, awful stillness. But this gave him hope. If the bear were alive it would by this time have made some movement. So he glided forward a little more boldly, his gun advanced and his finger on the trigger.

Presently the muzzle of the weapon touched something soft, and he knew it was either the bear or the dog; but he could not decide whether it was dead or alive. His eyes becoming more accustomed to the gloom, he could see by the bulk of the object that it was too large for a dog, and must therefore be the bear. The shock of the discovery almost gave him heart-failure. The time was at hand for a desperate life-struggle, or the termination of an adventure that would make him a hero.

Possibly the bear might be asleep, or comatose, for the hibernating season was not yet over. But there was no time to ponder a matter of that kind. He would soon know whether the bear was dead or alive, or merely sleeping.

Pushing his gun forward until its muzzle pressed against the bulky object, he touched the trigger. There was an explosion that made the cavern ring, but no movement of the inert mass. The bear was dead! Suffocated by the smoke and fumes of the fire!

For a moment the hunter became unconscious. The tremendous revulsion of feeling was more than his nerves could endure. When he came-to he was lying on the ground outside the cave, his companions rubbing and chaffing him to restore vitality. The sound of the gun had given them notice of the beginning of the combat, and they followed each other into the darkness to render such assistance as they could. Finding him insensible, they dragged him to the light, where he soon recovered. His comrades greeted him with shouts and blamed themselves for allowing him to undertake so desperate a thing; yet each felt within himself that he would have acted in the same way if the lot had been his. Years afterward, when Uncle Frank repeated the story to me, he said it was the biggest fool thing he ever did in his life, and he would not do it again for a thousand bears.

A Kicking Buck

There is another exciting story that Uncle Frank Skinner told me about a fight he and his brother Hugh had with a wounded deer. Hugh had shot a large buck, which escaped and concealed itself in a cane break; and having no dogs with him he returned home for them. Uncle Frank joined him, and accompanied by the dogs they repaired to the place where the deer had disappeared.

The dogs immediately struck the trail and in a few minutes ran the animal to cover. It was completely hidden from view by the cane and brush, but on being aroused it sprang up and charged the hunters. One of the dogs caught it by the under jaw and held fast, but the deer turned a somersault and broke the hold. Then as he was trying to gore the dog with his horns Uncle Frank ran in and caught him by the hind-legs. It was a ludicrous and very dangerous experiment, and might have cost the hunter his life except for the fact that the deer was already weak from the loss of blood.

With a ferocious kick the deer freed himself, and instantly turned on the hunter. As he lunged forward the two prongs of his horns passed on either side of Uncle Frank's thigh, ripping his buckskin pants and inflicting a couple of slight wounds. Being now in front of the deer he caught it by the forelegs and held it while the dogs worried it from the rear, and Hugh ran in with his knife and put an end to the struggle.

Remarkable exploits of the Pegrams

For the sake of variety I will now relate a series of incidents that happened to the Pegram family of Montgomery County, who were also good friends of mine, and I am sure they did not misrepresent a single item in their remarkable adventures.

Daniel Pegram, whose ancestors were Scotch, was himself a native of Petersburg, Va., where he reared ten children, six boys and four girls, each of them more than six feet in height. It is not an unusual thing in large families for one or more of the boys to attain six feet or more, but when every one of ten reaches that height, girls as well as boys, it may be accepted as a premonition of coming greatness. "In those days there were giants in the earth," and wonderful events followed.

James L. Pegram, one of Daniel's six foot sons, came to Missouri and settled in Montgomery County, and became a citizen in every way worthy of his sires.

Yellow Jackets, Bumble Bees, and Hornets

On a certain occasion, accompanied by one of his sons and a nephew, he drove down to Loutre Hills in his ox-wagon in search of flat rocks for a hearthstone. The things that happened to them, not only while they were away but also after their return, he related to me not long afterward, and as he was a class-leader in the Methodist Church I am sure he adhered faithfully to the truth. But the reader, not being personally acquainted with the family, is at liberty to think otherwise if he feels that way.

Expecting to be about for only a few hours they took no lunch along, and were consequently very hungry and in a generally dilapidated condition when they returned late in the evening.

Arriving at the scene of action, they overturned a nice looking flat rock and found a nest of yellow jackets under it. The insects, infuriated at the invasion of their vested rights, stung the oxen until they ran away and almost wrecked the wagon. But having recovered the oxen and repaired the vehicle, the men proceeded with their work.

When the next rock was overturned it revealed an extra-large bumble bees' nest, and these insects also objected to the manner of their treatment. Everybody got out of the way except the oxen, who were standing by chewing their cuds and wondering if anything more was liable to happen. Something did happen! Every bee in the nest lit upon those innocent cattle and stung them into fury. Again they ran away, and once more the wagon had to be repaired.

By this time the men were becoming a little discouraged, but with Scotch perseverance they lifted another rock and set free a nest of hornets. He who has been stung by a hornet remembers what these little beasts can do when aroused in defense of home and country. For the third time the oxen ran away, and when they were recovered only a fractional part of the wagon remained attached to them.

Rattle Snakes and a Pole Cat

After all this the average man would have returned home, but these descendants of wearers of the plaid were above the average man, and they resolved to have what they had come for or perish in the effort. When the fourth rock was lifted they discovered a nest of rattlesnakes, coiled and aching for a fight. But they were soon dispatched, and the old one skinned for a keepsake. The skin measured five feet in length and four inches in width, and was regarded as a pretty sizeable passive; but the men concluded it was about time to return home and come for flat rocks some other day. Patching up the remainder of the wagon so they could ride on it, they sadly turned their faces in the direction of home; but they had proceeded only a short distance when one of the wheels ran over a little striped cat, and the oxen, becoming frightened at the odor which began to permeate the air, ran away the fourth time and splintered up what was left of the wagon. This obliged the men to walk the rest of the way.

An Elusive Rooster

On reaching home, desperately hungry, they were informed by Mrs. Pegram that there was not a single thing left over from dinner; but if they would get a steak from the butcher's shop she would fry it for them. On applying to the butcher he said he had sold out completely, and had nothing left but a bite of dog eat, which the dogs ate with pleasure and profit.

Then Pegram got his gun and went hunting for an old rooster that had been a stench in the nostrils of the community for years; but the rooster became alarmed at the demonstration and flew into a neighbor's apple tree, where he could not be dislodged without damaging the fruit.

After this Pegram read a chapter in Lamentations, and the family retired for the night. But no sooner were they comfortably settled in bed than a young cyclone buzzed along and took the roof off the house.

For these and other reasons, that part of the hills down on Loutre Hills where the flat rocks grow, has ever since been known as the "Devil's Back".

Brazzelton's Race with a Bear

It has been said that when a bear or a lion gets after you, and you are not able to outrun it, the next best thing is to throw your hat in the mouth of the beast and trust to luck. But sometimes the plan will not work. You may have no hat, nothing but a coonskin cap; or you may lose your hat in the haste of departure. For these and other reasons the old pioneers preferred a flint-lock rifle or a sharp hunting knife. When so armed they were not afraid either of a lion or a bear. At least they told me so, and discretion seemed to imply that it was safer to take their word for it.

A man named Brazzelton came from Virginia to the Boone neighborhood to look for land, and while he was there a party was organized to take him on a bear hunt. He was especially warned not to fool with the cub bears when he found them alone, because the mother bear was generally close at hand and might be disposed to make trouble. But Brazzelton said he was an old hand at the business and understood the tricks of the animal. He was not afraid of bears and thought he could take care of himself. So they let him alone and said nothing more about the danger of fooling with cubs.

The party traveled away out into that wild region which is now John County, where it was well known there were plenty of bears, and likewise a few rattlesnakes and now and then an Indian. Brazzelton said it was just the kind of place he had wanted to find, and he would show them a thing or two that might surprise them. So the rest of the party let him alone and did not worry him with advice.

One morning after they had made their camp, Brazzelton went out before breakfast to see what luck he might have. The first thing he found was a cub bear taking a nap on a limb close to the ground, and he captured it for the sake of having fun. He pulled its ears and made it squeal; then he pulled its ears some more and it squealed a little louder. It was the most amusing little creature he had ever seen, and it brought him more fun than he expected. The more he pulled its ears the louder it squealed; and presently he learned a lesson about bears which he had not previously acquired.

While the little bear continued to squeal and Brazzelton enjoyed the fun, he heard a riot behind him, and turning in that direction he observed the mother bear approaching in a frame of mind that was calculated to arouse apprehension. She had been to a creek to get some fresh fish for breakfast, and hearing the cries of the cub was now coming to its rescue. Her bristles were elevated and her jaws distended, and out of the latter issued some of the most awful sounds that Brazzelton had ever heard. He said afterward that he believed the old beast was using profanity and very likely she was. At any rate, and taking her all in all, she was not the kind of animal to encourage familiarity; and Brazzelton arose and departed out of the place. He remembered that it was time for breakfast at the camp, and hastened to get there before it was over.

He flew along as if something was pressing on his mind. He did not stop to get his hat, which he had deposited on the ground while playing with the little bear. Therefore he had no hat to throw in the old bear's mouth.

There was a small prairie not far away, and he conceived the idea of exploring it, so he could tell his friends back in Virginia what a prairie looked like. He had a notion also that the old bear would not follow him into the open space, and as she was treading close upon his heels he did his best to get there first. It became a race between Brazzelton and the bear, with the prairie as the objective. He ran with a speed that was remarkable; he had never known himself to run so fast; yet he was not satisfied. He strained every nerve to see if he could run a little faster. Presently he ran over a rattlesnake, but he was going at such a rate that the snake had no time to pay its respects to him. Brazzelton was afraid he might be late for breakfast, and he did not want to keep his friends waiting. Just as he was about to launch into the prairie an Indian shot at him from behind a tree and bored a hole through his hunting coat. The sound of the gun frightened the old bear, and she turned back, leaving the remainder of the race to be run by Brazzelton alone. But he did not stop to bid her farewell or inquire after her health. He longed for breakfast and hurried on to camp, arriving in such a haste that he overturned the gravy and spilled the coffee. He told his comrades that an Indian, a rattlesnake, and two bears were after him, and that while he was not afraid of either alone, he did not care to fight the whole bunch at the same time.

Episode Number Forty-One

A Bear Cures Hugh Logan of Rheumatism

It is often the case when we are sick or in pain that relief comes from some unexpected source; and so it happened with Hugh Logan. He lived on Big Bear Creek in Montgomery County, a name which indicates the kind of animals that formerly hibernated there. Like many other elderly people, Hugh was afflicted with rheumatism, and his aches and pains were frequently near the limit of endurance that he longed to go where rheumatism flourishes not and the weary are at rest. As the years rolled on his sufferings became more acute, and there appeared to be no escape from them.

But relief was coming from a source entirely unexpected. One morning in the spring he felt better and decided to take a ramble in the woods, where he could put his aching feet on the grass and watch the violets as they pushed their modest heads above the earth. With the aid of his crutches he got along very well, better in fact than he anticipated; and was soon in the midst of the forest that surrounded his home. Now he could hear the birds sing, and the squirrels bark their defiance at one another, and he longed to be young again with a gun on his shoulder; for the spirit of the hunter never departs.

Presently he came upon three unexpected guests, whose presence reminded him that he had ventured too far. It was an old bear with her two cubs that she was training to climb a tree. Hugh would have been glad to stand by and watch the antics of the little ones and admire the intelligence of the mother, but she saw him about the time that he observed her, and objected to his presence. She did not like to be disturbed in the training of her family, and was not backward in making him aware of the fact. Leaving her cubs sitting on their haunches at the root of the tree, she advanced toward the intruder in a manner that was not intended to be friendly. As she approached nearer she rose on her hind-feet and frowned in a way that seemed to indicate a desire to polish him off; and as he had no gun and was unable to do any fancy running, he began to feel uneasy regarding his future state. He tried to move his legs and see if they could be persuaded to do something for him, but they remained stationary and tingled with pain. His case seemed hopeless.

But his mental facilities were alert, and when the old bear came near enough he pulled off his hat and threw it in her open mouth. Supposing that this was some part of his anatomy, she stopped long enough to tear and masticate it, and the interval inspired Hugh with some degree of hope. He began to feel as if he might run, and on making the effort he found that the inspiration was true.

So he "lit out" and did some fine and fancy sprinting. He was surprised and gratified to see how fast he could run. His crutches being no longer of any use, he threw them away, and found that there absence accelerated his speed. No man can do much running on a pair of crutches. He also gained another advantage. The old bear stopped to investigate the curious implements and lost a minute or two crunching them to splinters. This gave Hugh another respite, and his inspiration continuing to work he dashed for the yard fence. But the bear gained on him, and just as he reached the enclosure she was so near that he thought he could feel her hot breath on the back of his neck. Urged on to renewed energy, he went over the fence at a single leap and felt that he was safe.

The bear did not follow, but stopped and looked as if she admired his agility. In the yard lay a couple of hounds half asleep, and the old bear had discretion enough not to arouse a sleeping dog. But the noise and the calls of their master had already disturbed them, and in an instant they were on their feet and ready for battle. The bear now set out on a run on her own account, in the direction of her cubs, with the hounds gaining on her; and Hugh, no longer feeling any of the pains of rheumatism got his gun and joined the race. A bullet flies faster than any beast can run, and one out of Hugh's gun overtook the bear just as she came to her cubs. So the three were captured, and Hugh kept the little ones alive for pets. But the strange part of the story is, that he never again felt a twinge of his old complaint. He was definitely cured, and therefore took pleasure in recommending the remedy to his friends; but I never heard that any availed themselves of it. How strange it is that people will suffer the pangs of rheumatism rather than be chased by a bear!

William Ramsey Makes the Acquaintance of a Mother Bear

William Ramsey of Warren County had a singular adventure which taught him a good deal about the meaning of life. He had killed many a bear and thought he had a fair understanding of the genus of the beast; but he discovered that he had something yet to learn.

While hunting one day he wounded a half-grown cub and sat down to play with it. It is a singular thing that all those old hunters were so fond of the antics of young bears that they would frolic with them in spite of the fact that it was courting death to do so. In this case, although the little animal was suffering from the pain of its wound, it manifested the usual playfulness of the breed, much to the amusement and satisfaction of the hunter. But at the same time it was plaintively calling to its mother which it knew was not far away; and Ramsey soon made her acquaintance! She came upon him suddenly, and with great ferocity objected to his intrusion into her family affairs. Before he was aware of her purpose she took him in her arms and squeezed him until his ribs cracked, at the same time gnawing the back of his head until he felt reasonably sure he was about to lose his scalp. He had never met another bear that had ever hugged him, and in his struggles to keep the breath in his body he decided that something had to be done, quickly and without delay. In spite of the old bears' evident and intense affection, he resolved to puncture her hide with his knife if he could get his hand on it. But that was the question! How was he to get his knife while the beast hugged him closer and closer and combed his back hair with her teeth all the more fiercely? He could not even touch the hilt with the tip of his little finger.

But in her strenuous manifestations, the bear slipped on the edge of a ravine, and in her efforts to avoid falling let go of the hunter. Instantly he had his knife in hand, and when she came back he soon put an end to her recklessness.

Then followed a scene of the most touching character. The little bear ran to its dead mother with an intelligence that seemed almost human, and pressing its body against her whined and cried as a child would do. It knew what had happened; the common instinct of life taught it that its mother and protector was dead, and the hunter stood by with shame and regret for having been the author of its sorrow. But he had not long to wait. Slowly the little bear sank down under the effects of its own wound, until finally, with a last gasp and tremor, it lay dead on its mother's bosom. Humanity itself could not have been more human.

Ramsey was weak and trembling from the effects of the struggle, and although he was an old hunter and hardened by the scenes he had witnessed, it was with difficulty that he restrained tears of compassion. The affection which the two animals had manifested for each other gave him a new insight into life. Was love universal? Was it the same in the heart of a bear as in the bosom of a human being, differing only in the outward forms which it assumed? He never enjoyed hunting afterward. It seemed too much like killing his own kind. And in particular he never again played with a cub bear without a previous acquaintance with the old one.

Christopher Sanders is Suspicious

Christopher Sanders of Montgomery County was one of the many noted hunters of that region; but he knew so little about the proper care of a gun that he never kept one of his own. He preferred to borrow from his neighbors; and most of his borrowing was done of the Van Bibber boys. At last they grew tired of what they felt was something of an imposition, planned a scheme which they thought would put a stop to Sander's habit.

Among their other possessions was the usual old musket which their father had bought at a sale for ten cents, and they concluded it was just the kind of gun their neighbor ought to have. So when he called again they were ready and glad to accommodate him. It would be a pleasure to lend him a gun, and they had one which they knew would please him. It seemed to neighbor Sanders that they were rather too demonstrative in their wish to accommodate him, and his suspicions were somewhat excited. He inquired if the gun was all right, and they assured him it was. In fact it was the best gun of its kind they had ever seen, but they did not go so far as to recommend the "kind".

They rammed in a load of about six inches and handed the old fuse to Sanders. But he was still suspicious. Their manner was too effusively cordial.

"Are you sure she won't bust?" inquired Sanders, with a show of anxiety in his tone.

"No, indeed!" replied the boys. "You couldn't bust that gun with a keg of powder!"

But the more he thought about it the less confidence he had in the reliability and safety of the weapon. There must be something wrong, or the boys would not be so anxious to lend him a gun. Presently a deer got up and bounded away, but he did not have the courage to shoot. So he returned the musket and said he believed he wouldn't go hunting that day.

This put the boys in a dilemma. They did not dare fire the gun themselves, and they had no tools with which to remove the load. One of them suggested that they wait until Christmas, and touch it off with a slow-match, which would give them time to get out of the way.

Pat and the Old Musket

While they were discussing the matter, an Irishman called in a state of great excitement. He said there were four big bucks down in the woods and he would like to borrow a gun and try his luck on them. So they passed the ancient musket over to him and felt relieved. A few minutes later they heard a terrible crash down in the woods, and wondered if Pat was hurt. Then they began to get uneasy, for if the old gun had blown the Irishman to pieces they might be held responsible.

But their fears were soon relieved for Pat appeared, radiant and happy. He had bagged "three of the buggers, and would have got the fourth if the old fuse had had a descent load in her."

It had kicked him over, dislocated his arm, and otherwise damaged his anatomy, but what was that in comparison to getting three fine bucks at one shot!

William Strode Runs the Gauntlet

William Strode was a neighbor of Uncle Daniel, and himself a noted hunter and Indian fighter. But one day he fell into an ambuscade and was captured by a band of warriors led by Black Hawk.

The chief was glad to see him, for they had been friends before the war; and he said because of their former relations he would treat him with special distinction. He told him that he must first run the gauntlet, an honor bestowed only upon those who were known to be brave and worthy; and at the end of the lines he would find a good fire in which he would be roasted for the entertainment of the warriors.

Strode thanked him for his consideration, and said he would do his best to give them a good show.

"What do you mean by that?" demanded the chief, irritated at the prisoner's coolness.

"That's my business," replied Strode. "You go ahead with the preparations."

"Mebbe I give you something to change your mind," retorted Black Hawk. "Can you dance?"

Strode replied that being a Methodist he had never been taught that accomplishment.

"Then I show you how!" snorted the chief, and directed his warriors to proceed.

They gathered a lot of dry brushwood and piled it around a green hickory sapling, and having set it on fire they armed themselves with clubs, and forming two parallel lines a few feet apart, notified the chief that they were ready.

"Now," said Black Hawk, "you run between the lines of my warriors, and if you come out alive at the other end I show you how to dance."

Strode again thanked his old friend, and advance to the opening between the lines. The first warrior struck at him with his club, whereupon Strode knocked him down and took the club away from him. Then he walked down between the lines, whistling as he went, and not another warrior dared strike at him.

Having made the run of the gauntlet in triumph, he mounted a log in front of the fire and flapped his wings and crew like a rooster.

The Indians were so amazed at his coolness and delighted with the performance, that they set him free and adopted him as a member of the tribe. He remained with them apparently well pleased, until an opportunity came, when he escaped and returned home. After that at house-raisings and log-rollings it was his custom to entertain the men by imitating a rooster, while they did the work.

Strode claimed to believe in the migration of souls, and said he was the rooster that crew when Peter denied his master; but I was not there at the time and cannot vouch for the truth of the claim.

Conversion of Old Jane Pettingill

The reference to Peter's rooster reminds me of the conversion of old Jane Pettingill, who lived on Possum Flats down in the Missouri bottoms. She raised mosquitoes and rattlesnakes and was regarded as one of the worst characters in the whole Boone settlement. Some of the pioneers were also of the opinion that she could raise the devil, and they argued that the best thing to do with old Jane was to burn her at the stake. But they went no further than to hold public prayers in her behalf and petition that she might be stricken with some direful complaint that would keep her from doing any more mischief; or be captured by the Indians and carried away so far that she never could find her way back.

One of Jane's worst failings was making bad whiskey and selling it to the Indians, who generally went on the warpath immediately after; which was regarded as the most natural thing they could do, considering the kind of whiskey Jane made. This bad habit caused so much trouble that Uncle Daniel said he wished some stout warrior would get drunk and tomahawk Jane or carry her away and marry her. He didn't care which, for in either case she would not trouble the settlements anymore. This was probably the worst thing that Uncle Daniel ever said about anybody, for he was generally mild-mannered and soft-spoken; but you couldn't blame him when you consider that he had most of the fighting to do when old Jane brought on a fresh war.

Her nearest neighbor was Jack Sullivan, who lived five miles away and said he didn't care to get any closer while old Jane was alive. Jack had long since professed religion, was a deacon in the church, and an all-round good man; but he had an old mare named Juno that was almost as bad in her way as Jane Pettingill. She would get the stubborns and kick off the harness and play the mischief generally, and the only thing to do was to cut the bellyband and turn her loose and let her ramp until she kicked down a section of the forest. This usually quieted her nerves, and she would behave until another spell came on.

One hot day in July Jack hitched up and drove to camp meeting. It was a long drive and when he got there he was tired; so he sat down in the shade of the arbor, where the breeze was cool, and went to sleep.

Now it happened on this same day old Jane Pettingill had come to meeting, and becoming interested in what the preacher said, she went to the mourner's bench to see if the Lord would have mercy on as vile a sinner as he was. He did have mercy, and Jane began to shout and romp around until she roused Jack Sullivan. Being only half awake he imagined that something was the matter with his old mare, and he ran to the altar and caught old Jane and held her fast. It was the first time she had ever been hugged by a man, and the sensation was so peculiar that it made her shout and prance all the more. Jack on his part thought the old mare was having an extra spell, and he tried to soothe her by holding on tighter and speaking to her soothingly.

"Whoa, Juno, be still, old girl," he said. "Wait till I get my knife and I'll cut you loose and let you go."

The preacher now thought it was time for him to interfere, and going on:

"Brother Jack, it isn't your old mare that you've got—it's old Jane Pettingill. The Lord has blessed her and she's going to be good."

By this time Jack was thoroughly awake, and dropping old Jane, he looked the astonishment he could not find words to express.

"The Lord have mercy on us!" he cried. "And old Jane's got religion! Well! Well!" Then turning to the congregation he shouted: "Brethren, praise God from whom all blessings flow! If he can convert old Jane Pettingill there ain't nothin' he can't do!"

From that time onward "Sister Jane," as she came to be called, was transferred into one of the best women in the settlements. If any good was going on she was there to help, and Uncle Daniel confessed that he didn't see how they could get along without her.

Years afterward, when she died, several of the brethren and sisters who were present, said they saw her spirit ascend and sit down on the right-hand of the throne and commence playing the harp just as if she had known how all her life. It was a wonderful event and much to do with the subsequent good name of the Boone settlements.

Pigs' Tails and the Moon

During the course of my father's life he gave a good deal of attention to pigs' tails, and worked out a set of philosophical principles that seemed to be well-grounded. He had observed that if he cut their tails off in the dark of the moon they would bleed but little, sometimes not at all; but if the tails were amputated in the light of the moon they would bleed profusely. It was his custom therefore always to trim his pigs' tails in the dark of the moon, and I never knew one to die from loss of blood.

This led some of the neighbors to infer that Uncle 'Ligy's pigs' tails had something to do with the phases of the moon; but Father Barnett, the circuit rider, said it was clear as gospel to him that pigs were possessed of devils, as the scripture declared, or the Lord never would have given them the kind of tails he did.

There was indeed some ground for these various opinions, for I myself had often observed that when there was to be a cold spell the pigs would huddle together in the fence corners and squeal; and on several occasions some of them were observed to twist their tails the wrong way. Hayden Boone, a nephew of Uncle Daniel, said it was his belief when Uncle 'Ligy's pigs did that way it was a sign we were going to have a yelping hard winter, and it was time to prepare for the worst. Father claimed that it took as much corn to fatten a pigs' tail as it did to fatten the pig itself, and considering the kind of a tail the pig had he wondered why Provedence had given him any at all. And, finally, why does a pig curl his tail? It is easy enough to understand the purpose of a mule's tail, especially in fly-time or when you get too close to it; in either case it is a warning to keep away. But there is no philosophy in the tail of a pig, and the instinct which makes him curl it is pure vanity. This was the way father argued, and having reached a basis of sound reason it was his custom to excise his pigs' tails in the dark of the moon than take the chances.

A Rattlesnake in the Biscuit Oven

In the days of the pioneers rattlesnakes were very numerous, and the pigs used to kill and eat them; and father said he would rather eat the pig that had devoured the snake than to eat the snake itself. Now and then a snake would invade a cabin and warm itself by the fire, or get under the covers of the children's beds, and in other ways make itself at home. This usually happened in the fall when the weather was beginning to get frosty and the snake did not like to go into lonely hibernation; for even a snake has some idea of comfort and sociability.

One morning Sam Cobb, of Montgomery County, got up to start the kitchen fire for his wife to get breakfast, when he found a rattlesnake coiled in the biscuit oven. He slapped the cover on before it could strike, and baked it crisp and brown. But none of the family would choose snake for breakfast that morning; they would not even eat biscuits baked in the same oven, and Sam was obliged to go to town and get a new one. As a rule I have very little use for snake stories, but if I left them out you would not get a clear idea of how the pioneers lived and what they had to endure.

Uncle Abner Goes West

My Uncle Abner, who was something more than a year younger than my father, crossed the plains with his family in a covered wagon before gold was discovered in California. It was expected they would have trouble with Indians, but they were molested only twice, and no one was harmed on either occasion.

At that time the plains Indians were armed mostly with bows and arrows and flint-pointed spears, which were a feeble assortment of arms to contend with rifles that would do execution at two hundred yards or more. Yet those Indians would ride up by the side of a buffalo and shoot a flint tipped arrow clean through its body.

The savages of the plains were known as "Horse Indians", because they hunted and fought on horseback; while those with whom the Boone settlers were familiar had but a few horses, and as a rule the warriors did not know how to ride.

Fighting "Horse Indians" and Rattlesnakes

The plains Indians rode tough little ponies and were expert horsemen. But they beat their ponies and rode them to the limit of endurance, and in winter turned them out to graze on the snow-covered prairies or starve, as many of them did. Yet the ponies were gentle, even affectionate, and much devoted to their masters. They were wild descendants of Arabian horses which had been imported by the Spaniards, and as the Arab's horse is almost human we have an explanation of the characteristic of the Indian pony. He was not only hardy and devoted, but very sensible.

In attacking the emigrants it was the custom of the Indians to ride in a wide circle around the wagons, gradually contracting their lines until they came within range of their bows and arrows; meanwhile protecting themselves by lying flat against the bodies of their ponies on the outer side.

As soon as an attack was made, the emigrants would assemble their wagons in a circle, with the women and children in the center, and form a barricade of the heavy vehicles. The men stood close to the wagons and fired under or between them, and being well protected their aim was generally effective. In cases of emergency, which sometimes occurred, the women joined their husbands and brothers and took a hand in the fight; and as they were accustomed to the use of rifles the Indians had good cause to dread them.

An insidious enemy, which could not be excluded from the circle of the wagons, was the venomous little rattlesnakes. It burrowed in the ground as a companion of the prairie dog, never revealing its presence until ready to strike then injecting its poison into whatever object happened to be in the way. During a battle with Indians it was the duty of the women to look after the snakes on the inside, while the men attended to the circling and yelling savages in the open prairie.

There were one hundred and forty wagons in the train to which my uncle's family was attached, and as they had an average of two fighting men to each wagon it constituted a formidable force.

I have before me an old letter in which Uncle Abner gives a picturesque account of the trip across the plains, and as experiences of that kind are now ancient history I am sure it will interest you to know how our forefathers traveled and fought and conquered.

The train was made up in Jackson County, near the present site of Kansas City, before there was a cabin or hovel in that place. In fact no one imagined a city would ever built there, owing to what was supposed to be insurmountable hills and rocks. It was not even a steamboat landing at that time, but merely a wide space in the landscape.

The emigrants remained in camp for several weeks, waiting for the assemblage of the designated number of wagons; for the government would not allow them to depart until they were strong enough to ensure safety.

Their first encampment after starting was "on the bank of the Kaw River", as Uncle Ab writes, but he does not give the location. It could not have been more than a few miles from the heart of modern Kansas City. Here they turned their oxen out on the prairie to graze, and just before daylight they were aroused by the yells of Indians and the bellowing of the frightened cattle as they were being stampeded. Instantly the men were armed and on horseback, and in hot pursuit. As the oxen had opportunity they dropped out of the herd and came running back to the camp, bellowing with fright. In this way, even before the savages were overtaken, most of the cattle had returned. The blooded Kentucky and Missouri horses had no difficulty in overtaking the little short legged Indian ponies, and as they came upon them their riders fled in every direction to avoid the deadly rifles of their pursuers.

A Plumed Warrior

All the cattle were recovered, and only one of the Indians showed any disposition to fight. This was a tall warrior, decorated with feathers and plumes, who turned his pony and made directly for my uncle, who was mounted on a noted gelding that could have easily circled the pony without danger to himself or rider. Uncle Ab halted his horse as his movement would not interfere with his aim, and shot the tallest feather out of the chief's war-bonnet; whereupon he wheeled his pony and yelling as if old Harry were after him. That bold chief was never known to attack another pale face.

The other warriors who were already in the race, joined their chief and the whole cavalcade disappeared behind the cover of a ridge. With one exception this was the only "battle" they had during the entire journey.

The second adventure occurred while they were encamped on the Big Blue, where a party of Indians stole seven "horse creatures" while they were grazing, among the number Uncle Ab's favorite gelding. All the other horses were recovered, but there was nothing on the plains at the time that could equal the speed of his splendid animal, and the lucky Indian who captured him made good his escape. In his letter my uncle laments the loss of his beloved saddle horse, but consoles himself with the belief that Providence will look after and care for the beast.

Death of Aunt Mary

When the train reached the North Fork of Platte River Aunt Mary was taken ill of severe cold and never recovered from its effects, though she lived until they came within nine miles of the South

Pass of the Rocky Mountains, where she died and was buried in a lonely grave by the side of the trail. Concerning this pathetic incident my uncle writes:

"Her name was cut in a stone and planted at the head of the grave, at which time we held singing and prayers over the grave. She told me a short time before she died that she was willing to die, and she gave me her two little boys, Jonathan Marion and Thomas Jefferson, and that she was going to heaven."

Good Little Boys with Large Names

Aunt Mary was a widow when she and Uncle Ab were married, and had two sons by her former marriage. It seems the boys were all "little fellows", for he proceeds in his letter:

"My five little boys, Henry Clay, George Washington, John Madison, Jonathan Marion, and Thomas Jefferson, are still living, fine, hearty, stout boys, and have been called good boys."

I have not the least doubt that they were "good boys", considering the names with which they had been decorated. Years afterward, when one of them, Thomas Jefferson by name, visited us he had never heard the sound of thunder or seen a flash of lightning. One morning while he was reading the paper, a storm arose and he wanted to know, with some irritation, "what was making all that noise out there?" On being informed that it was God's way of doing things in Missouri, he seated himself on the porch and watched the storm until it was over, when he announced his intention to return to California, where God was not so boisterous in carrying on his works. He said he did not mind an earthquake now and then, but thunder and lightning rattled is nerves. Tom was a fine fellow, and we all loved him; but he returned to California by the next train and never came East again. One Missouri thunderstorm was enough for him.

Plenty of Food

Rumor came back while Uncle Ab's party was crossing the plains, that they had run out of provisions, and that Aunt Mary's death was caused by lack of nourishment. But Uncle Ab denied the rumor with vehemence, and in the same letter enumerates the supplies of food they had on hand at the time:

"We had bacon, flour, hams, dried punkins, rice, buffalo meat, sugar, coffee, tea, lard, corn meal, butter and milk a-plenty. We had milk all the way to California."

Their supplies of milk and butter were maintained by attaching cows to some of the wagons, or driving them in a separate herd; and it would seem there was no danger of starvation with such a store of provisions as they had on hand. The journey was more like a picnic than a trail of hunger.

Not too long after his arrival in California Uncle Ab was married again to another widow with two children, and a large family grew up around them. There never was any discord among "her children", "his children", and "our children", but they all lived in harmony and were very happy.

Uncle Ab was effusively religious, as were many others of Uncle Daniel's neighbors; and in his letters he mentions the results of several camp meetings in California, conducted by the Baptists and Cumberland Presbyterians. I do not know which denomination he belonged to, but think it was the latter; and as father was a Methodist he seems to have had some anxiety about the state of his brotherly soul, as expressed in these fervid terms:

"Dear Brother Elijah and Sister Lydia Ann: I am told you are an exorder; if you are not you ought to be; you ought to do all you can to bring sinners to a sense of feeling of the situation they are in. He that believeth not is already damned; repent and believe and you shall be saved."

Uncle Ab sometimes missed fire in his spelling, but there was no false ring in his orthodoxy.

Uncle Ab Buys a Ship

He was present at Suter's Mill when gold was discovered there, but was not carried away by the excitement, as many others were. Instead of getting a pick and pan and going in search of the fascinating yellow metal, he bought a few hens and went to raising eggs, which he sold to the miners at a dollar a piece; and as his flocks increased and the flcod of population poured in, he was soon amazed to find himself a millionaire. Then a sharper induced him to put his money into a ship to sail around Cape Horn and bring passengers from the States. The ship sailed in due form, with a large part of Uncle Ab's fortune in it; but never came back. As there was no telegraph then, and it took a year to get a reply to letters, he had no means of tracing the errant vessel. It was reported that the captain landed his passengers in San Francisco without the formality of notifying his patron, and in this way transferred my uncle's fortune to himself. Others claimed that the ship was wrecked on its first voyage, and that the captain departed for the place which had been prepared for him. However it may be, Uncle Ab never saw or heard of his ship which had sailed in the night.

Wonderful Products of California

While Uncle Ab was not a success as a ship-owner, he understood the business of farming and raising hens. When the gold excitement began to subside he bought a farm in Santa Clara County, and made a second fortune before he died; for agriculture paid then.

Uncle Jim was younger than the other two brothers, and one of the finest story-tellers I ever knew. After "Ab" had bought a farm in California Jim paid him a visit, and some of the yarns he told after returning to Missouri would have made Baron Munchausen blush. As I am about to repeat some of these stories I wish to give warning in advance that no reader is under the slightest obligation to believe them; although in a certain sense they do throw considerable light on some of the wonders of the Golden State.

Uncle Jim was greatly pleased with his brother's farm in Santa Clara County. He said it would produce a hundred and fifty bushels of wheat to the acre every season, and Ab sold the wheat for $2.00 a bushel; yet you could buy all the land you wanted in the same locality for five and ten dollars an acre. When father asked him why he didn't buy an acre and settle down he replied that he didn't have the five dollars. Moreover, he preferred Missouri, where the thunder stirred his blood and you were not shaken out of bed every-other night by an earthquake. He said he was fond of thunderstorms, but had no use for earthquakes.

Uncle Jim's Potato Story

In addition to raising a hundred and fifty bushels of wheat to the acre on his California farm, Uncle Jim said Ab's potatoes were so large that he had to drag them into the kitchen fire with a little Mexican donkey and roast one end at a time. While the second end was roasting the family ate the first one, and in this way all had potatoes enough to keep them in fine condition. One potato would last the family a week, and the labor of pulling them into the fire gave the donkey so little exercise that he would get skittish occasionally and ran away and wrecked a whole tuber. Father said that didn't sound reasonable, because a raw potato is tough and hard to wreck. "Yes," assented Uncle Jim, "that applies to the kind they raise in Missouri, but they don't raise that kind in Californy. In Californy potatoes are so mealy that the farmers have to sack them while they grow to keep 'em from scatterin' over the ground."

Waxey Maple Sugar

Uncle Jim was fond of maple sugar, and he said he didn't see a single maple tree in Californy. That was one reason why he came back. Which reminds me of a joke he played on Preacher Welch, who was a close friend of Uncle Daniel Boone and officiated at the latter's funeral. Like many other pioneers, Welch had a growing family. So he depended a good deal on contributions "in kind" and it was his custom at sugar-making time to leave his saddle bags at Uncle Jim's camp to be filled. Eventually Uncle Jim got tired of the arrangement, and one day he poured the saddle bags full of a waxy syrup, which became as hard as rock candy when it cooled. There was no way to get it out except to gnaw and lick it, and Uncle Jim said Welch's children wore all the hair off their heads licking the wax out of the saddle bags.

Uncle Jim was one of the finest men I ever knew, and also one of the most expert liars. That is to say, he did not lie with malice aforethought, but he told stories for the amusement of the public, that had no foundation except his own imagination. At the age of ninety-one he lost his mind, got religion, quit lying, and is now numbered with the saints.

Uncle Jim Founds a City

He founded and surveyed the town of Nevada, in Vernon County, laying out the blocks twice the usual size in order to play a perpetual joke on the citizens who have to walk them. He also built the first courthouse in the place, burning the bricks on the ground and laying them with his own hands. The house stood for many years, until the growth of population required a larger building for the safety of the county records. There are several old-style brick residences still standing in Nevada that Uncle Jim built, all of precisely the same style of architecture; for he had only one plan. When you see one of Uncle Jim's houses you do not need to ask who was the architect, for they resemble no other houses in the world; all are exactly alike, even to the number and color of the bricks.

When he removed his family to southwest Missouri that whole region was a wilderness, inhabited only by wandering savages, buffaloes and rattlesnakes; and he said he chose the location instead of returning to California because he wanted to find a place where he could build a country to suit himself.

Providence and the Southwest

On his first visit back home I heard him tell father some of the things Providence had done for the new country. As a foundation it had the finest soil that the lord knew how to make, and just under the top dressing there was a bed of the best coal in the world. All that was necessary to do on a cold morning was to take a bucket to the back-yard and fill it with coal and kindle a fire; which was literally true in his own case for there was an outcrop of coal in his yard. When you needed meat you went to the front door and shot a fat buck, or if you preferred a bear steak, the animal was there ready for the sacrifice. In case you wanted something more delicate for Sunday or Christmas, you could take in a brace of prairie chickens, which were as tame as domestic hens. As for eggs, they had them in abundance, without trouble of expense. The prairie hens laid them fresh every morning on the front door-steps.

If you dropped a watermelon seed anywhere it would take root and grow, and next summer you would have several acres of melon, the smallest of them weighing more than a hundred pounds. The large ones had to be cut into sections and dragged to the house with a jackass.

The Chief and His Watermelon

He mentioned an old Indian of whom he had become very fond, who claimed to be 106 years old. The chief borrowed a melon seed of him and planted it, and when the melons got ripe they were so large that the chief had to tomahawk a tunnel to the meat. Then he got lost and couldn't find his way out, and when winter came he froze to death in the center of a melon. The only way they could bury him was to dig a hole in the ground and roll the melon into it; and the next summer that whole region was covered with water melons six feet deep.

Uncle Jim said the bees in the southwest were a perfect nuisance. They made so much honey that it saturated the surface of the ground and gummed up the plows at corn-planting time. One day he left his hat in the barn while he went to the house for luncheon, and when he returned to work the hat was full of the finest comb-honey he ever tasted. As it was the only hat he had, he was obliged to go bareheaded until the family ate the honey.

He told such marvelous stories about the southwest and its products and free land, that several of Uncle Daniel's neighbors moved their families to that section, and when the Civil War commenced it was fairly well populated. The contending armies marched and fought over the country, sometimes one and again the other being in control; but Uncle Jim maintained friendly relations with both sides. When the Union boys came he was extra loyal, and when they were followed by the boys from the south he pulled the wool over their eyes to such an extent that they declared he was the jolliest old rebel outside of Dixie. His eldest son was an officer in the Confederate army, and the other wanted to go; but that did not affect Uncle Jim's politics. He was a wonder!

Brother Jim Has a Call to Preach

Beside my Uncle Jim I had a brother of the same name, though different in character. I do not suppose brother Jim ever told a lie in his life and if he is not in the place that good people go to it is a waste of time for anybody else to try.

Brother Jim was converted at the great revival in Marthasville, and received a call to preach. He was then a youth of eighteen, and I a very bad boy of eight. By reason of his superior age and higher moral state he assumed the right to chastise me when he thought I needed it, which I regret to say was almost every day in the week except Sunday, when I was on my good behavior. The fact is that in his efforts to train me up in the way I should go brother Jim stunted my growth. I was planned for a six-foot man, but was never able to attain the extra six inches.

Soon after his call to preach Jim made known the fact to father, who had suspected something of the kind from outward manifestations. He had just bought a farm in "the bottoms", two miles from home, and if Jim went to preaching it would leave him without adequate help; for brother John and I were boys of only eight and ten and not much account on a farm or anywhere else. Father himself was lame and could do nothing more than overlook the farm and direct the boys what to do; and Wilse was riding around the country with Dr. Paulk exhibiting himself as the greatest hero of the Boone settlements. It was a dismal outlook for the cultivation of a farm of more than a hundred acres, with fences in bad condition and sprouts and briars growing wherever they listed.

The time was at hand for spring plowing and corn-planting, and brother John told me he believed this had something to do with Jim's call to preach. But he was careful not to say it publicly where Jim might overhear, for he also thrashed John when he thought he needed it.

The situation was tense with possibilities, with Jim preaching at one end and starvation looking around the corner at the other. But Jim said he was bound to preach, no matter what happened, because the Lord was constantly ringing in his ear, "Go, preach my gospel, or I will hold you responsible for the soul that may be lost."

It did not occur to father that the Lord could save the souls without Jim's help as well as with it; so he took Jim's word for it and told him he supposed he might as well go. Father was a philosopher, and always submitted to what he knew was going to happen anyway. So he said to Jim, "Go my son, and preach, and save those sinners. I would rather give up the farm than be the cause of any one going to the place where there is weeping and wailing and gnashing of teeth."

He also said he would rather see Jim a Methodist preacher than President of the United States. I was present and heard the conversation, and soon afterward repeated it to brother John. The effect on John and his remarks in that connection will be related further along, space being inadequate in a single Episode.

Brother Jim Prepares for the Ministry

When I told brother John what father had said about preferring to see Jim a Methodist preacher rather than President, he said there might be some doubt in the premises. If Jim had a call to be president he thought father would mortgage the farm to raise the necessary campaign fund, but as he had heard no talk about mortgage because he was going to be a preacher, he imagined there must be some difference in the propositions.

It was a habit of John to make wise cracks of that kind, and I think now that if he had received a call to be president instead of a first-class doctor he would have done honor to the place. Any way, father knew he couldn't change the plans of the Almighty, so he decided to let things take their natural course. Jim promised to work on the farm until corn was planted, when he said he would be obliged to go about the Lord's business; but before that time arrived an incident occurred which came near wrecking the machinery, and John was responsible for it. However, there are several other things to be mentioned first.

As soon as it was decided that Jim was to preach instead of being President, he went about preparing for his new occupation. This consisted in acquiring a ministerial cast of countenance and a voice with the proper twang to it; also in modifying his feelings with regard to mirth and some other sinful habits which he had acquired. He might smile, because that was an outward expression of his inner state; but he must not laugh or be hilarious. How could he be merry with souls trembling on the verge of the tropics? He must also abandon the old swimming hole and bathe in a tin cup, for it was deplorable to go splashing around in a pool of water with no clothes on your sinful person.

As an evidence of the change which had taken place in Jim's moral nature; one day when a broken root flew back and barked his shin while he was plowing, instead of swearing, as he would have done in his former condition, he nursed the smarting member in his hands and called loudly on the name of the second member of the Trinity. He also whipped old Phebe, the leading plow animal, because if she had not pulled so hard the root would have been less flexible, therefore old Phebe needed punishment. Altogether Jim was having a melancholy time getting himself fitted into the proper niche.

An Incident of Vital Importance

And now came the incident which almost wrecked Jim's preparatory work, in which John was the moving spirit and I received my just need of discipline. We three were planting corn in the bottom field, Jim laying off the rows with a plow, I dropping the grains in the checks, and John covering them with a hoe. When Jim made the turn at the end of the rows it gave me a fraction of a minute to sit down and rest, and meanwhile John brought his part of the work up to time. I don't know how or why it happened, but in one of those turns I got mad and sulked, and refused to follow Jim when he started out with a fresh row. He had advanced about fifty feet, when he stopped and ordered me to drop the corn. I declined and pouted. Then he got a limber switch and corrected me, and I howled until Rover, the dog, caught the infection and howled too. We were indeed having a howling time. But eventually I reconsidered, and remembering the injunction about valor and prudence, proceeded with the dropping of the corn.

As soon as John got the chance he asked me how I liked the licking, and if it was any better than it used to be in the old days of sinfulness. I told him I couldn't tell the difference, and if he didn't keep still I would lick him and let him judge for himself. But we managed not to come to blows before luncheon, by which time my feelings were considerably modified and peace prevailed in the community.

We retired to the barn, and having fed old Phebe, ate our basket dinner and we were about to take a nap; when something else happened. Phebe had a colt just old enough to begin to feel that he might some day be a horse, and John took it into his head to play a trick on the colt. So he buckled a saddle on its back, then got a stick about a foot long and put it cross-wise under Phebe's tail. She clamped her tail down on the stick and began to ramp around the lot, kicking and squealing in a very remarkable manner. Every time she kicked she squealed, until John said he couldn't tell whether she was kicking at the squeals or squealing at the kicks. The colt, observing the evolutions of his dam, entered upon a round of kicks and squeals on his own account, until the saddle turned under his belly, when he demonstrated a regular tornado of excitement. Finally he kicked the saddle loose, and Phebe, having kicked the stick from under her tail, peace and order were restored.

The colt thereupon proceeded to get his natural consolation and nourishment, Phebe munched her hay and fodder as if nothing extraordinary had occurred, while I resumed my usual angelic state of mind. At the beginning of the proceedings Jim smiled in a reverend sort of way, but as they progressed he realized the comicality of the situation and laughed as any other person born in iniquity would have done. It required several days for him to restore his features to their proper ministerial setting, and I am sure that the memory of the occasion never quite departed out of his mind.

John was the only member of the assembly who was not seriously disturbed. He said he had no idea that a little thing like that would cause so much excitement; but he would do it again if the opportunity came his way.

John Saves Me from a Merited Flogging

Brother John's superior talents began to develop early in life, and I shall never forget the time when he made a display of them in my behalf. Our nearest neighbor was a German named Ulfries– peace to his ashes–who had a son Adolph about the same age as brother John. Adolph had received from his father as a Christmas present a small, single-barreled, pot-metal shotgun, and we were expressly forbidden to handle the thing or go near it, because it was regarded as unsafe and riotous. Especially were we forbidden to visit Adolph on Sunday, when it was his custom to shoot birds in the orchard with his wicked gun. But there was a screen of woodland lying between the Ulfries place and ours, and one Sunday John and I went into this woods to look for flowers. We wandered on until we were out of sight from our side, and came in view of Adolph shooting birds in the apple orchard. Of course we had no intention of visiting Adolph when we entered the woods but the sound of his gun led us astray. We were soon with him and as happy as truants usually are.

Adolph shot and killed a sparrow, and John shot at another sparrow and missed it. Thereupon I displayed my skill by bringing down a redheaded woodpecker. Never in my life have I felt more important than I did at that particular moment. If I had shot a lion I could not have been more puffed up. Other people might shoot sparrows, but it required genius to bring down a red-headed woodpecker. So I strutted and swaggered.

We Visit the Swimming Hole on the Sabbath

I was so much pleased with myself that on our way home I asked John how he would like to take a plunge in the swimming hole, and he being agreeable, we wended our way thither. Now the swimming hole was the last place that we were permitted to think of on Sunday, and I was duly punished for my indiscretion. As we were coming out my nose began to bleed, and several drops fell on my shirt. I was afraid to go home with these marks of disobedience plainly in view, but John said if I would keep still and trust him he would pull me through. He had me in charge and would be the spokesman, and I had confidence in him and felt relieved.

The first thing mother asked was how we got our hair so wet, and John replied that the weather was warm and we sweated a great deal, although it was a pleasant day in June. Then mother observed the spots of blood on my shirt, and inquired about them. John relieved the delicate situation by explaining that my nose got to bleeding while we were picking flowers in the woods, and the wind blew the drops on my shirt. But mother called his attention to the fact that there were drops on the back of the shirt too whereupon John displayed his remarkable genius in a very wonderful manner. He said the wind was blowing both ways at the same time—a sort of whirlwind. Mother knew there were occasionally such disturbance of the air at that time of year, and she let us off. But I still believe that her leniency was due to her admiration for the genius of her son John. We certainly needed a switching, and ought to have had it.

Sinking of the Kate Swinney

The following incident is not connected with anything that has gone before, or that may follow after, but it fits the space and is therefore available. Our bottom farm fronted on the Missouri River and extended back a mile, and it was a common thing for us to run this distance two or three times a day to see the steamboats go by. It was good exercise and built up our physical corporation for the long years that were to come.

Opposite the farm and across the river was a large island covered with tall cottonwood trees, and beyond the island there was a chute or short-cut with a rapid channel through which boats sometimes passed. When they took that channel the trees and undergrowth hid them from our view, and we felt that we had been deprived of a natural right. The chute had a dangerous reef near the mouth, and John and I prayed hopefully that every boat passing that way would strike the rocks and sink. The old Kate Swinney was one of the chief offenders, for she took the chute every time and we never did have a chance to see what kind of craft she was. But we understood that she was an old hulk, and I cannot measure the depth of hatred that we acquired for her. The fact of the matter is, that in her halcyon days the Kate Swinney had been one of the finest boats on the river, but in our time she was getting old and shabby-looking, and we thought she deserved sinking on general principles.

So one day she struck the reef and got what was coming to her. The wreck was so complete that there was nothing left worth salvaging. In this catastrophe John very clearly saw the hand of Providence. He pointed out that if the old boat had come on our side of the island, where we could see her go by she would not have struck the rocks and might have been afloat even unto this day.

However, she was so old and ugly that she deserved sinking, and Providence acted accordingly. It was a clear case of the manifestation of the wisdom of the Lord.

Episode Number Forty-Six

Adaline Bryan and Her Pet Pig

Adaline Bryan was the prettiest girl in the Boone neighborhood, and as full of mischief as her pretty skin would hold. Somehow or other she came into possession of a cute little snow-white pig, which she brought up by hand. The pig loved Adaline as much as the lamb loved Mary, and everywhere that Adaline went the pig was sure to go. He would trot along by her side and squeal and grunt for something to eat, for no matter how much he was fed he was always hungry. It is the nature of pigs to be that way.

One day Adaline was rummaging around in her grandmother's trunk in the attic, and found an old-fashioned "poke" bonnet. It was not the kind that pretty girls wear now, but such a bonnet as our great-grandmothers wore when they were crazy. It flared outward and upward in front and was emblazoned with ribbons and streamers until it looked like a garden of hollyhocks in bloom.

The next Sunday morning Adaline put on her grandmother's bonnet, and calling her pig sallied forth to Sunday school. Over in the woods across the creek stood a little cabin which had been furbished up for a house of that kind, and on Sundays the young people came there to make love and study the scriptures. All the pretty girls were there, and the boys came to see how pretty the girls were.

On this occasion Adaline and her pig and bonnet attracted more attention than Mathew, Mark, Luke and John, with the result that school had to be dismissed without prayers. Whereupon all the girls and boys went into the woods to gather flowers and laugh at the antics of Adaline's pig.

The circuit rider was so humiliated that on the next meeting day he preached a sermon on the frivolities of worldliness, warning the young people that if they disturbed religious exercises with unseemly displays of ribbons and animals out of which the devils had not yet been cast, they might expect nothing better than a very hot climate in the world to come, with water to cool their parched tongues. The sermon was an effort in behalf of beautiful but wicked Adaline, and she so understood it; but none of her friends observed any change in her demeanor; and her pet pig ever had any devils cast out of him I was not present to witness the operation. He lived a year or two longer, in the full pulchritude of pigdom, and was then made into sausages and eaten with thankfulness.

Brother Jim Gets a Ducking in his Sunday Clothes

I might have forgotten the story about Adaline and her pig except for an accident that happened to brother Jim the same day. It was sometime before he had received the call to preach, while he was still in the bonds of sin and iniquity; but he knew that Adaline was to be at Sunday school, and made up his mind to go over and see her.

Having dressed himself in his best, he invited the junior members of the family—John, Robert, and I—down to the creek to see him cross. There was no skiff or canoe, not even a raft, but Jim was going to perform the trick on a floating log, which he had hitched to the bank for the purpose. This explains why he wanted an audience.

The spectators having arrived and been seated, Jim mounted his log with a flourish and pushed out into the middle of the creek. There he lost his balance, the log turned over, and Jim went head-first into water six feet deep. The exhibition was perfect; it could not have been better after when he swam ashore puffing and blowing, and crawled out of the muddy bank. The glory of his Sunday clothes had departed and his features were drooping; but none of us dared to laugh, because we knew he would whip us if we did.

Jim sloshed home and put on dry clothes, but he was too late for the frolics at Sunday school and was not included in the reprimand two weeks later.

Lightning Strikes a Skeleton

Although my brother Jim had a habit of thrashing me whenever he felt that I needed it—which was quite frequently, and in my more mature years I became convinced that in this respect his judgement was rarely at fault. I am sure he had a genuine affection for me. Being ten years my senior he probably combined the tender love of an older brother with the thoughtful care of a father. At any rate he was resolved that I should walk in the path of the religious as long as the switches held out. It was a difficult task, considering I was a thorn in his flesh.

Jim nearly always took me with him when he went into the woods to get a "mess" of squirrels, my duty being to pick up the game as it fell out of the trees and tie it into a string with a sliver of pawpaw bark. He was a good shot, and the string often became as heavy as my infantile strength could manage; but the pride of being a hunter so early in life nerved me to the task, and I would have carried the game if it had weighed a ton.

One hot day in August Jim took me with him to the post office in Marthasville, to get the Weekly Christian Advocate and inquire if the annual letter from Uncle Ab had come. For some reason not immediately obvious he did not stop at the post office, but trudged on a quarter of a mile further to the verge of a high bluff, overlooking the river a mile away. Now I understood that he had come to this place for the purpose of giving himself and me the pleasure of seeing a steamboat go by, and I was duly and properly grateful. But no boats were due that day and none passed. We waited half an hour in anxious expectation of hearing the melancholy sound of a steam-whistle, when suddenly the sky was overcast by dark clouds; and almost before we knew what was about to take place one of those hot, blasting thunder storms of August was upon us. Jim gathered me in his arms and ran to an unoccupied house, which had been roofed in but not finished, and there we obtained shelter from the pouring rain.

The building belonged to the estate of the late Dr. Briscoe, who had died several years previously; and as usual on such occasions the local carpenter had constructed a wooden coffin for him. But it proved to be small, and another had to be provided, the extra one being stored on the joists in the vacant house. Jim and I observed it in trembling arms as the storm hissed and roared on the outside, and wondered if anything would happen.

Presently a sheet of lightening came through the roof, sizzling and snapping with a bluish-green hue, accompanied by a simultaneous crash of thunder that seemed destined to rend each particular log in the house; and out of the coffin protruded a grinning skeleton! The electric current had struck the coffin, splitting it open and revealing its horrid contents.

Again Jim gathered me in his arms, and rushing out into the black storm and pouring rain carried me to the post office, where he told the story of the fearful incident at the old house. By the time the storm had passed the whole village had heard the amazing revelation, and the population gathered to see for themselves. The shattered coffin, the grinning skeleton, and the hole in the roof through the bolt had come were sufficient to confirm all that Jim had said. The sensation was tremendous; nothing like it had ever been known in Marthasville before.

The mystery was soon explained. Dr. Briscoe, like most of the country doctors of the period, had a human skeleton which he kept in a closet at home, but after his death, his widow not caring for that sort of furniture had it carried to the old building and deposited in the empty coffin, where it remained until it was so miraculously revealed to Jim and me.

The Briscoes

The Briscoes were Virginians of the first order of First Families, and came west under the magic influence of the name of Uncle Daniel Boone. They were to be members of his great Palatinate which he hoped to establish in the wilderness, in imitation of those on the Hudson and in North Carolina. Dr. Briscoe stood at the head of his profession in his day, and his accomplished family would lend polish and charm to the society of the Palatinates.

It was a custom then for every prominent country doctor to hang a skeleton in some convenient closet about the house, not because it was of any service, but it gave standing to the doctor and helped to frighten pilferers away from the room where it hung. It was evidence that the owner was a surgeon of the first water, and the inhabitants supposed that any man who understood the form and construction of their bones ought to be able to cure their ills. In the estimation of the pioneers Dr. Briscoe stood next to Dr. Paulk as a life-saver. While it was true that nothing had been invented which could compare with "Paulk's Pink Purgative Pills" in chasing ills out of the suffering neighbors of Uncle Daniel, it was admitted by all that Briscoe's blue-mass pellets stood next to them in power and efficacy; therefore when a pink pill could not be had a blue-mass pellet was substituted, and the pioneer felt that a crisis had been averted.

The chief value of the skeleton in the closet was the protection it afforded valuables stored in that room. No body with a pilfering mind was bold enough to venture there alone, either in the gloom of night or the bright light of day; so that the lady of the house could deposit her silks and jewels in the room of the skeleton with perfect confidence that she would not lose them. It was the safest place in the house. But although lady Briscoe understood and appreciated the convenience of such an arrangement, she was inoculated with some of the superstitions of her servants, and as soon as the doctor "passed on" she and the skeleton parted.

The old unfinished house was a relic of a custom still prevailing in some parts of Virginia. The traveler who passes through the "Northern Neck" will be surprised at the number of builders of that description standing on the farms and along the roadsides. It would seem that about every tenth planter had started to build a house, and after raising the walls and putting on a roof had changed his mind and left the building to the ravages of decay or the fierce assaults of some rambling cyclone. Why such a peculiar custom should prevail no one can tell, but it is there to speak for itself, and it follows Virginians wherever they go.

It was a custom of lady Briscoe to attend all the camp-meetings within her reach, and to make the journey to and from them in a style befitting her station. Clothed in silks and ribbons, she sat in the midst of her old fashioned Virginia wagon-bed which swayed down in the middle and reared up at each end, was painted red on the outside and was devoid of ornament inwardly. Seated on the flat place at the rear end of the tongue, where it joins up with the "hounds", sat "Old Dick", her trusted servant of all work, a sharp stick in his hands with which he prodded the oxen at intervals between dozings, and drove them along the well-known road to the destination. At the end of the journey Madame B. descended in state and made her way to the arbor where the services were held, while Dick went fast asleep and the oxen lay down and contentedly chewed their cuds. No provision was made concerning the souls of Dick and the oxen, because it was not supposed they had any worth bothering about.

My First Funeral

It was about this time that I attended my first funeral and became acquainted with some of the mysteries of death. The German Methodist preacher in Marthasville had lost his wife, and father took me with him to observe the funeral exercises and show our respect for the bereaved. A coffin had been constructed out of black walnut boards, which have a peculiar odor, and over the boards the carpenter had plastered a thick coat of varnish. The combination produced a smell that was penetrating and peculiar, and somehow I got the idea that all dead people smell that way. I wondered if it was really so, and would I smell like the preacher's wife when I was dead. It is curious what singular ideas sometimes enter into the mind of a child.

There was a little boy in the family about my size and age, and he wept over the loss of his mother. I also wept in sympathy with him. When the services were over the coffin was loaded into a farm wagon and driven down a hill and across a valley and up another hill to the graveyard. The little boy walked close behind the tail of the wagon all the way, I by his side holding his hand; and we both wept as if our hearts would break. But all the time I wondered why his mother smelled as she did, and to this day I have not been able to disabuse my mind of the belief that it is the proper way for a corpse to smell. I thought it might be due to the fact that she was a German lady, but when I asked father about it on the way home he said German ladies didn't smell any different from those born in America.

At the grave, after the coffin had been lowered, the little boy and I stood on one side holding each other's hands and weeping. We must have been a pathetic couple.

But the little boy did not remain long in mourning. At the end of two weeks his father got a new wife, and she became as truly fond of the little orphan as though he had been her own.

Freezing God's Water in Summertime

I remember very well when the first ice-house was built in the Boone settlements, and the manner in which it came about. Nearly every family that had no springhouse, as my grandfather had, substituted in its place a cellar-pit in the yard, roofed over with puncheons and covered with earth. This made a cool place in which to store food and keep the milk and butter sweet and good; and it was also a safe retreat in case of storms. Cellar-pits were the forerunners of cyclone cellars and ice-houses.

Hayden Boone was the first man in the community to transform a cellar-pit into an ice-house; and people traveled many miles to view the wonder and see how ice-water tasted. Most of them thought it was too cold to be healthy, and some suggested that, to their way of thinking it would be more in accord with the scriptures to let nature take its course and drink your water fresh as God made it. If God had wanted us to drink frozen water he would have made it that way in the beginning.

But in spite of all the suggestions to the contrary, Hayden Boone and his family continued to drink their frozen water, even bathing in it and washing their faces with it, until the middle of summer when the real hot weather came, the ice gave out and they were obliged to return to the kind of water that God made, until he froze some more the following winter.

Uncle John Smith Goes Into Action

As soon as the report reached Uncle John Smith that Hayden Boone's folks had ice-water in July, he said that people who did such things were flying in the face of Providence and were no better than infidels. So he rode twenty miles the hottest day in the month to see if such a thing could really be. He drank a quart of the cold water in order to satisfy himself, and set out for home. But he was taken with cramps and died the following day, consoling himself to the last with the thought that he would no longer be required to live in a world where the people had become so wicked as to freeze their drinking water in summertime.

That particular summer was long and hot, with a good deal of moisture, and mosquitoes and miasma flourished to such a degree that many new graves were made before Christmas came. A large part of the illness was laid to Hayden Boone's ice-house, and the idea of "havin' frozen water out'n the course o' natur' and flauntin' it in the face of the almighty" was so unpopular that it was years before any other ice-houses were built in Femme Osage District. Finally, when the Germans began to come, they brought the custom with them, and Uncle Daniel's neighbors concluded that if frozen water wouldn't kill a Dutchman they might as well have it themselves. Now every family in that whole country has ice-water every summer.

Professional Bullies

The pioneers never bothered themselves much about work. Why labor when one could live as well at ease? The men spent the time hunting, trapping, wrestling, racing, jumping, fighting, and too often raising the mischief in general. One of their sports had a practical side to it and was essential in creating good marksmen; I mean shooting matches, which will be considered in their proper place.

Each neighborhood had its "bully", who considered himself the "cock of the walk," and believed he was monarch of all he surveyed. At house-raisings and log-rollings it was the custom of these gentry to pull off their coats, strike an attitude and challenge the community. When they failed by these methods to attract attention, they would strut around and crow like roosters and scratch up the ground with their feet in the fury of their ardor.

Such evolutions were preliminary to the fight which was sure to come, for no "champion" would disregard such a challenge. Each community had its nick-name. Those who lived on Elk Horn Creek were called "Heel Strings", those on Camp Branch "Shake Rags", and those on South Bear Creek "Anaruges." When a gentleman felt disposed to try his mettle with some other gentleman of the profession from any one of these localities, he would "licker up" to the fighting point, claw the earth and crow, and announce in a loud voice that he could lick any of the severally designated nick-names on the ground. Then the fighting would begin, and the champion who crew the loudest and clawed up the most of the ground was generally disposed of by some quiet little fellow who said nothing and fought like a wildcat.

When a champion knocked another down, it was the rule for him to jump on his helpless adversary and bite off the end of his nose, or chew one of his ears, or gouge out one of his eyes. Then swinging the trophy in his hand he would strut, crow, scratch the ground and wonder if any other gentleman would like to try a round with him. No red savage was ever more brutal than one of those self-styled champions, and the custom was carried to such lengths that it was a rare thing for a fighter to live to middle-age without the loss of an eye, while missing ears and trimmed noses were not uncommon. These one-eyed "Jakes" and "Petes" were looked down upon by the decent part of the population as the bullies who had been whipped. No sympathy was wasted on them, because other one-eyed and one-eared men owed their deformities to them. The man who lost a member in a fight became a retired bully, was shorn of his glory and ceased to crow. As a rule they were cowards who never fought except when they believed they had the advantage. When it came to real fighting with the red enemies of the forest, they had business elsewhere, or hid behind the walls of the forts.

Shooting Matches

On the other hand, there was something commendable in shooting-matches, for they demonstrated who were the best marksmen in the community; and these were selected as leaders when it became necessary to trail Indians. The matches also trained men and boys in the art of shooting, and prepared them for defense in the time of need. Girls and women participated in these exercises and learned the use of the rifle so perfectly that it became a deadly weapon in their hands when necessity demanded it.

A wild turkey was generally trapped and used as a mark, the merit being to shoot its head off at a distance of seventy-five to one hundred and fifty yards. This was done without "resting" the gun, in other words, it was "off-hand" shooting. When it became necessary to go after Indians it was a rare thing for the rifleman to have a "rest" for his gun; he must fire off-hand and be quick about it. The same rule held good in hunting the fiercer wild animals. In many instances the first intimation of the presence of a panther or wildcat was the slight noise it made in crouching for the fatal spring. Then with a single movement the gun must be brought into line and fired. There was no time for hesitation! The idea was to practice with the rifle until it would seem like a part of the hunter's anatomy, and come as spontaneously into action as the hand or the arm.

Not many turkeys lived to remember the ordeal through which they were called to pass, but it is comforting to remember that when a turkey lost his head by the amputation of a bullet he was not conscious of the fact. He was more fortunate than the modern chicken that has its neck wrung by the circling gyrations of the cook's hand. The chicken no doubt has a brief moment of intense suffering, but the turkey passed over into the place prepared for him without being aware of the change. It is true that no one with a conscious mind has ever taken the place of a turkey under such circumstances, for the purpose of acquiring knowledge; but reason teaches that the zip of a bullet is too instantaneous to afford time for mental action. Therefore it seems well established that the turkey was justified in congratulating himself that his neck was not wrung when the bullet clipped his head off.

Shooting matches were not merely cruel sport, like some of the games that the pioneers indulged; were a necessary drill in the acquirement of a practice that made perfect.

I hesitated to mention the gouging of eyes and slitting of noses that often took place in encounters among bullies, lest the reader might get the idea the pioneers were cruel and of low order. But such was not the case. The mass of the people had no more sympathy with the ruffian who indulged in such things than the refined and cultivated men and women of the present day would have; but in the great stream of emigration that flowed westward there was necessarily a good deal of drift-wood, which, finding itself free, gathered into a small and restricted place of its own, and was in no sense representative. The bully and the "gouger" were no more respectable than the gambler and the common outlaw, but they had greater freedom of action and did not hesitate to make a show of themselves. They were the commonest kind of common people, and were no more representative of the pioneers than they were of the cultivated and refined sections from whence they came.

Episode Number Forty-Eight

Weddings and Wedding Costumes

In his autobiography Black Hawk throws some very interesting light upon the domestic and religious customs of his people, and by way of comparison it will not be out of the way to mention some incident along the same line among early white settlers beyond the Mississippi. The reader will be surprised to observe how little difference there was between the Indians and ourselves.

I have before me a letter written by a pioneer lady to her friends "back home" in 1810, and its sincerity and detail of description will guarantee its genuineness. It is a picture of things with which the lady was familiar in her every-day life. She writes:

"The <u>men</u> and <u>dogs</u> have a fine time, but the poor women have to suffer. They have to pack water from one-half to one mile, and do all the cooking and washing. So my advice to you is, stay where you are. But if you see any one coming to this part of the country please send me a <u>plank cradle</u> for poor little Patrick. His poor little back is full of hard lumps and skinned all over, lying in nothing but a cradle George made out of one half of a hollow log, with a piece of wood in one end for a pillow. The poor child has a hard time, for he hain't got but two shirts in the world, and both of them is made of nettle bark that almost scratches him to death. Great dents and whelps are all over the poor little creature's back. I don't want to have any more children if the poor little things are to be treated this way. I told George so last night, and what you reckon he said? He said it was the very thing, it would make them tough, and they could stand Bare and Deer hunting. George has got him a buckskin hunting shirt and pants, and he is gone hunting day and night.

We have got some good kind neighbors, and we visit each other when we can. I forgot to tell you of a wedding I and George attended last week. They were married by an old Hard-Shell Baptist preacher by the name of Jabe Ham. He had on a long buckskin overcoat that looked so funny. The man was in his shirt sleeves with white cotton pants that just come below his knees, and white cotton socks and buckskin slippers on his feet. The girl was dressed in a short-wasted, low-necked, short-sleeved white cotton dress that was monstrous short for a tall girl like she was, for I don't recon there was more than five yards of cloth in her dress. She also had on buckskin slippers, and her hair was tied up with buckskin string, which is all the go out here. And when Mr. Ham was spelling and reading the ceremony from the book, the girl commenced sneezing, and the buckskin string slipped off and her hair flew all over her face, and everybody laughed."

The wedding costume as portrayed by the lady was "all the go" in those days. Some years after the date of her letter my mother was married in such a costume, but she had no buckskin string to bind her long silky brown locks. The strings had gone out of style, and her white dress was long and full enough to be modest and becoming.

On the same occasion my father was dressed in a white cotton suit, the pants reaching well down around the tops of his shoes. He had made the shoes himself, one at a time, owing to his habit of never finishing anything he undertook until the first half of it began to get old. The first shoe was finished a month before the wedding, and the other the day before. He came very near going to the wedding with one foot bare, as he did not think of the second shoe until the last moment. Then he went to plowing the next morning and would have forgotten the wedding altogether if a neighbor had not happened along and reminded him. His delinquency was not due to any lack of affection; it was just "his way". He and mother reared a large family, and he made all the children's shoes one at a time, because it was utterly impossible for him to make two at once. I never had a pair of new shoes until I was able to buy them myself, but always wore a new and an old one together.

Camp Meetings

There were no churches in those times, and the cabins of the settlers being too small to accommodate the crowds that came, they resorted to camp meetings. These supplied the need not only of worship but also as places for social gatherings and recreation, and during the camping season everybody went. Each family took a stock of provisions for the common lot, to which was added the game that was killed from day to day, so that no one went hungry.

The open forests afforded a means of escape from the stuffy cabins, and when one camp-meeting had run its course the people gathered up their belongings, got the children and dogs in line, and "trekked" to another. Sometimes in changing base they would walk as far as fifty miles, camping in the woods at night and living the wild life of nomads. The wanderlust was in their blood. The women carried the babies in their arms and walk barefoot to save their shoes, while the men and the older children and the dogs brought up the rear. No member of the family was more important than the family dog. He ranged the woods in quest of game, tantalizing "painters" and wild cats, and stood guard at night. The head of the family marched in the center of the cavalcade, his long rifle on his shoulder and his shoes or moccasins suspended across its shining barrel; for he too marched barefoot as a means of economy. On approaching the place of meeting all stopped and bathed their feet in some running brook or cool spring and made ready for the services. Those who had foot-coverings put them on, while those who had none retained the costumes which nature had given them. There was no distinction in dress or fashion; all stood on the same level and each was as good as the other. No freer or more independent way of living could have been devised.

Similar Ideas Among Whites and Indians About Children

While there was nothing in the religious beliefs or ceremonies of the Indians which compared with the regulated customs of the white people, their ideas of an overruling Providence were very similar. The Indian reverenced his Great Spirit, and the white man his God; but in all essentially they were practically the same. The dances of the Indians were as religious in character as the revivals of the whites, and in most instances lend to demonstrations of a similar nature. The red dancers became unconscious or ecstatic and while in this condition saw visions and heard voices. Their prophets foretold coming events with some degree of accuracy, and in this way gained a large influence over the people; while their medicine men represented the faith-healers that have prevailed in all nations. Both were equally faithful in their devotions. Black Hawk says that after his father was killed in battle he spent five years fasting and praying in his honor before receiving the spiritual baptism that made him also a great chief.

The two races were likewise very much alike in their views about children, both regarding the little ones as valuable assets. But there was much less parental discipline among the Indians than among the whites. Indian boys hardly knew what discipline meant, and the little they had was administered by their mothers until they were old enough to assert their independence. They were taught and trained by word and example to imitate the deeds of their fathers, but in personal restraint they were as free as the animals in the woods. They roamed together in troops, learning the use of the bow and arrow and the habits of the wild animals of which they were soon to become hunters. All their training looked to the future, when they were to be braves and warriors and take the places of their fathers as they passed off the stage. Therefore children were welcome and large families were common.

Among the white pioneers there was no lack of children, and every little newcomer received a cordial welcome. Families of ten or a dozen were not uncommon, and some by special providence acquired fifteen or twenty. At the beginning of the Civil War a man in Callaway County led twenty-one sons into the Confederate army, and he and one of the sons were all that lived to return. Judge Edward Bates, who was Attorney-General in President Lincoln's Cabinet, was the father of seventeen children by one mother. He lived a busy life, but always had time to look after the little folks.

The country was broad and fertile and needed population, and there were no unwelcome children. It cost little or nothing to bring them up to an age where they could care for themselves, and later in life they became the comfort and support of their parents. There was not much work to do, but each did his part, even to the tiniest toddler. At night the family sat or squatted around the great fireplace, shelling corn to be ground into meal, or rolling cotton for the spinning wheel. The little ones were kept awake with promises of supper when the task was done, the supper to consist of buttered corn bread and a cup of milk. But it was wholesome and sweet and the children were as eager to get it as if it had ben cake and tea.

Not many of the pioneers had earthenware vessels, except a few remains of chinaware—pronounced "chaney"—which had survived the accidents of overland travel and were treasured by Grandma as examples of former opulence. They were so precious that no profane hand was allowed to touch them, and none but mother or grandma could cleanse them after use. Plates were made of molded pewter and scoured until they shone like silver. Knives and forks were as rare as they were in the days of Queen Elizabeth, the head of the house utilizing his hunting knife in reducing the meat to particles small enough to serve to the individual members of the family. Drinking cups were made of horn, and "taking a horn" was a well-known custom. If the horn happened to be a little too large the pioneer made the fact known by taking his gun and going after a wild cat, with the remark that he could "whip his weight" of them. If wild cats were scarce he substituted Indians or bears with similar self-confidence. Without "horns" to stiffen their courage the red men and the wild cats were no match for him. Every family had one of more wooden spoons, reserved for "stirring things" and were never put to the plebeian service of conveying soup to the mouth. When they had soup they drank it out of their pewter plates.

The Family Skillet and Piggin

It was not an unusual thing for the family to have a skillet in which their bread was baked. This also was a treasured relic from "back home". I remember our family skillet with emotions that are sacred. It baked the best biscuits that ever came from over the coals, and to them a flavor which could not be otherwise obtained. I remember with reverence a certain Christmas when a young man who had come to visit one of my pretty sisters celebrated the event by shooting fire crackers in the yard. Next morning my sister was baking biscuits in the skillet, and I having picked up the stump of a cracker which had failed to explode, struck the end of it into the coals under the vessel. The biscuits were still in the form of dough and my sister was in the act of covering them with the lid when the cracker went off. I also went off into the yard in a hurry, and the lid slipping out of my sister's hand scattered ashes and burnt the powder over the tops of the raw biscuits. She was badly scared and scolded me roundly, but her good temper returned as I departed, and she laughed at the joke more than I did. I was penalized by being denied a biscuit for breakfast, but sister slipped one to me under her apron; and I went out into the cold, cold world and ate it with much satisfaction, ashes, powder and all.

Every family had a piggin. It was a wooden vessel not quite as large as a wooden bucket, with one of the staves extending several inches above the others for a handle. The uses of the piggin were quite universal. Dishes were washed in it, chickens and other feathered animals were scalded in it before being "picked", little boys and girls used it in place of a bathtub (when they bathed), and when mother and father had colds in their heads they bathed their feet in the piggin before going to bed. It served also as a washtub for small articles like socks, "nose rags," etc. If there was any service the piggin was not subjected to I never found it out.

The Coming of Biscuits

Biscuits were scarce among Uncle Daniel's neighbors, because they raised but little wheat. Corn was their principal output in the way of cereals. It was easier to raise and harvest than any other grain, and had more fattening qualities for stock, and could be utilized for beverage purposes as well as food. Neither were the primitive mills adjusted to grinding wheat; there were no "bolting chists" to bolt the flour. Corn bread was the staff of life, and if you didn't like that kind of food you were at liberty to eat hominy.

Afterward when a little wheat began to be raised and biscuits made their appearance, they were regarded as a sacred delicacy and reserved exclusively for Sunday. Each member of the family was limited to one biscuit. The biscuit also became the "mass" in the sacrament which had previously been administered with corn bread and whiskey, or wine made of the juice of poke-berries. When the change came some prophesied that the last days were at hand.

Those who were never called upon to emerge out of an era of corn bread and fat meat are not in position to appreciate the ecstasy of biscuit and honey on Sunday morning; neither can they fully comprehend the tremendous influence it had on the public mind. A forward step in culture was taken with the coming of the biscuit. It is true we had different kinds of corn bread, such as "pone bread," "ash cake," "corn pudding," "crackling bread," etc., but none of the several varieties had the refining influence of the wheat biscuit.

Threshing Floors

Even when wheat began to be raised, there were no machines to thresh and separate the grain from the straw; a process which had to be performed with flails, the same as they did in Babylon and Egypt before the time of Moses or Homer. Afterward the threshing-floor was substituted, although it was old when Genesis was written. It consisted of a circular place about thirty feet in diameter, beaten hard with mauls and dried by exposure to the sun. On this space the wheat in the straw was thrown, and horses or oxen driven round and round upon it until the grain was trodden out. When horses were employed it was the custom of the boys to ride and make them trot and "cut up"; it amused the boys and it did not hurt the horses. But the oxen were allowed to take their own time, which they did in their usual methodical way, munching the straw as they traveled the circle. " Muzzle not the ox that treadeth out the grain." Thus came the voice of Moses and of the still more ancient Babylonians down to Uncle Daniel and his neighbors. By the time the grain was trodden a considerable part of it had gone into the oxen, who in turn contributed their mead to the product. The output may not have been as clean as could be desired, but the pioneers were a hardy race and could digest almost anything that passed into their stomachs.

A few years later the more enterprising farmers began to build threshing-floors in barns, but at the time we are considering there were no such buildings in existence. Barns were a later evolution. One of the first was built by a man who was supposed to have descended from Croesus, and had wealth to burn. A foundation was excavated in the side of a hill, so that the second floor was on a level with the ground; and there the threshing-floor was constructed. It was made of stout beams and boards, or puncheons, with large auger holes bored through them, by means of which the wheat sifted through and fell on the first floor. This was a long step toward cleanliness, and also saved a good deal of work, and treading of the grain could be done when it was raining.

After the wheat had been separated from the straw it was partly cleaned of chaff by holding it aloft in a bucket and shaking it out in a thin stream, this way the wind would blow some of the chaff and dirt away. If there was no wind a faint breeze was created by flapping a sheet or quilt back and forth in front of the falling grain. What remained in the wheat after this process and went thence into the mill and the biscuits, I am not at liberty to say; but the pioneers made no objection and I can see no reason why we should. The biscuits were sweet and good, and we did not allow our imaginations to work while eating them. Any way, it is said that every one must eat a peck of dirt during his lifetime, and why not eat it early and be done with it?

Coming of the Threshing Machine

At last the threshing machine made its advent. It was a wonderful contrivance that people traveled far and near to see. Barefooted women came with babies in their arms, and wondered if the times that try men's souls were at hand. The first of these machines were of the endless-chain variety. A couple of horses or oxen—sometimes two cows—were confined in a slanting, box-like contraption several feet above the ground, the floor being composed of moving blocks of wood fastened to an endless-chain at each end. When the animals were safely housed in their elevated position, a plug was pulled and their weight carried the machinery forward; if they stopped their legs became entangled in the moving platform, and they soon learned that the only safe way was to watch their step and keep going. A long band connected this part of the machinery with a buzzing cylinder into which the straw was fed and the grain separated. But the chaff remained with the wheat. A later invention in the form of a fanning-mill blew the chaff away and left the grain clear and clean. This was a separate machine operated by hand; and it was years before another genius conceived the idea of combining the fanning-mill with the thresher and letting the animals do the work.

By the cooperation of these two wonderful inventions as much as fifty bushels of wheat could be separated from the straw and chaff in a single day, and those who were possessed of prophetic instinct asserted that the world had but little further to travel before coming to its end. The sacred threshing-floor had been relegated to the background, men were becoming idle and dissolute, and instead of earning their bread by the sweat of their faces were letting animals do it for them. But the world continued to turn round and things got worse instead of better. Men said they would rather hunt bears and wild cats than turn the crank of a wind-mill. Let the cows and the oxen thresh and clean the wheat while they civilized the wilderness. This was the philosophy of the men who had grown tired of eating their bread in the sweat of their faces.

Yet the world continued to make its revolutions as in the days of old. Grain was still harvested with a sickle, as it had been ten thousand years before in the valley of the Euphrates, and the wisest of the prophets did not imagine that anything better ever could be invented. Uncle Daniel Boone cut his first crop of wheat with his hunting knife, and it took him three days to harvest an acre. This was certainly not so good as the sickle, and he was advised to stick to the good old instrument that had come down through the ages. An expert sickler could reap an acre in a day, though most of them were satisfied if they did half as much. So harvest your wheat with a sickle, Uncle Daniel, and keep your hunting-knife for bears and wild cats. Such was the advice of wisdom.

Thus slowly do we progress from one thing to another. As the earth goes round and round so do the affairs of men advance. Recently when I mentioned a sickle to some school boys and girls they did not grasp my meaning until I told them it was the crooked little knife that they used in cutting grass on their lawns. Yet when I was a boy the sickle was our only harvester.

The "Cradle" and the Harvester

Then came the "cradle", another wonderful contrivance. The man who invented it believed that he had reached the utmost limits of labor-saving implements in the harvest field, and that any further effort in that direction would be a waste of energy and brain matter. An expert with the cradle could harvest as much as two acres a day, which made it possible for the farmer to raise ten or even fifteen acres of wheat in a single crop. If production kept on that amazing rate wheat would soon be so plentiful that it would cease to have any value, and instead of eating it in biscuits we would be obliged to feed it to the pigs. We have seen some of the prophecies fulfilled. No family could consume ten acres of wheat in a single year. One crop would last four or five years, and meanwhile idleness would flourish and the world go to the hot blazes. These arguments actually prevailed as harvesting machinery gradually advanced from one good thing to another that was better.

My father opposed the cradle at first because it was not mentioned in the scriptures, and afterward because most of his neighbors adopted it and he did not care to be like other people. He claimed that a man ought to cut as much grain with a sickle as he could with a cradle, if he kept his mind on his work and worshipped God according to the Methodist Catechism. The cradle was also wasteful; it left too much straw and grain on the ground, which produced worthless "cheat" the following season. It was true that the cradle did miss more straw than the sickle, but it doubled the capacity of the harvester and so won its way. Father argued that the cradle might be admissible if the women would go into the fields, as they did in the days of Ruth, and glean the wastage. In that case he would not object to the newfangled invention; but the women had quit doing that way and he did not know what the world was coming to. The women were getting as lazy as the men.

But he found that by turning his hogs into the field after harvest they would do the gleaning as well as Ruth did, and fatten themselves at the same time. Previously it had not been supposed that wheat would add flesh to a pig's corporosity; the fact had to be discovered by experiment. And so at one step after another he was finally won over, and actually bought a cradle for use on his own farm. It lasted until the McCormick reaper made its appearance and slashed the wheat down at the amazing speed of ten acres a day. After that father looked for the deluge.

He was constitutionally opposed to all kind of innovations. When I first became acquainted with him he had but recently discarded knee-breeches and long stockings, because mother declined to make them in that style. But he had his trousers cut with a large flap or "barn door" in front, and he stuck to it until the day of his death. All the other men except Uncle Daniel had their trousers made with an opening straight up in front, and he would have gone without pants rather than imitate other men. But it was different with Uncle Daniel; father did not mind imitating him; so the two were the only men in Femme Osage district who continued to wear their trousers with barn-door flaps..

The Profane Irishman

One of Uncle Daniel's neighbors hired an Irishman to "break up" a piece of new ground. The land being fertile was infested with large numbers of stumps and roots, and the oxen that pulled the plow were but newly broken. In fact they were hardly "broken" at all, and were a source of worry to Pat. First one thing and then another happened. The oxen ran away and broke the chain that drew the plow, and a new link had to be obtained from the shop. Then the plow hung fast to a root and had to be backed out. A nest of yellow jackets was plowed up and made life interesting for Pat—also for the oxen, which ran away again. A root broke in the middle and the loose end flew back and almost broke Pat's shin. While rubbing the wound he danced on the other leg and emitted blasphemy two ways for Sunday. At this critical moment the priest came along.

"Ah, Pat," he said, "if you swear that way you'll go to purgatory."

"Yes, begorry!" retorted Pat, "and so will these dom'd oxen, and that'll be a saving grace fer me."

Pat kept on until the land was broken, then the river took a turn and washed the field away, roots, stumps, and all. After that Pat returned to Ireland. He said he didn't care to live in a country that had to be held together by roots, and fell into the river as soon as the plowing was done.

Beds and House Furniture

Uncle Daniel's neighbors were sparingly provided with chairs, tables, beds and house furniture in general, and these conveniences had to be supplied with similar articles manufactured in the wilderness. Beds were made of rawhide cots fastened to the walls of the cabins with wooden pins, which sometimes pulled loose during the night and let the sleeper down with a thud on the floor. Those of an effeminate nature who wanted something softer than rawhide, provided themselves with bearskin or buffalo robes, which being placed on top of the rawhide foundations made beds almost as comfortable as a modern mattress. But these people being regarded with disfavor, the husky ones spread their rugs on the floor and went to bed.

Large gourds and punkins, as well as stumps and sawed off sections of logs, were utilized as seats. Punkins and gourds were thought to be softer than wood, and they were accordingly reserved for the aged and infirm. There is a record of a pioneer who was too lazy to remove the seeds from his punkin, and the rats ate holes in the rind until it gave way and let him fall through; whereupon the soft interior squashed out over the seat of his pants until his wife had to wash them before he could attend camp-meeting.

Bees Nest in a Punkin-Seat

In another case a swarm of bees made a nest in a pioneer's punkin, and he tamed the little workers until they never would sting the children. There upon they filled the punkin with honey, so that at mealtime he had nothing to do but reach down and dip out the honey enough to spread on his biscuits. The pioneer became so much attached to the arrangement that he dried the punkin to keep it from spoiling, and civilized the bees until they were s tame as house-flies. If the children left any honey on their plates, the bees worked it over for the next day, and by reason of their industry the family always had an abundant supply.

When the population became too dense for comfort, the family moved further west, and the bees went along with them. By this time the old punkin was thoroughly dry and sweet, and the man's wife made it into pies, and so much honey adhered to the punkin that Uncle Daniel said the pies were the sweetest he ever ate. The bees meanwhile were provided with a new punkin, and remained satisfied and docile.

Merit of this kind was sure to have its reward, and when the pioneer died he left an estate of two picayune and three pennies, which being put at interest became the foundation of a celebrated art gallery whose <u>chef-d'oeuvre</u> is a painting of bees making honey in a punkin, with a benevolent-looking pioneer sitting on it in the midst of his family.

Employing a Mule as a Churn

Uncle Daniel's neighbors had plenty of milk, but only a few churns, and they were obliged to adopt substitutes. In place of churns they used large gourds, with a capacity of several gallons. Some of the gourds had crooked necks, and were hung on limbs while the milk soured. If there happened to be a good deal of wind, as in January and March, the shaking of the limbs churned the butter. But the wind could not always be depended upon. Sometimes the family needed butter when there was no wind. In such cases the men had to shake the gourds until the butter came; but it was a laborious process, and the men struck and wouldn't work on account of it. They said they would do without butter all their lives rather than shake a gourd for it.

Then an enterprising pioneer thought out the plan of separating the milk into two gourds, and hanging them in opposite ends of a sack across his mule. Thereupon he would ride around and visit the neighbors, while the trotting of the mule churned the butter. When the butter "came" he would stop at a neighbor's and borrow salt enough to dress it, sharing part of the butter for the loan of the salt.

Uncle 'Ligy Thoroughman and the Indian

This method of churning became so popular that most of the men adopted it; but the credit was in fact due to Uncle 'Ligy Thoroughman. He was of a sociable disposition, and took pleasure in churning while calling on the neighbors. But one day as he was trotting through the woods he was ambushed by an Indian, and lost half his butter and came near losing his scalp also. The warrior fired on him at close quarters, and the bullet made a hole in one of the gourds, so that the milk on that side escaped. This left the other end of the sack loose, and it flopped up and down until all the milk turned to butter and left no buttermilk; which was a great disappointment to Uncle 'Ligy, who liked buttermilk better than butter. Besides, the butter was so hard that he couldn't dress it and was obliged to throw it away; so the day's churning was a failure.

The Buttermilk Treaty

But he had his revenge. A few days later he treed the same Indian in a tall sycamore, which he had climbed to rob a bee's nest. Not liking to kill the savages he ordered him to come down, and made him shake a gourd full of milk till the butter came. The warrior turned out to be a great chief, and was so humiliated by having to do such menial labor, that he promised if his captor would release him he would go home and stop the war, for he said there was no telling how many other warriors might have to shake gourds if it continued. So they entered into a treaty to that effect, and the chief faithfully kept his promise. He declared that he would rather never fight again than shake a gourd for butter. The agreement was known as the "Buttermilk Treaty", and it never was broken; and by reason of its great benefits to the community Uncle 'Ligy became a very noted man. He declared that he would rather be the author of such a treaty than win glory by shooting his fellowmen.

Sketch of Uncle 'Ligy Thoroughman

A brief notice of so distinguished a man will not be out of place. Uncle 'Ligy and Matilda were married while they were young and quite handsome, and he took his bride to a pole-cabin in the woods, on a piece of ground that he had entered from the government. The cabin was about twelve feet square, with ventilation enough between the poles to supply sufficient oxygen for two persons, which obviated the necessity for a sleeping-porch.

'Ligy observed that Matilda was disappointed in the size and general outlines of the house, but he told her it was only temporary; he would soon build a commodious double-log mansion that would be the pride and envy of the community. As there were plenty of trees in sight to build such a house, she felt it would not be long until the mansion arose. Therefore she made no complaint, but went about her household duties with a song in her heart.

The months and years came and went, and the voices of little children were heard in the pole-cabin; but there was no sign of the spacious double-log house. The dimensions of the cabin became strained to accommodate the numerous little ones, but still Matilda made no complaint. It required time of course to plan such a house as 'Ligy had in his mind, and she knew he was planning every day. So time went on, until 'Ligy and Matilda had reared nine children and made good citizens of them; and now they lie side-by-side under a tall linn tree that stood in the yard; but their only mansion is the one that God provided for them.

Uncle 'Ligy Thoroughman was a good man in every respect, and also a useful citizen. He not only invented the process of churning without having to shake a gourd by hand, but he never failed to supply his family with all the butter and buttermilk they could consume; and he said grace regularly before each meal.

Neighbor Groeby's Before Dinner Speech

One day a flock of wild geese flew over the cabin, and at a single shot Uncle 'Ligy brought down three of them. It seemed like a Providential supply of extra meat, coming down from the sky; and he and Matilda resolve in solemn council that it would not be proper to consume it all without the circle of their own family. So they decided to invite neighbor Groeby and his wife Katrinka to dinner.

When the guests came and were sat down to the table, groaning under the weight of three fat wild geese, Groeby said he had never seen anything like it in Germany. The aroma of the meat and the large dish of gravy that stood by it gave the old German a keen appetite, and he could hardly restrain his impatience while awaiting the conclusion of 'Ligy's lengthy grace. When at last it was done, Groeby, wishing to say something that would be appropriate to the occasion, arose and bowing formally to the head of the house, remarked:

"To me your grace of Gott was very goot; but I shall like me better the grease of the goose."

The memory of those three wild geese never passed away from the gallant old German, and by strict economy he lived to acquire a gun and powder and shot, and thereafter he and Katrinka ate goose until they grew wings and sailed away to a better land.

Black Hawk's Account of Religious and Domestic Customs Among His People

So many are unaware of the fact that the Indians were a religious people that some account of their beliefs and ceremonies will no doubt be appreciated. The social and domestic customs that prevailed among them are also highly interesting, and I have therefore compiled a number of items under these heads from Black Hawk's autobiography. It is quite natural of course that the old chief should express his sentiments in the most favorable light for his own people, yet he seems to have striven to fairly represent the truth as he understood it.

Their season for Thanksgiving, he says, comes in the spring, when the warm sun begins to start the young tendrils into life. After corn is planted the people enter upon a round of feasts, which are served publicly for all the tribe. At such times they have an abundance of beans, dried squashes, hominy, and other foods that have been left over from winter, and these being cooked with fish and meat are set before the people with invitations to come and help themselves. The festivals continue until corn is ripe, when another series of feasting begins.

The time is spent meanwhile in visiting one another, and with dancing and games. Some of the more pious offer a daily feast to the Great Spirit, accompanied by ceremonies and forms of worship which the whites would not understand. By this he means the religious mysteries of his people. Every one makes his feast according to the way he thinks will please the Great Spirit, who, being a good spirit, must be approached with a clean heart and good intentions. But they also have an evil spirit, which many of the Indians worship, hoping by their devotions to appease his anger and persuade him not to interfere with the good intentions of the Great Spirit.

Commenting on these matters Black Hawk says, "For my part I am of opinion that so far as we have reason we have a right to use it in determining what is right and wrong, and should pursue that path which we believe to be right, believing that whatever is is right. If the Great Spirit wished us to believe and do as the whites, he could easily change our opinions. . . We have men among us, like the whites, who pretend to know the right path, but will not consent to show it without pay. I have no faith in their paths, but believe that every man makes his own path."

Toward the end of the season, when the corn is beginning to ripen, the young people watch eagerly for the signal to pull roasting ears; but none dare touch them until the proper time. As soon as the corn is fit for use another great ceremony takes place, with feasting and thanks to the Great Spirit who has been so good to them. "We thank the Great Spirit for all the good he has conferred upon us. For myself I never take a drink of water from a spring without being mindful of his good-ness." He further illustrates his sentiments by saying that "even the birds and chickens acknowledge their obligations to the Great Spirit by raising their heads toward the sky when they drink."

Origin of Beans, Corn, and Tobacco

His description of how the Indians obtained corn, beans, and tobacco is so unique that I copy it in his own language:

"A beautiful woman was seen to descend from the clouds and alight upon the earth, by two of our ancestors who had killed a deer and were sitting by a fire roasting parts of it to eat. They were astonished at seeing her, and concluded that she must have smelled the meat and was hungry. So they immediately went to her, taking a piece of the roasted venison with them, which on presenting it to her she ate. Then in gratitude for their kindness she told them to return to the spot where she was sitting at the end of the year, and they would find a reward for their kindness and generosity. She then ascended into the clouds and disappeared. The two men returned to their village and explained to their nation what they had seen and heard, but were laughed at by their people. When the period arrived for them to revisit the consecrated ground, they went with a large party, and found where her right hand had rested upon the ground corn growing, and where the left had rested beans growing, and immediately where she had been sitting tobacco. The two first have ever since been cultivated by our people as our principal provisions, and the last used for smoking. The white people have since found out the latter and seem to relish it as much as we do, using it in different ways, smoking, snuffing, and eating."

Ball Playing Among the Indians

The most popular amusement among the Indians was ball playing. There would be from three to five hundred young men on a side, playing for guns, blankets, horses, or any other kind of property they might possess. The successful party took the stakes and they all retired to their lodges, either to lament their losses or rejoice because of their success. Then came horse racing, accompanied by feasting and overtures of friendship among the people. They bet on the results of the races, the same as the white people, and also in playing ball; but no chagrin was manifested by the losers, as their good luck might come afterward.

Sugar Making among Indians and Whites

At the beginning of the hunting season the warriors and some of the young women repaired to the hunting grounds, the women to look after the camp and prepare food. The old men and women and children were left in the towns with provisions enough to last them until the return of the hunters.

When the season was over the warriors proceeded first to the traders, where they sold the skins and peltries which they had acquired. Then began another round of feasting, gambling, races, card playing, and other pastimes until their money was gone; when the young men repaired once more to the hunting grounds, some to catch beavers, others raccoons and muskrats. But the bulk of the people went to the sugar camps, where sugar was made out of the sap of the maple trees. These trees formerly grew in large groves in many parts of the country, and the sugar produced from their sap was highly prized by the white settlers as well as the Indians. The art of making maple sugar and syrup was acquired from the red people, being unknown at the time of the discovery of America. The season came early in the spring when the sap was beginning to rise, the Indians obtaining the sap by cutting notches in the trunks of the trees, in which it collected. These notches sometimes killed the trees and destroyed portions of the forests; so the white sugar makers resorted to the plan of boring auger holes in the trees and driving "spiles", made of alder wood from which the pith had been removed, into the holes. The sap collected in the spiles and dripped into wooden troughs, whence it was conveyed to the camp to be boiled. Sugar making time was an occasion of joy and frolic among the whites as well as the Indians, and was anticipated especially by the children of both races for the good things which they knew would come to them.

Indian Burial Customs

Indian burial customs and ceremonies are next treated by Black Hawk, in the following terms:

"When we returned to our villages in the spring we would finish trading with our traders, who always followed us to our towns. We purposely kept some of our finest furs for this trade, and there was great competition among them who should get these skins. After this trade was over the traders would give us a few kegs of rum, to encourage us to make a good hunt and not go to war. Our old men would make a frolic of drinking the rum, but at this time the young men never drank.

When this was ended the next thing was to bury our dead, such as had died during the year. This was a great medicine feast. The relations of those who had died gave up all the goods they had purchased as presents to their friends, thereby reducing themselves to poverty in order to show the Great Spirit they were humble, so he would take pity on them.

We would next open the caches and take out corn and other provisions and commence repairing our lodges. As soon as this was done we repaired the fences around our fields and cleaned them off ready for planting corn. This work was done by our women. The men during this time are feasting on dried venison, bear's meat, wild fowls, and corn prepared in different ways; and recounting to each other what took place during the winter."

One of the most quaint and entertaining passages in Black Hawk's book relates to their marriage customs, which in several respects were not much different from our own. A good deal has been said of late about "trial marriages," which prevailed to a considerable extent among the first of the German immigrants; and we learn from the old Chief's writings that they had been common among his people for centuries. His remarks on the subject are therefore edifying.

"Our women plant the corn, and as soon as they are done we make a feast and dance the 'Corn Dance', in which they join us dressed in their best and decorated with feathers. At this feast each young brave selects the young woman he wishes to have for a wife. He then informs his mother, who calls on the mother of the girl, when the arrangement is made and the time appointed for him to come. He goes to the lodge when they are asleep (or pretend to be), lights his matches, which have been provided for the purpose, and soon finds where his intended sleeps. He then awakens her and holds his light to her face, that she may know him, after which he places the light close to her. If she blows it out the ceremony is ended, and he appears in the lodge next morning as one of the family. If she does not blow out the light, but leaves it to burn out, he retires from the lodge. The next day he places himself in full view and plays his flute. The young women go out one by one, to see who he is playing for. The tune changes so as to let them know he is not playing for them. When his intended makes her appearance at the door of the lodge he continues his courting tune until she retires. He then gives over playing and makes another trial at night, which generally turns out favorably.

"During the first year they ascertain whether they can agree with each other, and can be happy; if not they part, and each looks out again. If we were to live together and disagree, we would be as foolish as the whites. No indiscretion can banish a woman from the parental lodge; no matter how many children she may bring home she is always welcome, and the kettle is over the fire to feed them."

The Crane Dance

No young man could take his place as a warrior until he had killed an enemy in battle, or proven his prowess as a hunter. These ceremonies were enacted in the "Crane Dance," which the chief describes in the following terms:

"The Crane Dance often lasts two or three days. When it is over we feast again and have our National Dance. The large square in the village is swept and prepared for the purpose. The chiefs and old warriors take their seats, which have been spread at the upper end of the square, the drummers and singers come next, and the braves and women form the sides, leaving a large square in the middle. A warrior enters the square, keeping time with the music. He shows the manner in which he started on a war party, how he approached the enemy, he strikes and describes the way he killed him. All join in applause. He then leaves the square and another enters and takes his place, much of our young men have not been out on war parties and killed an enemy, stand back ashamed, not being allowed to enter the square. I remember I was ashamed to look where our young women stood before I could take my stand in the square as a warrior. What pleasure it is to an old warrior to see his son come forward and relate his exploits! It makes him feel young and induces him to enter the square and fight his battles over again."

"When our National Dance is over, our cornfields hoed and every weed dug up, and our corn about knee-high, all our young men start in a direction toward the sundown, to hunt deer and buffalo, being prepared also to kill Sioux if any are found on our hunting grounds. Part of our old men and women go to the lead mines to make lead, and the remainder of our people start to fish and get mat-stuff. Every one leaves the village and remains away about forty days. Then they return, the hunting party bringing in dried deer and buffalo meat, and sometimes Sioux scalps when they have been found trespassing on our hunting grounds. At other times they are met by a party of Sioux too strong for them and are driven in. If the Sioux have killed the Sacs last, they expect to be retaliated upon, and will fly before our warriors, and the same with us if it is the other way. Each party knows that the other has a right to retaliate, which induces those who have killed last to give way before their enemies, as neither wishes to strike except to avenge the death of their relatives. All our wars are predicated by the relatives of those killed, or by aggression upon our hunting grounds."

"The party from the lead mines brings lead, and the others dried fish and mats for the winter lodges. Presents are now made by each party, the first giving to the other dried buffalo and deer, and they in exchange presenting them lead, dried fish and mats."

It will be observed from the old chief's descriptions that many other customs of his people were very similar to our own, and if they had horses and opportunities of schools and education they would have been but little if any behind us in civilization. In fact, when we read the history of civilization in Europe at the time and before Columbus made his famous voyage, we are forced to blush at the comparison. In very many respects the red people were better civilized than those who came in ships to discover them; and even at the present time we would lose nothing by placing our own ways of living by the side of those of the early Indians and exchanging some of our bad customs for their better ones. No Indian was ever a beggar among his own people, and it was not necessary for them to have jails or police to protect the weak and innocent from the vicious. Perhaps a look backward might help us in our march toward a perfect civilization, which, however, cannot come until selfishness is banished from human nature.

An Indian Hero

The following incident reads like a classic story of Greece or Rome in their era of glory, but Black Hawk vouches for its literal truth. He tells the story in mere outline, but it is not difficult to fill in the details.

An Indian and a Frenchman at Prairie-du-Chein drank together as they gambled, then they quarreled and the warrior, feeling that he had been insulted and cheated, plunged his knife into the heart of his opponent. The British were in charge of the place at the time, and the savage was arrested, tried by the quick process of court-martial and condemned to be shot at sunrise the next morning.

When night came he begged the commander to let him go home and spend his few remaining hours with his wife and children, promising to return in time for the execution. The officer was disposed to grant the request, but his lieutenant said it would be an act of folly.

"If you let that Indian go you will never see him again," remonstrated the lieutenant. "I know the tricks of these critters."

"I wouldn't care if he did deceive me," replied the officer. "Then I wouldn't have to shoot him."

So he let him go, on his personal pledge to return by daylight. "I would give a month's pay if he never came back," said the commander, with emphasis. "It's bad enough to shoot men in battle; the firing squad is barbarism."

"You needn't worry," responded the lieutenant; "you'll never have a chance to shoot that Indian!"

The warrior spent the night with his wife and six sons. What passed between them none but themselves can know. "I cannot describe the meeting and parting," writes Black Hawk, "so as to be understood by the whites, as it appears their feelings are acted upon by certain rules laid down by the prophets, while ours are governed only by the monitor within us."

The father gathered his sons about him and told them of his exploits in war and the chase, and begged them to imitate his example. "Be brave warriors and great hunters!" he exclaimed, "and when you come over to the happy hunting grounds I shall be there to greet you."

As day began to dawn his wife begged him not to return. "They are not good people," she cried; "they are our enemies and would kill us if they could. Why should you go back to be shot?"

But the warrior replied: "You are a woman and do not know. I killed a man and must pay the forfeit. It is the law of our people, as well as theirs, and I am no coward to run away from death!"

The firing squad had already been detailed, and the men were drawn up in line at the place of execution.

"Has our man come?" inquired the British captain as he appeared on the ground.

"No," replied the lieutenant, there is no sign of him, and you'll be a much older man than you are when you see him again."

But at that moment the warrior appeared. His war-bonnet was on his head, and his face was painted as if he were going to battle. Taking his place in front of the line, he signaled that he was ready.

The lieutenant advanced with a handkerchief to bind his eyes, but the warrior pushed him aside.

"Me no 'fraid!" he exclaimed; me look gun in face when he shoot!"

The officer waved his sword and cried,

"Ready!"

Six muskets fell into place.

"Aim!" cried the officer.

Then reluctantly came the last hesitating command,

"Fire!"

There was a crash of six muskets as their fire leaped into the face of the hero, and with a smile upon his countenance he sank to the earth. Another human soul had fled into the unknown.

"You may say what you please", said the commander to his lieutenant as they walked back to their quarters; "you may call that Indian a savage and a barbarian, but if you search the pages of history you will not find a nobler example than this. There may have been something like it among the ancient Romans, but they were soldiers with a soldier's instincts, while this savage was only a man. God help me to be as brave as he was when my time comes!"

Black Hawk adopted the family of the dead warrior, and he and other members of the tribe supplied them with fish and game and corn and beans, until the boys were old enough to take their places as hunters and warriors. And the memory of the warrior who kept his promise even unto death was ever after treasured by the tribe to which he belonged.

Black Hawk concludes the account with these words:

"Why did the Great Spirit send the whites to this island, to drive us from our homes and poison our young men with liquors, disease and death? They should have remained on their own island, where the Great Spirit first placed them."

Black Hawk's Opinion of War

The old chief had but little respect for the methods of warfare practiced by the English and Americans. It seemed to him like making a play of something that was desperately tragic.

"Instead of stealing upon each other," he says, "and taking every advantage to kill the enemy and save their own people, as we do, they march out in open daylight and fight, regardless of the number of warriors they may lose. After the battle is over they retire to feast and drink wine as if nothing had happened. After which they make a statement in writing of what they have done, each claiming the victory, and neither giving an account of half the numbers that have been killed on their side. They fight like braves, but would not do to lead a war party with us. Their chiefs can paddle a canoe, but they do not know how to steer it. The Americans shoot better than the British, but their soldiers are not so well clothed or provided for."

Black Hawk did not visit his home during the entire war with the white people, but at its conclusion he returned home to see his wife and sons. It seems from the way he introduces the subject that he expected to find that they had been driven away, but he found them at home and they gave him a warm and affectionate greeting. He says: "I found them, and my boys were growing finely. It is not customary for us to say much about our women, as they generally perform their part cheerfully, and never interfere with business belonging to men. This is the only wife I ever had, or ever shall have. She is a good woman and teaches my boys to be brave."

It seems that during the chief's absence the wife and mother taught the boys the art of war and the use of weapons; also the habits of animals in the forest and how to trail them. This is what Black Hawk means when he says she taught his boys to be brave. The Indians not only regarded war as honorable, but looked upon it as a glorious profession, their only path to distinction. When the father was away therefore, on the warpath or the hunt, the mother taught the boys to emulate his example and grow up to be brave and useful members of the tribe.

The Tomahawk

The tomahawk was the weapon used by them more than any other, and their proficiency with it was truly amazing. This was gained by long and persistent practice, representing daily exercise and duty, the same as with our boys in attending school. Before the coming of the white traders they had only stone hatchets, which descended from father to son, and in the use of which they were highly proficient. The stone hatchet took the place of an axe, and was the emblem of great achievements in the past. But when steel implements were introduced it did not take them long to recognize their superiority, and the stone hatchet became a thing of the past, to be treasured as a memory of glorious deeds.

The steel tomahawk had a keener edge than the stone implement, and was therefore more deadly. It not only broke the skull of the opposing warrior, but it penetrated to the brain and produced instant death. The Indians were more expert than the white rangers in handling this weapon, owing to their early and persistent training. A warrior would hurl his tomahawk almost with the accuracy of a bullet at any object within thirty to fifty feet. They preferred prisoners as mark for practice, but when these were not available they substituted marks on trees or other stationary objects. One of their amusements was to tie a prisoner to a stake or sapling and see how close they could come to grazing his ears without cutting them off. If they happened now and then to clip an ear it only added to the zest of the experiment. A partly clipped ear was a good mark, to be entirely cut off at the next throw. Or if the whizzing tomahawk happened to split the head of the prisoner it did not disconcert the warrior. A new victim was produced and the lesson resumed.

Uncle Daniel was not an expert with the hatchet. With him it was more an implement for the camp than a weapon of war. But when it came to the rifle or the knife it was a wise Indian who got out of the way.

Wild Pigeons

With the coming of civilization many changes took place. The Indians learned much from the white people, and they also learned some useful things from their red neighbors. The good continues, and the evil or the useless disappears. Life also accommodated itself to the new environment. Many wild animals and birds that peopled the forests in the time of Boone and his neighbors have been exterminated or found refuge in unknown regions. One of the most mysterious and remarkable of these is the wild pigeon. Two generations of boys and girls have grown to maturity without ever having seen a specimen of this curious bird; yet when I was a boy there were billions of them in this same country where we are now living. I have seen flocks so immense that they extended laterally beyond both horizons and were so dense as to hide the noonday sun as effectively as a cloud in the sky. They were so numerous that they could not be estimated. When they lit in the forest the sound of their wings resembled distant thunder, and they stripped every nut from the trees. In many instances they would light in such number as to break limbs of considerable size, and in some cases it is claimed that they even broke down small trees. Pigeon pie might have been a daily dish with the pioneers, but the supply was so abundant that they were satiated. There was something mysterious and awe-inspiring in the flight of these birds, and hunters have told many amusing stories about them, as we shall observe in later Episodes. But where are the wild pigeons now? It is claimed that they migrated to Honduras, where they collected in such amazing masses that there was not sufficient food for them, and they perished of hunger. So utterly has this mysterious bird disappeared from the wild life of our country that later cyclopedias make no mention of it.

Buried Treasure

Like many other localities, the Boone neighborhood had its legend of buried treasure. There may have been truth enough for the foundation of the myth, but as it passed from hand to hand it grew and expanded until those who gave it a start would hardly have recognized their own child.

The place of the buried treasure was about two miles east of the farm where my father lived when I can first remember, and the story existed in several forms. At the spot indicated there was an ancient excavation and several "Indian graves", the latter having been covered with rocks to prevent depredations by wild animals. There were also other graves near by, indicating that a battle might have been fought there.

The story is curious enough to be worth repeating, and it may contain enough truth to justify a more careful search than has yet been made. The pioneers cared so little for "treasures" that they did not bother their brains with such stories; and they were also superstitious about opening ancient graves. The story is to the following effect:

Adventures of Six Priests

About the middle of the sixteenth century (1700) a company of six French priests left New Orleans and traveled northward, mainly with a view of converting pagan Indians to Christianity; but they also believed that they might discover deposits of gold, as the Spaniards had done on the southern continent. In order to make sure of a supply of the precious metal with which to purchase their freedom in case of capture by any of the wild tribes, they filled several sacks with gold coins and loaded them on the backs of donkeys which they drove with them. The money was in gold coins of the values of that date, and was variously estimate according to the quality of the imagination of the relator. Some said it was not less than a hundred thousand dollars, while others painted it as millions. It seems strange that a small company of poor priests could raise so large a sum, or that it could be safely carried through swamps and across rivers by a few donkeys. But the larger and more unreal the story the better it pleased a lively fancy.

It was claimed that the priests believed the possession of so great a treasure would win the respect of the savages, and lead more easily to their conversion; or in case of capture it would go far toward securing their liberty.

Indians with brilliant fancies, from the unexplored regions of the north, had reported that in their country gold existed in large nuggets that might be dug out of the ground by hand; and the priests believed that if this new El Dorado could be found it would almost immediately secure the conversion of the world to their religion. Also that the discovery would cause a rush of population to that mysterious and fascinating region, and carry civilization with it. Therefore they were stimulated in their undertaking by a double purpose.

Defense of the "Buried Treasure"

They traveled by slow stages, inspecting every indication of gold on the way, and were fortunate enough not to be molested until they reached a range of hills out of which flowed a small stream, to which they gave the name of Teuque Creek. The place is near the eastern line of Warren County, about three miles east of the village of Marthasville. Here they were attacked by Indians and oblige to defend themselves; which accounts for the ancient graves. In raising their defenses they found what they believed to be indications of gold in the rocks; and as soon as the Indians were driven away they established a camp and commenced digging. Slowly and painfully they burrowed their way down through solid rock to a depth of thirty or forty feet, when they were again assaulted by a band of savages. In this engagement several more of the Indians were slain, but being armed only with bows and arrows they could not make headway against the muskets of the besieged. None of the latter were killed or wounded, and the savages soon took their departure. But they drove the donkeys away with them, leaving the priests no means of transportation for their gold. There was formerly an ancient strain of donkeys in that locality, and some contended that they were descendants of those captured by the Indians.

The priests now decided that it would be wise to return home, as they would probably be assaulted again by new bands of savages; but what should be done with the treasure? Their donkeys were gone, and the coin was too heavy to be carried on their backs so great a distance. So they decided to place the sacks in the bottom of the shaft, and cover them with the rocks which they had taken out. Afterward they would lead a party back and recover the gold.

This seemed to be the only thing to do, and accordingly the plan was hastily carried out, after which they planted shrubbery and trees over the spot and set out on their return. I can remember when cedars grew there, and these would be the most natural plants to utilize in such a case.

Having completed their arrangements, they shouldered their muskets and blankets and made their way to the Missouri River, which flows a few miles to the southward. There with their tomahawks they constructed a canoe out of a cottonwood log, and embarking in it submitted themselves to the water in their long journey down the great rivers. Two of the priests died on the way, or were killed by savages, and the remaining four, having kept no record of their exploration, the memory of it died with them, except as a dim and uncertain legend.

No effort worthy of the name was ever made to solve the mystery, but the story had a wide circulation and there must have been some incident to serve as a foundation. There may be sacks of Spanish gold at the bottom of the shaft, or there may be nothing but worthless rocks.

Poncho's Weird Story

A story that old Poncho used to tell, when extra potations of fire-water loosened his tongue, probably had some connection with this incident. Poncho declared that "many moons ago,"

Long before he was born, a party of his countrymen left Rock Island where the villages of his tribe were located, and crossing the great river proceeded westward many leagues, far beyond any place ever visited before by man. There they found much game, deer and elk, and bears and wild cats, and the big cat that cries like a baby. While engaged in hunting these animals they came unexpectedly upon the camp of some men who had descended from the sun, and had many sacks full of bright round rocks which they guarded with great care. They wore long black robes and were bald on the top of their heads, showing that they had been scalped in their own country.

They offered some of the yellow rocks to the warriors, and told them about a God they worshipped who had come from the skies to show all men the path to the happy hunting grounds; but the warriors did not take kindly to their story, because they thought these must be bad men or they would not have been scalped by their own people before leaving home.

At length, through some misunderstanding, a battle began, and the men brought out some crooked sticks out of which they caused fire and smoke to issue, accompanied by loud crashes of thunder; and every warrior who happened to be in front of the thunder-sticks was killed. Finding that their bows and arrows had no effect on such men, the Indians ran away and returned home. When they told their story many brave warriors asked to be led to the place, in order that they might see those strange beings and fight with them, for they boasted that they had no fear of their thunder-sticks. So the head medicine man of the tribe anointed them all over their bodies with oil as a protection against the smoke and fire of the men from the sun, assuring them that nothing could penetrate beneath the oil. Even if a snake should strike at them the smoothness of the oil would turn it aside and its venom would spit into the air and do them no harm. The Great Spirit had blessed the oil for the medicine man, and if the men from the sun turned their thunder-sticks upon them they would be broken and rendered useless.

The warrior had faith in the medicine man, and set out on their long journey with much noise and great boasting; but in a single moon they returned and reported what they had seen. They had no difficulty in finding the place where they also saw the graves of their countrymen who had been killed in the former battle. But no sooner did the men from the sun see them than they pointed their crooked sticks at them, and made the sticks smoke and blaze fire, and thunder also issued from them and killed several of their party. Realizing then that it was useless to fight such men, they gave up the battle and returned home. The medicine man's oil was powerless to turn aside the thunder of the sun-men, and he was disgraced and sent into the woods to live by himself.

Such was the substance of Poncho's story, and it seems to connect directly with the legend of the French priests. There also was the creek with a French name flowing at the foot of the hill on which the priests had encamped; and it was known as Teuque Creek when Uncle Daniel first came to that country. Nobody could tell who named it, and there certainly had been no Frenchman there before the time of the priests.

All these facts and legends seem to fit in with the character of the story, and every legend must have a beginning. It cannot be born out of this air. I know very well where the place is, and if I were a younger man I would go there and dig to the bottom of that shaft and satisfy myself if there is Spanish gold there, or merely the windy nothing of an imaginative brain. Even to this day people are searching the islands of the sea and going down in diving-bells to the bottom of the ocean, looking for lost treasure; while those Spanish dollars lie there undisturbed.

A Pioneer Hermit

Whatever there may be of fancy or truth in this curious story, it had the effect of upsetting the brain of one of the most picturesque characters that ever came into the Boone country.

George Baughman was a native of Carroll County, Ohio, the seventh son in a family of ten children—a lucky number, as prophets and seers are generally supposed to be seventh sons. He had heard the legend of buried gold, and it interested him so much that when he was in his thirty-third year he came west to investigate for himself. He had no idea of the true location but only knew that it was on a range of hills near a small stream. Those who are familiar with the expansive territory of the great state that has been carved out of Upper Louisiana, will smile at the idea of finding buried treasure in so vast a space with so indefinite a description; but Baughman believed he could find it, and he worked on it until his brain became like a basket of scrambled eggs.

Searching For Gold

Baughman first located in Christian County, where he labored for several years as a hired man on a farm. Then he returned to his native state on a visit to his family, but was soon back in Missouri again looking for buried gold. This time he located in Montgomery County, near the head waters of Loutre Creek, because he believed the treasure was there. In fact he claimed to have received information to that effect during his absence, and the hills and topography, and especially the French name of the Creek, impressed the idea on his mind so deeply that it never departed.

He came this time with a cart and yoke of oxen, and was accompanied by a nephew who had traveled with him from Ohio. The poor boy imagined he was about to become heir to one of the most colossal fortunes in the world but it did not take long to discover that he was merely dreaming.

Baughman himself was secretive as to his purposes, but he told several persons that he knew the location of a great deposit of gold, and expatiated upon it to such an extent that they believed him to be demented.

In their progress westward the two men camped one night at Loutre Lick, and when they awoke in the morning one of the oxen was gone. It never came back, and this proved to be the end of their travels.

Their only means of subsistence was a flint-lock rifle and some fishing tackle, and hunger soon brought disappointment and hopelessness to the boy. He deserted his uncle and returned home, and was never afterward heard from.

Baughman now began the life of a hermit, which lasted through a long period of fifty years, until his death. He became a veritable Rip Van Winkle, expecting to wake up some morning with wealth enough to but the whole State of Missouri.

He chose as his place of residence a small cavern formed by shelving rocks in the side of a bluff. At the opening he built a rough stone wall, with a doorway for admittance to the interior, and having no money to buy nails or hinges, and being too proud to beg, he substituted strings and strips of bark peeled from adjacent pawpaw bushes. It was a gloomy abode at best, and as time went on smoke and dirt collected until it was no fit place for a human habitation. But it suited the character of the occupant, whose mind was solely devoted to the riche which he believed lay just under his feet. He was lord of all he surveyed, and if his gun or his hook failed to supply him with food today he was sure of better luck tomorrow.

A Weird and Romantic Character

During the first years of his hermitage he refused all offers of assistance, proudly maintaining that he could feed and clothe himself until he came into possession of his great estate. But when the feeble years of old age began to creep upon him he condescended to accept small gifts of food and second-hand clothing, and contrived to continue his independent way of living.

Each year he raised a little patch of corn, which supplied him with roasting ears, and when the grain ripened he ground it into coarse meal between a couple of rocks, and ate it in the form of hominy or "pone" bread baked in hot ashes. He made salt at the "licks", boiled syrup and sugar out of the sap of the maple trees, and lived with more comfort and luxury than some who regarded him as an object of charity. Several peach trees sprang up from seeds which he had thrown out through his door, and when these reached maturity they decorated his home with the glorious beauty of their blooms and brought him an abundance of fruit for his table.

As the years went by his gun grew old and decrepit like himself, but he patched it together with strings and wooden wedges and made it shoot straight enough to supply him with fresh squirrel and possum to season his fish and hominy.

His style of dress was peculiar to himself. For shoes he wore rough leather tied with thongs to clapboard soles, without socks to soften the rasping leather or the rigidity of the boards. In this respect Caesar's soldiers were no better clad than he, and they would not have known what to so with socks if such articles had been included in their kits.

In the side of the hill near his cave he dug two large wells, about thirty feet deep and most of the way through solid rock. Having neither powder nor blasting tools he cut the rock in pieces with the blade of an old pocket knife and fragments of scrap iron, and carried them to the top of the ground in his pockets, ascending and descending by means of an "Indian ladder". It was a slow process, but he had an abundance of time and lots of perseverance.

At length he announced that he found the treasure at the bottom of one of his wells, and had notified the French Government to send an army for his protection while he lifted the precious pieces out. I saw him a short time before his death, when he informed me confidentially that he had written the "Boss of Paris" to send the army as soon as possible, as he was getting old and feeble and might soon become unable to guard the treasure. He spoke with such assurance and earnestness that I could hardly doubt his word, or resist the belief that he had in fact discovered great wealth at the bottom of his well in the rocks.

During the last failing years of his life he was looked after by the county, but continued to cultivate the small tract which he had cleared with a horse as infirm as himself, that some kind-hearted person had given him. But everything in the way of charity had to be conveyed under cover; he was too intensely proud to accept anything as a free gift. As soon as the "French Army" came he would be a millionaire, when he would pay for everything that was delivered to him "on account". To the day of his death his old gun continued to supply him with an abundance of game. Squirrels, rabbits, wild turkeys, ducks and geese frescoed the walls of his "palace," and when he needed groceries or other domestic supplies he exchanged some of his game for what he wanted. All that was lacking to paint a grand romance of disappointed love was the absence of the beautiful girl. There was no intimation that he had ever been in love. His mind was too thoroughly saturated with the infatuation of buried treasure to leave room for the tender passion.

A German Count

And now let us consider the career of a German Count, who in some respects resembled Baughman the hermit. When he came to America and was corraled in the Boone settlements his chief visible possessions were a pair of leather boots with wide flaring tops, into which the rain poured when storms came. But he had treasures back in the old country, and unlike the hermit, he acquired and enjoyed their comforts before he died.

Revolution and Romance

Count Benting was a grand old character. He had fought against the King in the revolution of '48, and after the fracas was over he found that he needed a change of climate for the benefit of his health; so he migrated and landed in the little town of Marthasville, where he had a daughter who had married a commoner. This commoner could not live pleasantly in Germany as husband of a countess, and they too migrated and found refuge in Marthasville, where he established a small country store and sold whiskey and molasses without prejudice or partiality. When I became old enough to entertain the divine passion I fell desperately in love with one of their pretty daughters, and might have married a countess if her fancy had run parallel with my own. She sleeps now, and has slept for many years, in ground that is sacred, where roses bloom and purple violets modestly decorate the little mound that covers a heart which was very beautiful and good.

Count Benting found a place in Teuque Creek where he built a six-story water mill, in such a way that the first freshet washed a new channel around the end of the dam and left the Count without power to turn the wheels of his mill. Then he spent the rest of his life in having a high time and recounting the glory that was Germany.

He came to our house one night at bedtime, out of a soaking rain, wearing the boots with flaring tops. Being unlike anything I had ever seen except in pictures of cavaliers, the boots captivated my infantile fancy. The rain had filled them with water, and the Count being of small stature might have drowned except for the timely help of my father, who pulled the boots off and let out a flood. Mother prepared a hot supper for him, against his earnest protest, which she could see was only for politeness' sake, he remained with us all night. Where he slept I do not know, for long before he retired I was snuggled in the trundle-bed by the side of brother John and his cat-switch. It would have been in keeping with the Count's character to sleep in the open passage, or in the loft over the kitchen; but there were obstacles. Wilse reposed in the kitchen and might have objected to sleeping under the Count's boots, and the remainder of the family occupied the rest of the house. The open passage was the only vacant space, and he must have slept there. But it is not material. It makes no particular difference where the Count slept on that memorable night. All I remember is his flaring - topped boots, the water that came out of them, and a remark he made about Sam Jones. Sam was a son of Dr. Jones, and having absorbed some knowledge of medicine from his father, had engaged in the practice of the profession. When my father communicated the information to Benting, he threw his hands in the air and remarked that "Sam Yones didn't know enough about medicine to doctor his old boots," from which I understood that the boots needed doctoring and Sam was not qualified for the job.

A few years later the German government became pacified about the Count's exploits in the revolution, and offered to restore his confiscated estates. Whereupon his son-in-law crossed the ocean with a power-of-attorney and a plug hat and effected a settlement that enabled the Count to live happily ever after.

Fritz Sachs

Among other Germans who came to the Boone neighborhood as a result of the fracas of '48 was Frederick Sachs, whom we knew as Fritz Socks. He was a bricklayer by trade, and father hired him to finish a chimney that he had started and knew he would never complete. Brother John was assigned to Fritz as "helper," and when he was not busy carrying bricks and "mut", as Frita called the plaster, he amused himself by throwing clods and soft brick bats at his boss. Fritz was not pleased with John's conduct, and told father that "that boy, Yohnnis Daniel, was a rapscallion, and he was going to lick hell out of him." Father replied that he might lick anything he pleased out of John Daniel, as he never could keep the boy still long enough to do it himself. But the chimney was finished without an eruption, and when Fritz collected his pay he found that he had enough to retire and live comfortably in Germany. So he returned to the Fatherland and never came back. But we heard that he married a nice German girl, and between them they reared a family of little Socks, one of whom was named Johannis.

Episode Number Fifty-Five

Gotfried Duden and His Book

During the summer of 1824 an educated German named Gotfried Duden came to the Boone country on an inspection tour. It was the third year after the death of Uncle Daniel, but his neighbors were still there, also his sons, General Nathan and Daniel Morgan. The latter had studied surveying and was employed by the government for a number of years in running the meridian and boundary lines in the eastern part of the State.

Duden was accompanied by another young German named Louis Eversman, who was so well pleased with the country and its people that he married a pretty American girl, a Miss McLane, and settled down for life. Eversman was a fine man, and his son Julius who came after him, was a wit and story-teller of the first water. Fun bubbled out of Julius like water out of a spring, but it was not always as pure as nature's liquid. It had the sparkle and the shimmer, but sometimes it had also a bad smell. But it suited the times in which he lived and the rough characters for whom it was intended.

Julius Eversman the Fun Maker

I was at a log-rolling one day where Julius was the principal character, as he generally was wherever he went; and he told so many stories that the men neglected the work and had to come back another day to finish it. Although I was a mere child, barely able to understand their meaning, some of the stories he told that day shocked me so that I have never been quite as good as I was before. There is no telling how good I might have been if Julius had not told these loud yarns. They were not the kind that are repeated in ladies' sewing circles, but the men and the older boys seemed to enjoy them immensely. No promiscuous company of men in our day would tolerate such stories, but those men stood or sat and listened with shouts of laughter to the smut that bubbled out of Julius Eversman at that far-away log-rolling. If Julius had had an opportunity to go on the vaudeville stage he would have made a hit, provided he had toned his yarns down to meet the requirements of an advancing civilization.

The affair occurred at the home of Hayden Boone, a class-leader in the Methodist Church, and no man there enjoyed the jokes more than he did. The world of today is certainly better than the one I knew eighty years ago; and morals are of a much higher order.

When dinner came there was a great spread of good things to eat, and father was asked to say the blessing. He did not make it a lengthy affair, for he knew the men were hungry and eager to return to the field and entertainment. They longed for the wide-open spaces where Julius' jokes could circulate without tainting the atmosphere. Yet when all the others were through, father continued to eat in his usual slow and methodical way. He was not only a slow eater, but also a very hearty one, two qualifications which enabled him to reach ninety-seven years in his span of life. Therefore he did not hurry. He took his time to thoroughly masticate each mouthful before swallowing it, until the men became impatient.

"Oh come on, Uncle 'Ligy,' they growled; "there'll be something for dinner tomorrow."

"Uncle 'Ligy, it ain't healthy to eat everything at one time."

"Uncle 'Ligy, how long has it been since you had something to eat before?"

But father paid no attention to them, or their jabs. He continued the mastication of his bacon and greens, his cabbage and pork, his pie and pudding, until he felt that he had enough to last him to another meal. Then he rose and followed the gang to the field, where Julius continued his slippery yarns until the sun went down.

Results of Duden's Book

Duden made his headquarters at the Boone mansion, as it was called then and still deserves to be; and engaging Daniel M. as a guide they traveled widely over the country. The better part of two years was consumed in the work, and as usual with his countrymen, Duden did it thoroughly and with system. He drew maps of the roads, rivers, streams and topography; located farms and gave the names and characteristics of their occupants; so that afterward when the immigrants began to come, each family with a copy of Duden's book, they could travel without guides and knew the names and kind of people they would meet at each farmhouse. It was probably the most accurate and complete land and real estate prospectus ever written.

On his return to Germany Duden published his notes and maps in a book of 350 pages, and its sale was so large that it is said to have enriched the author. Its influence was soon realized in the appearance of the first immigrants, who as a rule were men of character and means. Following Duden's advice, they came to the Boone neighborhood for investment and speculation; but land was so abundant and easy to obtain that many of this class suffered a loss. When the real settlers arrived they sought out their own locations and bought from the government direct, thus getting farms at less cost and avoiding litigation over titles.

The First Germans

These German farmers were mostly of the peasant class, who had turned everything they possessed into cash in order to pay their way across the ocean. They brought their families with them, and when they reached the Boone country their money was generally exhausted. But they had been accustomed to hard living in their native land, and now hiring out to the Americans they worked and saved until they were able to get a little piece of land of their own. Then their future was assured. Bringing into play the same habits to which they had been accustomed in Germany, living on food that the Americans too often threw away, they soon gained a competence, and in many cases modest wealth. In a few years they had money ahead and became money-lenders to their American neighbors, whom they had regarded as rich people when they first came.

Men and women worked together in the fields and clearings, even the little children doing what they could, for there were no idle hands. Children of four and five would pile brush that their fathers and mothers cut, and while they were all slow of movement they kept everlastingly at work; so that at the end of the day the results would more than equal those of their more expeditious neighbors.

After frost came and nuts began to ripen, the children were sent into the woods to gather and pile them in cones and ricks, to be fed to hogs later in the season. Nut-fed bacon was sweeter than corn-fed and brought a better price. Neither were the nuts salable in the markets, while corn was worth so much a bushel; the result being that the Germans got more for their meat than the Americans did and turned their corn into cash. This economical system has not been maintained as it should have been, even by the descendants of the people who originated it; probably owing to the fact that nuts are not as plentiful as they used to be. But it is said that a man by the name of Smith, living in the mountains of Virginia, has made a large fortune by fattening razor-back hogs on chestnuts and selling the bacon at fancy prices. There are more ways of making a living than robbing banks or resorting to the mean and cowardly crime of kidnapping.

Eugenics, But No Birth Control

Those early Germans were a prolific race. Each little stranger was welcomed as a new unit in the family hive, and soon took his place in the work of filling the hive with the good things of life. Child-bearing did not worry the women. They were healthy, strong and muscular, unhampered by corsets and long skirts; and they bore their children with the ease and safety that nature intended. My father hired a young couple, just arrived from Germany, to work on his farm, and one day while they were in the field their first heir announced his arrival. The mother wrapped the little one in a petticoat, and after a few minutes of rest proceeded with her work of piling and burning brush, the little fellow meanwhile sleeping contentedly on top of a stump. He grew to be a prosperous citizen and in the after years bought off my father the field in which he was born.

The apostles of eugenics might have learned much from those thrifty Germans. Where land is abundant enough for each citizen to have a piece of his own there will be no danger of over-population; and if our women will continue their present sensible style of dress and recreation for a generation or two the penalty of child-birth will become a forgotten curse. Neither will there be any over-production when every one has enough to eat and none are hungry.

In his book Duden laid special stress on the abundance of game, and at the same time referred to the red men of the forest in such a way that some of his countrymen formed the idea it would be necessary for them to defend their families against ambushes and sudden assaults. So when they began to arrive it was no uncommon thing to see a stout burgher marching in the lead with an immense sabre buckled around his portly form, a flint lock pistol or two in his belt, and a musket or "yager" on his shoulder. But they soon learned that such armaments were unnecessary, and while they beat their swords into plowshares they reserved their shooting irons for the deer, elk, wild turkeys and geese with which the country abounded.

Arnold Krekel and Brother Sherman

Among those early Germans was the Krekel family, a sister and two brothers, who landed at my father's farm penniless. But they went to work at whatever they could get to do, meanwhile persistently studying our language and customs so as to be able to communicate their ideas. Arnold, the elder of the two brothers, split rails for my father at twenty-five cents a hundred, and saved enough to pay his way through St. Charles College, where he obtained the education that made him one of the distinguished jurists of the west.

Arnold was an Evolutionist, though that science was not then understood as it is now; and he and father had many arguments on the subject, father of course feeling that he was on the solid ground of scriptural truth. He could not comprehend Arnold's philosophy about man having ascended from an imperfect being, when Genesis said that he was created perfect in the beginning. So he turned the young German over to the circuit rider the Rev. W. T. Sherman, whose experience with the "talking bear" has already been mentioned.

"Mr. Krekel," he inquired, "if you reject Genesis how do you account for the origin of man?"

Arnold was silent for a while, turning over in his mind how he could make a Methodist circuit rider understand Evolution; then an idea coming to him he said:

"Perhaps at some distant period in the world's history there was an island in the sea, with conditions of climate and soil that produced life spontaneously; and from this beginning man progressed to his present status."

It will be observed that Arnold himself was not well posted in the theory of Evolution as it is now understood, and he opened his armor to the thrust of the preacher.

"Accepting your theory as true," replied Brother Sherman, "will you please give me the location of that island in the sea, as I would like to make a trip there and see the little fellows grow?"

Arnold made no reply. He looked at the circuit rider, picked up his axe and maul and started for the woods, with the single remark:

"Gott im Himmel! Vat iss?"

Curious German Names

Ilove to look over the list of names of those old Germans, and consider the days when every boat brought accessions to their numbers. It was the era of "cholera times," and many who set sail for America died on the way and were buried at sea; while others unconsciously brought the germs with them and found graves in a land that was foreign to them.

A complete list of the names would require more space than is available, but a few will suffice as a sort of tonic for the others. In the Berlin colony were Charles Madler, Charles A. Mueller, William and Ferdinand Roch, Henry Waulks, Louis, William, and Conrad Haspes, August Rizrath, Jerry Scheiper, Daniel Benner, Justus Muhn, Charles Lippross, Philip Benner, Jacob Sachs (father of Fitz), Henry Schaff, Harmon Stuckoff, Charles V. Spankern, and others. Nearly all of these settled in the south western part of St. Charles County, near my father's farm, where they become neighbors and friends. The old family burying grounds contain their remains, and the rude headstones recount their deeds and preserve the memory of their quaint German names. Henry Schaff built a mill which he operated with oxen on a tread-wheel; and as the oxen became fat with eating the "mill-stuff" he sold them for beef and made a fortune.

There were others who came with these or followed soon after, among whom I find the names of Charles Wincker, George H. Mindrup (who became Judge of the County Court of St. Charles county), Fredrick Winsker (who was a merchant and postmaster at Agusta), Bernard and Henry Stuckoff, Arnold Voelkerding, William, August, and Julius Schart, Francis Krekel (father of the afterward famous Arnold Krekel), and Julius, Emile, Herman and Conrad Mallinckrodt. Julius married my Aunt Mary, a sister of my mother who was reputed to be the prettiest girl in the Boone settlements.

The Mallinckrodt brothers were well educated and became men of influence in the communities where they settled. They had studied English in the Fatherland, but it was not the same English they found in America. It had to be unlearned and a new idiom acquired before they could converse freely with the neighbors of Daniel Boone.

France and Germany Meet in St. Louis

When Julius Mallinckrodt arrived in St. Louis he encountered an intelligent looking man on Main Street, and wishing to obtain some information, addressed him in what he supposed to be classic English. The man was amazed to hear a good-looking stranger utter such barbarous lingo, and seemed in doubt as to whether he should use his gun or run away. Then Uncle Julius (as he afterward became) addressed him in German, but the man was not pacified. Whereupon he tried the classics and spoke in Latin, still without penetrating the man's understanding. At length, in desperation, he cried out: "Parlez-vous Francais, Monsieur?" (adding in an undertone, "Gott ver dom jackass!" for Uncle Julius had a temper.) This produced more than he expected. It came as a revelation, for French was the man's mother tongue. With the impetuosity of his race he threw his arms around Uncle Julius and kissed him on both cheeks. They then repaired to the old Barnum Hotel and parley-voused and drank wine until they were filled with emotion.

Frederick Meunch and the Gissen Society

In 1834 the Gissen Society came, under the lead of Frederick Muench. They settled in the eastern part of Warren County, where Muench exercised a large influence as writer and speaker. He was chosen a member of the Legislature and State several times, and through his influence his people established a high-grade German College a few miles east of Marthasville, which is still flourishing. Muench was a convincing speaker and profound thinker and philosopher. He was born and reared in the Province of Upper Hesse, educated for the ministry, and served as pastor of a Protestant liberal church for thirteen years: but having advanced beyond the orthodoxy of the times he organized the Gissen Society and came to America. Among the members of the society were Gotlieb Beng, John Kessler, Jacob Jeude, Frederick Beck, Dr. Frederick Kruge, Henry Becker, Charles Kesel, Jonathan Kunze, Mr. Guhlemann, Frederick Feach, Andrew and Louis Klug, Pressner Goeple (whose son Gelt represented Franklin County in both houses of the Legislature), Frederick Bruche (whose son represented Cape Girardeau County in the Legislature), and August Kroell, who removed to Cincinnati and became pastor of a German Protestant church there.

These people were highly religious, but their faith was rational. They believed that Christ was a good man and teacher, though not divine, and that we make our own future by the kind of life we live here. In other words, we are saved by works, not by faith or belief. They discarded the account of creation as given in Genesis and taught the natural origin of man, which made them Evolutionists without being aware of the fact.

At a later date the following families came: Jacob and Frederick Ahman, Charles Winkelmeir, Frederick and Erasmus Hyeromymus, Ulmfers and Frederick Blantink, Erastus Grabbs, William Barez, who had been a banker in Berlin and was a very intelligent man, Henry and George Berg, Mr. Fuhr and his five sons, Harmon, Lucas, Henry, Luke, and Hermann; Mr. Tueperts, Mr. Oberhellmann, and I think Franz Rainbow was also a member of this company.

Eggs and Butter, Calico and Whiskey

Erastus Grabbs had been a druggist's clerk in Berlin, where he became acquainted with and married the beautiful Countess Benting. But her family felt that she had disgraced herself by her union with a commoner, and the young people came to America, the land of freedom. They settled in the village of Marthasville and prospered. Grabbs began as a clerk for Harvey Griswold, afterward acquired a small store of his own, was appointed postmaster and elected Justice of the Peace. He planted an orchard and a vineyard, bought and sold everything for which there was any demand, from eggs and butter to calico, molasses and whiskey, and prospered out of all expectation. The family that disowned him and his wife in Germany were subsequently under obligation to the druggist's clerk for the salvage of their estates as already related. His pretty little daughter was my first sweetheart, though I never had the courage to say anything to her about it, and now that she has been dead fifty years I can express my sentiments without hurting her feelings.

A New Era in Agriculture

The German immigrants brought a new era into the Boone country. The methods of agriculture were more intensive and productive than those of the Americans had ever been. Large farms poorly cultivated were not in accord with their ideas. They preferred small tracts well tilled and fertilized, and they made them produce more, with less labor, than the broad acres of the Americans. Before they came no farmer thought of using fertilizers; the soil was supposed to be rich enough to take care of itself. When a field "wore out" another was cleared to take its place, and thus the wheels went round and round from year to year.

I knew a German who bought a "worn out" farm whose owner regarded it only as worthless land. It would not even grow grass. But when the German asked him his price he named three times the he would have been willing to accept, and the German thought it was a bargain.

The man laughed among his neighbors and said there was one "Dutchman" who had parted with his money. The "Dutchman" hauled all the manure he could get from neighboring stables and spread it over the field, the farmers considering it a favor to have him "move the stuff out of their way". The manure having been well spread, the German plowed the land with deep furrows, and harrowed and pulverized it. When planting time came he produced a new-fangled sort of a machine and drilled the seed instead of sowing it broadcast. No farmer in the Boone country had ever seen a wheat drill, and they shook their heads. It left too much space between the rows, which of course was nothing but "waste land," and would grow up in weeds. If the Dutchman got back his seed he would be lucky. But when harvest time came he reaped an immense return. He got more than three times as much wheat per acre as had ever been raised in that country before, and the price happening to be good, his first crop brought him enough to pay for the land and leave a neat surplus to buy another field. Then the Dutchman laughed, and his neighbors took note.

But some of the Germans thought they knew more than they really did and they suffered loss in consequence until they learned better. Along the lines to which they had been accustomed they were superior to the American farmers, but they had never seen a crop of corn until they crossed the ocean. Herman Groeby and his wife worked for my father the first summer after coming over, and helped him cultivate a field of corn. The next year Groeby rented the same field for himself, and told my father he would show him how to raise corn. The Americans were behind the times; they wasted too much space between the rows. So he sowed his corn broadcast and very thick, and it soon covered the field with a rich dark-green matting. Groeby wagged his head, and father wondered if he had been raising corn all his life without knowing how. But when harvest time came Groeby had a big lot of fodder and no corn. He did not get as much grain as he had sown; but he fed the fodder to his cows and got a big return in butter and milk. He lost his bacon, but saved his butter.

The Germans did not care so much for the quality of the soil, provided there was enough of it to hold the manure they put into it. They would take a barren hillside and convert it into a blooming orchard or vineyard. They also opened little farms in the woods, and each year added a few acres to them. Swamps and marshes that an American would not have as a gift, were drained and converted into fertile fields, thereby adding to the wealth of the country and the health of the people. The very swamps in which Uncle Daniel heard the ducks and wild geese gabble the day he crossed the bottoms on his way to the spring at the foot of the bluff, have been cultivated in wheat and corn for many years, and are worth more per acre than any other land in that locality. The snakes and mosquitoes have also disappeared, and the doctor does not call as frequently as he did in former times.

Villages and towns have sprung up where solitude and pestilence reigned, and the study of philosophy has taken the place of considering the phases of the moon. There were no newspapers or magazines until the Germans came, and no one had ever heard of a circulating library until Cousin Willis Bryan gave one to the local Sunday School. But it was a small affair and did not concern itself with mundane conditions. The Gissen Society introduced a library of scientific and historical works; and now there are schools and colleges there and every child in that region can read and write. America gained much in the coming of the Germans, but the loss to Germany was irreparable.

Pioneer Literature

There was nothing that could be called literature in the Boone country when the Germans began to come. Across the water Sir Walter Scott and the great English and German poets were at the height of their fame, and Dickens came a little later; but these books were not to be found in the libraries of the pioneers. In our family the reading of Dickens was prohibited, and when "Uncle Tom's Cabin" appeared it was like throwing a live coal into a keg of powder. Shakespeare was also ostracized; he did not come up the circuit rider's standard.

By some occult means a paper-backed novel called "Cruising in the Last War" was smuggled into our house, the "Last War" meaning that of 1812. It belonged to the blood and thunder class of literature and was about the weakest mental broth I ever essayed; unless it might have been Sylvanus Cobb's "Gunmaker of Moscow", which also slipped into our house through the back-door. The first book I ever read was Weems' "Life of Washington," which I spelled out and wept over at the age of five. It was truly a great book, an American classic, and no one can read it now without feeling the patriotic blood stir in his veins and wondering if the great Washington, who could not tell a lie, will ever return to save the country he established.

From Weems' classic to "Cruising in the Last War" was a tremendous and hazardous descent, but I made it without completely wrecking my mental faculties. After I was grown and had written and published a dozen books of my own, I tried my hand at a story along the same lines; and although I wove into it a number of valuable historical facts about our Navy and compiled what I conceived to be a really good story, no publisher would risk his reputation by printing it. Public taste had risen to greater heights, and my story still remains in manuscript. But after all, it is not quite as crazy as Cooper's "Pilot," and sometimes I think it is almost as good as Scott's "Pirate".

In actual civilization the American pioneers were superior to the German immigrants. It is difficult to understand why this should have been, but it was due to the fact that the first of the Germans belonged so largely to the peasant class. They knew how to make the earth yield her fruits, but had not acquired the art of using them for their own betterment. Their descendants, however, have succeeded beyond anything that might have been expected, and as intelligent men and women they have no superiors in the world. They constitute a new generation, risen under better conditions out of the suppressed elements of their predecessors. For centuries the latter had been held in virtual slavery by the aristocratic classes of the Fatherland, but in their transplantation a wonderful change was wrought. The elements of greatness were within them, but there had been no chance for development. Now a virile race was planted in virgin soil, and the good which had been suppressed blossomed into life and greatness.

An Intimate View of Slavery

This explains also why German immigrants were so bitterly opposed to slavery. They had realized its withering effects in their own persons, and had no desire to impose it on others. The slavery which they found among Uncle Daniel's neighbors was generally mild and beneficent, resembling the condition of minor children in a patriarchal family. Yet there were instances of the meanest sort of oppression, and these increased with the progress of the "institution". It was not the old masters who oppressed the black people, but a later generation of pampered and spoiled spendthrifts. A lady who came to the Boone settlements with her family in 1839 wrote back to her friends at home:

"The two greatest evils today are intemperance and slavery. We hired a slave woman at one dollar per week, but paid the money not to the woman, but to her master. She brought her bedding along; a sack filled with hay; and no covers except some old rags. She sleeps in the kitchen, where the white folk's victuals are kept."

This was a common custom. Wilse slept in the kitchen of my father's house, where the "victuals" were kept and cooked and eaten. He had no bed, but lay on a buffalo robe, which he spread near the fire to keep himself warm. But Wilse never imagined that he was badly treated, even though he had no interest in the products of his own labor. He felt that what he helped to produce belonged to him as much as to "'Ligy", as he called my father, and was intensely proud when the home products happened to be above those of the community. But his lot was better than the average of his race, because he had been raised as a member of the family and was devoted to it. There was a genuine affection between him and the children, and when he found and saved little Jane he rose to a height that no other slave ever attained. Moreover, Wilse was a hero, even in the estimation of so great a man as Uncle Daniel. He was above the level of the common slave.

The Mormons

The lady from whom I have quoted wrote again in 1848:

"Great excitement here about Mormons and Indians. The Mormons are persuading the Indians to adopt their doctrines, and then use them against the whites."

But her fears were groundless. The Mormons and the Indians "Went West" and grew up with the country, and now the Indians are among the wealthiest of our citizens and the Mormons are orthodox. They have a church in the town where I live, and their pastor is a member of the "Ministers' Alliance". A bright and somewhat charming lady missionary of the Mormon faith tried to convert me last summer, and my inability to absorb the civilizing influences of Joseph Smith's revelation provoked her almost to the point of consigning me to the everlasting blazes.

Honey and Flies

Among the progressive Germans who found homes in the new world were Jacob and Henry Ahmann, tall, handsome brothers, each of whom reared a large family. Jacob and his son Henry, who though a little older than I, was one of my most cherished school chums. Henry was not brilliant, but that was no fault of his; nature made him as he was. He used to bring honey to school to eat with his lunch, in a big quinine bottle without a stopper. Flies, being sensible creatures, found their way into the honey, and Henry "ate them alive". He was not especially fond of flies, but was too brave not to eat them on a "dare". One day when I hungered for honey I offered to eat half the flies if Henry would divide the honey equally with me; but he declined. He said he could eat his own flies.

A Dashing German Major

Marriage customs among the Germans of that date were different from what they are now. My father hired a German named Billy Spruziker to work on the farm, but he proved to be so expert a rail-maker that he soon devoted all his time to that occupation. He had been a major and engineer in the German army, and understood the art of blasting. So when he made rails, instead of splitting the logs with maul and wedge, he blew them open with gunpowder. It was quicker than the old way, and much more picturesque; and Billy made a military maneuver of it. When he was ready to touch off a blast he would hold up his hand and shout, "Fire!" and the logs came open with a bang which the boys thought was very grand. Sometimes Billy would split as many as two hundred and fifty rails in a single day.

He had a comely German wife and they lived happily in the cabin on the bank of the creek at the back of the farm. But he had participated in the revolution, and one of the King's cavalrymen had slashed his skull with a sabre, leaving a wound that caused frequent headaches. As time went on the headaches became more frequent and painful, until at last he died in one of the paroxysms. On the day of the funeral I opened the big gate for the passage of the wagon carrying the coffin, on which sat the widow dressed in her best and weeping bitterly. I thought she was quite beautiful, and her sorrow excited my sympathy. In the afternoon she returned and brought with her a new husband, who had no sabre-slashes to cause pain. The late widow seemed radiantly happy, for why worry over a dead husband when there were plenty live ones? There is something to be said in favor of this old German custom. A dead husband is of no further use, and why not supply his place with one who can be of service?

Cholera Days

Those were cholera days, and husbands went so rapidly that the widows were obliged to step lively in order to keep a supply on hand. The Germans had founded a town about fifteen miles from where we lived, with a population of a hundred or two; and some fresh immigrant brought the germs of the dread malady with him. It spread through the village and about half the inhabitants died. Whole families would be stricken and die in a single day. The terror became so great that the doctors refused to attend the sick; but there was no panic among the inhabitants themselves. They met the grim reaper with the stolid courage characteristic of the race, and their common sense view of things relieved them of much sorrow and worry. When a man lost his wife, or a woman her husband, it was their custom to find a new mate the same day, in order that there might be no rift in the domestic arrangements. In one instance a man who was burying his wife met a woman who was performing a similar service for her husband in an adjoining lot, and when the graves were filled they plighted their faith and were married before leaving the cemetery. The new wife cooked the funeral dinner, and the domestic affairs flowed on as if nothing had occurred to disturb them.

"Trial Marriages"

Those early Germans had another custom which no doubt would interest some of our modern up-to-date people. It was what they called "trial marriages," or "accommodation nuptials". Young couples, desiring to be assured of future happiness, went to house-keeping without the intervention of priest or preacher, under an agreement that if either became dissatisfied with the other, he or she, as the case might be, could sever the relation and go free. But if both were satisfied at the end of six months or a year, they had a marriage ceremony performed and became husband and wife. In the meantime if any children were born they took the name of the mother and belonged to her. It was practically the same as a similar custom among the Indians, mentioned by Black Hawk.

There were several such marriages in the Boone neighborhood, and they all turned out satisfactorily. There were no separations and no trouble, and the young people suffered nothing in the way of social standing.

They had a somewhat similar arrangement in the German Methodist Church, where members were received on probation. If they held out for six months, and their characters stood satisfactory inspection at the end of that time, they were then received into full membership with all the rights and privileges of the older members. This was to guard against "backsliders", of whom there were too many. Meanwhile if they backslided during the trial term they had no assurance of salvation, but they were given full time to make the effort, without prejudice and with the help of the church. The American Methodists had the same rules at that time, but they have discontinued it. A member told me not long ago that it was too much like an application for fire insurance with time to investigate the character of the applicant, and many objected to having their characters exposed to public inspection in that way.

Episode Number Fifty-Eight

The "Slicker" War

About 1844 a series of difficulties occurred between the citizens of St. Charles and Lincoln Counties, which led to a diminutive war, known at the time as the "Slicker War". It lasted about three years and resulted in several battles or skirmishes and a number of incidents and adventures, some of them tragic and others amusing.

By this time the settlements had extended to the western line of the State, adjoining the unoccupied territory of Kansas, and the Slicker War no doubt had considerable influence in the greater conflict between the North and South which was soon to come.

The name "Slickers" originated in Benton County, where a company of vigilantes was organized for the purpose of breaking up the band of horse thieves and counterfeiters who had their headquarters in the Ozark Mountains. Among the crimes that seemed to have the greatest fascination for the criminal-minded were horse stealing and counterfeiting, yet the punishments were generally of the severest kind. Hanging was the usual penalty for stealing another man's horse, and while this extreme was not resorted to in the case of counterfeiting what they did receive was generally severe enough to induce them to immigrate to more congenial lines.

The mode of punishment inflicted by the Slickers was to tie the culprit to a tree or sapling and "slick" him down with hickory withes until he promised to leave the country, and it was from this custom that the name originated.

The success of the Benton County Slickers in ridding their part of the state of undesirables led to similar organizations in other localities, where counterfeiters and horse thieves were more or less active. At that time St. Charles and Lincoln Counties were especially infested by such characters, owing to their proximity to St. Louis, which afforded a ready market for stolen horses and a place of hiding for those whose fancy ran toward slick dollars and clipped quarters. There had also been a certain degree of rivalry among the settlers themselves, almost from the beginning, due to differences in racial origins. Most of the pioneers in Uncle Daniel's immediate neighborhood were of English extraction, with a considerable percentage of French; while some parts of Lincoln were settled almost exclusively by immigrants from Scotland. The rivalries of the old countries had been transplanted to the new, and while they were gradually dying out there was still enough to make Englishmen laugh at the eccentricities of the Scotch neighbors, and both were united in declining full fellowship with the French.

The first company of Slickers was organized in St. Charles County near the border of Lincoln, and contained a number of men with grudges against their neighbors to the north, several of whom were "Slicked down" without cause. This led to the organization of an anti-Slicker company and retributive measures, until the country along the borders of the two countries suddenly blazed into an incipient civil war. Neighbors became suspicious of one another, and as the organizations were more or less secret no one knew whom to trust. Houses and barns were burnt by unknown enemies and good citizens were taken into the woods at night and whipped without mercy.

Two armed bodies were now organized and operating against each other in a limited region; several skirmishes ensued, and several men on each side were killed. Others were wounded and mal-treated, and conditions created which could not be endured. The thieves and blacklegs for whose suppression the first company had ostensibly been organized, exercised an evil influence on both sides; for their leaders were men of standing and good address. So far goats had not been separated from the sheep, and the former advantage of the conditions to fight out their own rivalries and at the same time punish good citizens against whom they had a grudge. It resembled the more recent wars of Racketeers in some of our larger cities, but was never carried to such extreme. In several instances it developed that leaders on one side or the other, or both, were active circulators of "slick" money.

The Versatile Mr. Grammar

During the high waters of 1844, which subsequently became known as the "year of the flood", a little steamboat called the <u>Bee</u> came up from St. Louis, and turning into Cuivre River landed at the village of Chain-of-Rocks, where there were several stores, a mill, hotel, blacksmith shop, and a number of residences. A good-looking stranger left the boat and registered at the hotel as Hal Grammar, and announced that he represented a company of developers who were planning to invest largely in real estate in that part of the country. Mr. Grammar wore fine clothes of the latest pattern, and was so polished and suave that most of the citizens felt themselves honored by his acquaintance; but a few wondered if his morals were as good as his clothes and his grammar. He spent money freely, treated liberally to the best cigars and whiskey, and while the money that he personally dispensed was of first-class purity, it was soon observed that counterfeit coins had multiplied in the community.

At length a citizen whose suspicions had been aroused put a mark on a good Spanish dollar and passed it to a neighbor whose morals were not above reproach. The transaction was made in payment for some seed corn. The next day the citizen who had marked the coin was invited to drink with Mr. Grammar, and he noticed that the entertainment was paid for with his good dollar. Of course this was nothing in the way of evidence, yet it seemed strange that the coin has so soon found its way from the pocket of a suspect into that of the elegant Mr. Grammar. The incident was regarded as significant enough to justify further effort along the same line.

But before anything more was discovered the <u>Bee</u> made another trip and landed a peddler with a pack of goods, which he left in the office of the hotel while he ate his dinner. When the peddler returned his pack was gone, and Mr. Grammar had disappeared also. The pack and the man seemed to have had an affinity for each other.

Grammar was pursued and arrested, but none of the stolen goods were found in his possession. So far the evidence indicated he was an innocent man; but he concluded the climate was getting too warm for him and left for parts unknown. The peddler's goods also remained out of sight. He never recovered a single article. There could not have been much value in a pack of goods, but they evidently had some sort of mysterious affinity for the polished Mr. Grammar and followed him into seclusion.

But although he had folded his tent and silently stolen away, his influence remained. Where he had located or how he operated was never known, but the country soon became flooded with base coin; and horses, cattle, hogs, and other livestock were driven away and sold in St. Louis.

Such operations were not difficult in those days, when there was no telegraph or telephone systems and no regular mail deliveries. A drove could be rounded up and driven to market in a couple of days, and the proceeds safely lodged in the pockets of the thieves before the owner discovered that his stock had disappeared from the range. The thieves became so bold that they even butchered cattle and hogs on the farms of their owners at night, and before daylight shipped the dressed meat in flat-boats which had been prepared in advance. It was a matter of impossibility to prove ownership of a skinned ox or dressed pig, and for a while this wholesale piracy flourished and expanded. Those who made any effort to prove their stolen meat were so threatened and intimidated that they dared not proceed and an independent company of rangers was organized to protect the community. But it was soon discovered that among these were some of the very blacklegs they were endeavoring to hunt down, who were serving as spies and informers. Two or three of the worst of them were hung to limbs and their carcasses left as a warning to others; and these extreme measures had their intended effect. No thief likes to feel the halter draw, regardless of his opinion of the law. Peace and security were restored; but still the whereabouts of Mr. Grammar were unknown. It was the common opinion that he was the leader of the whole lawless movement, but kept himself so well concealed in the background that no trace of him could be found.

Mr. Grammar Reappears

When the lines became too closely drawn for the security of the hidden leader, reports came of the greatest revival of religion in the Salt River section, led by a distinguished evangelist from the East. Simultaneously the circulation of slick dollars increased out of proportion, and citizens of the Flint Hill neighborhood remembered that Mr. Grammar had been of a pious turn of mind. He had led prayer- and class–meetings and had preached a sermon or two on special occasions; and their suspicions were aroused. Several citizens of an inquiring disposition journeyed to Salt River, and were not surprised to find Mr. Grammar on the rostrum. Recognizing them at the same time he excused himself with a plea of sudden indisposition, and retired to the privacy of his tent, which he entered by the front and evidently passed out at the back. When the citizens followed they found the tent vacant, and Mr. Grammar was never afterward seen or heard of in that part of the country. He may have continued his operations elsewhere until the end of his career, but if so he was shrewd enough to hide his identity. Mr. Hal Grammar was one of the slickest and boldest rascals that ever wore sheep's clothing and played the wolf among Uncle Daniel's neighbors.

The Redoubtable Sarah

It was time now that the Slickers should have disbanded, if indeed there had ever been any reason for their organization; but such incongruous disturbers of human society and peace do not always disappear for some time, even after the disappearance of the counterfeiters and horse thieves and trouble followed as a natural result. In the vicinity of Flint Hill there lived a Mr. James Trumbull, who was wrongfully suspicioned of being in sympathy with the lawless elements and it was reported that two of his sons were actually engaged in the manufacture of base metal dollars. About noon one day in April a company of Slickers appeared at Mr. Trumbull's house and demanded entrance, but the family barred the doors and prepared for assault. However, Mr. Trumbull and his daughter Sarah came out and expostulated with the men, nearly all of whom were known to them personally.

They asserted the innocence of every member of the family and offered to give bond for their good behavior; but in reply they were advised to leave the country and be quick about their going. The result was a battle in which tragedy and comedy both played a prominent part; but it will be necessary to defer the account to another Episode.

Episode Number Fifty-Nine

"Lamp-Lighter of the Twelve Apostles

Among the Slickers who came to attack the Trumbulls were two brothers, John and Malcom Davis, who tried to force an entrance into the house. In the scuffle that ensued John was severely wounded on the head by a corn knife wielded by Sarah Trumbull; while Malcom received two gunshot wounds from inside the house. He died the following day. His brother John, enraged at what happened, and disregarding his own hurts, fired through the door and wounded the two Trumbull boys, one of whom died a few hours later. The other brother was shot through the mouth and neck, and fell apparently dead; but he recovered and lived several years, though a paralytic. Several of the Slickers were wounded, but none severely, and they finally left without accomplishing their purpose.

Among them was a man named Kinchen Robinson, who styled himself "The Lamplighter of the Twelve Apostles". He was a gasser and boaster, and his courage needed certifying. On this occasion he wore a long dress-coat with a split-tail, so as to be prepared to light lamps when called upon. When the retreat was sounded Kinchen was among the first to retire, and he went with such haste that as he rose to jump the yard fence the long tails of his apostolic coat spread out behind like a fan; whereupon Sarah Trumbull, who was in close pursuit, cut them off with her corn knife. What eventually became of the "Lamp Lighter" is not revealed; he may be running yet with no tails to his coat. But for several years it was Sarah's custom, when she rode into town, to pin the tails of Kinchen's coat to the skirt of her riding habit and parade up and down the streets.

In this affair the sympathies of the community were with the Trumbulls and it led to the organization of a new company to put down the Slickers. Several clashes took place and two or three men were killed and others whipped. But in the end the good sense of the people prevailed, the bands lost their enthusiasm, were dispersed, and peace once more was restored to the community.

A Moonlight Adventure

In subsequent times I became well acquainted with the people of that section, and found them to be the very salt of the earth; but still retaining some of the fiery characteristics of their Scotch ancestry. I remember one instance very acutely, when I was called to the door of my father's house at midnight by a man who I recognized as a near neighbor. He fancies that he had a grudge against me, and had come to "settle".

I could see him plainly as he sat on his horse outside the gate with a gun in his hand, which he tried to conceal behind his body. He inquired the way to the village, which was a sight, and he had left the road in order ot come to our house. It was a sorry trick on his part; but for the sake of neighborliness I gave him the necessary directions, being careful to remain in the shadow of the doorway. He complained that he could not see me, and demanded that I come out into the yard; but feeling that I was too young to die, I closed the door and went back to bed. Afterward when the irate neighbor understood that I had done him no wrong, we became the best of friends; but neither of us ever referred to that moonlight adventure.

The incident that caused the rupture was to this effect: It was a year or two after the close of the Civil War, when that locality was pretty well filled with "free niggers" working for a living. The man had hired one of that class, and becoming disgusted with his laziness discharged him without pay. I remonstrated and took the negro's part, claiming that he ought at least to have received as much as he had earned. The neighbor said it was none of my business, and came to "shoot it out" according to the code of the olden times. It is probable that the negro was not worth any more than his "keep", and it was really "none of my business," as the neighbor claimed.

What Time Did Sall Have Her Chill?

The coming of freedom threw upon the country a lot of lazy, half witted relics of slavery, as unlike the industrious colored people of our time as a Senegambian is different from a civilized human. Only those who were familiar with both eras can appreciate the real difference. In the days "befo' de wah" there lived in Troy a physician named Linn, who was a fine man and had a large practice in the surrounding country. One day he was called to see Aunt Sall, who had had a chill the day before. Wishing to locate the time, the doctor asked her when the chill came on. "Jes' when Ike come frum de mill," she replied. "And what time was it when you brought the wood?" the doctor asked of John. "Jes befo' Bill come home," said John, with great precision and visible importance. Turning now in desperation to Bill, the doctor inquired what time it was when he came home. "I golly," said Bill, "it was jes' befo' Sall had de chill." "And how in thunder!" exclaimed the irate doctor, "am I to find out when Sall had the chill from you blamed fools?" Bill drew a long breath and replied, "God knows, Boss, I wan't dar."

Such was the kind of timber that my choleric neighbor had to deal with, and it is no wonder that he felt like shooting somebody.

I Attend a Revival

When I was quite a small boy my father took me with him to the night services at the German church, where a revival was in progress. The church was very plainly furnished, for the Germans of that time were poor. A dim light was obtained from tallow candles dispersed in wooden holders around the walls, emphasizing the darkness just enough to make it visible. The preacher stood in a wooden pulpit at the far end of the house, and appeared to be in a dim haze, which I interpreted as the nimbus which we see surrounding holy pictures. The seats or pews were composed of oak poles with the bark on, having legs driven into auger holes on the under side to keep them in place. The bark was rough and uncomfortable to my tender flesh, and on the way home I asked father about it. He said regular members had the privilege of sitting in the same place until they wore the poles smooth, but as we were not even probationers we had to take things as we found them. I understood this to mean that you could not begin to smooth your seat until you were a regular member, and he said I had the correct idea. If you expected a smooth seat in the German church you had to be something better than a probationer, for it took more than six months to smooth the bark by sitting on it.

During the services I had observed a young man sitting next to me who seemed to be deeply moved, but when they called for mourners he did not go forward. I inferred that he was smoothing his seat and wept because it was so rough, and said as much to father; but the old gentleman said he thought he had given me information enough for one time, and declined to answer my question. Older people do not always understand children. I was genuinely sorry for that young German, and have sympathized with him all my life. Some people may think this is not so, but it is. There are soft cushions in church pews now, but I wonder if the religion that occupies them is any more sincere than that of the young German who sat on the oak pole and wept because it was so rough?

Louis Helgerdick and His Son Otto

One of our best German neighbors was Louis Helgerdick, who spelled his name "Hellofadick," but did not pronounce the way he spelled. He came to our house one day to borrow some turkey eggs, which he said he wanted to set under a "schicken hen" and raise some turkeys. When my sister gave him the eggs he asked her if a "schicken hen" would sit on a turkey's eggs as well as her own, because he had no turkey hen and he was not sure as to results. My sister told him a chicken hen would set on any kind of eggs if you approached her when she was in a "setting" mood. She knew an old hen that sat on some snake's eggs and hatched out a nest of rattlers. This had a discouraging effect on Louis, who was mortally afraid of snakes; and he was not sure but his "schicken hen" might gather up some eggs of that kind. But he persisted in his original purpose, and in due course of time became the proud owner of a dozen young turkeys.

Helgerdick had a son Otto, who was a playmate of mine, and the very apple of his father's eye. Otto and I were fond of each other, but he had never been baptized, and I asked him one day if he thought it was safe to live that way. Not long afterward he took the measles, and was very sick, because the measles did not "break out". His father said he needed two things, baptism, and for the measles to come out. So he tenderly folded Otto in a sheet, and carried him down to the creek, where he submerged him in the cold water until he was chilled to the bone. That night Otto died, and the next day his father died of a broken heart. The two were buried in a single grave, and every one admitted that it was the saddest tragedy that had ever occurred in the Boone country. The poor father said with his last breath that he did the best he could for Otto, but measles and baptism would not sleep in the same bed.

Tobacco and Gunpowder

Andrew Davidson, who lived near our farm, believed that the Indians had been badly treated, especially in not having been baptized in their youth; and in order to make amends as far as he could, he showed the warriors special favors. He invited them to his house as honored guests, and when the weather was warm he accompanied them to the creek and showed them how to bathe, which he told them was the white man's baptism. The warriors became so fond of the exercise that they would go to the creek and get baptized several times a day when the weather was uncomfortable.

He also kept a supply of tobacco for them, which they regarded as the "plant of peace", and as Davidson offered them none but the best, raised by his own hands, they became very much attached to the good white man. But he had a son who was mischievous, and often got him in trouble by the pranks that he played on other people. So one day when a delegation of chiefs and warriors were coming to smoke the pipe of peace this boy mixed a pound of gunpowder with the tobacco, and waited around for results. When it was time for the smoking party, and the warriors lit their pipes, several of them had their noses almost blown off and their eyes dimmed by the flashing powder, and a battle would have been staged except for the opportune arrival of Uncle Daniel, who was to be the guest of honor for the day.

He explained the matter to the satisfaction of the chiefs, saying it was merely a boyish prank, such as their own boys sometimes played for the sake of a little fun. They were so well pleased to know that it was nothing worse than a joke that they insisted on being introduced to the boy, whom they patted on the back and invited to visit them in their own country, where they would "give him plenty good powder to smoke." But the boy never found a convenient opportunity to accept their courtesy, and so escaped what probably might have been something more than a joke for him.

Missouri's First Legislature

Some of the incidents recorded in the pages that follow may excite the inquisitiveness of the reader; and while most of them are true, it may be well to consider the brilliance of the pioneer imagination in passing judgement. In a large measure the incidents illustrate the personal characteristics of Uncle Daniel's neighbors, and in that respect are valuable historical reminiscences. We should also remember that the men whose eccentricities now seem so amusing, were the ones who laid the foundations of our government and social institutions, and we can hardly appreciate what we have without an impartial view of the things that went before.

Missouri was admitted into the Union of States during the session of Congress of 1820-1821, and the first Legislature met in St. Charles the following winter. I believe the old house on Main Street where the members held their sessions is still standing; it was the last time I visited St. Charles; and if it is there yet the ladies of the D.A.R. have undoubtedly given it prominence by placing a tablet upon its walls.

Uncle Daniel had been dead about a year when his neighbors met and organized the State Government; if he had been living at the time he would undoubtedly have been a member of the Legislature and very likely the first Governor. At any rate his spirit dominated the proceedings of the assembly.

A majority of the members came on horseback from their homes in the wilderness; others walked and carried their guns and camping outfit, and all of them subsisted for the most part on the game they encountered.

On arriving in St. Charles they experienced difficulty in finding accommodations in so small a place. Those who had horses hired them kept by a Mr. Watson, who lived in "the point" below the city, and was the only man in the country who was able to care for so many animals at one time. When the legislative session was over he returned the horses to their owners in such good condition and so frisky that several dignified members were obliged to re-tame their steeds before they could mount them.

Mr. Watson was a fine old gentleman and a staunch believer in the moral influences of the Sunday school. Early in life he prepared and committed to memory a speech on the subject, and thereafter attended every convention within his reach and delivered the speech for the good of the public. He never changed a word or sentence, and probably repeated the oration several hundred times during the remainder of his life. It affected him so keenly that he wept during the exercise, and some of the audience also wept when they remembered that a scrumptious basket dinner was waiting.

Style in Food and Clothing

The members of the Legislature secured accommodations for themselves among the citizens and at boarding houses, at the uniform rate of $2.50 per week; and it is claimed that those who supplied the entertainment lost money. The honorable gentlemen were a healthy lot, and seemed to have eaten their hosts out of house and home. Mr. Uriah Devore, who boarded several of them, declared that he lost everything he had except his hopes of heaven, and they were jeopardized by the morals of his guests. Yet the low prices of food might indicate that a householder ought to have been able to board a member of the Legislature without going into bankruptcy. Pork sold for one and a half cent per pound; venison hams 25 cents each; eggs five cents a dozen (employed mainly); honey was a drug on the market at five cents a gallon, and was used mainly for sweetening liquids because there was no sugar in the market. Several families had small stocks of maple sugar, but it was too precious to waste on members of the Legislature.

Most of the members were dressed in suits of buckskin, or homespun coats and knee breeches, with buckskin leggings and moccasins. A few wore rough leather boots of their own manufacture–shoes were unknown–but they were regarded with suspicion as being inclined to foppishness. A duel was fought on the river bank early one morning by two members, one of whom had called the other a "feather-head dandy" because he wore boots. Although both of the gentlemen were regarded as dead shots, neither was hurt, owing to the fact that they had stimulated their courage so liberally that it interfered with their aim.

Caps made of the skins of raccoons or wild cats were the prevailing style of head-dress, though there were a few slouch hats and one or two Revolutionary cocked-hats of the style worn by Washington and Napoleon. The French emperor had but lately died in exile, and the death of Washington was of such recent occurrence that the fame of both was still fresh in the memory of the pioneer statesmen. Indeed it was claimed that several of the legislatures had not heard of the death of the great American until their arrival in St. Charles, and they were visibly affected by the sad news.

Gov. McNair set the style for upper-tendon with a blue-cloth coat, cut square at the waist and rounding back to a split pigeon-tail. Two rows of brightly polished brass buttons ornamented the front, and two single buttons of the same kind marked the center of the waistline in the back. It was claimed that the rear buttons were placed there as targets to be shot at, but as no Missouri Governor ever ran away from a gun this slander was attributed to personal animosity. The buttons might have served as a point of fascination for the fair sex as the Governor receded from view, for he was reputed to be a very handsome man. His feet were decorated with highly polished boots, the trademark of the polish being a rampant rooster fighting his own reflection on the surface of the leather, while a gleeful negro enjoyed the fun as he brushed the other boot. The Governor wore short breeches of the same color as his coat, and on his head sat a tall beaver hat with a flaring crown, which was soon to be made famous as the hat of Jackson and Jacksonian Democrats. Beavers were plentiful, their fur abundant, and the proportions of the hat were adjusted to the supply.

The Honorable Jacob Groom

One of the unique characters of this first Missouri Legislature was the Hon. Jacob Groom of Montgomery County. He wore short buckskin breeches with homemade woolen stockings and deer-skin moccasins tanned with the hair on. A buckskin hunting coat of ample proportions adorned his upper person while on the top of his statesman-like head rested a round-topped hat of no particular style and also made at home. The brim of the hat was extra narrow to avoid interference with his aim in shooting wild cats. Throughout the session he carried a heavy hickory cane, with a knob on the end formed by the roots of the sapling which had supplied the timber for the staff. He walked from his home in Montgomery County to St. Charles, subsisting on the game that his rifle supplied, and sleeping at night under the stars or in hollow logs.

MR. GROOM ARISES TO A POINT OF ORDER.

Jacob and the Piano

Jacob became a noted character in the Assembly, and was invited to several social functions where his wit and common sense attitude toward things won him great favor. Early in the session he and several other members received an invitation to a tea at the hospitable home of Mrs. Dr. Young, whose first name, Martha, gave title to the village of Marthasville. Her beauty and wit made her the leader of the fashion of the time, and it was no small honor to be asked to take tea at her house.

It had also been noised abroad that Mrs. Young had a piano, the only instrument of the kind west of St. Louis, and the honorable Jacob's imagination became excited. He longed to see the wonderful instrument that "howled when you touched its ivory". Therefore, on being ushered into the parlor and while awaiting the appearance of the lady herself, he critically examined every article of furniture in the room, and observing an old-fashioned bedstead in one corner, with curtains and valance, he concluded that it must be the musical instrument which had so excited his fancy.

Soon the charming hostess appeared, and welcomed the guests with a gracious courtesy that put them all at their ease. She had heard of Mr. Groom, and to him she showed special favor, a courtesy which he relished. Feeling at ease in her presence, he introduced the subject of music, declaring that he was passionately fond of the divine harmony and often played the fiddle at home to while away the lonely hours. Having thus paved the way to the subject which he had in mind, he informed Mrs. Young that he had heard of her piano, and it would fill his soul with rapture to hear its melody under her delicate touch. Would the lady therefore be so gracious as to favor the company with a performance? Whereupon, with a flourish, he arose and offering her his arm led her to the side of the bed. The lady blushed and stammered, caught her breath, and tried to explain; and then availing herself of the universal feminine privilege, burst into tears and fled from the room.

Jacob was overcome. He had not the slightest idea why or how he had offended the hostess, for his intentions were complimentary in the highest degree. He appealed to his fellow-guests, who, being better posted, explained the situation. Then Jacob was even more embarrassed than the lady herself had been; but there was no way to clear the atmosphere without making the matter worse. So it was allowed to drift along and take care of itself. By the time tea was ready Mrs. Young had recovered her equanimity, and being a sensible little person she made no reference to the unfortunate incident, but rattled along with the conversation as if nothing had happened. Later in the evening she went to the piano and with delicate touch showed her guests how it could be made to "howl" by the touch of the ivories.

Jacksonian Democrats

The first Legislature held its session during the time that the "Old Hickory" excitement was at its height. The hero of New Orleans was the political idol of the South and West for his great victory at New Orleans; but he had been defeated by John Quincy Adams in his first effort to win the Presidency. His friends everywhere were sore from center to circumference, and just as determined that their leader should win at the next turn of the political wheel. In every group of men a majority would be "Jacksonian Democrats", and they were systematically concentrating their force for the next effort. Jacob Groom was in the movement over his head, and during the session he made a memorable speech setting forth his ideas. It was so remarkable a performance that one of the members took it down in short-hand, and it was published in "The Missourian", a paper which had been established at St. Charles to report the proceedings of the Legislature. A friend gave me an aged, yellow copy of the paper, and I shall now endeavor to give the speech the immortality which it deserves.

Episode Number Sixty-One

Jacob Groom's Immortal Speech

T he honorable member from Montgomery had the floor, and probably there never was another speech like his delivered before a legislative assembly. It is unique in language and thought. But we are anticipating; let the honorable Jacob speak for himself:

"Members of this Meeting:"

"You don't know me, I 'spose: well, it's no matter! I tell you my name is Jacob Groom; I live at Big Springs Postoffice in Montgomery County. I air the postmaster, being a Jacksonian Dimmycrat of the upright principle. You see I am a big man—can eat a heap—can eat green 'simmons without puckerin'. Salt don't keep me, nor licker down me. I air a tearin' critter of the catamount school, and a teetotal porker in pollyticks. In religion I am neutral and masculine on the upright principle."

"Gentlemen Jacksonians and fellers of this conflicacious community in this land of concuss-edness and supernaciousness, Jacksonians, I say, exaggerate yourselves and support the inefflica-ciousness of the oracle of Jackson. My friends, the cause of the vote of the veloniciousness of the United States Bank was the perlicution of the Clay party, and when Jackson has spyficated the confi-dence of the present Congress, he will rise in his superscilious majesty and crush the growing pow-ers of these illusionable states. This, gentlemen Jacksonians, was adequate to the circumference of Jacksonianism."

"And I now previse you to exaggerate yourselves and let them that you left behind see the doin's of this 'Sembly, the first that has ever met in this town of St. Charles. Just before we all got to this place we stayed all night at our friend John Pittman's on the road, where we enjoyed the good eaten', drinkin', and dancin' of the hospiculities of our old friend Pittman."

"I am no book larnt man, but there is few can beat me swappin' horses or guessin' at the weight of a b'ar. I have come here because my people voted for me, known' I was a honest man, and could make as good whiskey and apple brandy at my still as any man. I want you all to commit the same like feelin', and finish the whole job on the Jacksonian principle; and if you don't do as I previse you will come short and it will be harder for you to git to this place ag'in than it would be to ride down from the clouds on a thunderbolt through a crab apple tree and not git scratched."

Mr. Groom took his seat in the midst of thunderous applause, and the 'Sembly proceeded with its Jacksonian efflorescence. The gentleman's constituents were so well pleased with his efforts in the first Legislature that they reelected him to several subsequent terms, and though uneducated and without experience in public affairs he had common sense enough to make himself useful. He remained all his life a leading "Jacksonian Democrat", and exercised an influence that gave his distinction among our earlier statesmen.

A Personal Glimpse

And now it will be interesting to get a personal glimpse of the character of Mr. Groom's constituency at the time. The Rev. Timothy Flint, a Presbyterian minister of Connecticut, came to the Boone settlements in 1816, five years before the delivery of the great speech. He was an educated man and a missionary; a close observer and wrote much about the habits and customs of the people. But what he wrote should be weighed with care, as he gave his imagination a wide rein and was naturally prejudiced against the unrestrained freedom that he found in the West. Yet for the most part of his pictures are true to life as he saw it:

"In approaching the country," he wrote, "I heard thousands of stories of 'gougings,' and robberies, and shooting down with rifle." (But in fact there were not a "thousand" gougings, shootings, and robberies in the whole Boone settlement during its entire existence. If each of them had been counted they probably would have numbered less than a hundred; but there were enough to give tone to the realities, and brother Flint allowed his imagination to do the rest. However, he makes amends for some of his stories, but stretches the blanket again in saying that he "traveled thousands of miles" through the region.) "I have traveled thousands of miles through the region," he says, "under all circumstances of exposure and danger, I have traveled alone, or in company only with such as needed protection, instead of being able to impart it. . . I never have carried the slightest weapon of defense, and I scarcely remember to have experienced anything that resembled insult, or to have felt myself in danger from the people. I have often seen men that had lost an eye. Instance of murder, numerous and horrible in their circumstances, have occurred in my vicinity." (Again his imagination travels with a loose rein. There were not twenty murders in the Boone country during its entire history, and they were not any more "horrible" than shootings that usually take place among rough and unhampered peoples. But he proceeds to soften the impeachment in the following terms.) "But they were such lawless encounters as terminate in murder everywhere, and in which the drunkenness, brutality, and violence were mutual. They were catastrophes in which quiet and sober men would not be involved. . The first Sabbath that I preached in St. Charles, before morning worship, directly opposite where worship was to take place, there was a horse-race. The horses received the signal to start just as I rode to the door."

The gentleman does not tell us whether he participated in the race or not, but he does say that the people who engaged in the pastime were orderly and devout. A horse-race at the place of religious services and just a moment before its commencement, was a very unusual experience for a New England Presbyterian minister, and we are not surprised that he was shocked. His leading member may have owned the winning horse. He proceeds to relate that when he visited the same place six years later he preached in "a decent brick church" which had been erected in the meantime. Evidently the pioneers believed there was a time for all things, horse-racing a well as preaching, and they did not allow one to interfere with the other. When the race was over the participants repaired to church and listened reverently to the sermon.

A few years later Mr. Flint engaged in farming, and did much to encourage the industry of cotton growing in the community. He also made wine from grapes, and shared it freely with those who came to see him, a course of conduct which sent many other good men and women to prison during the reign of prohibition. And thus we see that things which are regarded as immoral and even criminal in one age, may be evidence of friendly hospitality in another.

The Rev. Jabez Ham

Probably you will remember the pioneer lady who wrote back home describing a wedding at which the Rev. Jabez Ham officiated, and her account of his dress and appearance. He was one of the most original characters that came to the Boone settlements, and he made an impression which lasts even to the present time.

Hunting and preaching were his chief occupations, and wherever he traveled he carried his gun with him. It supplied him with venison and bear meat and afforded him protection from wild cats and "painters". He was stout and robust and emphasized his sermons by pounding on the pulpit, or the table when there was no pulpit at hand. On a certain occasion he forgot the text from which he had intended to preach, and announced the dilema to the congregation in a brief address; meanwhile hammering the pulpit so vigorously that he split the boards. "When I left home this morning," he said, "I had a tex', but I've lost it and can't find it, and Hannah looked for it and couldn't find it; but to the best of my belief it was some'ers in the hind-end a' Job, or thereabouts, and went about like this: Do any of you'ns know the good woman they call Mary, or Sol of Tarkus, who said you must not put new wine into old bottles, or the bottles will bust and the good stuff run out."

Regardless of the liberty construction of his sermons, his delivery was so energetic that he had no trouble in driving home his thoughts into the minds of his congregations. They understood what he meant, and no man had a wider or healthier influence than Brother Ham. He compared his sermons to a shotgun loaded with beans, which "was sure to hit some sinner when it went off, and make him remember to obey the scripture."

One of his favorite expressions was, "Shoot him with a pack-saddle," applied mainly to those who would not join his church. One of his sermons has been preserved in its original form and idiom, and it will afford some idea of the power he wielded over his audiences:

A Sample Sermon

"And my sheep shall know my voice, and when I call they will come; but a stranger's voice they know not, and therefore they won't come, Ah."

"Now my brothering, my sheep is likened unto a little goat named Cato, that my father had, Ah. One day Cato came up missing, Ah, and the thunder, and lightnin', and wind was a-comin' on at a mighty rate, Ah; and we children went out and called Cato, Ah, and no Cato answered we children, Ah. But Pap just poked his head out'n the winder, Ah, and called Cato one time, Ah, and Cato said baa, Ah. So you see, my brethering, Ah, poor Cato knowed Pap's voice, and as soon as he called him he answered, Ah. Just so it will be with us at the great day of judgement, Ah. When the Master shall call his sheep, Ah, they will answer, Ah; and a heap of 'em will answer, Ah, that he did not call, Ah; and a heap of 'em will answer, Ah, that he did not call, Ah; and a heap of 'em will have wolves skins, Ah and pretend they are sheep, Ah; but the great Sheperd will know which of 'em wears the wool, Ah. So Pap called poor Cato and he said baa, Ah. Tes, my brethering, when Gabriel shall stand with one foot on the ground and the other on the water, Ah and blow that long trumpet, Ah, that will wake up the dead and the livin', Ah, and the livin' will start a-runnin', Ah, and callin' on Brother Ham to save them from the blue blazes of hell, Ah."

"I think I hear some brother say over in that corner, Ah, Brother Ham can't preach, Ah; and think I hear some brother in that other corner say Brother Ham can preach, Ah; but if you'll wait a while Brother Ham will turn himself loose, Ah, and lumber, Ah. And when Pap called poor Cato he said baa, Ah. "

"We are told, my brethering, Ah, that we must not put new wine into old bottles, Ah; and it becometh us to fill full all righteousness, Ah, and not to back bite our neighbor, Ah, nor our neighbor's ass, nor anything that is his, Ah. And the Bible says, wives, do good to your husband Ah, and husbands do good to your wives, Ah, and children obey your father and mother, Ah. And I want to know tonight, Ah, how many of you have done these things, Ah. And Pap called poor Cato, and he said baa, Ah."

"Now in conclusion I want to say to you, my brethering, Ah, that if any of you get to heaven, Ah, before Brother Ham, Ah, just say that I'm a'comin' too, ah. And while I have been a-preachin' this night, Ah, some of my sheep have gone to sleep, Ah; and I will ask Brother Logan to say to that man talkin' at the door not to talk so loud, Ah, or I'll shoot him with a pack-saddle, Ah; and he may wake up Sister Cobb, Ah, who is setting there in the corner asleep, Ah."

"And my sheep will know my voice, Ah, and when I call they will come, Ah. And Pap called poor Cato, Ah, and Cato said baa, Ah."

Brother Ham's Farewell to Marthasville

For several years Brother Ham had a regular appointment at the log church at Marthasville, which stood on the hill above the spring, where the old graveyard can still be seen. But as the other settlements grew and his congregation increased in numbers he could not serve them all as well as he wished; so he prepared a farewell sermon to the people of Marthasville in the following terms:

"Brethering and sisters, Ah, it happens in the course of human events, Ah, that Marthasville is too far away from the center of the universe, Ah, to remain permanently in my list of appointments, Ah. Therefore I have concluded to preach you a farewell sermon, Ah, and prepare you to meet the Lord, Ah, to whose tender mercies I consign you, Ah.

"As I rode along this mornin', Ah, on my old mare Sal, Ah, all nature seemed in harmony with my feelings, ah. A doe and her fawn came out of the woods, Ah, and stood in the road ahead of me, Ah, and waited until I was almost up to them, ah, when they jumped back into the woods,Ah, and shook their tails at me, Ah, and seemed to say, 'Fairwell, Brother Ham,' Ah.

"And as I rode along an owl poked his head out'n a hole in a tree, Ah, and said, 'Who-who-air-you,' Ah, and I said, 'I'm the Rev. Jabez Ham, Ah, goin' to preach a farewell sermon,' Ah. And he tucked his head into his hole, ah, and seemed to say, 'Farewell Brother Ham,' Ah.

"And after a while, Ah, I come down from the hills into the valley of the crick, Ah, and a bullfrog was a-settin' on a log, Ah, and he jumps into the crick, Ah, and says, 'Jug-a-room,' Ah, which means 'Farewell, Brother Ham ,'Ah.

"And when I come to the ford of the crick, ah, the water looked so clear and cool, Ah, I got down to bathe my face and hands, Ah, and as I was a-bathin', Ah, Old Sal runs away, Ah, and as she went over the bank of the crick, Ah, she waved her tail and seemed to say, Ah, 'Farewell, Brother Ham,' ah.

"And now my dear brethering and sisters, Ah, being obleeged to walk the rest of the way, Ah, and the day bein' warm, Ah, I am somewhat weary in the service of the Lord, Ah, and will dismiss you to his tender mercies and go home with Brother Callaway, Ah, and refresh myself with a horn of his peach brandy, Ah. So, my brethering and sisters, Ah, I bid you an affectionate farewell, Ah, admonishin' you to beware of the wiles of Satan, Ah."

The earthly remains of Brother Ham probably occupy some obscure burial place, covered with weeds and briars and unknown to mortal man; but wherever it may be he deserves a monument for the good he intended to do. No matter how secluded the place may be, or how much it is covered with unfriendly growths, it is pleasant to know that once a year the brairs blossom, and again once a year the ripe fruit hangs from their gnarled branches; and that every year and at all seasons the birds rest there and sing their songs of glory. Every life is worth living that is devoted to the good of others, regardless of what or where the end may be.

Murder of an Indian Boy

Indians were not as bad as they too often were painted. Some of course were bad enough for any purpose, but their worst deeds were generally provoked in retaliation for wrongs done them by whites as cruel and savage as themselves. If all white men had been like Uncle Daniel, and all the red ones like Black Hawk, there would have been little if any trouble between races.

In the first instance, the Indians regarded the forests as their natural hunting preserves, in as true a sense as the whites considered their farms their own. The white pioneer would have died in defense of his farm and home, and the Indian tried to do the same in punishing the pale face whom he found trespassing upon what he felt belonged to him; each in his own way.

The rangers who were organized for the protection of the border during the war with Black Hawk and his red followers, did many brave and noble deeds, and their heroism makes a romantic page in the history of our country; but they were not all anglic. Some of them were as bad as any Indian that ever lived, and take them singly or in bands and companies there were not many of them who had feathers enough to make even the wing of an angle.

A ranger named Thomas Massey, a member of Nathan Boone's command, crossed the Mississippi one day with several companions, and invaded a region which was regarded by the Indians as their special hunting ground. Here they encountered an old warrior and his son chasing a deer, and pretending that they were in forbidden precincts Massey and his companions took the boy across the river to the Missouri side and shot him, in full view of his father. Subsequently Black Hawk assembled a band of warriors and followed Massey to his home in Loutre Island, but failing to find the leader of the company that had slain the boy, they ambushed and shot his brother as he was plowing in a field.

This was purely an act of retribution, justified by Indian law and custom. Indeed the Indians would have considered themselves cowards and renegades if they had neglected to avenge the old warrior for the death of his son. In many instances the rangers themselves acted in a similar manner. It was understood that retribution would follow every overt deed in that era of savagery when men's passions made their customs. It was the age-old law of an eye for an eye and a tooth for a tooth, with no thought on either side of loving your neighbor as yourself.

The leaders on both sides were opposed to such retaliatory measures, but they could not control their men when beyond the reach of their immediate command. The reference to Massey being a member of Nathan Boone's company, might give color to the belief that the latter was himself of a savage disposition; but nothing could be further from the truth. Nathan Boone was like his father. He loved peace rather than war, and was disposed to go even to extremes in preserving amity and justice between the two peoples. If he had been present at the time there would have been no aggression on the part of his men, and no new incentive would have been given to the spirit of hatred. The old Indian would not have had cause to mourn the death of his son, or to feel that his Gods demanded vengeance for the wrong.

Black Hawk's Pathetic Account

Black Hawk was a personal friend of the old Indian whose son was murdered; and in his autobiography he gives an account of the deplorable affair. The great chief throws a degree of poetic fancy into his story that would do honor to an educated philosopher.

There was no war prevailing at the time between the whites and the red people, but Black Hawk and a party of his warriors had been on a visit to the Indian settlements on the Wabash River, where hostilities had been practically decided upon. As they were returning home the chief observed smoke arising out of the wigwam of his friend who was mourning the death of his son; then follows his account of what took place:

"In three days we were in the vicinity of our village, when I discovered smoke ascending from a hollow in the bluffs. I directed my party to proceed to the village, as I wished to go alone to the place from whence the smoke proceeded, to see who was there. I approached the spot, and when I came in view of the fire I saw a mat stretched and an old man sitting upon it in sorrow. At any other time I would have turned away without disturbing him, knowing that he had come there to be alone, to humble himself before the Great Spirit that he might take pity upon him. I approached and seated myself beside him. He gave one look at me and then fixed his eyes on the ground. It was my old friend. I anxiously inquired for his son, and what had befallen our people. My old comrade seemed scarcely alive; he must have fasted a long time. I lighted my pipe and put it in his mouth. He eagerly drew a few puffs, cast up his eyes, which met mine, and he recognized me. His eyes were glassy. He would again have fallen off into forgetfulness, had I not given him some water, which revived him. I again inquired what had befallen our people, and what had become of his son. In a feeble voice he said: 'Soon after your departure to join the British, I descended the river with a small party, to winter at the place I told you the white man had requested me to come. When we arrived I found a fort built, and the white family that had invited me to come and hunt near them had removed it. I then paid a visit to the fort, to tell the white people that myself and little band were friendly, and that we wished to hunt in the vicinity of their fort. The war chief who commanded it (Nathan Boone) told me that we might hunt on the Illinois side of the Mississippi, and no person would trouble us; that the horsemen only ranged on the Missouri side; and he directed them not to cross the river. I was pleased with this assurance of safety, and immediately crossed over and made my winter's camp.

"'Game was plentiful, we lived happy, and often talked of you. My boy regretted your absence, and the hardships you would have to undergo.'

"'We had been there about two moons, when my boy went out as usual to hunt. Night came on and he did not return; I was alarmed for his safety and passed a sleepless night. In the morning my old woman went to the other lodges and gave alarm, and all turned out in pursuit. There being snow on the ground they soon came upon the track, and after pursuing it some distance they found he was on the trail of a deer that led toward the river. They soon came to the place where he had stood and fired, and found a deer hanging on the branch of a tree, which had been skinned. But here were found tracks of white men. They had taken my boy prisoner. These tracks led across the river and then down toward the fort. My friends followed them, and soon found my boy lying dead. He had been most cruelly murdered. His face was shot to pieces, his body stabbed in several places, and his head scalped. His arms were tied behind him.'

"The old man paused for some time, and then told me that his wife had died on her way up the Mississippi. I took the hand of my old friend in mine, and pledged myself to avenge the death of his son. It was now dark, a terrible storm commenced raging, with heavy torrents of rain, thunder and lightning. I had taken my blanket off and wrapped around the old man. When the storm abated I kindled the fire, and took hold of my old friend to move him near it, but he was dead."

Black Hawk was faithful to his promise. He led the band that slew the brother of the man who had caused the death of his friend's son, and this incident had more to do with the outbreak of the war that came so near destroying the white settlements than anything else.

When we go to the bottom of human nature we find that all men are very much alike in the emotions and passions that control them. And who would have thought that an unsettled savage like Black Hawk could have dictated so fine a panegyric as the one he devoted to his old friend? There is little in the Greek or Roman classics that surpasses it.

A Tragedy of Profound Influence

The tragedy that sank deepest into the hearts of Uncle Daniel and his neighbors, and was longer remembered than any other, was the ambushment and death of Captain James Callaway and three of his men at Loutre Creek, in what is now the southwestern part of Montgomery County. It occurred on the 7th of March, 1815, a year that was marked by more fighting and bloodshed than any other during Black Hawk's campaigns against the white settlements.

The resourceful chieftain had resolved to make life among the pale faces so certain and dangerous that they would abandon their homes and return to the older states; but his efforts were opposed by a still greater leader in the person of Daniel Boone; and the contest ended by the red chief and his warriors being driven back to their own country beyond the Mississippi, with losses much greater than they had been able to inflict upon their opponents.

James Callaway was a grandson of the famous white chief, his mother being Jemima Boone, around whose name so much romance had been woven in connection with the capture of herself and two girl friends while they were living in the fort at Boonesboro. The other two girls were daughters of Colonel Richard Callaway, a friend of Daniel Boone; and his son, Flanders Callaway, was a member of the party that pursued and rescued the girls. In this way the two families had become related, and in the romantic annals of the West the name of Callaway is as prominent as that of Boone. Flanders Callaway married Jemima Boone, and their son James, destined to a brief but glorious career, was born in Kentucky in 1783. When he was fifteen years of age his parents removed to Missouri, and settled on a tract of land in the Missouri River bottoms near Marthasville. Their farm adjoined one owned by my father at a later period, and it was here that I absorbed much of the romance of those stirring times in memories related by him as we sat by the winter's log-fire.

As there were no schools in that locality at the time, James returned to Kentucky and spent several years in study there, rejoining his parents when he was twenty-two years old. Handsome, well educated, genial and full of life, he seemed destined by his family connections to a career above average. A year or two later he was married to Frances Howell, a charming beauty who lived with her parents a few miles distance from the Boone home; and the young couple entered upon a life of promise and usefulness. They made themselves a home in the northwestern part of Howell's Prairie, where, after his untimely death, his widow continued to live until she attained the unusual age of ninety years. I remember "Aunt Fanny" in my boyhood as a sweet-faced old lady who made the best maple sugar candy that anybody ever ate. But what a long and lonely life she lived! Perhaps that was why she was so good and sweet.

At the first intimation of trouble with the Indians in 1813, young Callaway organized a company of rangers and was chosen their captain, a position which he maintained with honor until his tragic death two years later. He seemed to have inherited a genius for leadership from his famous grandfather, and came into it naturally without effort on his part. But he did not possess the strategy and wise discretion that were such distinguishing features of his great ancestor, and for lack of them he came to an untimely death.

During the forepart of 1815, when Indian hostilities had assumed their most threatening proportions, Captain Callaway was stationed at Fort Clemson, on Loutre Island, with a small command of rangers, recklessly desperate characters as their adventures soon demonstrated. Clemson was an outpost of a chain of forts which had been established on the recommendation of Uncle Daniel, and his grandson was stationed there, not because of any favoritism, but owing to the exposed position of the place and the confidence the people had in the young commander. Lieutenant Riggs second in command, had already proven himself a brave and wise leader on several trying occasions; and with such men and officers in charge of the most important outpost, the settlers felt that they were safe.

Episode Number Sixty- Three

A Desperate Adventure

On the 7th of March, 1815, a scout reported that a band of Indians was in the vicinity of Fort Clemson, and that they had stolen several horses from the settlers. Their trail indicated a force of between eighty and a hundred, besides several women; and it was later ascertained that Black Hawk himself was their leader. The presence of the wiley chief might easily have been inferred by the fact of women in the party, for it was a theory of his that men would fight better under the observation of their women than when alone.

Callaway immediately selected a party of only fourteen of his best scouts and set out in pursuit, accompanied by Lieutenant Riggs. Going after a hundred armed savages under as shrewd a leader as Black Hawk, with only fourteen men, was a daring adventure; but the men of that age held the courage of the savages in content and cared but little about their numbers.

Loutre Island is formed by a slough of the same name, which flows out of the Missouri River, and after winding its course for several miles through the bottom turns and empties again into the larger stream. It is a deep, sluggish bayou, dangerous by reason of its muddy banks; and at this season of the year its waters were chilled by the ice of winter. In order to reach the mainland it was necessary for the men to cross the slough, and without hesitation they plunged their horses into the icey flood and crossed to the opposite side. It would seem that such a baptism would cool the ardor of the stoutest hearts, but it only added new fire to the courage of these hardy rangers. Proceeding eastward they came to Loutre Creek, which empties into the slough from the north at almost right angles. Here they found the trail leading northward along the west bank of the creek. It was broad and plain and showed no desire for concealment. The red warriors were inviting pursuit!

Presently they came to a small stream called Prairie Fork, a tributary of Loutre flowing into it from the west, as it lay between them and freezing water and swam across. Even at this distant day it makes one shiver to read of such exploits.

It was now about noon, and feeling sure they were near the enemy they proceeded with more caution. Two hours later they came upon the camp, located in the bend of Loutre Creek. Not a warrior was in sight, but there were several women who fled into the woods on the appearance of the white rangers. So far they had met no opposition, but it was evident that they were being enclosed within an ambuscade planned by a shrewd leader. Lieutenant Riggs suggested as much to his commander, who assigned two of the best men to assist Riggs in searching the woods. No sign of an Indian was discovered; yet at that very moment a hundred savages lay in concealment in plain view of the white pursuers. They might easily have ended the affair at once with a single volley; but Black Hawk had but little faith in the old-style muskets with which his men were armed, and he chose to await a more favorable opportunity, when the knife and the tomahawk might also be brought into action.

Massacre of Callaway and His Men

On the return of Riggs and his men, they secured the stolen horses and started back to the fort. Riggs protested earnestly against following the same route by which they had come, as the Indians would undoubtedly resort to one of their old tricks, by doubling back on their trail and firing upon them from concealment and at close quarters. The very fact that he had been unable to find a single warrior convinced the shrewd Lieutenant that they were in numbers and would make themselves visible at their own chosen time and place. But Callaway declared that he did not believe there were half-a-dozen Indians in the country, and that he would return by the way he had come. Riggs said nothing, and the rangers were soon in the saddle and threading their way homeward on their trail in the morning.

About a mile before reaching Prairie Fork they stopped to rest their horses and eat their lunch; and once more Riggs remonstrated with his commander against following the old trail. He represented that they would undoubtedly be attacked at the junction of the smaller stream, which they could avoid by making a detour and crossing at a point higher up. But although Callaway was himself a shrewd Indian fighter and should have learned wisdom from the experience of his ancestor, on this occasion he seemed to have lost all discretion, and flying into a passion he accused his assistant of cowardice; asserting at the same time he would return the way he had come if he had to go alone.

Riggs keenly felt the injustice of the accusation, but restrained himself and made no reply. When the order to mount and proceed was given he felt that they were about to ride into the jaws of death. Three men were sent in advance with the stolen horses, the rest of the company following at a distance of about a hundred yards. This was the shrewdest maneuver of the entire adventure, for it would oblige the Indians to fire on the small party in advance and thus uncover their ambuscade and it turned out precisely that way. It was all that saved the entire party from massacre.

Prairie Fork, though a small stream, was swollen by the spring thaw and recent rains, and as soon as the men in advance drove their horses into the water they became unmanageable. Plunging and rearing they refused to enter the cold water and endeavored to make their way back to the rear; when instantly from both sides of the stream there came a crash of musketry.

But neither horse nor man was harmed by this fired volley! Black Hawk's estimate of the quality of his men's guns was verified. The three rangers now spurred their horses across the stream, but were all killed as they attempted to ascend the bank on the opposite side. Whether they fell from point-blank discharges or were hacked to death with tomahawks is not known; but the latter would seem the more probable from developments of the following day. With their horses struggling in the mud in the very presence of the Indians, it was impossible for them to offer the least resistance, and they fell helpless victims to the ferocity of their foes.

At the first crash of musketry Callaway spurred his horse forward and plunged into the creek, followed by his men. He had almost reached the other bank when his horse was killed by a shot fired within ten feet of him. He himself was wounded in the left arm, just over the heart, but his life was saved for the instant by the ball striking his watch and glancing off. Then he seemed bereft of all sense of judgement. Leaping from his dying horse to the shore he threw his rifle into the creek, muzzle downward, and running down the stream a short distance plunged once again into the water and tried to swim to the opposite side. But as he reached midstream a shot struck him in the back of the head and he sank out of sight.

Meanwhile Riggs and the remainder of the men were hotly engaged by forces of the enemy on both sides of the stream, but retreated, firing at random as they ran. In this way they killed and wounded several of their assailants, as they discovered later; but not a single ranger was hurt. Again Black Hawk's estimate of the shooting qualities of the guns carried by his men was confirmed. It had been his plan to bring the contending parties close enough together to use the hatchet and the knife, but it was frustrated by the strategy of the white commander.

During the retreat two of the men, Scott and Wolff, were separated from the main body, and the former was killed in a combat with two savages who closed in upon him with their knives. Wolff was the first to reach the fort, where he reported that he was the only survivor of the party; but about dark Riggs and the others came in.

Grim Reminders of Savage Warfare

Early next morning Riggs led a rescue party to the scene of conflict, where a horrible spectacle met their view. The bodies of the three men who were killed in the creek had been hacked to pieces and the parts hung on limbs of adjacent trees, ghastly reminders of the ferocity of their foes. Two of the men, Hutchings and McDonald, had quarreled several days before, and agreed to settle their differences in a duel with rifles as soon as their terms of enlistment expired; but Black Hawk's savage warriors had put an end to their strife. Such a duel as they contemplated would probably have resulted in the death of both, so that the forestallment of their plans by a few days made but little difference.

Captain Callaway's body was not found until several days after his death, when it was discovered hanging in a bush two hundred yards below the scene of action. His gun had been previously recovered, sticking muzzle downward in the mud; but having a waterproof lock it remained in perfect condition and fired as clearly as though it had not been subjected to such a trial.

As soon as news of the disaster reached the settlements, Flanders Callaway led a company of rangers to the scene in search of the body of his son, and was present when it was found. Wrapped in blankets it was buried on the side of a hill overlooking the scene of his last exploit, and a small monument of rough stones now marks the place.

And so ended a life of promise that seems a failure. A strange fatality has attended every Indian massacre of importance from Braddock to Custer, where the stubbornness or inadvertence of a commander has resulted in disaster. The defeat and death of Callaway was a greater blow to the little Boone settlement of 1815, than the larger disasters of Braddock and Custer were to the greater countries which they served; for it left the border open to the assaults of a large body of savages encouraged by what seemed to them a splendid victory. But it was fortunate for both sides that the issues were in the hands of so able a leader as Black Hawk. If his men had been armed with rifles and on an equality with their white opponents, it is probable that he would have made a general assault upon the settlements; but he had no faith in blundering muskets that made a loud noise and did but little execution. The chief took advantage of the lull that followed to lead his warriors back to safety. He relied more on small parties, well armed, who could dash into a community and capture a few scalps and vanish into the wilderness before they could be followed and punished, and it was only a brief space of time until he headed such a foray in the massacre of the Ramsey family near Marthsville.

Massacre of the Ramsey Family

Robert Ramsey had been a soldier in the Revolution, and lost a leg at the battle of Saratoga. Imigrating to the Boone neighborhood, he bought a tract of land about two and a half miles west of Marthasville and built a cabin to shelter his family, which consisted of himself and wife and five small children. There was also an Indian boy named Paul, whom they were rearing as their own.

Ramsey's missing leg was supplied with a wooden "peg," which enabled him to hobble about the little farm, hunt game and support his family in comfort. The oldest of the children, a little girl of thirteen, noted and loved for her beauty and gentleness of disposition, assisted her mother with domestic duties and in the care of her two brothers and sisters. Each member of the family except the baby of two years, did something for the general welfare; the industry of each adding to the contentment and happiness of them all.

They had good neighbors in Mr. Jesse Caton and his family, who lived at Marthasville; and Aleck McKinney, Jr. and his young wife, who had been bold enough to venture five miles further into the forest. Nancy McKinney (Bryan) was a niece of Rebecca Boone, and thus closely related to the great pioneer and hunter. Their home was so far away from the center of the settlements as to be regarded as a point of danger, but at the same time it served as an outpost for the Ramseys, who felt safer by reason of the fact. If the Indians came, the McKinneys would most likely be first to receive the blow; but they were close enough to be neighbors in those times of scant population. There were several other neighbors within call of the alarm trumpet, and Fort Charrette stood on the bank of the river only two miles away, strong enough in estimation of the pioneers to withstand a thousand red skins. Under such conditions no one thought of danger, or if such a thing were suggested it was smiled away as incredible.

But the rangers believed that Ramsey's place was unsafe and on the first day of March, 1815, Captain James Callaway visited them to consider the matter. It was only a week until his own tragic death, but fate revealed no warning of its approach. He told the Ramseys that the rangers had information indicating an early raid by Indians, and he advised them to abandon their home temporarily and seek safety in Fort Charrette. But Ramsey laughed, and his wife smiled. What had they to fear from a few red skins? The older soldier pointed to the loaded French rifle that hung in the rack over the door, and reminded the Captain that he had carried it at Saratoga and Yorktown, and if danger came it would do its duty again.

But Callaway shook his head. If Indians came it would not be a fair fight, such as the continentals had at Saratoga or Yorktown. Indians were prowlers, crawling through the woods like serpents, and coming upon their victims suddenly, without warning, probably in the darkness of the night, when defense would be impossible. It was better to take no chances with that kind of an enemy.

"There's my trumpet hanging by the door," responded Ramsey, pointing to the large tin trumpet which had been supplied by the rangers to be blown in case of danger; "if they come I'll blow my trumpet and scare the liver out of 'em."

Callaway smiled, but was doubtful.

"They might run from the sound of the trumpet," he said, "and again they might not. In any case they would come before you had time to sound the alarm. If they ran away, as they doubtless would, they would shoot you and your family first. You are not safe here, and I shall at least send a man to help you stand guard."

"And how about McKinney and pretty Nancy?" inquired Ramsey; "their place is five miles further out than ours."

"That doesn't excuse you," remonstrated Callaway. "Nancy thinks that because she happens to be a niece of Grandpa she can whip her weight in wild cats; but as a matter of fact I have stationed one of my men there, and shall do the same for you."

"Let him come and welcome, Capin'. We'll make him fat with our good living; but as for the red skins, I'm not afraid of them. If they don't run from the trumpet I'll take my wooden leg and beat their brains out, and the old woman can tan their hides and make them into moccasins."

Then, after a moment's hesitation, he continued, as if uttering a prophecy: "Better look out for yourself, Cap. You need protection more than we do. Day and night you are riding through the woods, in all sorts of weather and every possible condition of danger. How do you know when you may ride into a nest of them and be stung before you know it? Better keep an eye to yourself, capin'!"

"Oh, that's your business," laughed the young officer. "If we get shot there's somebody else to take our place; but when it comes your turn that'll be the end of you."

And swinging himself into his saddle, he rode away with the careless indifference for which he was distinguished.

After the massacre at Loutre the following week, nearly three months passed without any further alarms in that locality. Then, on the 20th of May, 1815, came the bloody attack on the Ramseys which marked an era in the history of the items.

On the morning of the tragedy Jesse Caton, Jr., was hunting his father's horses in the vicinity of the Ramsey place, and discovered Indian "signs" while crossing a ravine. Hurrying home, he gave the alarm, when at the same instant came the sound of the guns and the blowing of the trumpet at the home of the Ramseys.

In an incredibly short space of time the country was aroused. The news flew on the wings of the wind, by calls from house to house and the blowing of trumpets; and in less than half an hour Uncle Daniel himself was told of the disaster. In even less time a company of rangers had assembled at the Ramsey home, ready to pursue the trail. They were "minute men," trained Indian fighters, and learned in the tricks and stratagems of the red enemy.

The attack came suddenly, just at break of day---as Callaway had warned. Mrs. Ramsey was in the lot adjoining the house milking cows, which gave the first intimation of the presence of danger by shaking their horns and endeavoring to break out of the lot. At the same instant six savages burst out of the woods with whoops and yells, and rushed forward with the intention of slaying their victims with their tomahawks. But as Mrs. Ramsey started to run the leader of the band, Black Hawk himself, fired and mortally wounded her; than as she attempted to crawl under the bars he threw his hatchet, but missed the mark. She succeeded in reaching the house, but was too severely wounded to blow the trumpet. Her husband, who had been in the lot with her, started to run at the same time, but being without his peg leg he could make but slow progress, and was shot just as he came to the door of the cabin. As he fell he reached for the trumpet and blew a blast, whereupon the savages fled.

But they left death and horror in their wake. Three of their children had been tomahawked in the yard, and the eldest little girl scalped. She lingered four days in agony before death came to her relief. The other two children had been killed instantly, each with a single stroke of the hatchet; but they were not scalped. The baby, just old enough to be trotting around, squatted like a frightened quail in a bunch of weeds and escaped unhurt. The Indian boy Paul and the other Ramsey child had gone to the spring for water, and alarmed by the yells and musketry firing fled to the house of a neighbor and escaped.

Such were the details of the horrible affair as related to me by my father, who arrived on the scene three hours after its occurrence. Mrs. Ramsey, though desperately wounded, lived until the next day. Out of a family of eight, three were dead and three so badly wounded that none believed they could live. The father himself was the only one that recovered, to live for several years afterward. The whole murderous transaction had not occupied more than a couple of minutes.

A Close Call

As soon as news of the massacre reached Femme Osage settlement, sixteen miles to the eastward, Aleck McKinney the elder and my father mounted their horses and set out for the scene. The road was nothing more than a buffalo path through the tall grass and peavine, which in many places grew so luxuriantly as to reach a horsemen's waist as he sat in the saddle, while the dense undergrowth made it impossible to see more than a few yards on either side. As the man and boy were advancing at a rapid trot, McKinney leading the way, they were startled by the sudden flashing of two feathered heads a few steps to their right, sinking out of sight as suddenly as they had appeared. The ranger was close and a shot might have been deadly, but nothing came of the alarm. Two Indians were making their way to the home of Daniel Boone, hoping to destroy at a single blow the man whom they most dreaded and hearing the approach of horses they raised their head above the grass to see who it might be. Their curiosity satisfied, they ducked down again into their concealment and continued on their way to the fate that met them the next morning at the hands of two women, as related in a previous Episode.

Meanwhile the man and the boy paid no attention to the incident, but trotted on as if nothing had happened. So far as they knew there might be a dozen savages hidden in the grass, and it would be folly to fight an enemy whom they could not see and whose numbers were indefinite. If they had known there were but two, a fight might have ensued, with unknown results. The Indians were no less willing to let them go than they were to get out of the zone of danger, and so the incident passed without further excitement.

At the time of the massacre my father's younger brother, Abner, was living at the Caton's attending school, and as the alarm occurred he was sent to Fort Charrette to warn the garrison. There he found Uncle Daniel, then in his 81st year, pacing back and forth in an open space in the stockade, with his gun on his shoulder and whistling softly to himself. For several days previously he had been visiting at the home of his daughter Jemima, two miles from the fort, and knowing there was an unfinished gap in the palisades he hurried to the scene at the first intimation of danger. There his nephew found him an hour later filling the breach. As soon as he learned the conditions at the Ramsey home he hurried there, and having dispatched the rangers in pursuit, gave his attention to the wounded members of the family.

Episode Number Sixty-Five

Pursuing the Indians

Thirty rangers were soon on the trail, but a difficult task lay before them. Directly after begging their flight the Indians had separated into parties of two, and these again into one, each pursuing his way alone. One man in passing through a forest leaves but a slight trail.

The rangers counceled if they should adopt similar tactics, which hindered their progress and made the pursuit more uncertain. The Indians would probably come together again at some designated point, where an ambushment would be staged; and as this meeting place could not be determined, the rangers decided to march in a solid body in the general direction of the retreat.

The savages did meet at a point near the present site of Troy, where the signs showed they had spent the night; but there were only four of them instead of the six who had been engaged in the massacre. What had become of the other two? We have already accounted for them in the pursuit by Wilse and their fatal meeting with the two women at Grandfather's house.

The rangers did not reach the camping place until the following morning, after the Indians had left; and soon afterward their path showed that they had been met by a much larger party, how many the pursuers could not determine. But it was enough to make them feel safe, for they no longer made any effort to conceal their trail.

The woods seemed filled with savages. A fight took place the following day with a considerable body near Howard's Fort, on the north bank of Cuivre River, about two miles west of Old Monroe. Although it was an outpost in the direction of the enemy's country, it was manned by only a small garrison, and the men, as usual with the rangers, where careless to the point of recklessness. It was reported that the Indians were collecting a large force with a view of making an attack on the post, and the report was subsequently verified; but Indians are superstitious, and the mystery of the disappearance of their two warriors disconcerted their plans. The little affair in which Grandmother and Aunt Jemima had played so important a part proved the turning point of the campaign. If it had not taken place the settlements would have been overrun by a force so large that the rangers would have had difficulty in controlling it.

Making a "Good Indian" Better

The small garrison at Howard's Fort was under command of a Captain Craig, who had permitted his men to straggle and form an undefended camp two miles further up the river. During the day following the Ramsey massacre these men heard what they supposed to be the "call" of wild turkeys. They had no difficulty in finding them! Scarcely had they reached midstream when they were fired upon by a band of savages concealed in the woods, who had imitated the call of turkeys as a decoy.

McNeice and two of the men were killed, but a ranger named Webber escaped unhurt. Plunging into the water he swam to a raft near the fort, where he was quickly followed by a warrior who professed extreme friendship.

"Me good Injun!" he cried; "me no hurt!"

But close behind him came another, with a knife between his teeth, and Webber, not liking the presence of such friends, dived under the water and swam to the side of the savage with the knife. He was badly frightened when the ranger came up almost touching him, and cried out, as his comrade had done,

"Me good injun! Me heap good injun!"

"And I'll make you a heap gooder," growled the ranger, plunging a knife into his body.

By this time Webber had drifted some distance below the camp, and being within hearing of the fort he climbed into a tree on an island and called for help. His call was heard and several men came off in a canoe to his rescue; but it capsized in the middle of the stream and left the men struggling in the water. At that moment a keel-boat rounded the point of the island, and its occupants, observing the situation, rescued all the men and conveyed them in safety to the fort.

A Tomahawk in the Head

But the Indians lingered in the vicinity. The day following the incidents just related, a man named Burnes and three Frenchmen went down the river in a canoe to Old Monroe to get a grindstone. So reckless were they that they paid no attention to the fact that the woods were swarming with concealed savages. The grindstone could have waited until another day, but these rangers seemed to value their lives as little as feared the painted enemy. On their return they stopped in the woods to peel some pawpaw bark for stretching deer hides, and while so engaged they were fired upon by a party of Indians who had been watching their movements. Two of the Frenchmen were killed, and the other, in attempting to escape, was struck in the back of the head with a tomahawk. The weapon stuck fast in his skull and he ran about a hundred yards before falling. Meanwhile Burnes got away and returned to the fort unharmed.

Subsequently Black Hawk claimed to have witnessed the throwing of the hatchet—indeed he may have thrown it himself, for he was an expert in that line—and when he saw the man running with the weapon sticking in his head it horrified him so that he decided to go home and put a stop to the war. This may be true, and it may not. Black Hawk was a wiley old chief, and when engaged in war he was as cruel as he was shrewd. It took a good deal to melt his heart at sight of an enemy in trouble.

Battle of the Sink-Hole

Burnes was followed to the fort by a large band of savages, yelling and firing their muskets; but no execution was done other than the flattening of several bullets on the palisades.

The rangers sallied out of the fort and in their turn pursued the Indians into the woods. Each man went on "his own hook," believing they knew how to "take care of themselves." But the sequel proved that they did not. On the contrary, they were reckless beyond the limits of reason.

Part of the band of Indians fled to a sink-hole about a mile from the fort, Black Hawk being among the number, as he afterward related. There at the bottom of the sinkhole they fortified themselves with rocks and by scraping holes in the ground; so that while they could see the rangers they themselves were completely hidden.

Amazing Recklessness

Surrounding the circular declivity, the rangers advanced from tree to tree on all sides, firing at random; for not an Indian could be seen. The latter, however, returned the fire with deadly effect. Captain Craig and Lieutenant Stevens were killed and several of the men wounded. Their recklessness was amazing. Finding that the trees did not afford full protection, and that much time was lost in trying to keep under cover, they boldly advanced in the open, each man challenging the others to follow. But finding this method of attack ineffective as well as hazardous, they constructed a movable breastwork on a couple of wagon wheels, and tried to push it before them. But the sides of the sink-hole were so thickly lined with trees that they could not guide the vehicle around them. In this effort they succeeded in killing one of the Indians, but in turn lost another of their own men, whose death was due to his disregard of the rules of common sense. Addressing a comrade next to him, he said he could see an Indian at the bottom of the sink-hole "whose teeth needed plugging," and he was going to do the job for him by shooting him in the mouth. Stepping out from the breastwork into open view, he coolly took aim and fired, and an answering yell indicated that his dental work had been successful. But at the same instant there was a return flash from the bottom of the sink-hole and the ranger fell with a bullet through the center of his forehead. This shot was fired by Black Hawk, who always carried a dependable rifle when he was hunting or on the warpath, and it was a rare thing for him to miss his mark.

A Fire-Wagon

Seeing they were getting no satisfactory results from their mode of attack, the rangers withdrew their wheeled breastwork and loading it with brush and dry wood set them in fire and started it down the declivity. When the Indians saw the fire-wagon coming they supposed their time had arrived, and praying loudly to the Great spirit for help, they promised to be better Indians in future if he would get them out of this crape. Black Hawk refers to the prayers of his men and adds that he believed they were efficient, for the Great Spirit guided the fire-wagon against a tree, where it burnt to the ground without harm to them.

Shortly before night a scout came in and reported that a large army of Indians, supposed to number eight hundred or a thousand warriors, had crossed the Mississippi and was moving on the settlements. The report subsequently proved to be unfounded, but it was alarming enough to cause serious apprehension. Black Hawk alone could have raised an army of that size among his own people if he had possessed the organizing talents of his great contemporary, Tecumseh; and although the latter was now dead, the bands which he had formed were still in existence and might be called upon if needed.

The rangers therefore took shelter in the fort, and during the night sent out runners in every direction to warn the settlers. Most of them heeded the alarm and collected at Boone's Fort, the strongest in the country. In this way nearly all the outposts were abandoned, and the way opened for the advance of the Indian "army", which never came.

In the morning when the rangers returned to the scene of their previous day's encounter, their opponents were gone, leaving a trail that pointed toward their homes beyond the Mississippi. But they left a gruesome reminder of their presence. On the margin of the sink-hole lay the body of a ranger who had performed the dental service for the Indian, and sitting astride of him was the dead warrior. It was the savage way of proclaiming a victory and defying an enemy.

The excitement produced by the report of an approaching army soon died out and the settlers returned to their homes; but months passed before active hostilities ceased. In fact they continued as long as white hunters invaded grounds that the Indians claimed as their own. Actual peace did not return until the country became so thickly populated that it was no longer a hunting ground, and the Indians realized that they were too weak to resist the flood of immigration that poured in upon them. Meanwhile Tecumseh had fallen, and Black Hawk, his able successor, was growing old and weary of the warpath. Gradually hostilities died away, like the dashing showers of a receding storm; but in their trail a number of incidents occurred of the most thrilling character.

Episode Number Sixty-Six

Battle of the Petticoats

One of the most unique battles ever fought occurred in 1815, at a place in Callaway County known as Cote-sans-Dessein; and it is probable that the attacking force of Indians was the same that participated in the massacre of Callaway and his men at Loutre Creek. They were about the same in numbers, and the two engagements occurred within a few days of each other.

The fort was an outpost which had been established by the French, as the name indicates; and it consisted merely of a small blockhouse standing on the bank of the Missouri River. Its proximity to the river afforded protection on that side, and it was here also that the garrison obtained their supplies of water. At the time of the attack nearly all the settlers had sought safety from threatened inroads of savages by removing to the stronger forts to the eastward, and especially to Boone's Fort near the Femme Osage.

Therefore when Black Hawk and his little army of red warriors came, there were only five persons in the blockhouse, a Frenchman named Baptiste Roi, another man whose name is not given, Roi's wife and her sister, and an individual who took no part in the proceedings. His name also has escaped fame. Roi and his comrade and the two women defended the castle. But it was the courage and resourcefulness of the women that saved the fort; not casting any reflection whatever on the two men, who were as brave as the bravest. But they could not have driven the savages away except for the very efficient and somewhat picturesque assistance rendered at a critical moment by their feminine associates. The third man, who took no part in the battle, spent the time praying to the Higher Powers for celestial help; and when victory came he claimed the credit through his alliance with providence.

It is a serious mistake in not providing water inside the palisades, for when the crisis came they had only a few gallons for domestic use, and none to spare for putting out fires. According to their custom, the Indians made the assault early in the morning, suddenly rushing their entire force against the land-slide of the blockhouse. There had been no intimation of their presence, until they came out of the cover of the woods, firing their muskets and yelling ferociously in order to inspire the garrison with fear. They knew there was a small number of defenders within the blockhouse, and they hoped to capture the place at a single rush. But they met with a reception that amazed them. A volley from four rifles blasted out through the portholes, and four red warriors bit the earth with leaden bullets in their hearts or heads. Instantly there was another volley with similar results, and before the surprised assailants could retreat to safety, fourteen of their number had been killed or wounded. This astonishing result had been achieved by the active participation of the women, who could shoot as accurately as their male companions. Also as a matter of precaution all the rifles in the fort had been kept loaded, so that volley followed volley with such quick succession that the savages concluded they had a larger force to deal with than they had expected.

When the first attack had been driven back with such heavy loss, and the little garrison began to reload their guns, they made the unpleasant discovery that they were short bullets. But Mrs. Roi began to cast new ones, while her sister aided the men in reloading the rifles; so that when a second rush was made the enemy met the same deadly fire that had been poured upon them in their first attempt. They were now satisfied that a considerable force was within the blockhouse, and instead of charging forward in mass formation they spread out in a thin line and came on under cover of trees and stumps, or anything else that afforded protection. But again they met with disaster. Every feathered head that peered around a tree or above a log or stump became the recipient of a leaden bullet, and the owner of the unfortunate head lost interest in the subsequent proceedings. The deadly fire of the little garrison made the path to glory rough and uneven. Already the savages had lost nearly a third of their original force, and the battle was hardly begun. They could easily imagine that there were a hundred men inside the walls of the little fort.

Meanwhile the praying man continued his supplications, until Mrs. Roi, finding him in the way, took him by the collar and lifted him into an adjoining apartment, where she locked him in. But as the battle proceeded he could still be heard soliciting aid from on high.

Flaming Arrows

The Indians resorted to the stratagem of burning the blockhouse with flaming arrows, which they shot into the roof. Soon the flames burst out in several places, and the warriors announced the success of their experiment with loud yells of exultation. But the garrison put out the fire by a judicious use of their limited supply of water.

Again the burning arrows came, and once more the dry roof was blazing; but it was extinguished with a little more of the precious fluid. Anxiously they watched the water as it receded towards the bottom of the bucket. They had only enough for one more effort, and when that was gone no one could tell their fate.

Meanwhile the besiegers guarded the river bank to see that no fresh supplies came from that quarter. Roi looked toward the river and wondered if he might venture out. He had no lack of courage, but could he afford to risk his life where the numbers were so small? Presently, as he peered through a porthole he noticed a tuft of grass, or young sprout that seemed to be alive. As he watched, the object slowly sank until it was hidden behind the bank, a curious thing for a sprout to do, which generally prefers to grow upward. Presently it began to grow again. Slowly the leaf rose above the ground, followed by a bunch of grass and a feather-tip disappeared. When the battle was over, they found a dead Indian there with a bullet hole in the center of his forehead. He had tried one stratagem too many.

The Last Drop of Water

Again the flaming arrows came, and the last drop of water was gone. The men looked at the women and fingered their rifles. Death would be better for them than captivity by the savages. The roof was beginning to blaze and yells of triumph came from the surrounding woods. Roi and his companion looked to their priming and nodded significantly. The time was at hand! Did they have the courage? God would decide!

Viva la Petticoat!

But the time had not come! Pretty little Mrs. Roi came out of the kitchen with a bucket of milk, the last liquid in the house; and once more the flames were subdued. Now nothing could save them if more arrows were shot!

The answer was two more arrows that stuck fast in the roof and began to blaze! Beyond all question the end had come! But not yet! Mrs. Roi lifted her skirt and with a deft motion of her hand unbuttoned a quilted petticoat and let it fall to the floor. Handing the garment to her husband, she motioned him to smother the flames with it; and like a dutiful husband, he obeyed his wife's order.

On descending from the ladder by means of which he had climbed to the roof, he kissed his wife on her blushing cheek:

"How many petticoats haf you?" he inquired.

"I haf mysekf seex petticoats,: she replied; "and my seester she haf also six."

Roi threw his hat in the air and danced around the floor shouting:

"Vive la petticoat! Vith twelve petticoats we shall vip the whole tribe! Come on, you bloody scoundrels! Py tam! Vive la petticoat!"

It was an era of quilted petticoats in the fashionable world, and Mrs. Roi and her sister had made a supply for themselves with their own fair hands. The grace and charm which these garments had lent to their persons could now be employed in saving their lives!

Twice more the arrows came, and two more petticoats were sacrificed. Then the savages, yelling with rage and despair, vanished into the woods burdened with their wounded, whom they carried along with them. But before leaving they broke several of their earthenware camp kettles into fragments and piled them around an unbroken one, as a sign to others of their countrymen that it was not safe to attack that place.

When the war was over and the neighbors had returned to their homes, there was a quilting at Mrs. Roi's house, and more than a dozen new silk petticoats were wrought. Then as the years went by the brave little woman and her husband and sister lay down to rest in the little French cemetery where side-by-side they sleep in peace with no fear of savage yell or burning gun.

Legend of Chief Keokuk

It may be added in conclusion that there is a legend to the effect that the Indians in this affair were commanded by the Chief Keokuk, who was wounded and carried away by his men, but died a day or two afterward. At any rate, it is said that as late as 1826 the remains of an unusually tall man, such as Keokuk is said to have been, were exhumed in the prairie a short distance from the town of Wellsville, in Montgomery County, and on the breast was a bronze medal bearing the name of that chief. The jawbone was so large that it would fit over the face of an ordinary man, and Keokuk is known to have been of extraordinary proportions. But all the facts do not agree. Keokuk was a friend of the whites, and went with the tribe when they were removed from their ancient home at Rockford, and Keokuk, Iowa, was named in honor of him. Black Hawk claims that he was at the "Battle of the Petticoats," and if he tells the truth a chief of his force of character would not have permitted another to command. It was Black Hawk also who told about the breaking of the earthenware and piling the fragments around an unbroken vessel. The legend about the finding of the tall skeleton is probably only an idle tale; yet it afford ground enough for a romantic suggestion. Why not find the place—if it can be found—and erect a monument there representing a tall chief leading his men to the assault and waving a petticoat? It would be an appropriate tribute not only to Keokuk but to the brave little women whose ingenuity saved the lives of a sorely tried garrison. But it has been more than a hundred years since the lone grave on the prairie was found, and it is not probable that any definite information can be had of it now. The place for the moment is at the grave of the heroine in the cemetery at Cote-sans-Dessein.

Massacre of the O'Neil Family

On the bank of King's Lake, in Lincoln County, there lived a Scotch family named O'Neil. Besides the father and mother there were two sons and two daughters, and a little orphan boy two years old whom they had adopted. He was at the most attractive baby age, the pet and playfellow of all the family, whom he ruled by the golden bonds of love. They could not have been any more devoted to him if he had been their own. All the children were still in the age of childhood, and they were as faithful to the parents as the latter were to the little family which had gathered about them. All who knew the O'Neils liked them, because they were the kind of people who strove to love their neighbors as themselves. If any savage had appealed to them for food or comfort they would have denied themselves to help him.

King's Lake, on whose borders they lived, is near the Mississippi River, runs parallel with it, and was formed by the river in some past age. In those early days the lake was well stocked with fish, and during the winter months thousands of wild geese and ducks came there to feed on the wild rice and return thanks with their incessant honking and quacking. In the woods were squirrels, foxes, deer, and now and then a wild cat or bear, but never hungry enough to be fierce. All these, with other game, and wild fruits and nuts in lavish profusion, made an Elysium for those who longed for peace, piety, and happiness. It seems to these simple Scotch people as if they had found a new Canaan, and there they planted their staff with no desire to wander further.

But the location was regarded as dangerous, lying near the main trail between the Indian towns and the white settlements; and the rangers had warned O'Neil that it was not wise or prudent to expose his family there. But he had probably never seen a red Indian, had no idea as to their savage character, and wishing harm to no one he could not understand why other should disturb him.

But when reports of depredations began to reach him, and especially after the massacre of the Ramsey family, he concluded it would be wise to consider the safety of himself and his family. So one day he visited a neighbor to consult with him about combining forces for their mutual defense in case of trouble, and the neighbor, being of the same opinion, their plans were soon formed.

But it was too late!

During O'Neil's brief absence a party of warriors had crossed the river on the ice and murdered his entire family. Not a soul was left alive. Such was the fearful spectacle which met his gaze when he returned to his desolated home. His wife and all the children had been tomahawked and scalped and their mutilated bodies left lying on the floor. The cabin itself would have been destroyed except for the fact that the red friends were afraid to linger long enough to apply the torch.

The little orphan, with the natural instinct of self-preservation, had crawled into the great chimney and hid himself; but on being driven out by heat and smoke the monsters threw him alive into a kettle of boiling water, and there his tiny body was found by his foster father.

This was perhaps the most cruel and unnatural of all the acts committed by the Indians during the war, and it aroused a spirit of revenge and hate that demanded retribution. But the band had disappeared as quickly and noiselessly as it had come, leaving no sign of identification; and peace being declared soon afterward, the miscreants escaped the punishment they so richly deserved.

The Scout's Revenge

After the armistice had come a great council of officers and chiefs on both sides was sitting at Rock Island to devise terms of peace. One day during the proceedings a ranger named McNair, a countryman of O'Neil, who understood the Indian tongue, overheard one of the warriors boasting of the part he had played in the murder of the O'Neil family. He declared that he himself had tomahawked and scalped one of the children, at the same time mimicking the death agonies of the little one.

McNair kept his eye on the boasting warrior as he strutted among his companions, and planned vengeance. But an overt act at a peace convention would be regarded as a crime, no matter how great the provocation, and punished accordingly. So the ranger bided his time, nursing his resentment until it boiled into uncontrollable rage.

At length, no longer able to govern himself, he faced the savage and told him in his own language that he was a coward and a monster. The warrior resented the imputation and made a motion as if to resist, whereupon McNair struck him in the face, and as he reeled from the blow the ranger stabbed him to the heart. Then mounting his horse fled into the woods and disappeared.

Instantly the counsel was in turmoil. The bugles of the whites and the tom-toms of the savages sounded the call to arms, and both sides prepared for what appeared to be an inevitable clash. But the leaders got together, and when the incident was explained to the chiefs they admitted that the man's vengeance was just as commendable. He had acted like a warrior and a brave man, and in accordance with their own laws and customs. Had he not executed vengeance when the opportunity came he would have been a coward and fit to associate only with women. Such was their view of the matter. An eye for an eye and a tooth for a tooth; he who slays shall himself be slain.

So the council continued its sittings, and a treaty was entered into. The peaceful termination of the affair was due, in a large measure to the influence of Black Hawk, who reminded his people of what they themselves would have done under like conditions. "The man who will not avenge his friend or brother," said the great chief, "is not worthy to associate with warriors. His place is in the wigwam with the women."

The massacre of the O'Neil family left a bitter memory in the community, which did not die out until a new generation came that was not influenced by the hatreds of the past. Both sides were inflamed, the whites claiming that every warrior who had participated in the affair should be hunted down and punished; while the Indians took the ground that it was merely an incident of war. Among themselves they argued that the white family was living on ground which they claimed as a special hunting preserve, and they were justified in disposing of them in a manner that would deter others from committing a similar offence. So, Indians being about the same as white people, except in color and custom, each watched the other for opportunities to "get even".

Retribution

Not long after the massacre, when the spring sun had thawed the ice in the river, a keelboat came up from St. Louis, and turning into Cuiver River was fired on by a band of Indians concealed in the woods, and a ranger named Reeland was severely wounded. Several weeks later, when his wounds had healed sufficiently to permit him to be out, he rode to the home of a neighbor named Keeley; and while sitting on his horse talking to his friend he was shot and killed by an Indian who had hidden himself in the woods for such an opportunity. This particular savage was braver than some others of his race, for he ran forward and was in the act of scalping his victim when Keeley put an end to his activities by a shot from his rifle.

Indian Superstition

This incident led to the revelation of a curious superstition among the Indians. The warrior in question was a member of a band which had come on a raid into the white settlements, and a few days before his death they had attacked the home of Christopher Hostetter, a neighbor of Keeley. In their efforts to break into the house the warrior fell into a well in the yard, and was nearly drowned before his comrades could get him out. The mishap convinced the remaining members of the party that the Great Spirit did not approve of what they were doing, and they left for their homes the following day. But the warrior in question decided to remain and continue on the warpath alone, in spite of the fact that during the night he had a series of remarkable dreams which would have deterred any but the boldest of spirits. He dreamed, in the first place, that he shot a large buffalo, but when he ran forward to stab it the animal rose to its feet and scalped him with its horns. Next he dreamed that while passing under a tall bluff a stone near the top was loosened and came crashing down so close to him that it tore the scalp from his head. His third dream was even more startling than either of the two preceding ones. It was to the effect that while chasing an antelope in the prairie he stumbled on a grass-root and was thrown into an open grave, which was so deep that he could not get out.

In the morning he consulted the medicine man of the party about his remarkable series of dreams, and was told that they were all parts of a single warning; and that if he hunted any more scalps before the setting of the third sun he would lose his life.

The interpretation so discouraged his companions that they set out for home the same morning, as already explained; but the lone warrior, being a bold spirit, decided to remain and see what would come of the adventure. Wishing to obey the warning as far as he could, he made a bed of leaves in a hollow tree near Keeley's house, and lay down to sleep three days before engaging in any new enterprise. On the second day however, he was awakened by hunger, and seeing the ranger sitting on his horse, the mark was so good that he could not resist the temptation to shoot him. So far he was safe from the warnings of his dreams, but in his eagerness to secure a fresh scalp he forgot the whole matter, and rushing forward out of his concealment became a victim of Keeley's rifle.

Indian lore is highly colored with superstitions and warnings of this kind, but not many of them are so complex in character as the one just related. In addition to falling into a well, this Indian had been warned in three separate dreams of his impending fate, and yet he was bold enough to risk his life for the sake of getting a fresh scalp. Many white men of that period were so imbued with superstition that they would not have dared to neglect the warning of the dreams. In fact dreams, and signs, and portents exercised a strong influence over their conduct; and in a number of instances warnings seemed to come from some weird outside intelligence that could see and interpret the future. The people lived lonely lives, much of the time in the woods, where they dreamed dreams and saw visions, and dared not neglect warnings of approaching calamities.

Episode Number Sixty-Eight

Sportive Red Men

Wood's Fort stood on the present site of Troy, County Seat of Lincoln County, and was then the most northern garrison of white settlers, and naturally the most exposed. It was in a state of almost constant siege. Black Hawk's bands prowled about the country, killing cattle and hogs, picking up an occasional straggler, and doing all the mischief they could in a time of ostensible peace. In this respect the Indian had no fixed principles; he made his declarations of war and peace to suit his own convenience. War existed whenever a red man wanted to steal a horse of kill a pig—or scalp a pale face; and peace returned as soon as he found himself in a tight place.

It was one of their favorite sports on dark nights to charge up nearly to the walls of the fort, yelling and firing their guns and raising Cain in general; and while these exuberances did no particular harm except to flatten a few musket balls against the palisades, it kept the inmates in such a state of nervous tension that they could not get their natural rest. This of course had a tendency to break down their spirit of resistance, which was precisely what the savages desired. No Indian was killed or hurt in these raids in the darkness, for they dashed up and were gone again before the sentinels could locate them. It was fine sport for the warriors, but nerve-racking to the rangers. During the day the Indians hid in the woods and slept, so as to be fresh for another jollification during the darkness of the night.

The rangers had cleared a small field adjoining the fort, in which they planted corn, beans, and potatoes, and a little tobacco for the comfort of the garrison. But the nocturnal activities of the savages and fear of ambuscades in the day, obliged them to cease cultivating the plants, and the little field grew up in weeds. This threatened suffering in the future, and as several of the men had their wives and families with them they dreaded to think of hearing their little ones cry for food when winter came.

But necessity is a promoter of wisdom, and when winter did come and the boats could not bring food because of the ice, the men went into the woods and dug up the roots of the sassafras, out of which they brewed a fragrant and nourishing tea. They also brought back with them fresh game and ripe acorns picked from under the leaves, and pounding the latter into a course meal they baked it into a bread that was palatable and nourishing in case of emergency. Walnuts and hickory nuts were plentiful, and during lulls between the festivities of the frolicsome red men they ventured forth and gathered them for luxuries. By these several contrivances they met the necessity for food, and their little children did not cry because of hunger. All were reasonably happy, though no one knew what moment the crash of a musket might land him in eternity.

A Battle at the Lick

At that time there was a "lick", or a salt spring, a short distance east of North Cuiver River—probably it is there yet—and deer and other game came to lick the salt. Bears and panthers also assembled to eat the deer and antelopes and occasional buffaloes that assembled there, the arrangement being sort of mutual convenience contrived by nature. It was believed also that the waters of the spring were good for various kinds of diseases, as nearly all pure water is; for in addition to the salt, it was impregnated with Sulphur and iron, which made it taste bad enough to be medicine of some kind or other, and therefore good for something.

On a certain fatal day, before there had been any declaration of war, four young rangers left the fort and went to the lick to hunt deer and purge their systems of accumulated humors. They were Hamilton McNair, Peter Pugh, and Big and Little Joe McCoy. The preponderance of "Macs" indicates a settlement of Scotch, with the hardihood of the race as well as its peculiarities. Hamilton McNair was a brother of the man who subsequently stabbed the Indian during the sitting of the Rock Island Peace Council.

While they were encamped at the spring, hunting and frolicking and having a good time, with suspicion of danger, they were furiously assaulted by a large band of Indians under the ever-present Black Hawk, as he subsequently related in his autobiography. Big Joe McCoy was in the woods at the time, a short distance from the camp, and being first to discover the savages as they were preparing for their grand rush, he hid himself under the turn of a log, and the Indians ran over without observing him.

Neither of the three men at the camp was hurt by the first volley. McNair fled to the woods, but in crossing an open field he was over-taken and killed and scalped. This left Pugh and Little Joe McCoy alone, and they put up a fight that surprised their adversaries. Pugh screened himself behind his horse, firing only when he could get a good aim, and four of the savages became victims of his accuracy. Then they made a rush, and overcoming the two men by weight of numbers slew them with their hatchets.

A Race with Black Hawk

Meanwhile Big Joe McCoy's hiding place had been discovered, and the savages began to close in upon him. Having no gun he could make no defense, and springing up he started on a race through the woods, hoping to reach the fort. Among the rangers he was noted for his fleetness of foot, and now he brought his energies into full play as he ran for life. It was the purpose of the Indian to capture him alive and serve him on the altar of fire as a sacrifice to their Gods; so several of their fleetest runners went howling after him. He easily outran all but one, who proved to be the redoubtable Black Hawk, himself no mean sprinter. Slowly the chief gained on the white man, and in another spring or two they would be together. But at the critical moment McCoy came to a big oak tree which he had recently fallen across the path, its branches still covered with a screen of brown leaves. Over the tree McCoy went at a single bound, and Black Hawk stopped and looked in wonder. He could not imagine any man being able to cover such an obstruction, and he gazed in amazement at the feat. Then turning back, he cried in broken English,

"Whoopee! Heap big jump! Me no go!"

Whereupon he abandoned the chase and returned to his companions. Afterward in describing the adventure he gave it a slightly different version from McCoy! He said that the tree had been cut and split into rails and these piled across the path higher than a man's head: adding that he so admired the white man's dexterity in leaping over such an obstruction that he no longer cared to capture him, and so let the ranger go. But it is no strain on the imagination to believe that if the chief could have jumped that pile of rails he would have done it.

McCoy ran until he met a party of his comrades, who, alarmed at the prolonged absence of the men, were coming in search of them. Guided by McCoy they cautiously approached the camp, but the Indians had observed them and fled. Before doing so they hacked the body of Pugh into pieces and hung the fragments on limbs, as an indication of their resentment for the death of their companion.

Tragic Death of Three Little Boys

William McHugh, who lived near where the road from Cap-au-gris crosses Sandy Creek, had three sons just turning into young manhood; and near the McHugh place there lived a famous scout and hunter named Dixon, whom the boys greatly admired and were never more pleased than when listening to his stories of adventure.

One summer day the boys went into the woods to hunt the horses and drive them home to be salted. They found them on the opposite side of Salt Creek, and by the offer of a little salt in their hands each of the boys caught a riding animal, mounting without bridle or saddle they set out in a wild race for home. Jesse being the youngest, and less expert than his brothers, had brought with him a light pack-saddle; but the other boys preferred the bare backs of their half-tamed steeds. It was glorious fun, this racing through the woods, the horses knowing the way as well as their riders, and bounding over logs and ravines no doubt enjoyed the sport as much as the boys themselves.

In the midst of their fun they met their friend Dixon, and insisted that he should accompany them home for the hospitality of a good supper and an evening's entertainment of stories. Glad enough to accept such an invitation, the scouts mounted into the saddle in front of Jesse, and the race was resumed.

When they came to the ford at Sandy Creek the horses stopped to drink but scarcely had they dipped their brown noses in the water when a volley of musketry flashed out of a thicket of willow trees on the bank, and the two older boys and their horses were instantly killed. Frightened by the crash of the guns, the horse that Dixon and Jesse were riding reared and in its struggles to climb the steep bank, the girth of the saddle broke and the riders fell to the ground. Dixon pushed the boy in front of him to shield him from danger, and they started on a run for home, followed by the yelling savages. If the scout had been armed there would have been a different story to tell, but he had left his gun at home and they must now run for their lives. Jesse fell behind, whereupon Dixon lifted him to his shoulder, and at the same instant the little fellow was struck and killed by a flying tomahawk. Pausing a moment in horror at the catastrophe, the scout bent his body low to avoid the bullets of the savages and dashing through the woods reached the house in safety. The Indians followed him to the surrounding fence, when McHugh appeared in the door and shot one of them dead, whereupon the others turned and fled.

It was a sad story that Dixon had to relate to the afflicted parents. In a single short hour they had been deprived of their sons in whom their affections and their lives were centered, and the promised comfort of their old age swept away. The bodies of the boys were assembled and buried in a single grave near the spot where Jesse had fallen, protected by wooden puncheons and covered by the warm earth of summer; and there they still sleep. Long afterward an oak tree grew up by the side of the grave and bent its trunk as if weeping over their untimely fate and the tree still marks the place of the tragedy.

Episode Number Sixty-Nine

Safety In a Hollow Log

Nine years after the murder of his sons, William McHugh came near losing his own life at the hands of a band of savages, among whom were several who had participated in the death of the boys.

One day in the early spring McHugh and five other men went out to gather greens, and one of the men, named Durgee, took his two little boys with him.

As they were returning to the fort they were fired upon by some Indians concealed in a cane-brake near the path, and Durgee was killed. No one else was harmed. They had been following the winding course of a small stream known as McLean's Creek, and when the little boys saw their father fall they sprang into the creek and waded to the other side, where they hid themselves in a hollow log. A tall warrior soon came along, and standing on top of the log shaded his eyes with his hand, as if looking for the fugitives. The boys could see him plainly through a crevice in the log, and expected to be discovered any moment. At one time they felt that he was gazing directly at them, as he was in fact; but a moment later he gave a loud yell and jumping to the ground disappeared in the woods. When he was gone the boys came out of their concealment and ran to the fort.

Years afterward Black Hawk described the scene in his book, for it was he who had given the boys their fright. He had seen them when they first sought refuge in the log, and intended to toma-hawk them; but his sense of humanity overcame his lust for blood and he let them go.

The Naming of Bear Creek

Let us turn now to other subjects of a less gruesome character, and more intimately representa-tive of the pioneers and their manner of life.

Bear Creek in Montgomery County was named by Uncle Daniel Boone because of the large numbers of bears that he found there. The location suited the tastes of the animal, and the pickings in the way of food supplies were abundant. Also when winter came there were canebrakes in which he could hibernate and be comfortable until the season for warmer weather came around again. So when Uncle Daniel wanted fresh bear meat, or a new robe for his sleeping room, he knew where to find it.

Treed By a Bear

There is another stream in the same locality called Little Bear Creek, because it is not quite as large as the other; but in former times it was a favorite resort for bears and their families. One day while hunting along the banks of this smaller creek, Presley Anderson came upon two cub bears playing and frolicking among the branches of a tall maple tree. He had heard of other hunters getting in trouble by fooling with baby bears, but believing himself to be an exception to the rule, he climbed the tree and made the acquaintance of the little fellows. They were not averse to having some fun with this new specimen of their species, and the three were enjoying themselves hugely; when the hunter heard a noise below which intimated that they were about to have an addition to their party. Looking down he saw the mother bear climbing the tree below him, and her manner indicated that he was in for a different kind of fun. The old bear had the advantage of being between him and the ground, and he did not see how he could avoid making her acquaintance, much as he would have appreciated doing so. Fighting a bear on solid earth is one thing, but it is another thing up a tree. It was too far to jump, and he could not climb higher without breaking the slender limbs.

So there he was! He must either slide down and make acquaintance of Mrs. Bear, and endeavor to come to some sort of an understanding with her, or jump to another tree. It was a slim chance either way, but the attitude of mother bruin was so forbidding that he did not care to become intimate with her; so he decided to jump. It was a desperate undertaking, but it seemed to have advantages over fighting a mad bear in the top of a tree. Nerving himself for the effort he made the leap, and landed among the tangled limbs of a near-by tree. Sliding down thence to the ground he got his gun and settled matters in his own way with mother bear. But it was the last time Presley Anderson was ever known to climb a tree to play with cub bears.

An Absent Minded Man

John Charlton was a native of Ireland by birth, and probably the most absent-minded man that ever settled in the Boone country. After having persuaded the girl of his choice to marry him, he forgot all about it, and on the day of the wedding she was obliged to send a company of rangers after him before the ceremony could proceed. Then having spent an hour or so very pleasantly with his bride and her family, he said he thought it was about time for him to go home, and was surprised when the young lady said she would accompany him. She explained that it was her intention to stay at his house now and forever, and having promised to take him for better or worse she would do the best she could with the material at hand.

He never discovered that he was really married until his first son was about to be born, when he started for the doctor and did not return until the little fellow was two years old. When he came back he saw a little boy playing in the yard, and asked who he was.

"I ain't nobody," replied the boy. "My pappy went for the doctor when I was born'd and hain't come back yet, and Mother says I won't be nobody till he comes."

"Well, I guess I'm the man," said John; and taking the little fellow to his heart they were the best of friends ever after.

Going To Market Without His Breeches

One winter Charlton drove his hogs to market at St. Louis, and forgot to put on his buckskin breeches before starting. The weather was very cold and he suffered a "right smart," but did not discover the cause of the inconvenience until he got back home and his wife asked him what he had done with his pants. His long buckskin hunting-shirt was all that saved him from freezing, and the market men asked him no questions because they supposed it was his custom to go without breeches.

But his most outstanding adventure was the time he went to the country store for a sack of salt, and did not return until eighteen months later. When he came back he was carrying a broadaxe on his shoulder, but could not remember where he got it or what he was going to do with it. When his wife asked him what he had done with the salt--

"By thunder!" he said, "I left it at the store!"

Returning there he found it lying on the counter where he had placed it a year and a half before. But he never did remember where he got the broadaxe or what use he expected to make of it.

Making Sure That He Was Dead

As he began to grow old he worried a good deal about what might happen when he died, for he had a horror of being buried alive. So he told his wife that when his time came he would tell her that he was dead, and then she must shoot him with his rifle to make sure of it. But the catastrophe passed without the dire necessity, for he lost his mind so completely that he never knew what happened when he died.

The pioneer from whom I obtained these items may have enlarged them a little, but he said they were true to the best of his knowledge and belief; and as he was just starting out after a bear I thought it was prudent not to question him too closely.

A Candidate For the Legislature

William H. Russell of Boone County, was a candidate for the Legislature at several elections, and was finally chosen through the friendly service of an owl. It happened in this way; He went hunting with a party of friends and got lost in the woods, and like many others in such cases he wandered in a circle. Presently he came upon his own tracks in the snow, and supposing they had been made by one of his comrades, he cried out, "Hello! Here's one of the fellows!" and hurried on to overtake him. Having completed the circle again he found three sets of tracks. "Well!" he said, "the boys are getting together! Pretty soon I'll have votes enough to elect me to the Legislature!"

He continued walking for several hours, and found at each completion of the circle that another one of "the boys" had joined the crowd. Finally as dark was approaching an owl called out of a tree, "Who-who-a-o-i-u ?

"I'm William H. Russell," he replied urbanity, "formerly of Kentucky, but now of the grand old state of Missouri. I'm a candidate for the Legislature and hope you'll vote for me."

At that moment his friends found him, and the joke about the owl was so good that it elected him.

Russell built one of the finest steamboats that ever plied the Missouri River. To my youthful imagination it was a floating palace, and I ran a mile many a day to see it sail by. He named the boat for himself and in this enterprise did much to atone for being a member of the Legislature.

Steamboating Days

Those old steamboating days were a grand era. I have seen as many as twenty boats pass my father's farm in a single day, and brother John and I knew every one of them by the sound of their whistles. There was one old tug named the Henry Lewis, with a six-foot draft and so slow that we had to sight by a tree to determine whether she was going or standing still or coming back. The Lewis spent most of her time on sandbars or tied up waiting for a rise.

There was another boat the name of which I cannot recall, whose steering gear had been so badly adjusted that she had to be guided by her side-wheels. She wound her way up and down the river with the uncertainty of a pig with the blind staggers. We never could tell whether she was going to land or continue on her course.

Still another boat was called the Meteor, because, like the Henry Lewis, she ran so slow that it was difficult to decide which way she was going. Just in front of our landing there was a "sawyer," so-called because it "sawed" up and down with the force of the current. At its extreme end there was a sort of projecting hook of the proper height to catch the guards of a passing boat and rip them off. One day the Meteor sidled up to this hook and it laid hold of her guards and shattered them from stem to midship, with a noise that sounded like the old boat was in her death agonies. The passengers all rushed to that side to see what was the matter, and would have capsized the boat if the Captain and mate had not intervened with canes and profanity and driven them back.

At that time all the furnaces were fired with cordwood, the utility of coal not having yet been recognized. In fact the public was just beginning to learn that the "black rocks" would burn. The earlier boats landed once or twice a day while the deck hands went ashore, under command of the cherubic mate, and cut down trees and split them into sizes and lengths that would fit the furnace. This was soon followed by wood-yards, where the farmers prepared and stacked the wood ready for the boats. It was a landing of this kind that my father owned, and many "shin- plaster" bills were exchanged for wood that would make steam. It was the days of "wild-cat banking," and father never knew whether he had money or plasters until he tried them on some merchant who kept his eyes open. It was "boloney" money without hope or expectation of redemption.

Remindful of Baron Munchausen

Some of the stories which I shall relate in conclusion may excite the incredulity of the reader; but I shall endeavor to tell them precisely as they were told to me by the pioneers themselves. Only a genius of the highest order could imagine such things, and I do not profess to be that kind of a person. Some of the stories would make Baron Munchausen turn over in his grave and gasp for breath, but they are neither dull nor stupid. On the contrary they represent the manner in which the pioneers entertained their friends around the campfires and by the hearthstone, and if the reader thinks some of them need modification he is referred to the old fellows themselves, who I am told are still lying in their graves. In any event, there is nobody alive who can dispute what they say, and no man who wanted to remain alive would have done it in their time.

Famous General Burdine

One of the most picturesque characters of early times was General Burdine of the Kingdom of Callaway, as Callaway County is sometimes called. I knew the General very well, and greatly admired his courage and gallantry; but he never told me how he won his title. Everybody called him "General" and I shall not disturb his slumbers by asking unnecessary questions.

When he first began to relate his adventures I thought he might possibly be drawing the lines a little heavy, but he repeated the same things several times afterward in the same way, and was so sincere about it that I was forced to the conclusion that if he was lying he was unconscious of the fact.

A Peculiar Gun

The General had a gun constructed in such a peculiar way that when the bullet struck an object it produced no shock, and the victim did not realize that it was dead. It was a merciful scheme for hunting without producing unnecessary pain, and I felt that the General was entitled to much credit for the invention.

As an illustration of the operations of the gun, I might mention the following incident: While hunting one day the General came upon a large buck eating acorns out of a tall oak. The buck was so large that the General could not at first decide whether it was a deer or an elephant, but as elephants did not range in that part of the country he decided that it must be an animal of the deer species but of extraordinary size. So taking aim with his patient gun he fired, and knew by the natural instincts of the hunter that he had hit the mark; but the animal did not fall or move, or show any sign to indicate that it knew anything unusual had happened. Reloading his gun, the General cautiously approached the deer, and found it was stone dead, but owing to the absence of shock, it was not conscious of the fact. He was obliged to pull the buck over by one of its ears before it came to a realization of the conditions whereupon it remained as dead as any other buck would have been under similar circumstances.

An Intemperate Doe

But the gun had a serious defect. It was a single-barreled muzzleloader, and when discharged it had to be reloaded before it could be fired again. This defect sometimes proved inconvenient when game was plentiful, as it always was where General Burdine hunted. For instance, that very day as he was returning home carrying the huge buck on his shoulders, he came upon a doe that happened to be the dead buck's wife. She was eating poke berries, a species of intemperance that the deer acquires in countries where prohibition prevails. In a tree immediately over the poke-berry bush he observed a large turkey gobbler sitting on a limb picking his teeth; and wishing to get the turkey as well as the doe, he began to contrive some plan to accomplish his purpose. If he shot the doe first the turkey would fly away before he could reload, and if he fired on the turkey first the doe would escape. He was greatly puzzled over the situation; for he felt that it was a moral duty to take the doe along with the buck, and at the same time he did not want to miss hitting the turkey. While considering the matter a brilliant idea flashed into his mind, as was often the case with General Burdine, a faculty which had much to do with his fame as a hunter. He would put a second charge in his gun, on top of the one it already contained; then shoot the doe first, and by the time the second charge ignited he could bring his gun to bear on the turkey and get it too. The plan was so simple that he wondered he had not thought of it sooner, instead of wasting time trying to think what he should do. But he told me afterward that he knew it would take darned quick action to get a bead on the gobbler by the time the second shot came out; but he felt competent to meet the emergency and the result proved his sagacity. He shot the doe as it was reaching for another mouthful of poke-berries, and though he knew he had killed it, it stood perfectly still with its neck outstretched. Then he brought his gun to bear on the gobbler, and shot it while it was still picking its teeth. But it did not fall, and he was obliged to climb the tree and pull it off the limb. This was another inconvenience of the gun; the absence of shock not disturbing the game, left it just as it was when the ball struck it. The General told me confidentially that he was at work on another invention that would knock the game over and save him the trouble of climbing trees to get it. He remarked that these two shots were about the best he had ever made, and he doubted if he could do it again, unless the conditions were especially favorable.

On this occasion, however, his good luck remained with him, though he found that the two deers and the turkey made a pretty heavy load. Loutre Creek lay between him and his home, and as there had been a freshet he was obliged to swim the stream with the game on his back; but he succeeded even beyond his expectations. On landing he found that the set of his breeches was filled with a fine assortment of trout, which he had caught while crossing the creek. This good fortune was not due to any foresight on his part, for the pants had been made large in the seat for the sake of comfort with no expectation of using them for fishing purposes. The General admitted as much when he related the circumstance to me.

He now had a fine stock of fresh meat, and concluded to take a rest for perhaps the remainder of the season. But the old fascination for hunting returned, and in a few weeks he felt once more obliged to indulge his passion for the sport.

Powder But No Bullets

On examining his ammunition he found that he had plenty of powder but no lead or bullets; and knowing that he could not kill game with powder alone he was troubled in his mind what to do. However, no matter what the emergency might be the General always found a way out. In the present case he remembered that a traveling man had left a box of shoemaker's awls at his house, and on examining them he concluded that they might be made to fill the place of bullets. So loading his favorite gun with the implements, he set out to try his luck. He had gone less than a quarter of a mile when he saw three deer standing under a pecan tree eating nuts. They were a tall buck with his wife and daughter. The buck was cracking the nuts with his horns while the fawn and doe picked the kernels out with the points of their hoofs. It was such a happy family that the General hated to disturb them; but remembering that everything was fair in hunting, he fired at the group. The doe and he fawn ran away unharmed, but the buck remained standing against the tree as if something held him fast. Reloading his gun in order to be ready for an emergency, the General cautiously approached, and found that the buck was nailed to the tree by his right ear, which had been penetrated by one of his awls.

A Gentle Buck

It proved to be a nice, docile sort of buck, and he decided to take it home and tame it; though in fact it needed but little taming on account of its gentle disposition. The awl had been driven so tightly into the tree that in pulling it out he shook down several bushels of nuts, which he carried home in the seat of his leather breeches as food for the buck. He was careful also to lead the animal by the left ear, so as not to cause it unnecessary pain; for the awl having passed through the right one he naturally concluded it would be sore. I mention this as evidence of the General's humanity and tenderness of heart.

He and the buck became the best of friends, but he made the mistake in feeding it too liberally with the rich and meaty pecans; for in the course of a few months it became so fat it could not walk. The deer would often eat as much as a bushel of nuts at a single feed, carefully picking the kernels out with his horns and placing them in a china plate which he kept for the purpose; and the General never could determine whether it was the nuts or the plate that made him so fat.

Finally the buck made signs to intimate that he was in great pain on account of his fatness, and he begged his friend to shoot him and put him out of his misery. But the General did not have the heart to kill the animal he loved so well, so he hired a Dutchman who was passing that way to do the job for him. The buck had eaten so many pecans that when his flesh was made into venison and well smoked, it tasted precisely like the nuts, and the General declared to me that when he closed his eyes he could not tell whether he was eating venison or pecans.

Adventure In a Buffalo Hide

One cold winter General Burdine met with an adventure on the bank of Loutre Creek which came near costing him his life. Just before sundown he shot a large fat buffalo that had been to the creek to drink, and as night was near at hand and the weather extremely cold, he removed the hide and rolling himself in it fell asleep. During the night several inches of snow fell and the buffalo hide froze stiff, so that when the General attempted to get up in the morning he found that he could not move. The situation was perilous. He must either get rid of the frozen hide or starve to death.

While anxiously considering the matter, he remembered that there were several warm springs in that vicinity, which emptied their waters into the creek; and he resolved to take the chance of rolling himself into one of them in order to thaw the frozen hide. By great good fortune he happened to hit the right spot, for on rolling down the bank he splashed into a spring that was almost boiling hot. In a few minutes the hide became soft and pliable, and extricating himself from his perilous position he carried it home and tanned it. It made the finest buffalo robe that had ever been seen in that part of the country, the freezing and subsequent thawing in the hot water being just what was required. Thereafter all the General's neighbors tanned their buffalo robes by that process, first sleeping in the hides until they froze and then thawing them in hot water; which explains why Callaway County buffalo robes were superior to all others and brought better prices.

A Woodpecker and a Snake

Geneneral Burdine's whole life was attended by marvelous circumstances. Even while he was a small boy things happened that indicated his future greatness. When he was ten years old he saw a woodpecker fly into its hole in a sycamore tree, and as its head was more brilliant than any other woodpecker's he had ever seen, he decided to climb the tree and get it for experimental purposes. He knew also that birds of that species are very intellectual, and he believed he might get a good price for it at the Zoo.

But when he had climbed the tree and thrust his hand into the hole he caught a large black snake instead of the bird, and it frightened him so that he let go his hold and fell twenty feet into the crotch of a limb. His body was wedged in so tightly that he could not move; but on calling for help a man who was digging fish-worms in the vicinity heard him and came to his relief. The man was getting old and so stiff that he couldn't climb the tree, but he called to the boy that he would cut it down and let it fall into the creek and the crash into the water would loosen the limb and he could crawl out. As this seemed the only solution of the difficulty, the boy assented; and in the course of half an hour the tree began to tremble and sway and fell with a great splash into the creek, as the man had intended. When the limb struck the water it sprung apart and let the boy out, and he swam to the bank. But on the way he caught a catfish that weighed three hundred pounds, and brought it along with him. The fish had been hanging around to see what was going to happen, and a limb struck him and knocked all the sense he ever had out of his head; so the boy had no trouble managing him.

The old man said he was very fond of catfish, and begged the boy for half of it; but the future General was so grateful that he gave him the whole fish, and he carried it home and he and his family had it for Thanksgiving instead of turkey.

A Famous Pony

General Burdine had a pony that he called Ned, who knew almost as much as some people; and his master was very proud of the fact, as he had a right to be. The pony had been bred in Kentucky, which accounted for his knowing much. But in his youth he had acquired two bad habits, as will appear in the course of the story, and they increased to such an extent that the General was finally obliged to sell him to a circus.

The pony was as fond of hunting as his master, and could trail a bear or tree a wild cat as well as any hound dog. But he could not climb trees to get cats, and owing to this defect several wild cats got away and ravaged the neighboring pig-pens and sheep-folds. Finally the blacksmith invented a pair of shoes which he said would enable Ned to climb trees the same as a wild cat, and the pony felt much encouraged when he heard about it.

The very day that the blacksmith fitted the shoes to the pony's feet he and the General went in pursuit of a herd of buffaloes, which swam a deep creek with steep banks and escaped. This obliged them either to abandon the chase or cross the creek, and the banks were so high and steep that the General was in doubt what to do. So he cut a sapling and threw it across the stream in such a way that it made a foot-bridge for himself, but he motioned to Ned that he would have to swim, because his shoes would not hold fast to the pole. The pony shook his head and intimated that he was able to take care of himself. "Very well," said the General, "if you don't want to swim you may stay where you are."

But he was not more than half-way across the creek when he felt the pole shake and tremble behind him, and turning his head, behold, there was the pony right at his heels! The blacksmith's shoes had been constructed so that he could either climb trees or walk poles, as the case might be! Ned smiled at his master's bewilderment, but shook his nose for him to go on, or their double weight might break the pole. So they passed over in safety to the other side, where Ned struck the trail of a wild cat and chased it up a tree. But he could not follow, because it was a shell-bark hickory and his shoes would not take hold of the hard, slippery bark. He made a desperate effort however and succeeded in climbing up about ten feet, when a piece of the bark pulled loose and let him fall. He struck a large rock at the foot of the tree and knocked out one of his molar teeth, which so enraged him that when the General shot the wild cat and wounded it, the pony caught it in his remaining teeth and shook it until the hide came off. The General tanned the hide and made it into a saddle cover, and after that when he went hunting wild cats the cats would come running to see if the saddle-cover belonged to any of their relatives; and in this way he soon killed all the wild cats in that part of the country.

Ned's Bad Habits

It has been intimated that Ned had two bad habits, which will now be considered. One of these was his fondness for Kentucky whiskey, which he would drink in spite of everything his master could do. As he grew older the habit increased, until occasionally he would wander off alone into the woods and stay drunk for several days at a time. But the General did not blame Ned, because it was the result of his raising in a State where everybody took a nip now and then. Moreover, the pony had not voluntarily acquired the habit, but having been bitten by a rattlesnake when he was quite small, they gave him so much whiskey to cure the bite that he never entirely recovered from the effects.

Ned's other bad habit was is fondness for blood. In fact he was almost as bloodthirsty as a panther, and always licked the blood of the game that his master shot. The General did everything he could to break so disgusting a habit, but never succeeded; because the pony's ancestors had inherited it while fighting Indians under General Boone. Ned's passion for blood was so uncontrollable that when he could not get it from wild cats and other game he would kill a pig or a sheep in order to satisfy his unnatural thirst.

At length a circus came into the neighborhood, and the agent, hearing about Ned's remarkable talents, offered to buy him for any reasonable price. He said that a pony that would get drunk and drink blood like a civilized human being was almost worth his weight in gold; and by such arguments he induced General Burdine to part with his beloved Ned. But the pony did not long survive the separation. He was not accustomed to the kind of society he was obliged to associate with in the circus, and having to stay drunk most of the time in the performance of his stunts he fell into a decline and at the end of six months died of a complication of tuberculosis and delirium tremens.

General Burdine as an Indian Fighter

Much of General Burdine's fame was won as an Indian fighter, but in all his exploits there were none that quite equaled the following adventure, or resulted in greater good.

It was late in August, and the summer had been unusually hot; in fact the General asserted that in all his life he had never experienced another summer like it. He had been trailing a large band of warriors, and coming to the bank of the Cuivre River he decided to take a bath. It was a dangerous thing to do under the circumstances, but the General's courage was of such a character that he never allowed himself to consider a risk.

Placing his loaded rifle on the bank of the stream, he divested himself of his clothing and entered the grateful waters. But scarcely had he done so when the very Indians whom he had been trailing came out of the brush, and observing his clothes and gun, sat down on the bank to see what would happen. In order to escape their observation, the General dived under the water and watched their maneuvers. But they were in no hurry. Supposing that the owner of the gun and clothes must eventually appear and fall under their hands, the Indians stretched themselves out on the grass to rest; and several of the chiefs lit their pipes and took a smoke. Their leisurely movements caused the General a good deal of apprehension, for he would soon need a supply of fresh air, and he could not push his nose above the water without danger of discovery.

Presently a black snake came swimming along and gave him an idea, which he put into immediate action. Catching the snake, he tied its head and neck into a noose, with which he lassoed his gun and pulled it to him. He now felt considerably relieved, for with his trusty rifle in hand the General felt that he could manage a thousand savages.

He now took note of the position of the Indians, and finding by actual count that they numbered a hundred and five, he laid his plans for their extermination. Meandering slowly under the water to avoid making ripples, he reached the left wing of the enemy, where he unlimbered and slew thirty-five of them. Then meandering back to the right wing he slaughtered thirty-five more, which left only a similar number to be accounted for. On reloading his rifle, however, he found to his dismay that his powder was wet from having been so long under water, and he began to feel uneasy as to what the result might be. But his fears were groundless; the remaining thirty-five warriors were so terrified by the death of their companions that they fled in dismay and never stopped running until they were safe in the British dominions. Never afterward could they be persuaded to go on the warpath, for they argued among themselves that if one pale face could slay seventy braves while swimming under water, what chance would they have in the open against equal numbers? It will be seen, therefore, that this single achievement of the great General brought the war to an end and restored peace to the troubled nation.

Our country has produced many noble warriors and astute statesmen, but General Burdine was the only one who had the ability or the opportunity to end a war single-handed and alone. The history of his achievements therefore well worth the study of the rising generations, in order that they may be inspired by his career to imitate his example.

I shall be able to recount only one more of his exploits, which appeals to me as authentic and valuable as any of the preceding. It refers to the General's first appearance on the pioneer stage, and reveals several peculiarities which I hope will be interesting and instructive.

Episode Number Seventy-Two

Remarkable Happenings to General Burdine

Gieneral Burdine was a native of Kentucky, which State, according to the belief of many of its citizens, has produced most of the great men of our country; but after his marriage, and a family began to accumulate around him, he came to Missouri to assist Uncle Daniel in populating the West.

He settled first in Dog Prairie, and immediately afterward the New Madrid earthquakes occurred. Whether these were caused by the General's arrival has never been scientifically determined, but the two events happened so nearly at the same time convinced him that there was some sort of connection between them. The violent commotion of the earth shook the General's cabin until the boards on the roof rattled and he concluded that Indians were making an assault on the place. So, arousing his sons, they commenced firing their rifles through the roof, and kept it up so vigorously that when daylight came they found that they had shot the boards to splinters, and were obliged to put on a new roof in place of the old one.

An Accommodating Earthquake

The quake did one good turn for the General and his family. By an oversight he had built his cabin some distance from the spring, which made it inconvenient for Mrs. Burdine to get water for domestic uses, especially as she was a very fat lady and somewhat clumsy. But during the evolutions of the earthquake it picked up the spring and planted it at the corner of the porch; and if there are any who do not believe this statement, or have any doubts concerning its truthfulness, they may go and see the spring still bubbling in the same place. Some say it was there all the time, but I prefer to accept the General's account of the matter.

Circumventing the Witches

Like many of his contemporaries General Burdine was a believer in witches, and in order to protect his cattle from their evil influence it was his custom to brand them on their heads with a hot shoe hammer; for he said that he had made a close study of the matter and had never known a "cow-brute" with such a mark on its head to be harmed by witches. Since then I myself have made a number of observations along the same line, and it affords me pleasure to say that I have never seen an animal of any kind, marked as the General explained, that was troubled in any way with witches. I am therefore disposed to believe that the remedy is infallible; but I cannot explain why witches should be afraid of the sign of the shoemaker's hammer, unless it might be because it is their preference to go barefooted.

Domesticating Wild Geese

Wild geese were so plentiful when the General first came to the Boone country, that he caught a flock one day and tamed them for domestic purposes. But being of a naturally wild disposition, they pined away in captivity and nearly all the flock died of some disease peculiar to the goose family, which the General decided was due to the evil machinations of witches. He therefore built a large fire and collecting the dead birds threw them into it, for he had been told that witches could not stand excessive heat. When about half the dead birds had been consumed one of them came to life, and flew around the fire and drove the witches away; and the strangest part of it was that as soon as they were gone all the rest of the birds except one also came to life. On examination, the body of this particular bird it was found that the witches had left an egg in it which was noncombustible, and of course it was impossible to burn the birds while the egg was there. So the General removed the egg and fed it to his pigs, whereupon the goose came to life and flew away with the rest of the flock. But by some curious freak the pigs were so infected that they twisted their tails so tight they had to walk on their forelegs, and the General was obliged to manufacture them into sausage, which he sold to a Jew named Isaac Samuels in St. Louis. I believe the descendants of Mr. Samuels are still in business, and if any one wishes to verify these facts he might consult them. General Burdine told me that he never heard what effect the sausages had on the people who ate them but to the best of his knowledge and belief several were affected like the pigs and walked on their hands instead of their feet, although they had no tails to curl.

Naming Trees

The General hunted so much, and killed such quantities of game, that it was impossible for him to carry it all home; so it was his custom to send the boys out after the extra supplies. In order that they might be able to find the animals, he adopted the plan of naming the trees in the woods where he hunted, and when he sent the boys after the game he would direct them in the following manner: "At the foot of 'Sarah Sycamore' you will find two fine fat bucks; and there are six wild cats under 'Jim Walnut'; and just beyond the creek you'll find the fattest buffalo I ever drew a bead on hanging on a limb of 'Dick Hickorynut'. The boys knew the names and locations of the trees so well that they never made a mistake, and when Uncle Daniel heard about it he said he would adopt the same plan if he were only a few years younger; but he was too old to be learning new tricks.

Imitating the Calls of Wild Animals

By long practice General Burdine had learned to mimic the cry of any bird or wild animal so accurately as to deceive the animals themselves, and he found it a great convenience. It saved him much walking, for he could stand in one place and call the game to him to be shot. There were several other ways in which this talent served him a good purpose. For instance, a party of hunters came over from Kentucky and camped in a forest which he had reserved for his own use, and as they were not experienced in the art he was afraid they would scare the game and make it leave the country. So one Sunday morning, just before daylight, he secreted himself in the woods near their camp and began to scream like a panther. The hunters were so frightened that they left in haste, and ran all the way back to Kentucky, swimming the Mississippi and Ohio Rivers on the way. One of them left a frilled shirt hanging to a limb, which the General adopted as his own and wore it at the wedding of his daughter. Another left a night-shirt, but the General did not understand its use, so he hung it on a stake in the middle of his cornfield, and no crow ever after bothered his corn.

General Burdine Weighs His Wife

BURDINE'S ATTEMPT TO WEIGH HIS WIFE.

In spite of his great reputation and prowess as a hunter, General Burdine was of small stature. But his wife was large and fleshy, as previously intimated, and so good natured that she was always smiling or laughing. As she grew older her flesh increased, and one day she asked the General to rig up his steelyards and see how much she weighed. So he fastened the steelyards to a rafter of the porch with a grape vine, and arranged another vine for his wife to sit on. When all was ready she sat down suddenly, but was so much heavier than her husband that he was hoisted by the beam of the steelyards into the air, where he hung kicking and struggling in his efforts to get down. Unfortunately Mrs. Burdine was hard of hearing, so that she remained unconscious of her husband's appeals, and sat smilingly waiting for him to announce her weight. The General admitted subsequently that it was one of the most trying experiences of his life, and he did not know what might have happened; but at the most critical moment one of the boys came home to get his dinner, and finding his father in such an uncomfortable position he took hold of his legs and pulled him down. This released the other end of the scales and Mrs. Burdine fell so hard that she broke through the floor, and it required the combined efforts of the whole family to pull her out.

But it is time to give attention to other pioneers whose exploits were as famous as those of General Burdine. At the same time I leave him with reluctance, for if all his adventures should be recorded I suppose that the world itself could not contain all the books that would be written.

Jim Stewart's Turkey Trench

Jim Stewart of Montgomery County, becoming tired of ranging the forests in quest of wild turkeys, of which he was excessively fond, conceived a plan by means of which he became famous above all his neighbors. But it was so simple that when he applied for a patent the Patent Office refused his application, and the way being left open everybody in that part of the country adopted the plan, with the result that in a few years there was not a turkey left in the entire county.

Stewart's plan consisted merely in digging a trench about three feet deep under his barn, and just wide enough to admit one turkey at a time. Having completed his trench, he baited it by sprinkling corn along the bottom, after which he lay down to take a nap and did not awake until next morning.

On examining his trench he found it was filled with turkeys, ground hogs, pole cats, and an old sow that belonged to a neighbor with whom he was not on good terms. Firing into the assortment, he brought down sixteen turkeys, ten ground hogs, five pole cats, and the old sow; but the cats made such an odor that he could not approach the place to get his game.

To make matters worse, his disagreeable neighbor, whose name was Jack Billops, sued him for fifty dollars for killing his sow, and having proved by several witness that the animal was worth that much if she was worth a cent, he got judgement for the full amount. Jim said the judgement was in excess of all common sense, and he moved across the river to Benton County in order to escape legal process.

There he built a barn with a roof so constructed that he believed it would get more turkeys than a trench, and at the same time prevent pole cats and old sows from mingling with his game. At the peak of the roof, where the boards came together, he planed the ends so sharp that when a turkey lit the keen edge would cut its feet off, and reduce the bird to a condition which would enable him to catch it without the trouble and expense of shooting.

When his barn was finished he filed the edges of the boards and whetted them with his razor-strop until he said he believed he could have shaved himself with them. Then he spread molasses along the edge and stuck grains of corn in it to entice the turkeys; and when he woke up next morning his barn lot was full of fat turkeys without legs. He caught and dressed several of them for immediate use, and picked a hundred and sixteen for future emergencies.

Turkeys were plentiful in Benton County, and Jim caught and ate so many that feathers began to grow on his legs; and when he applied to a doctor for advice, the doctor told him to quit eating turkeys and confine his diet to corned beef and sauerkraut. After several weeks of this fare the feathers came off and Jim's hair fell out until he became as bald as a turkey's egg; whereupon the doctor advised him that if he would diet himself and not eat more than two or three turkeys a day, his hair would probably grow out again.

Some of Mr. Tate's Adventures with Wild Pigeons

Mr. Calvin Tate of Calloway County, was one of the most conscientiously truthful pioneers I ever met, and I think therefore that a good deal of reliance may be placed in the following stories he told me about wild pigeons. He said that quite frequently the pigeons would come to his woods-pasture and light in such numbers that the oak trees would be bent to the ground by their weight, and that when they flew away large limbs would be broken off and hurled several hundred yards with great force. In one instance a limb as large as his thigh and twenty-two feet long was thrown half a mile. It passed through the air so rapidly that he could not see it, but it roared like a battery of cannons, and when it struck the earth the concussion shook the ground so that several panels of his new rail fence were destroyed. In reply to my question, Mr. Tate said he had never seen a cannon or heard one discharged, but the limb roared that way. Without intending to hurt his feelings in the least, I asked him if he measured the half-mile. He was profoundly moved to think I would doubt his word, and replied that he guessed he knew half-mile when he saw one.

One Tuesday morning about ten minutes before nine o'clock, a large flock of pigeons lit in his woods-pasture, and they made so much noise with the fluttering of their wings that he thought a thunderstorm was brewing though there was not a cloud in the sky at the time. As soon as he discovered the cause of the disturbance he loaded his gun and rode out to the pasture, hitching his horse to a large hickory tree, which seemed to be the center of operations. He did not notice at the time that the tree had been bent over until the top branches touched the ground, and it was to one of these branches that he tied his horse. Then he fired at random into the tree and killed a hundred and thirteen pigeons at a single shot. He counted them so as to be sure of the number. The rest of the birds flew away, and the tree on being relieved of their weight straightened up to its natural position and carried his horse with it. There hung his favorite riding animal by the bridle fifty feet in the air, with no derrick or other machinery to get him down. Mr. Tate said he wouldn't have had it happen for all the pigeons in Callaway County; but while he was considering the matter and planning how to recover his horse, another flock came flying along and lit in the same tree, which bent over again until he could untie his horse. Then he gathered up the pigeons he had shot and rode home with a thankful heart; but after that when he went pigeon hunting he was careful not to tie his horse to loose limbs. I myself have seen pigeons enough to perform this act, and the fact that they did not do it in my presence is no reason why I should doubt Mr. Tate's story.

Ben Barnes Creates a Panic

Benjamin Barnes the elder was a pioneer of two counties, Boone and Callaway. I knew him when he was quite an old man, and became acquainted with his son Benjamin at a later date. Young

Ben moved to St. Louis and made a large fortune betting the right way on the future prices of grain but lost every cent of it not long after by betting the wrong way. Then he went into the brokerage business and made another fortune telling other people which way to bet. Nothing could keep young Ben down.

He and his father were both of small stature, and one day while the Indians were bad and most of the pioneers had sought safety for themselves and families in the forts, little Ben and some of the other boys climbed over the palisades and went swimming. Ben was so small that the other boys decided he should watch the clothes and give the alarm if Indians came; but he was peeved at what he regarded as unfair treatment and although no savages were in sight he yelled "Indians!" as loud as he could, and ran to the fort. The other boys did not take time to put on their clothes, but lit out for safety and tumbled over the palisades in their natural state. Several maiden ladies who happened to see this had fits, and others fainted, until the whole fort was in a state of commotion. The trumpets blew and the garrison was called to order, but when no Indians appeared the commander demanded an explanation from Ben. He was obliged to own up, and they put him in the guard house for a week so that he might have time to repent of his sins.

A Champion Liar

The elder Barnes had a cousin named Azel, who was a blacksmith by trade and was regarded as the champion liar of the community. According to his own account he took a bar of cold iron one day and beat it on his anvil until it was so hot he had to leave the shop a half an hour to let it cool off. Then he beat it into a scythe seven feet in length, and attaching it to a sneath of the same length he had a scythe that would cut a swath fourteen feet wide. With this magic scythe he mowed fourteen acres of timothy in one day, without stopping to wet the blade or take a drink. I think it was the combination of "sacred sevens" that enabled Azel to perform such wonders, for I am quite sure he would not tell a lie in a case of that kind.

Azel Mowes Down a Column of Indians

As Azel was on his way home after his day's work, he was waylaid by six Indians, who observing that he was unarmed did not shoot at him, but came out of their concealment and demanded his surrender. According to their custom they marched in single file, one behind another; and Azel, on pretense of obeying their order, gave his scythe a sweep and mowed down the whole column. He then buried the six warriors in a single grave, but was never able afterward to find the grave in proof of his claims.

After Azel had slain and buried his Indians, he proceeded on his way home, but on coming to the horse-pond he was so thirsty that he lay down and drank forty quarts of water. On rising to pursue his way, he observes a sheepskin floating in the pond with the wool upward, and remembering that he had only one air of socks, he took his scythe and shaved off the wool and carried it home so his wife could knit him another pair. He got thirty-one pounds of wool at a single sweep of the scythe, and by putting this with some cotton that she picked up under the cottonwood tree she spliced out enough to make her husband a pair of socks; though she was obliged to leave the legs so short that they barely covered his ankles, and when cold weather came he caught chilblains in both feet so badly that he had to stay in bed most of the time while his wife did the work.

Some Corn and Some Turkey

The next summer Azel raised five acres of corn, which was admitted to be the finest crop that was ever grown in that county. But one day after the corn was ripe, a turkey gobbler came up to the outside of the fence, and poking his head through a crack between two rails ate every grain of corn in the field. He ate so much that he couldn't run, and Azel caught him and wrung his neck; a just punishment for being so greedy. The turkey weighed six hundred and four pounds, allowing for the corn that was inside him, and yielded seventy-three pounds of feathers; so that Azel got more money out of the gobbler than he would have received for his corn if he had sold it in the open market. In proof of his statement he always wore one of his tail-feathers of the turkey in his cap, and it made him look so fierce that it did not consider it would be prudent to express any doubt as to the character of his stories.

Aleck Weant and the Big Cannon

Aleck Weant was a native of Kentucky, and a gunsmith by trade, and having decided to come to the Boone country he loaded his family and effects in a small flatboat and floated down to Louisville, where he landed for liquid refreshments. The river of course was full of water, but it was not the kind Aleck wanted at the time.

In looking about the city he came to a park where there was a very large cannon, which a Kentuckian had captured at the battle of New Orleans. He became much interested in the great gun and its history, which the keeper of the park related in a circumstantial manner; and as he seemed to be a very conscientious man, Aleck felt that he had no reason to doubt his word.

The keeper explained that the cannon had been captured from the British in the following curious manner, by a Kentucky rifleman: As everyone who is familiar with the history of that great battle is aware, the British made an attempt to turn General Jackson's left wing, but they got entangled in a swamp and were obliged to retreat. Quite a number of the soldiers sank in the mire and were drowned, and altogether it was a very sad and lamentable affair. They had taken this big gun with them, intending to enfilade the American line and reduce it to cannon fodder. But the wheels sank in the quicksand and became immovable.

It so happened that General Jackson suspected the enemy would attempt a movement of this kind, and he sent one of the Kentucky riflemen to this point to guard his left wing and give the alarm in case an assault should be made. This result proved the sagacity of the General, for scarcely had the Kentuckian reached the place assigned to him when he saw the column of attack approaching; and in front was this tremendous cannon with sixteen men dragging it with a rope. The Kentuckian observed that the men were all of the same height, for there was a fad then in armies to have everything uniform. He accordingly stationed himself on a line with the sixteen British soldiers, and at a single discharge of his rifle shot every one of them in the middle of the forehead. He said afterward that it was a cruel thing to do, and when the war was over he taught a class in Sunday school for sixteen years as pence for what he had done.

When General Jackson learned the facts, he complemented the soldier and shook him by the hand in presence of the entire army, and said if he had an army of that kind of men he could whip the whole of Europe, including Napoleon and Wellington and Blucher. When he was afterward elected President he promoted the soldier to corporal, and directed that on his retirement from the service he should have a pension of five dollars a month for the remainder of his life, in order that he might live in the style of affluence becoming so brave a citizen.

The keeper of the park explained to Mr. Weant that the chamber of the gun was so large they were obliged to draw the ball in with a yoke of oxen, and when he inquired how they got the oxen out of the cannon he was told that as soon as the ball was in place the oxen unyoked themselves and came out one at a time through the touch-hole. It happened that the cannon was being loaded at the same time, and the keeper obligingly fired it off to please his visitor. The vibration was so great that Aleck's clothes were torn off, and as there were several ladies present he was placed in a very embarrassing position. Some of the ladies laughed and peeked through their fingers, until a motherly old lady pulled off one of her petticoats and pinned it around him so he could go down town and buy a new outfit, and get something to steady his nerves.

Adventure with a Buck, a Turkey, and a Panther

Shortly before coming to Missouri, Aleck Weant met with a series of adventures of the most curious and remarkable character. One day while hunting he shot and wounded a buck, which in the paroxysms of its pain and rage jumped on him and almost stamped him to death with its sharp hoofs; but before completing its purpose it slipped and fell over a cliff overlooking the valley of the Kentucky River. The cliff was about fifty feet high and so steep as to preclude all idea of descending it; so Aleck felt that he would be obliged to suffer the loss of his game.

Soon afterward a turkey came and lit in a tree near the edge of the cliff, and when Aleck shot it the bird also fell over the declivity. He concluded, therefore, that he must be in an unlucky place, and decided to move on as soon as he reloaded his rifle. But at that instant a large, fierce-looking pantheress appeared on the scene, trailing the scent of the deer, and coming suddenly upon the hunter she crouched to spring upon him. In his excitement and haste he fired somewhat at random, and instead of hitting the beast in the heart as he intended his bullet cut her tail in two about the middle. This enraged her more than ever, and lashing the stump of her tail against her sides she crouched and made the fatal spring; but her movement loosened the rock on which she was standing, and both pantheress and the rock went crashing over the bluff.

Aleck now had an abundance of game, but so out of reach that he could not see any way to recover it. While considering the matter he heard a deep growl, and noticed a tree that grew on the side of the cliff shaking and trembling as though agitated by some heavy weight; and before he could determine the cause the head of the pantheress came into sight with the deer in her mouth. On reaching a point a little above the level of the ridge she crawled out on a limb and let the deer fall, evidently intending to recover it later. At present she was in the act of springing upon him he sent a bullet into her brain and put an end to her activities.

He now had the buck and the pantheress and began to plan some way to secure the turkey, as it was a fine fat bird and he did not like to lose it. At this moment a large bald eagle came soaring over, and observing the turkey at the bottom of the cliff, it swooped down and grasping it in its talons carried it to the top of the ridge. Then as the eagle was preparing to make a dinner of the turkey Aleck brought it down with a crack of his unerring rifle.

Raising Panthers for Pets

Picking up the turkey, he started for home, intending to return later with his pony for the rest of the game. But as he was passing the mouth of a cavern he heard a purring and growling inside, and on investigating the cause he found two pretty little panther kittens playing and frolicking together.

As soon as they scented the turkey they came mewing for their dinners, and Aleck, supposing they belonged to the pantheress which he had just shot, decided to take them home and see if he could domesticate them. So trailing the turkey along just out of their reach, they followed him all the way, mewing the same as tame kittens would have done.

Then while he returned for the rest of his game his wife fed the little panthers with warm milk until they curled up and went to sleep in the corner of the fireplace. When Aleck returned and saw them sleeping there, he declared it was the most beautiful sight he had ever witnesses, and he told his wife it compensated them in a measure for having no children of their own.

So the little panthers were raised as pets, and never allowed to get a taste of meat or blood; but were fed exclusively on milk and molasses. The result was that they grew up with a mild tempers, and were as harmless and playful as any tame kittens would be.

A New Species of Cat-Panthers

It may be added that Aleck bred a species of cats from his panthers, which became celebrated all over the Boone country; and when strangers from various parts of the world visit that interesting locality they never fail to express their admiration for the beauty and gentleness of the animals. A celebrated scientist, after having studied them for some time expressed the belief that if men were reared in the same way, on a diet of milk and molasses and never allowed to taste meat or blood, they would probably be as docile as the panther cats, and in this way war might be banished from the world. He laid the matter before the Geneva Conference, but nothing came of it, because about that time Mr. Hitler said he wanted to do a little more fighting, and the subject was tabled for the time being. It will probably be taken up again as soon as the German Chandler cools off.

"Father Bratton" Visits "Uncle Daniel"

When I first met "Father Bratton", as he was affectionately called, he was ninety-six years and three months old, and his long white hair and venerable appearance gave me confidence in what he said concerning the stirring events of his busy life.

He was a Kentuckian by birth, but on coming West settled first in Iowa, believing that the climate would suit him better than that of a more southern locality. But his constitution was not vigorous, and the rigors of the first Iowa winter convinced him that he had made a mistake. So he removed to the Boone country in Missouri, where he found a climate which he said he did not think could be surpassed anywhere else in the world.

On coming to Missouri he spent several days as the guest of Uncle Daniel, who advised him by all means to locate in Montgomery County, where there seemed to be more fresh air to the square mile than anywhere else in America. So acting upon the advice of the famous old hunter, he located in that county, and attributed his long life and good health to that fact.

During my conference with him he mentioned several interesting incidents about Uncle Daniel, which throw light upon his remarkable character. He said that one day while he was a guest at the Boone home in Femme Osage valley, sitting on the lawn and talking with the venerable pioneer, a flock of little yellow-breasted, blue-winged birds settled in a tree just over their heads; and one of Uncle Daniel's little granddaughters who was playing near them, like all children, was delighted with their beauty, and wished she could have one for a pet. Thereupon the old hunter went into the house and got his gun, remarking that he would get one for her. But she said she did not want a dead bird, and it would be cruel to shoot so beautiful a creature. "I shall not hurt the bird," replied Uncle Daniel.

Then firing a bullet into the limb immediately under where the bird was sitting, it was stunned by the concussion and fell to the ground unharmed. The little girl caught the pet in her hands and pressed it to her bosom, but as soon as it came-to she let it fly away with the flock. The visitor was impressed with the incident, both as a manifestation of skill as a marksman on the part of Uncle Daniel, and of humanity in the little girl. {This is a true story}

Some Remarkable Skating

While Peter lived in Iowa the winters were so long and so much snow fell and froze to ice on the surface, that he became an expert skater. He traveled a great deal on his skates and saw much of the country; and acquired such speed that when he came to a valley, instead of taking time to walk down the declivity on one side and up again on the other, he adopted what he called a "running jump" and cleared the depression at a single leap. This is now called "skiing," but it was unknown in his time and he acquired much fame as the originator of that thrilling sport. He assured me that he acquired such dexterity that it was no trouble for him to jump a valley a mile wide. But eventually his confidence in himself came near costing him his life, and after that experience he was more careful. He had been skating for pleasure one Sunday morning, when on examining his watch he found that he was going to be late for Sunday school; so he put on extra speed and so on came to the valley of the Des Moines River. The sun was shining so brightly that its reflection deceived him regarding the width of the valley, and in attempting to jump from one hill to the other he fell into the river. The spring thaw had commenced and the ice was so rotten that every time he tried to climb on it it would break and let him slide back into the cold water. He made several efforts to save himself, but always with the same result; and finally believing that his time had come he resigned himself to the care of Providence for his many sins. Being a Baptist he was consoled with the thought that he would make the trip by water, and thus be more certain of gaining admittance through the gates of pearl.

But just at the moment, when he supposed he was about to draw his last breath, he found himself in the midst of a shoal of fish, which had been attracted to the hole in the ice for fresh air. Laying hold of two of the largest he put one under each arm, and directing their course toward the shore he soon made a landing. The delay caused him to be a few minutes late at Sunday school, but the superintendent excused him on the ground that he had done the best he could.

Some Remarkable Freaks of Lightning

While the winters in Iowa were long and cold, the summers on the contrary were short and hot; and owing to these conditions thunder storms were numerous and severe. One day Peter was hauling a load of steel rods for the local blacksmith, and the load being heavy he walked by the side of the wagon to relieve the team. Presently a storm arose and the lightning was so fierce and continuous that it flashed and crackled under his feet and all around him, as electricity will do when one strokes the back of a cat, though of course on a much larger scale. It was fortunate for Peter that he had the load of steel, for the electric current was endeavoring to get at the rods, and so passed by him without harm.

Feeling that he had made a Providential escape, as soon as the storm was over he knelt under a tree and gave thanks for his preservation. Meanwhile a turkey lit in the tree under which he was praying, when the lightning stunned it so badly that it fell down at his feet. The bird would no doubt have been killed except for the fact that feathers are a non-conductor, and for this reason it was merely stunned. It may be remarked in this connection that a feather bed is the safest place in a thunder storm, or if you have two feather beds it is well to get between them. They might be uncomfortably warm, but it is better to sweat than be struck by lightning.

The turkey in falling had struck Peter on the head and almost knocked him down, for it was fat and heavy. His first thought was that he had done something to displease the Lord, who had taken this method of administering reproof; but when he saw the turkey lying at his feet he realized the goodness of Providence, which had showered blessings upon him to an extent exceeding his merits.

Extraordinary Growth of Fur in Iowa

During his residence in Iowa Father Bratton hunted many of the fur-bearing animals of that region, and made some remarks concerning them which I have not seen recorded in the standard natural histories; but his sincerity of character is a sufficient warrant for their publication.

One thing that especially attracted his attention was the rapid growth of fur on fox skins after the beginning of winter, which in his opinion demonstrated the wisdom of nature's provisions. The fur grew in proportion to the state of the weather, in order to keep the animals comfortable. This phenomenon was familiar not only to the animals themselves, but also to the hunters, who confined their operations to the coldest seasons. The winter furs were also appreciated by the fair ladies for whose adornment they were intended, because they were softer and more brilliant than those obtained in mild weather. Thus nature worked impartially and without prejudice to any of the parties concerned.

One morning about the middle of January Father Bratton went into the woods near his home and shot four foxes by sunrise. On examining them he was pleased to find that their furs were of the highest grade, and he began removing the skins at once so as to have time to get more of the same kind. But as he was skinning the fourth animal he observed that the first three had grown new hides, and that the new coat of fur was better than the preceding ones. It was thicker and softer and less flea-bitten, and had a very brilliant gloss.

Encouraged by these facts, he continued skinning the same four foxes until noon, in each successive case getting better furs. He now felt that he could profitably remain there and skin the same foxes the rest of his life, or at least until the weather moderated; but at noon he began to feel the pangs of hunger, and fearing his wife might become uneasy at his prolonged absence, he ceased work and went home.

In the meantime he had obtained so many pelts that when spring came and it was time to market them the hides filled a large flatboat, and the fur was of such high grade that it brought an extra price and enabled him to pay the government cash for his land in Montgomery County.

I was so impressed by this story that I decided to go also to Iowa and engage in the fox hunting business, and if I could have carried out my plans I would soon have become a merchant prince; but a severe attack of rheumatism obliged me to return to a milder climate. Foxes were so plentiful that in a single night I counted no less than five thousand tracks, but the man at whose house I was stopping said these had all been made by one fox while looking for a rooster to make chicken and dumpling. The story got out and resulted in the production of fox-trot music; but I hope my friends will not give me away, as I do not wish to be translate until I am a few years older.

Father Bratton Goes on a Whaling Expedition

Soon after locating in Missouri, Father Bratton decided to go on a sea voyage for his health, and he embarked on a vessel bound for the Arctic Ocean. In due course of time they arrived in the land of whales, and the season being unusually good their tanks were soon filled with fine grade of oil. The captain was so impressed with his good fortune that he told Father Bratton he was going to write a book on the subject of whale fishing as soon as he returned home, and he believed it would have a large sale. While he was considering these matters, they had been sailing for several hours close by the side of what the Captain supposed to be an island, but it contained no verdure and was perfectly smooth all over; and on consulting with the sailing-master they could find no such land in the charts. On closer observation they discovered that the land was moving in the same direction as the ship, and there was no record of an island of that size being afloat. The sailing-master said there was no explanation for such a phenomenon unless they were bewitched, but the Captain quieted his fears by reminding him that Rev. Cotton Mather had banished all witches to Africa. The Captain feared, however, that they had mistaken their calculations and were lost in the great frozen regions of the north; but while they were considering the matter an explanation came in a perfectly natural way.

"There she blows!" roared the outlook from his lofty perch in the cross-trees, and on looking in the direction indicated a sight was revealed of the most astonishing character. The ship was now approaching the head of the supposed island, when suddenly two immense spouts of water were thrown two hundred feet into the air and roared like a flood. Everything was now explained! They had found perhaps the greatest whale in all the seas, and their proximity to it was sufficient to strike terror into the stoutest heart. By a single fluke of its tail the monster could wreck the ship and consign all on board to a watery grave.

But the Captain did not lose his presence of mind. Quickly issuing his orders, the ship was brought about and sailed a distance of two hundred fathoms from the whale, where he believed they would be safe. Then he ordered the sailing-master to luff and sail in the opposite direction from which they had been pursuing, which meant that they would proceed toward the tail of the fish instead of it head. The order was obeyed as soon as issued; whereupon Father Bratton approached the Captain and inquired his reason for reversing the course of the vessel, which he explained in the following manner: The covering of the whale is composed of a thick hide, in the form of scales, sloping from the head toward the tail. Therefore if the harpoon is cast from the front or side of the animal its point is apt to glance away from the smooth scales and not penetrate a vital spot; but if it is hurled from the rear it will find an opening between the scales and enter the body of the fish. It was therefore his purpose to gain a position beyond the middle of the whale, where the harpoon could be cast from the rear, and they would still be out of reach of the tail of the monster.

They had an enormously large beast to deal with, and prudence demanded that they proceed with caution. In concluding his remarks the Captain whispered to Father Bratton that it was highly probable they were in the vicinity of the fish that had swallowed the prophet Jonah, for plenty of time had elapsed for it to grow; and having a taste of the prophet it might be disposed to swallow the whole ship's crew. Father Bratton admitted the wisdom of the Captain's suspicions, and thanked him for his courtesy in communicating them to him.

In a short time they reached the desired position immediately beyond the waist of the monster, when the ship was luffed again and brought within reach of the harpoon; whereupon a shaft was sent hurling through the air. It took hold and sank nearly to the handle in the fatty integuments, when instantly there was a mighty commotion in the sea. The great fish floundered and lashed the water with its tail until the waves rolled as high as the masts of the ship, and the vessel would inevitably have been wrecked except for the wise precautions of the Captain.

Several other harpoon were thrown, each with deadly effect; until with a great bellow the monster turned on its side and ceased to breathe. It required several weeks to dispose of the blubber and make places for the oil. Every tank and empty vessel in the ship was filled, even to the empty rum casks and water buckets. The Captain was overjoyed with the results, so that as he ordered the ship to sail for home, he said he would now be able to live in comfort the rest of his days.

On their arrival in port, and as he and Father Bratton were taking an affectionate leave of each other, the Captain placed in his hand a check for five thousand dollars and begged him to accept it as a token of his esteem. Father Bratton had not expected any such reward, for he had made the voyage merely as a passenger and was not entitled to any of the emoluments. The Captain's generosity moved him deeply, and therefore until the end of his days he regarded him as one of his best friends. As a special mark of his regard he had three of his grandsons named for him; and in order to distinguish one from the other the two younger ones were called Jonah and Big Fish respectively.

Father Bratton reached home in time to plant his first crop of corn, which grew so high in the virgin soil of Montgomery County that when the grain was ripe and ready to be gathered, the ears were elevated so high in the air that he was obliged to shoot them off with his rifle. This practice made him so fine a shot that none of his neighbors ever dared enter the lists with him in their friendly shooting matches, and he worried over the deprivation so keenly that it shortened his life by several years.

Mr. Hudson Tames a Mad Bull

During my visit to Father Bratton he introduced me to his neighbor John Hudson, whom I found to be a very fine man. One morning he came over to see me riding a bull, and during our conversation I remarked on the apparent docility of the animal. He then related the following adventure, in explanation of the fact that the bull had not always been as gentle as he was at that time.

One Sunday morning Mr. Hudson rode his pony over to Dr. Briscoe's in Warren County, to get some of his famous blue mass pills for his wife, who had been suffering with toothache for several days. On his way back he was attacked by this same bull, who threw his pony into Charrette Creek and was climbing down the bank to finish him, when the pony contrived to make his escape and ran home, followed by the bull.

John was so frightened by the adventure that he climbed a tree, and fastening himself to a limb with his suspenders remained there until daylight. Then supposing the way was open, he came down and started home; but in a little while he met the bull returning for him. There was nothing to do but climb another tree, whereupon the animal lay down and commenced chewing his cud, knowing that John would have to come out of the tree sooner or later. But as noon approached he became very hungry, and tried to think of some plan to get rid of the bull. Finally, while the beast was looking up at him with his mouth open, John threw the package of pills down his throat, and when they began to take effect they made him so sick that he lost all desire to fight. John now cut a large hickory switch, and watching his opportunity slid down the tree and mounting on the back of the bull made him run all the way home, lashing him with his switch at every jump. After that, said John, that animal was as gentle as a lamb, and owing to his docility and easy gait he became the choice riding animal in all Montgomery County. Mrs. Hudson preferred him to her pacing pony, and rode him to church every Sunday.

Skilt and His Thanksgiving Turkey

SKILT AND THE TURKEYS.

Some account has already been given of the adventures of Mr. Calvin Tate of Callaway County, who, as his name indicates, was a Presbyterian; but nothing has been said about his little colored boy Skilt, who was born so deaf that he could hear the thunder only when there were especially loud cracks. He was a little fellow of such spirit and sound judgement, that his master had the utmost confidence in him; and his confidence was not misplaced, as the following circumstances will attest.

Thanksgiving day was approaching, and the family had not yet been provided with a turkey, a fact which seemed to affect every member of the household. Skilt especially wore a sad and even morose countenance, and appeared to be lacking in the spirit which usually characterized him. His mother remarked that she was sure something was going to happen, and she spoke to her master about it. But he told her not to worry, that the boy was able to take care of himself. In fact he said he would trust Skilt under all conditions.

These assurances quieted the mother for the time being, but there was no change in Skilt's attitude until the very morning of the annual feast. He arose a little earlier than usual, dressed himself with care in his best white and blue long-tailed shirt, which was the prevailing costume of the time for persons of his age and color, and seated himself by the kitchen table where his mother was preparing his bacon and eggs for breakfast. Casting a melancholy glance through the window he looked with abstraction toward the corn-crib, when suddenly he became a changed boy. There, in full view, was a flock of wild turkeys filling themselves with grain.

Immediately Skilt was on his feet. The time for action had come, and he was not slow in availing himself of it. Making his way through the brush to the rear of the crib, he crawled under it to the opposite side where the turkeys were collected, and seized two of the fattest gobblers by their legs. At once the entire flock took wing and flew away, including the two that Skilt had caught; but he was too brave a lad to let go. Manfully he held on as the birds rose above the treetops and then sailed away apparently into the blue sky.

At this moment his mother came out to tell him that the bacon and eggs were ready, when she observed her favorite son almost out of sight and apparently being carried to heaven by winged angels. Greatly excited, she called loudly to the family to come and witness the ascension of her boy, which reminded her more than anything else of the flight of the prophet Elijah in his chariot of fire.

Mr. Tate was the first to appear, and looking in the direction to which the anxious mother pointed he saw Skilt about to disappear behind a bank of clouds. He also realized his purpose in capturing the turkeys, for he had overheard him mourning the absence of the favorite bird on the day of our national festival. But realizing that it would be impossible for the boy to handle two birds of such great size, he made signs for him to let one of them go, in order that he might bring the other in safety to the earth. Skilt understood and obeyed his master's injunction, and in a few minutes was standing at the kitchen door with the larger of the two birds in his hands.

Skilt Becomes the First Airplane

As a reward for his courage and good sense he was given an extra portion of roast turkey at dinner, and his hunger having been excited by his activities he ate more than he should. The result was an accumulation of gasses in his stomach, until the pain became so great that he ran into the yard intending to roll on the grass for relief. But when he came into the heavy outside atmosphere the lighter gasses in his body carried him upward, and encountering an eastern breeze he was blown beyond the middle of Boone County. There he met the gasses that ascend regularly from that quarter, and being heavier than his own they formed a descending current and brought him safely down to earth.

It was several days before Skilt made his way back home, walking the entire distance and subsisting on grasshopper and frogs' legs; and when he appeared at the kitchen door his mother demanded where he had been. He told her a fanciful story about having visited heaven, where he talked with St. Peter and the angels; and might have had an audience with the Higher Powers, but they were busy showing the German Kaiser about the city and getting his advice concerning some improvements which he thought would add to the comfort of the inhabitants. But it transpired that this was merely a trick of the boy's fancy, for on that particular day, his Majesty was in the other place showing the head-master how to regulate his furnaces without interfering with the draught.

While stories of this kind had a tendency to make the boy's associate lose confidence in his veracity, his fame as an aeronaut increased and spread all over the country, until he was invited to country fairs and other places of amusement to "gas up" and distribute posters and advertising matter. This occupation was not only congenial but remunerative, and in a little while Skilt was able to have roast turkey every third day, whether it was Thanksgiving or the Fourth of July.

Uncle Daniel Goes Into Business with Skilt

Eventually Uncle Daniel sent for the boy and made him a proposition which proved to be highly remunerative. Skilt was to "gas up" and sail south of the Missouri River, where there were many bears and large herds of buffalo, and frighten them into swimming to the north bank of the stream where Uncle Danial would meet and attend to them. The partners were to share equally in all profits, which were so large at the beginning that they would soon have become wealthy; but Skilt fell in love with a colored girl in Franklin County, named Elvira Koontz, and neglected his part of the work. The girl's mother also refused to give her consent to the union unless Skilt would agree to quit filing himself with dangerous gasses and imperiling his life; for she claimed that when a man got married he should take care of himself in order that he might look after the wife and babies. She especially objected to her daughter marrying a mere gasbag, who probably would never amount to anything more than a small sized politician. As usual in such cases, Skilt gave up his profession rather than lose the girl of his choice, and of course the partnership with Uncle Daniel had to be dissolved. Skilt married and settled in Boone County, where he became the ancestor of most of the colored people in that section.

Captain Oxley and General Jackson

I must now give some attention to Captain William Oxley, who was a neighbor of Mr. Tate and a man of considerable renown. He won his title at the battle of New Orleans, where he had charge of the flatboat on which was stationed the famous six-pound gun that scattered round-shot over the battlefield. The shot did not hit any of the soldiers, but they lacerated several trees and broke off so many limbs that the left wing of the British army took fright and ran away. It was one of these shot also that wounded General Packenham and caused his death.

General Jackson was so well pleased with Oxley's performance that he commissioned him Captain on the battlefield, and when he was chosen President he appointed him postmaster at a salary of $6.25 a year. As there were only five or six letters annually coming to the post office, the inhabitants protested to Congress that the salary was excessive, and Congress accordingly reduced it to six dollars even, thus making a saving of two-bits annually in the public expenditures. It cost five thousand dollars to get the bill through Congress, but several members secured their re-election by pointing with pride to their industry in protecting the public interests.

Captain Oxley's Hickory Teeth

Captain Oxley was noted for his great strength, which enabled him to do things which other men could contemplate only with amazement. One day he shouldered a beech log six feet long and three feet in diameter, and started to carry it to the fireplace for a back-log. But his foot slipped on the door sill and he fell in such a way that his teeth stuck fast in the floor and were all pulled out when he got up. Being now toothless, his health began to decline from lack of mastication of his food; but one day he read in a newspaper that General Washington had a set of teeth made of hickory wood, and he decided to try the experiment himself. So he whittled the required number of teeth out of a well seasoned axe-handle, and fastening them together with a copper wire, found that they worked satisfactorily. But one morning while chewing a piece of tough buffalo steak his teeth came loose and went down with the steak. For several days he felt uncomfortable on account of the copper wire, but this soon passed away. However, his health declining once more, and made him another set of wooden teeth; but they were scarcely in working order when a young colt that he was breaking kicked them down his throat.

Then he made a third set, which were better than either of the others, but one morning when he got up he saw large deer grazing on the bluegrass in the front yard, and having no other gun convenient he shot it with the family musket. In its recoil the gun kicked his teeth loose and they followed the others into his stomach.

He now began to suffer excruciating pains from indigestion, and on consulting Dr. Paulk was advised to take a dose of his Pink Purgative Pills. These were so effective that they removed his three sets of teeth and several other organs that had been corroded by the copper wire, so that in a short time he recovered his health and became so fleshy that he could not button his pants. But his wife sent him to bed while she made him another pair out of the best buckskin in the house.

Meanwhile his natural teeth remained fast in the floor, where his wife polished them with her weekly scrubbings until they became very bright and beautiful. So he cut them out with an axe, and adjusted them until he could wear them with comfort; but they were so much more beautiful than his wooden teeth that he wore them only on special occasions, such as Christmas, the Fourth of July, weddings, funerals, and other festivities.

However, in the several catastrophes which had beset his teeth, one of the molars had become bent, until it made that side of his face appear larger than the other; and a friend suggested that perhaps an abscess was forming. But he overcame the defect by carrying his quid of tobacco in the opposite cheek, which gave him so much the appearance of being young and round-faced that his wife became jealous and he was obliged to quit chewing tobacco and have the defective tooth removed.

A Hollow Stump Full of Coons

Captain Oxley's health having been sufficiently restored to enable him to resume his former occupations, he went into the woods one morning. The weather was very cold, and he hunted nearly an hour without seeing a sign of a coon. Then concluding that they were in their holes keeping warm, he was about to return home, when he was startled by a peculiar noise. It sounded like a man splitting rails with a maul and wedge, though nothing like so loud. It resembled more the sound of a boy's ball falling to the ground after it has been tossed up.

Proceeding in the direction of the sound, he came upon a very curious scene. It was a hollow stump filled level-full of coons huddling together to keep warm, as pigs do in extremely cold weather. It seemed to the Captain as if all the coons in that part of the woods had assembled there which explained why he had not been able to find any.

He stood for several minutes watching them, and noticed that there was always one coon on the outside, owing to the fact that the capacity of the stump was not quite large enough to hold it. So this extra coon would run around as long as he could stand the cold, and then push his way into a hole at the bottom of the stump. This necessarily crowded out another coon at the top, and he would fall to the ground with the curious thumping noise which the Captain had observed.

The coons kept up this exercise with the regularity of a clock, and the Captain said he could have set his watch by it if he had known the correct time to start with. At length he threw his hunting jacket over the top of the stump and captured the whole outfit, except the one on the outside, which escaped.

The Tall Man of Callaway County

THE TALL MAN OF CALLAWAY COUNTY.

Owing to the excellence of its soil and the sterling character of its citizens, Callaway County had been known for a long time as the "Kingdom of Callaway," and one of the most distinguished residents of the Kingdom was a relative of Uncle Daniel Boone. Was known as "the tall man of Callaway" but as he had never been measured no one knew how tall he really was. After harvest the farmers hired him to stack their wheat and hay, because he could do the work while sitting on the ground and save the tallest stack so it would turn the rain, and of course a man of that kind had his own value. But he never over-charged his neighbors or put on style in the way of fine clothes, as he might have been justified in doing.

He even brought his own luncheon from home, because he said he liked his wife's cooking better than any other; and he hung the bucket in a tall tree where the food would keep cool and the flies would not bother. At noon it was his custom to reach up and squeeze water out of a passing cloud because it was cooler than spring water and free of germs.

The man's farm adjoined Montgomery County, and when he died there was a good deal of contention about getting him buried. He was so tall that while his body lay on his farm in Calloway County, his legs and feet extended over into Montgomery; and the land was so rich that the man who owned it said he couldn't afford to give it away for burial purposes. So they called a meeting of the County Court and agreed to pay him a hundred dollars for half an acre, although it was really not worth more than ten. But when they got the tall man stretched out in a grave his feet were still beyond the line, so that another quarter of an acre had to be purchased at the same rate. They came very near not getting him buried at all, and the farmers said they would not mind keeping a tall man in the county as long as he lived, if they only had a place to bury him when he was dead.

Joseph Lamb and His Wonderful Watch

Joseph Lamb was an old-time school teacher of St. Charles County, and he had a watch which was considered the most remarkable timepiece in that section of the country. It had a brass case and kept such correct time that the government offered to buy it to correct Congressmen when they were making speeches; but Lamb said he didn't feel like he could part with it. In fact he claimed that a thousand dollars in clean cash would be no inducement to him; which will afford some idea of the value he placed on his old brass watch. He said if he was sure another like it could be found anywhere in the western hemisphere he might consider a proposition to sell but he didn't believe there was another such watch in the world; and everybody who knew anything about it said he was right.

One day while the Professor, as he was called, was helping Isaac Fulkerson to bind wheat, his watch fell out of his pocket and was so completely lost that no trace of it could be found. Quite naturally he worried over the loss of his famous time piece, until he fell into a decline, and his neighbors were apprehensive that he was about to pass over. But the following summer while Isaac Fulkerson was plowing for another crop of wheat, he heard a peculiar ticking noise in the furrow behind him, and thinking it might be a rattlesnake he made the most famous jump that was ever known in the Boone country. But finding that no snake appeared, he cautiously approached the furrow, and there lay Lamb's old brass watch ticking away as if nothing had happened. For a full year it had not been wound or regulated, and yet it indicated the time as correctly as it had ever done; which is perfectly true. The incident was related to me by several of the Professor's former students, who said they would vouch for it but when I asked who would vouch for them, they replied that they were on the way to Sunday school and didn't have time that day.

A Buck Eats Hay with the Horses

Early one morning in August Mr. James Suggett of Calloway County, heard a peculiar noise in his barn, and on investigation found a large buck eating hay with the horses. Flies were bad, and in throwing his head around to brush them off, the buck's horns struck the roof and made the sound which had been observed by Mr. Suggett.

Wishing to trap the animal, he pushed the door shut; but the buck plunged through and carried the shutter away on his horns. As he ran across the lot Suggett laid hold of his horns and tried to pull him down, but he got away, jumped the fence and disappeared in the woods. That was the last Suggett saw of the buck or his barn door, until several months after when an Indian called at his house in a state of great excitement and said the devil was eating walnuts down in the woods. Suggett pacified him by telling him there were no devils this side of China, and finally persuaded him to show the way to the place where he had seen the apparition. They had scarcely climbed the fence into the woods when they were startled by a very peculiar noise, as if something were running and slapping the trees with a large board; and on looking in that direction they saw the buck with the barn door still on his head. But on turning to explain the matter to the Indian Suggett saw him a hundred yards away running with all his might and yelling, "Heap big devil!" at each jump.

SUGGETT AND THE BUCK.

Suggett shot the deer and carried it home, and his wife broiled one of the haunches for dinner. But the Indian would not come near. He would neither touch the meat nor stay in the house, but disappeared that afternoon and was never seen again in that neighborhood.

A few months later Black Hawk called on Mr. Suggett and said one of his warriors was "heap big fool" about seeing the devil with a house on his horns, and he had to come to see for himself. When the matter was explained he said the warrior was "heap much crazy" and he would return to the village and make him go with the squaws, as it was not safe for a man of that kind to run at large.

A Man Without Ears

James Ripper of Callaway County had no ears, and he was very sensitive about it. In order to hide the defect he wore his hair long, but when the wind blew the hair aside the deformity was painfully visible. Those who were not intimately acquainted with him supposed he had been in a fight and had his ears bitten off by his adversary, as sometimes happened in those exciting times. But when asked about it, Ripper explained that he had lost the members by trying to be good to a couple of young bears, and he used the incident as an argument against wasting sympathy on unappreciative subjects. He had found the bears in the woods, and wishing to domesticate them, placed one on each shoulder and started home. He got along very well for quite a distance, meanwhile petting the little bears and talking kindly to them; when all of a sudden, and without the least provocation, they reached down and bit his ears off. Their conduct seemed so ungrateful that he threw them down and killed and skinned them on the spot; and took a solemn oath that he never would fool with another bear as long as he lived.

Ripper said that the loss of his ears made no difference in his hearing, because it was not the "flappers" that conveyed the sound. They were merely for ornament. He claimed that if the flappers had been an essential part of the ear a jackass would hear better than a man, but he had compared several men and jackasses and could not see that either had any advantage over the other.

Sad Havoc of the "Hollow Horn"

In early days a disease known as "hollow horn" prevailed quite extensively among the cattle in Callaway County, and many of them died. The only remedy known was to bore the horns of the cattle with a gimlet and let the "bad air" escape. But Ripper thought he knew a better way, so he sold all his horned cattle and bought "muleys" in their place. He did not see how the hollow horn could operate when there were no horns to work on. But his cattle began to die the same as before, and in great distress he appealed to his neighbors for advice. They told him it was positively necessary for the bad air to escape, and as his cattle had no horns he would have to bore their heads instead. He tried the plan and every one of them passed out.

Then he went into the hog business. Now a hog has no horns and of course cannot have hollow horn. But Ripper found that it took as much corn to fatten a pig's tail as it did to fatten the pig, and it consumed all the profit. It seemed as if there was nothing that would pay on the farm. Then a man told him if he would cut his pig's tails off in the dark of the moon it wouldn't hurt the pigs and would leave him a profit. He tried it and it worked. Then the next thing was to raise corn enough to fatten the pigs, and he cultivated his corn until it grew so high he couldn't reach the ears. Thereupon his neighbor Hamlin proposed a partnership, Hamlin was short and stout, and Ripper was long and slim, and by standing on Hamlin's shoulders could reach the ears of corn without any trouble. So they went into business together and made so much money they didn't know what to do with it. Finally they bought a steamboat and loaded it with molasses, and the boat struck a snag and was wrecked, and the molasses made the water so sweet that people couldn't drink it. At last accounts Ripper and Hamlin were looking for jobs.

Episode Number Seventy-Eight

Potlicker Bill

One of the early pioneers of the Boone settlement was known as "Potlicker Bill" but there was a mystery about his name and the place of his nativity. Nobody knew what his name really was, or where he had come from, and as he was very reticent about everything concerning himself he remained to the day of his death a subject of speculation. He never married or left an estate, and no heirs came to claim the few little trinkets that he possessed. When he died he was buried in that part of the graveyard on the hill which had been reserved for strangers. Grandfather carved the name by which he had been known on a block of sandstone and placed it at the head of the grave; but when brother John and I visited the place in 1903 there were no letter enough still visible to enable us to decipher the name in full. Twenty-Five years later the stone itself vanished.

And so passed out of human knowledge a man who deserved something better than oblivion. At present his grave cannot be distinguished from the other indistinct mounds by which it is surrounded. Even if the stone had remained the letters by this time would have been obliterated, until one stone would have been no more eloquent than another in telling where sleeps a man who invented a dish which will carry his name into the ages.

As there may be some who do not know the meaning of "potlicker," I will explain that it is a species of thin soup in which cabbage and bacon have been boiled and seasoned with red peppers, until no good Christian can eat it without saying his prayers. My father was so fond of the dish that he often ate several platesful at a single meal; and I remember one occasion when he said he would like another plateful but did not wish to appear greedy.

Potlicker Bill had no home of his own, but divided his time between Uncle Daniel's and Grandfather's, where Aunt Rebecca and Grandmother Mary assisted him in the concoction of his famous dish. He had plain potlicker every day in the week except Friday, when he ate fish out of respect for the associations; but as time progressed he improved it with additions of several kinds of meat and vegetables, until a devotee of the original potlicker would hardly have recognized the new compound. He would put into the pot fragments of pork, beef, mutton, venison, possum, coon, squirrels, ducks, geese, turkeys, pheasants, quails, and bear and buffalo meat in such quantities as he could obtain; then he would chip in cabbage, garlic, onions, sweet and white potatoes, tomatoes, turnips, parsnips, ochre, beets, corn beans, and any other vegetables that might be handy, and boil the mess until it was reduced to the consistency of a thick soup or stew. He insisted on garlic and onions, because he considered them the most healthy vegetables that grew. Indeed, he declared that any human who would chew garlic as a daily habit would live to be a hundred years old; but those who have tried it tell me that they would rather die young than chew the garlic.

It was a habit of Potlicker Bill to have spells of melancholy, and when I asked him the cause he replied, with hesitation, that in early life he had been accustomed to a diet of garlic and onions, but after he was married his wife objected to the perfume and threatened to leave him if he persisted in the habit. As he could neither give up his wife nor his favorite vegetables, he built a little cabin for himself in the corner of the yard, and they lived separately for several years. In the meantime three beautiful children were born to them, and in order to remove the cause of discord between himself and wife, and insure long life to the little ones, Potlicker was at work on an invention to neutralize the odor of garlic and onions; when one morning they were attacked by Black Hawk and one of his bands, and his wife and children were murdered and their cabin set on fire. But when the chief burst down the door to Potlicker's cabin, intending to slay him also, he caught the scent of garlic, and fled into the forest yelling, "Whoopee! Heap big smell!" It was the "last round up" of the great chief, but all that Potlicker loved and held sacred was gone.

As he related the incident tears welled into his eyes, and he said in a voice filled with emotion, "If my wife and children had been as fond of onions and garlic as I am, they might still be living, instead of their bones bleaching in the ashes of our home." This was the only reference I ever heard him make to his home and family, and his memories of them appeared so sacred that I never mentioned the subject to him again.

Bill's stew was eaten with a spoon, or if no spoon happened to be in sight it was drunk out of plates or tin cups as the case might be. If you have ever eaten it that way don't fail to try, you will be surprised at the richness of the flavor and the fullness of the stew.

Jerry Simpson and the Frog's Legs

The first time that Bill tried frog's legs in his compound it happened that old Jerry Simpson was at our house for dinner; and he ate so much that he began to hop around the kitchen floor and croak like a frog. The family becoming alarmed about the safety of his mind, sent right away for Dr. Young at Marthasville, while another messenger was hurried across the river for Dr. Paulk. Young arrived first and found Jerry sleeping off the effects of his riotous living and a quart of brandy which had been prescribed on suspicion; and when Paulk came he was so furious because they had not waited for him that he administered an extra large dose of his Pink Purgative Pills. After Jerry's recovery he never could listen to the song of a bullfrog without melancholy reflections and unpleasant activities in his stomach.

Bergoo and Kentucky Dew

The stew was introduced into Kentucky in the name of "Bergoo", by which it is still known. It is a popular dish at the races and fine stock shows, where it is served freely to guests in whatever quantities they may desire, either in tin cups or wash-basins. A large pot containing Bergoo is placed on a stump, and every one helps himself according to his appetite and physical capacity.

In former times, before Prohibition, it was the custom to set an open barrel of the best Kentucky Bourbon by the side of the pot of Bergoo, with pint cups for the convenience of visitors; but when Prohibition came the barrel was concealed in a willow grove down by the spring branch and guests stole up through the woods and drank until they were full. Most of them preferred this plan, because it was easier to souse themselves in a barrel than it was with a tin cup. The new plan was so popular that Kentucky came very near going dry at the repeal election and it is claimed that Bergoo's popularity in the Bluegrass State was due as much to its association with first-class Bourbon as to its own merits. But as I never indulged in anything more exciting than sassafras tea, I do not feel myself capable of making a decision.

Potlicker soup was the favorite dish in Femme Osage District during the later years of Uncle Daniel, though it was not known by the Kentucky name. Uncle Daniel favored it because of its influence on bears and Indians. By this time Potlicker Bill had brought his infusion up to its highest state of perfection, but he did not combine it with Bourbon or any other kind of licker. If he had done so it would not have served its purpose as well as it did, for the licker and the garlic would have been about equal in their powers of attraction and propulsion, and thus have held the red warriors helpless in one position, and unable to run away. However, this would have given the pioneers a chance to shoot and scalp them, and the advantage might have balanced the discrepancy.

Repelling Indians with Garlic and Potlicker

Uncle Daniel observed the repugnance of the red warriors to the smell of garlic, and near the close of the war he was preparing to have the forts surrounded with ditches to be filled with the strongest blend of the plant. But when Black Hawk heard about it he came to terms. He realized that it was time to quit fighting; so he came on a friendly visit to Uncle Daniel and proposed to bury the hatchet if the white chief would discontinue his garlic and potlicker campaign. As peace was Uncle Daniel's great objective he gladly accepted Black Hawk's proposal, and the hatchet was buried with appropriate ceremonies.

During their conference the red chief claimed that he had trained his warriors to fight like German "shock troops", but they would not stand before the smell of garlic. It weakened their nerves, neutralized their ardor for battle, and in spite of everything he could do they would run beyond its range. He went so far as to say that if the pale face continued to use the "heap big smell" it would put an end to war and close the way for men to win glory by killing and scalping one another.

Efforts have been made to get this idea properly before the Geneva Conference, by suggesting that when nations feel that they can no longer restrain their ardor, they shall be required to load their cannons with garlic and potlicker; but so far it has not been successful. Herr Hitler claimed that he had been accustomed all his life to garlic as a daily food, and if he should now be deprived of its solace by reason of its military uses, it would excite his ferocity to such an extent that he would be obliged to fight the other nations alone and single-handed. So the proposition has been held up until some method can be devised to pacify the fiery German. It has been proposed that he confine himself to garlic for breakfast and supper, and at dinner eat sauerkraut and drink buttermilk, and see if it would have a restraining influence. But the Herr has not yet communicated his ultimatum.

Bears Flee from the "Great Smell"

As soon as potlicker became the prevailing beverage in Femme Osage District, it was observed that the bears began to migrate. In the short space of six weeks more than five thousand swam the Missouri River and fled southward. In their eagerness to get out of range they departed in droves and herds, not even taking time to pack and ship their furniture. Several ancient heads of families, who by long association had become much attached to their places of hibernation, endeavored to acquire the garlic habit; but their fellow-bears looked upon them with disfavor. A bear that would eat the "great smell", they said, deserved no better fate. Neither were they moved by the argument that it would lengthen their lives to a hundred years, for that would merely emphasize the unhappy conditions. Think of a bear eating garlic for a hundred years they exclaimed! Death itself would be preferable. So the hegira proceeded, until in a short time the country was relieved of their presence; whereupon the pigs held a convention and publicly thanked the growers of garlic for their efforts in bringing peace and security to their homes and families.

The Last Round-Up

Adventures and Romances in the
Last Days of Daniel Boone

Episode Number Seventy-Nine

Uncle Daniel a Failure in Business

In his old age Uncle Daniel had no means of support except his rifle and his traps, and it was his custom during the hunting season to go into remote parts of the country in quest of peltries that he sold for cash in the markets at St. Louis. The proceeds were used for his simple personal wants and the payment of the last remnants of what he considered honest debts in Kentucky and the Carolinas. These obligations had accrued by friends, acquaintances, and even entire strangers, entrusting him with sums of money to be invested in lands, the titles to which afterward proved defective. The failure of the titles was of no fault of his; it was due in most cases to legal chicanery and technicalities; yet he regarded every one of them as a personal debt, and devoted nearly the whole of his life after moving west of the Mississippi to their payment. When the last one had been disposed of, and he was left with four bits (50 cents) in the pocket of his leather breeches, he exclaimed, with a sigh of relief, "Now no man can say that Daniel Boone was not honest!" He said it was the happiest moment of his life, and he no doubt meant what he said. Now and then there are instances of such rigid personal honesty among men, but they are few and far between. It is the rule in such cases to say—and feel—that every one should take his own risk and look out for himself.

Many of these obligations represented, not cash, but preemption land warrants, issued to Continental soldiers in lieu of money, and authorizing them or their successors to preempt government land wherever they chose. Most of these warrants were utilized in the mountains of the Carolinas and Tennessee, where the descendants of the old Revolutionary heroes still live. But many of them were traded around among the early pioneers as "joke money", and were regarded as comparatively worthless. It was this class in the main that found their way into Kentucky and Missouri, and were given to Boone to do "the best he could" with them. If he secured a tract of good land, with a title that held, well and good; but when the titles failed and the warrants were gone, Uncle Daniel made the amount good in hard cash. That was his way of looking at things, and it shows the high character of the man. What percentage of the population now living would do as he did? I shall not judge, least I might be judged myself. But I do not wish to leave the impression that all of those old land-warrants were worthless. On the contrary, wherever the original title was sound the warrants were as good as cash, and many of the finest estates in the Middle West run their titles back to them. This was the idea that dominated Uncle Daniel in his conduct. He knew that the warrants were good, however little their owners might appreciate them, and he believed he was buying sound titles with them; but he was no lawyer! He lost all of his own land by reason of the same lack of professional knowledge and it was an actual fact that when he died he did not own even so much as a grave! He and Aunt Rebecca were buried in soil that belonged to a nephew.

Uncle Daniel Explores the Ozarks

Two years after the exploration into the south-western country, in which my father participated, Uncle Daniel made another venture into the region south of the Missouri River, though more to the northward, on the waters of the Osage and Gasconade Rivers. On this trip he was accompanied only by his black boy Dan, for whom I subsequently obtained most of the particulars. The old hero was now in his 83rd year, and feeling the need of more comforts than he had previously allowed himself, he took along with him a pony, on whose back was strapped the camp equipage and cooking outfit. There were also certain comforts and even luxuries, the whole constituting a burden that he and Dan could not have carried on their shoulders.

In this untrod region into which they were now penetrating, the old hunter expected to find not only an abundance of deer, buffaloes, and bears, but he knew by the nature of things that there were beavers and minks and otters along the water courses, and these animals were of great value because of their furs. On the other hand, it was a dangerous country, for it had been long in dispute as a hunting ground among the Sacs and Foxes of the Illinois country and the Osages of the western prairies; and numerous bloody battles had been fought there. It was in this region that the father of Black Hawk had died while leading his warriors to victory in a battle with the Osages. The red men regarded the forests in which roamed the game upon which they and their families subsided, in the same light that the farmer looks upon his home and the lands surrounding it; and they fought to the bitter end in maintaining their rights.

The Cherokees of the South also had a shadowy claim to the same region, and as they were civilized and better trained than the other tribes, war with them was essentially dreaded. No Osage or Sac or Fox dare attack a Cherokee alone; but when opportunity came, by ambuscade or capture, they never failed to wreak a savage vengeance. The principal towns of the Cherokees were in the vicinity of the modern city of Chattanooga, and in fact constitute a part of the city; and by means of the connecting water courses they traded to a considerable extent with the French and Spanish merchants at St. Louis. Here warriors of the several tribes often met, and while they dared not fight in the presence of the authorities, many an old score was settled under cover of the surrounding forests.

Uncle Daniel's Advice to Dan

Venturing into such a field was more than ordinarily dangerous, for every red warrior, regardless of his tribe, was an avowed and alert enemy. Uncle Daniel realized the fact, and cautioned Dan to be always on guard. "But," said he, in counseling his youthful companion, "it is not necessary or even advisable, to kill your opponent in battle; the better way is to frighten and make him run. The Indian is by nature superstitious, and if you shoot close enough to give him a bad scare he will run away and let you alone. He thinks, for instance, if you clip his scalp-lock, you could just as easily shoot him through the head; and a live Indian running and yelling with fright, is worth more than ten dead ones." Uncle Daniel declared, on this and other occasions, that in all his battles he had found strategy more effective than slaughter.

Dan observed the instructions, but thought to himself that if he saw an Indian about to get the drop on him he would lose no time in deciding where to shoot. Afterward, in his old age, he repeated the instructions to me in his own vernacular, at the same time describing a battle with a par of Osages who besieged them soon after they had gone into camp.

"Marse Dan'l he tole me," "effen we got inter tr'uble wid de sabages, I shouldn't try ter kill um, but jes' shoot close 'nuff terr skeer um; 'kase effen you kills a sabage dat's de eend ob him; he won't hab no erbove a logdozen oders wid him. Darfo', remahks Marse Dan'l, effen we git inter a fight, doan't shoot ter kill, but skeer um bad as you kin."

On reaching the hunting grounds they found a camping place under a shelving rock, overlooking the valley of the Osage River where they had a wide view of the surrounding country but could not themselves be seen. This was another of Uncle Daniel's stratagems. By keeping his own side concealed the enemy could not estimate his numbers, and firing rapidly or in turn, as in the present instance, they would create the idea of a larger force than actually existed. The Indian was never bold in attacking a concealed enemy.

Dan Describes a Battle with Osages

The pony was also taken into the cavern, so as to be out of the way and insure his safety; and having laid in a good supply of venison and bear steaks, they were prepared, if necessary, to withstand a siege. The following morning they were attacked by a band of Osages, and I will let Dan tell the story of what happened:

"So whin de sabages cum wid dar shootin' an' yellin', I 'members de adwice frum haidquatahs, an' de fus' nigger whut pokes his scalp-lock erbove a log, I shoots his top-knot off, an' he shore done some runnin'. Mebbe I tuk a leetle ob de hide wid de ha'r; leastways dat nigger suddenly he wus in a hurry erbout hit. Den 'soon's I git load'n'd an' primed ag'in. Mars Dan'l he shoots de bahk off'n de side ob a tree dat one ob de niggers wus lookin' eround, an' he yelps an' howls laik he had som'thin' painful on he min', an' he lites out fer anoder path ob de country. "Spec" de bahk flew in he eye, an' he wanted ter see a doctah. You see, cordin' ter ohdahs, we nevah bof' shoots at de same time, an' on dar recount de niggers couldn't tell how many we wus, but dey jes' nach'ully s'posed we wus a big lot."

"I bein' re'ddy cocked and primed ag'in, I shoots de scalp-lock offen anoder nigger's haid, an' he yelps an' runs fas'er dan any ob de odders, 'kase he know'd mighty well effen I could shoot off he scalp-lock I might's well plug him straight thro' he haid. Ouah bein' in a cave whar dey couldn't see us, made um kin' a' keerful, 'speshully as dar ole muskets wouldn't soot mor'n fify yahds, while ouah rifles 'd play de debil wid um t'ree times 's fur."

"Hit wus jes' fun fer me an' Marse Dan'l, settin' down dar an' shootin' at dem niggers at ouah le'sure. An' ouah not shootin' at the de same time so conflustered um dat dey didn't know Sunday frum nex' week. So hit did not take um long ter maik up dar min's dat wan't a he'lthy path ob de country, an' dey packed up dar belongin's an' lit out in a hurry. De way dey went wus remahkable. I speck whin dey got home dey tol' de res' ob de tribe dat dar wus a million ob us."

It will be observed that Dan refers to the "sabages" as "niggers", which was an epithet of contempt applied generally by the pioneers. To say that an Indian, or a worthless white man, was "no better than a nigger," was the utmost limit of disrespect; and the negroes used the term as freely and indiscriminately as their masters did. "A no 'count nigger" was the worst specimen of humanity that could be imagined.

Dan's account of the fight reveals Uncle Daniel's strategy at its best. He fought a hundred battles and never killed a man; and yet no other white chief was dreaded by the Indians so much as he. His philosophy that a badly scared Indian running away, was worth a dozen dead ones lying still, was certainly demonstrated in Dan's account of the battle on the Osage.

Dan Rescues a Cherokee Woman

The shadowy claim which the Cherokees asserted to the hunting-ground south of the Missouri River, often brought clashes between their warriors and those of the contending tribes; and as each was fighting what he considered to be thieves and dishonest intruders, these combats were of the bloodiest and most disastrous character. In addition to the glory of acquiring scalps, there was the universal urge to protect rightful property. Therefore no lives were spared, and if occasionally a prisoner was taken it was for the purpose of ending his life by torture at the stake.

In their hunting expeditions it was often the custom of the Indians to take a few of their women along with them, to cook the food, look after the camp, and nurse the wounded should there be any. These women did the hard work of the expedition, and gloried in it as much as if they themselves had taken part with the warriors in their boldest adventures. They also assumed the same risks, for in case of capture it was the rule for them to be tomahawked and scalped; though they were not subjected to the supreme test of the stake. No warrior would have sunk so low in his own estimation, or that of his fellows, as to apply the torch to a squaw.

Dan went out early one morning to look for fresh meat for breakfast, and while stealthily tracking a bear in a canebrake he was startled by the shrill cry of a woman only a short distance away. Anticipating that she was being pursued, and that he would doubtless soon have a combat on his hands, he turned a little to one side of the trail and threw himself on the ground in order to avoid observation. Expecting also that it would be a hand-to-hand struggle, in which his rifle would be of but little use, he drew his hunting knife and prepared for instant action.

The cries of the woman indicated that she was running rapidly and directly toward him, and the fact that there were no answering yells convinced him that she was either being chased by a bear or some lone warrior. It was not the custom of the warriors to make a noise when they pursued or killed a woman; there was no glory in the act. The yelling and the shouting were reserved for deeds of greater moment. Dan therefore concluded that he would either have a bear or a single red man to deal with and in either case a surprise attack on his part would be to his advantage.

Scarcely had he disposed of the matter in his own mind, when a handsome Indian woman, whom he recognized as a Cherokee by her dark color, with a scream more heartrending than any which had proceeded it, caught her foot in some tangled cane and fell at full length across his body. At the same instant the warrior in pursuing stumbled over her and fell; instead of reaching the ground in safety he encountered Dan's upturned knife, which by accident rather than by intention, penetrated his heart and brought the combat to a speedy end.

In order to be prepared for any others who might come, Dan sprung to his feet with his rifle in hand; but the woman, quickly recovering from her fright, assured him there were no others. Inferring by his color that he was a member of her tribe, she spoke rapidly in Cherokee tongue; but seeing that he did not understand her, she resorted to the sign language of her people, and explained that she had accompanied a party of warriors on a hunt; that they had been ambushed and all killed except herself, and that she had escaped by hiding in the cane until the victorious part had disappeared. Then on venturing out she had been discovered and pursued by the lone warrior who now lay dead at her feet. What became of the others she did not know, but they were gone and out of the way; for during the interval the sun had traveled the space of about an hour, as she indicated by pointing.

Dan made the woman understand that he was not an Indian, but "American", and would protect and lead her to safety; whereupon she poured out her gratitude in voluble Cherokee. Though he did not comprehend a word she said, and could communicate with her only by signs, he had no trouble in convincing her of his good intentions; and she gratefully followed him to the camp. There the venerable white chief spoke to her kindly, gave her something to eat, and soon dispelled any lingering fear or doubt that she might have entertained.

Having learned the conditions, and understanding that she wished to make her way to the "big village" on the river meaning St. Louis, where she would meet some of her own people, he and Dan constructed a bark canoe, and supplying her with food and a blanket sent her on her way rejoicing. It would require three or four days to paddle down the river to her destination, and as there were hunting parties of rival tribes in the country, Uncle Daniel cautioned her to travel only at night, and keep well in the middle of the stream where she would be out of range of their muskets. She made the trip in safety, as he learned on his next visit to the city; and having met a party of her own people accompanied them on the journey to her distant Southern home.

"Marse Dan'l, said Dan, a little shamefacedly, after the woman was gone, "I didn't kill dat nigger a-pu'pose. We done it hisse'f. I had my knife in my han' an' he didn't have no mo' sense dan ter fall down an' stick hisse'f wid de blade."

"All right", replied Uncle Daniel, "all rules have their variations, and if an Indian wants to kill himself I don't suppose there's any harm in letting him do it. Any way, this Indian deserved killing, because he was trying to kill a woman."

Friendly Animals

Not long after the incident of the Cherokee woman, the weather changed from balmy September to mid-winter. Snow fell to a depth of several inches, and froze with a glassy surface until it was almost impossible to walk over it. Hunting and trapping were no longer practicable, and Uncle Daniel said they would remain in camp until the weather moderated. They had their blankets and robes, their cooking vessels, and everything necessary for their comfort. Food was the only thing lacking, and that would be supplied. Dan thought of the prophet Elijah and the ravens, for he could not understand how they were to get something to eat without Providential interference. But it turned out as his master had said; food was supplied in abundance. Rabbits and quails come into the cavern seeking shelter and warmth, and as many of them as necessity required were utilized for food.

"It's a strange law of nature," commented Uncle Daniel. "The rabbit and the quail are two of the most inoffensive creatures in the world, yet all the carnivorous animals, including man, eat them. It is true that the quail eats bugs and insects, and perhaps thereby justifies her own fate; but the rabbit confines himself strictly to a vegetable diet. He is one of the cleanest of all the animals, and devours no living thing; yet he never knows what moment he will be eaten by some other animal. He lives his entire span in dread of a horrible death and annihilation; he seems to be about as happy as any of the rest of us, and is certainly just as fond of life."

They had plenty of food, which came to them of its own accord, and rejoiced in the shelter and warmth of the cavern. The birds and animals were a little shy at first, but they showed no real fear of their human hosts. They huddled around the campfire and slept and dreamed in its balmy comfort. "Animals are not afraid of us by nature", remarked Uncle Daniel; "they fear us only because we mistreat them and kill and eat them. For the same reasons we are afraid of the panther and the wild cat, whose conduct in some respects, resembles our own."

The Doe and Her Fawn

One day a doe came into the cavern with her little speckled fawn, and timidly approached the fire to enjoy its comfort. The fawn was so tame that it came and licked Uncle Daniel's hand, but the doe was more backward in her approaches. She stamped her feet and shook her head, as if in general warning of a disposition to fight in case of danger. She had seen her male companion stamp the ground on the approach of an enemy, and perhaps it was the proper thing for her to do. The little fawn would no doubt act the same way when it learned by experience to fear man and other meat eating animals. The deer thinks it is brave and wise to stamp its feet and shake its head in the midst of danger, just as a man gets his gun and makes loud and profane noises to scare away the burglar. When we study them we find that men and animals are very much alike.

Dan reported one morning that they were out of venison, and he proposed to kill the doe. But his master would not hear of such a thing; he said he would as soon kill and eat a member of his family. "We have plenty of rabbit and quail," he said, "and what more could we wish?" So the doe and her fawn continued in safety as welcome guests; and Dan, finding some grass in a secluded place, brought it to them for food. Thus they lived and were happy, until the ice was gone, when they trotted away to their natural element in the wild-woods.

Fight Between a Bear and a Panther

One day they had a visit from different kinds of animals. A loud, growling and snapping of teeth at the verge of the cavern announced the presence of contending beasts, and instantaneously a huge bear came into view fighting back at a ferocious panther. The panther would snarl and leap upon the bear, only to be hurled back stunned and wounded by the tremendous strength of the latter. Several such attacks were made and repulsed, when finally the bear caught his antagonist in his great arms and crushed the life out of it. Only a moment was consumed in the fruitful act, when the bear turned and calmly viewed the inmates of the cave. If he contemplated a similar fate for them it did not appear in his countenance, for he regarded them with a friendly smile. He had only done his duty in protecting his life, and now he was ready to sit down by the fire and warm himself. Bruin is a jovial fellow when he isn't hungry and thinks there is no danger. But when men were not looking for that kind of society, and as the bear began cautiously to approach the fire the crack of Dan's rifle laid its great body heavily upon the floor of the cave.

"Bear meat's better 'n bear company." He coolly remarked as he reloaded his gun.

The skin of the panther was removed and placed among the other peltries, and bear steaks were plentiful from that time until the end of the hunt.

Uncle Daniel Marks His Own Grave

During the time of their stay in the cave Uncle Daniel was taken ill and lay for a week or more in a helpless state, attended faithfully and tenderly by Dan. It was a new experience with the old hunter, and all his philosophy was required to sustain him.

"I am getting old," he said to Dan, as if he had not previously realized the fact. During the whole of his life he had never felt a twinge of rheumatism or any of the complaints that cause so much pain among elderly people. That which others would have called exposure and hardship had kept him healthy and vigorous.

His illness progressed until at length he believed himself to be approaching near to death, when the sun having at last made a rift in the clouds, he ventured out to enjoy its light and warmth. Leaning on the shoulder of faithful Dan, he selected a spot near the camp, and marking the outlines of a grave told the boy that if he died he wanted to be buried there. He showed him how to make a wooden shovel with which to remove the tender earth, and directed that when he was gone his body should be wrapped in his deerskin mantel and blanket and placed in the grave, and covered again with the earth which had been thrown out, to prevent wild animals from tearing or disfiguring his mortal remains.

"And yet," he said, "I have eaten them, and why should I complain if they in turn eat me?"

He further directed that when his body had been disposed of, Dan was to pack their effects on the pony and return to the settlements; but under no circumstances were his remains ever to be disturbed. It was his wish to rest in the woods that he loved so much, where the wild flowers grew and the birds warbled their songs.

The directions were given with the same circumspection and calmness that he would have exercised if he had been planning the last rites of a friend; but fortunately he recovered and returned home to die a year later in his little room in the stone house.

Evidently he had no sense of the fear of death. Descending from Quaker ancestry, he had inherited a philosophy which satisfied his aspirations. We regarded the future either as an evolution into a higher and better state of experience, or an eternal sleep with the rest from trouble and worry. Whichever it might be, he was ready to meet it with the faith of the philosopher.

Beavers and a Panther

As he recovered from his illness and milder weather advanced, he ventured out again to set his traps and resume his hunting operations. Furbearing animals were plentiful in that region, and they would supply the means for him to leave a modest estate at his funeral passing. He was especially desirous to acquire the peltries of beavers, which were more in demand than others and brought better prices in the market. Therefore he hunted along the water-courses where they built their dams and made their homes.

One day he came upon a new settlement of these industrious little animals, and sat on the bank of the stream, plastering the intervening spaces with mud which they carried on their trowel-like tails.

While he watched with intense interest, admiring the intelligence that directed the little workers, a panther glided through the brush that bordered the opposite side of the stream, intent on satisfying his hunger with the flesh of one of the busy throng. So stealthily had been its approach that no harm had been excited among the intended victims, who continued their work with no apprehension of impending danger. Crouching a moment to select one of the most desirable, the ravenous best was about to make his fatal spring, when the hunter touched the trigger of his rifle. There was a crash, a howl of disappointed rage, and the tawny body whirled over and fell with a splash into the brook.

Instantly there was commotion among the beavers, as with shrieks and cries of alarm they dived beneath the surface of the water to escape whatever danger might threaten. But soon regaining their composure, they began to poke their sharp noses into the open air, followed by their lithe bodies as they came to the surface and resumed their labors. They seemed to have no fear of the strange being whom they recognized as a friend, and paid no attention to him as they went about their business.

Death of the Fawn

Weary at last with watching the movements of the little animals, Boone began climbing the hill that sloped down to the brook, and on reaching the summit paused a moment to decide his further progress. Observing a canebrake near by, he started toward it, hoping to find a bear hidden in the thicket. But scarcely had he advanced a dozen paces when a sudden puff of smoke flashed above the cane, followed by the crash of a musket, and out of the thick screen of wild growth dashed the same little fawn which he had sheltered during the storm. It ran straight to him and rubbed tremblingly against the fringe of his leggings, begging protection. The terrified little creature seemed to recognize his as its recent protector, and showed no sign of fear in his presence.

At the same time there emerged from the cane an Indian warrior with his tomahawk in hand, chasing the fawn with the evident intention of hurling the weapon into its body. But seeing the white hunter, he stopped and let his hatchet fall, this being a sign of surrender.

"Me good Injun!" he cried. "Me no hurt white chief!"

Boone thereupon motioned him to advance, at the same time keeping on his guard against treachery. But the savage proved to be a member of the friendly band which had entertained him at the great dog-feast the year before, and the two men were soon on the best of terms. The Indian had gone into the thicket looking for a bear, which he had tracked to the covert; and coming upon the doe and her fawn as they were feeding he had shot the former. The little one, being thus left motherless, the old hunter decided to take with him to the cavern and let Dan care for it, as he had done on the former occasion with the orphaned bear.

The Warrior is Slain by a Bear

The Indian insisted that the bear was still in the canebrake, where it had no doubt gone in search of the doe and her fawn; and having secured his gun the two went in search of it. Following separate paths some thirty yards apart, they advanced cautiously into the lair of the invisible beast.

The little fawn meanwhile followed close upon the heels of the white hunter, trusting him with the same confidence which it had previously reposed in its mother.

The cane was so thick that they were obliged to open their way through the tangled mass with their guns, which they kept ready for instant use. They had proceeded in this way only a few rods, when Boone was startled by a vigorous commotion in the direction of his companion, whom he could not see for the impenetrable thicket. The disturbance was followed by angry growls from the infuriated bear a scream of terror from the Indian, and the stillness of death ensued. Boone knew only too well what it meant; the warrior had been crushed in the arms of the great beast.

Now it was the white hunter's turn, for the bear must be aware of his presence, and would attack him as soon as it was relieved of the fear of the other enemy. Already he could hear its lumbering approach through the cane, though it was still hidden by the thick entangled growth. But a moment later its ponderous bulk came into view only a yard or two distant, almost in reach of its great out-stretched arms, its eyes glaring with fear and the natural hate of the wild animal when driven to desperation. Suddenly it reared upon its hind-feet and bending forward was in the act of lunging upon its foe, when the hunter touched the hair-trigger of his rifle and sent a leaden bullet crashing into its brain. The great unwieldy body fell like an inert log among the cane, and the combat was over. It proved to be one of the largest of its species, the body measuring more than eight feet in length.

It required only a moment's search to find the mangled body of the poor remnant of humanity, the old hunter procured the assistance of Dan, and the two buried the warrior in a place of safety.

A Tragedy in the Widerness

Meanwhile the little fawn remained close to its protector, following him with the trusting faithfulness of a pet dog; at night sleeping close by his side for the sake of the warmth which it found there.

As the balmy weather of spring advanced, and the melting snow portended the annual floods, the hunters gathered their peltries together and loaded them on the back of the pony, set out on their return homeward. The little fawn remained a willing member of the party, browsing on the tender grass and buds which were beginning once more to freshen into life. Under all conditions it remained constantly near its white-haired friend, occasionally rubbing its silky fur against the fringe of his leggings, or licking his hand in tenderest expression of love.

One day, while passing through a long stretch of densely wooded area, Boone leading the way and the fawn as usual frisking by his side, they came near a large fallen tree, whose branches still retained the heavy foliage of the previous summer. When suddenly, without warning, a large black wolf lurched out of the leafy ambush, and with a single stroke of its teeth cut the jugular vein of the little animal. The attack was so sudden and unexpected as to leave no time or chance for defense, and with a gurgling moan of pain the little victim sank to the earth and lay still at the feet of its friend.

But sudden and ferocious as the rush had been, it was not too quick for the eagle eye of Dan, walking twenty paces in the rear. Before the wolf had time to enjoy the fruits of its victory, or poise its body for an assault on the master, the sharp crack of his rifle sent a bullet through the black heart of the black beast, and its body lurched upon the ground. So instantaneously had retribution come that it seemed a connected part of the same tragedy.

Uncle Daniel's Last Exploration

Late in the fall of 1817-18 Uncle Daniel made what proved to be one of the most remarkable excursions in his eventful life, out of which arose the legend of his having died at a deer-lick with his gun in his hands. He was at the time in his 84th year, but still as vigorous as an ordinary man of sixty.

Some of his Indian friends had told him there were "heap plenty" beavers on the upper waters of Grand River, in the region now embraced in the counties of Livingston and Daviess; and they so fired his imagination with the marvelous stories about this distant and unexplored country that he resolved to pay it a visit. Abundant danger lay there, not only from fierce wild animals by which it was infested, but it was in the heart of the hunting preserve which Black Hawk had set apart for the exclusive benefit of his own people; and although Boone and the red chief were personal friends, this relationship would not hinder him from wreaking vengeance if he found the white chief trespassing upon what he regarded as his personal property.

Therefore, Boone resolved to go alone, and not lead any one else into unnecessary peril. If danger and hardship, and possible death, were to be encountered he would meet them in his own person, as he had so often done in the past. His faithful black Dan was surprised at his old master's decision, and when I spoke to him about it in later years he confessed that he had never been able to solve the riddle.

"Marse Dan'l ought to've took me 'long wid him," said Dan, "effen fer no other reason than to paddle the canoe and cook the meat. But he wus clean gone an' out o' hearin' befo' I knowed anything about it."

Procuring a light bark canoe, he loaded his gun and traps into it and paddled up the Missouri River a distance of more than a hundred and fifty miles until he came to the junction of Grand River, which he ascended to a point a short distance south of the present city of Chillocothe. Here he found a cave in a bluff overlooking the river, and decided that it was a good place to camp for the approaching winter. So he proceeded to make the place as comfortable as circumstances would permit, by laying in a supply of meat to serve as food in case he should be besieged by bands of Indians whom he knew were accustomed to hunting in that region. Then he set his traps and began his usual occupation of collecting furs and peltries for the market.

In his daily trips to and from his traps he was careful to conceal his trail from any prowling warriors who might be in the vicinity; and it was well that he did, for only a few days had expired when a company of Indian hunters encamped on the opposite side of the little river, in plain view of his cavern home. They were separated only by the stream and a narrow valley at the foot of the bluff, and across this intervening space a rifle-bullet might easily have found its way. The red warriors would have been delighted to get the scalp of so famous a hunter, and Boone might easily have fired into the heart of their camp had he deemed it wise or prudent to do so.

Fortunately, the very night that the Indians made their camp, snow fell to a depth of several inches, effectually hiding both the trail and traps of the white man; and the savages, being thus unaware of the proximity of their distinguished visitor, spent the time in dancing, singing, and recounting to one another their exploits on other occasions. If they had known he was so close a neighbor the results would have been quite different.

Having plenty of food and pure water that trickled from the roof of the cavern into a pool, Boone withdrew to the most distant part of his quarters, and prepared to await developments. Thus the time went on for twenty days and nights, the white prisoner waiting and watching, while his unconscious captors continued their dancing and feasting. It was like a reversion to the life of the Cave Man, but Boone had been so long accustomed to danger and uncertainty that his present surroundings did not disturb his serenity. Having no need to hurry, he calmly resigned himself to the inevitable and patiently watched the coming and going of the days and nights.

In order to avoid discovery by the Indians, he made a fire to cook his meat only at midnight in the deepest recess of the cavern, where the light could not be seen from the outside; and as additional precaution he ate but one meal each twenty-four hours.

Finally the weather moderated and the snow melted, whereupon the Indians broke camp and took their departure. When they were gone Boone resumed his trapping and hunting, until he had secured what was to him a valuable cargo; whereupon he loaded it into his canoe and set out on his return. But on his way down the great river he met with an adventure which combined romance with peril.

Adventure with a Drunken Indian

Having passed out of Grand River into the Missouri, he landed one evening near the Salt Licks, in what is now Howard County, and there made his camp for the night. After cooking and eating his supper he was about to retire, when he was startled by the loud shrieks of a woman, evidently in dire distress. Seizing his rifle, he hurries cautiously in the direction of the sound, and soon came upon a teepee located on the margin of a spring. By this time the cries had ceased, and there was no sound to indicate that the place was occupied; but by the light of a fire in the center of the place he could see an Indian woman, naked to her hips, her arms tied with thongs to the center pole, and her body partly reclining on the ground. Observing her more closely, he saw that she was in a half-faint, her back bleeding from the blows of some instrument of torture; and as the hunter viewed her through the opening that served as a door, it seemed to him that she was on the point of expiring.

As he was about to go to her relief, a movement on a couch of skins near the opposite wall, revealed a drunken Indian, reclining in the stupor of intoxication. A moment later he arose and staggered toward the woman, a cruel hickory withe in his hand, with which he attempted to renew the torture of the prisoner. But he was so excessively drunk that as he struck at her he reeled and fell to the ground. Again the woman shrieked and struggled to release herself.

Unable longer to endure the scene, Boone pushed his way into the teepee, and stood threateningly over the prostrate form of the drunken savage. Terrified by the unexpected apparition, and supposing it to be an avenging spirit, he lay for a moment in frightened stupor, so paralyzed by fear that he could make no movement.

The aspect of the white hunter must indeed have been appalling to the warrior's guilty conscience, for having left his camp hurriedly without his cap, his long white hair fell to his shoulders, framing a venerable countenance with the appearance of a divine messenger of justice. Presently with a yell of terror, the savage burst through the door of the teepee and disappeared in the darkness.

Quickly slashing the thongs that bound the woman, Boone carried her to his canoe, where having deposited her among the furs, he pushed the craft into the middle of the stream. He knew enough of the habits of the Indians to feel assured that there were other warriors near, by whom he would soon be attacked unless he placed himself beyond their reach. His intuitions were correct, for scarcely had he reached the middle of the stream when a party of six appeared on the bank and discharged their muskets in the direction of the canoe. But the range was so great that the balls splashed into the water short of the mark, except one, which buried itself in the gunwale of the craft. Before the second volley could be fired he had passed out of the reach of danger.

Then letting the canoe float with the current, he examined the woman to ascertain her condition, and was glad to find that she was not seriously hurt. Weak from pain and terror and loss of blood, she lay quietly on the bed of furs, until he revived her with a little water; when she sat up and began to thank him in her own tongue for his kindness to her. Realizing, however, that her condition might grow worse, he arranged the furs into a soft bed, and covering her form with his blanket she soon fell asleep.

A Narrow Escape

Boone now turned his attention to propelling the canoe, for he knew that they were not yet out of danger. At this point the river runs south for some distance, then bends abruptly and continues its eastward course; so that a party on land, by hurrying across the angle, could easily intercept them after the turn had been made. This was precisely what happened! But by paddling as vigorously as possible he outran the pursuers, who appeared on the bank soon after the bend had been passed. Baffled in their purpose, they uttered yells of rage and fired their guns at the fleeing canoe. But the range was too great. The balls fell harmlessly into the water, and they soon retreated back into the forest.

Continuing on down the river for some distance, Boone landed at a point not far from the present city of Booneville, and there prepared breakfast for himself and the woman. By this time the rest and relief from fear had restored her faculties, and in a few words of broken English she explained the conditions under which the white chief had found her. She belonged to the Fox tribe, and had but recently been married to the warrior who had so cruelly abused her. For the first few months he was devoted and they lived happily; but having accompanied him on the hunt to the Licks, he there obtained whiskey and went on a spree, culminating in the wild orgy of brutal torture, some of which Boone had witnessed. Except for his timely interference her husband would undoubtedly have murdered her.

Boone conveyed the woman in safety to the settlements, where she was adopted by a prominent white family, who treated her as their own daughter. When restored to her normal condition and clothed in feminine apparel she was a comely person; and a few years later she was married to a promising young man who was sent as a teaching missionary to the Cherokees of Tennessee, by whom he and his wife were greatly loved for their kindness and devotion. They sleep now in the old Indian graveyard near Chattanooga, and the record of their good deeds is a benediction to those who remember them.

Before her marriage, while she was living with the family of her adoption, the famous Black Hawk visited the community; and on learning her origin tried to persuade her to return to her own people. But nothing could induce her to leave those who had been kind when she was in trouble. In her fancy the great white chief was a saint, sent by the Great Spirit to save her life; and when he died not long afterward the grateful Indian girl was one of the chief mourners at his funeral.

Last Days and Death of Daniel Boone

I t would be difficult to close these Episodes in a better or more appropriate way than with an account of the last days and death of the great pioneer, derived from the memories of my father, who was a youth of twenty-one at the time; and others of Boone's neighbors who were familiar with the circumstances.

The man who laid the foundations of two empires, and cleared the way for the future homes of millions of people, owned not enough land at the time of his death for a grave, and was obliged to borrow a place for his eternal sleep from a nephew to whom fortune had been more kind.

A fatality seemed to attend everything of a material character connected in any way with the name of Daniel Boone. The broad acres which he thought he owned in Kentucky melted away into the hands of strangers; and finally when he supposed that he was secure by action of our own government in the thousand arpents which the Spanish Government had given him in Missouri, the mad river whirled its eddying current and devoured its last square foot.

But who would not rather be Boone, with his purity of soul and the fame that grows brighter with each recurring century, than those who became rich as a result of his sacrifices? If immortality is the chief aim of man, Daniel Boone is richer than any of those who profited by his misfortunes; for the richest of all men is he who is known everywhere for the good he has done.

The immediate ancestors of Daniel Boone were English Quakers, who were persecuted in their native land because of their abandonment of the faith of the Established Church. For this reason they came to America, the land of freedom and religious tolerance. This explains why neither Boone nor any of his immediate family were church members, though membership came with subsequent generations. He was himself a poet of the wilderness and a philosopher whose thoughts were bounded by no creed except the love of humanity. One of his sisters, who remained in Kentucky, a devout Baptist, wrote him several letters urging him to be baptized and prepare for the future. A short time before his death he replied to one of these letters, saying that he had no desire to make a profession of religion, since he had nothing to confess. He had endeavored all his life to live as an honest man, and was willing to leave the decision to that Beneficent Power which had brought him into the world without his volition and had protected him in the many dangers to which he had been exposed. I saw and read this letter, but do not think there was any answer to it. Evidently the sister refrained from further efforts to convert her brother.

On the 18th of March, 1813, the old pioneer experienced the saddest bereavement of his long life, in the death of his beloved Rebecca. For more than half a century she had been an affectionate and sympathizing companion in all his toils and dangers and hopes, manifesting the same generous and heroic sentiments that animated him. She was his inspiration and a fit companion for so noble a character. In their youth they had loved with a devotion that is rarely equaled, and their intimate association had so closely knit their hearts together that they seemed to have but a single wish. In all respects Aunt Rebecca was as great a woman as Uncle Daniel was a man.

They were living at the time of her death at the home of their daughter Jemima, around whose name so much of romance had been woven. The daughter was the wife of Flanders Callaway, and their farm lay in the Missouri River bottoms a mile southeast of the village of Marthasville. When Rebecca closed her eyes and passed into her eternal rest, her body was submitted to the earth in the family burying ground of David Bryan, a nephew and a near neighbor. The spot occupies the end of a ridge, with so much the appearance of a tumulus of the Mound Builders that it was believed to be a cemetery of that ancient people. A small stream, called Teuque Creek, flows at the foot of the hill, and after touching it with a benediction meandering in its course through the bottoms until it empties into the river several miles away. There the old pioneer laid his beloved to rest, and marked a place for his own grave close beside hers.

Little now remained for him but the contemplation of his loss and the winding up of his affairs. The rest of his life was spent like that of the philosopher. In preparation for the final event, he had a coffin of black walnut made for himself, which he kept under the bed in his little room at the stone house. Now and then he would draw out the plain black chest and lie down in it, "just to see if it would fit." In winter he kept it filled with mellow apples, which he shared with the merry children whom he loved so much. Some months later a traveler came to the neighborhood and sickened and died, whereupon Boone, with his customary generosity, "loaned" him his coffin to be buried in. He then had another made of wild cherry, in which he himself eventually slept.

The closing years of his life were devoted to pleasant associations with his neighbors and relatives, and especially with the troops of children who played and romped around him. His experiences as a hunter and soldier had made him a fairly good surgeon, and he understood the medicinal qualities of several plants and herbs in their application to human ills. As there was at the time no regular physician in the settlements, he healed the sick and bound up the wounds of those who were hurt, always without money and without price. He never charged or expected pay for any good thing that he did. Modest as a sensitive woman, he made no pretensions to scientific attainments, yet he did a considerable practice in relieving the pains and ailments of his neighbors, or any stranger who came to him for help.

His spare time was given to occupations that would please or benefit others. He made powder-horns for his grandsons and neighbors, ornamenting them with much ingenuity and artistic taste. He repaired rifles and performed various kinds of handicraft, always without pay or the expectation of it.

Although a "silent man," he was a very genial one, and when he said anything, though it may have been only a word or two, it was always so much to the point that those who heard him thought he had said a good deal. He told stories to the children, but never of a doubtful character, or such as might lead them to admire what is generally termed the heroic. His stories were about nature, and trees, and flowers, and birds, and animals. He seemed to love all animals except the vicious and venomous species.

What a book might be written if these stories had been preserved! His disposition was gentle and refined, and although drinking was a universal custom among the men of his time, he was a total abstainer. No drop of intoxicating liquor ever passed his lips during his entire life, and he was equally abstemious with regard to tobacco. Yet he did not obtrude his opinions upon others. If his neighbors and associates liked a stimulant, well and good. As for himself he cared nothing for it, and made no display of his opinions.

After the death of Aunt Rebecca he removed from his home in the stone house and came and dwelt with his daughter, so as to be near the grave on the hill. But he made frequent visits to the homes of his sons and their families; and the coming of "Grandfather" was always an event of moment in the family history.

With the beginning of the summer of 1820 he paid his final visit to the home of his daughter, remaining there until the early part of September; and it was during this interval that Harding painted his picture. Soon after this incident he shouldered his rifle and walked back to the stone house on the banks of the Femme Osage. Here a lingering fever confined him for some time to the house; but one morning, feeling a little better, he walked over to nephew Jonathan's and sat on the porch talking to him and Mary about old times and the people they had known in former years. He was sad and retrospective, as if contemplating a journey from which he did not expect to return. He said it seemed to him as if his life had been a failure, and he could see no reason why he should longer cumber the earth.

The new crop of sweet potatoes had ripened, and Mary, knowing his fondness for the vegetable, baked a large yellow one for him; and splitting it open laid it before him with a dish of sweet butter and a bowl of milk from the spring-house. He thanked her, and said he believed she could bake sweet potatoes better than anybody else—except Rebecca. Then he lapsed into silence while he ate the delicacy and drank the milk that she had brought him.

That night he was taken with severe pains in the abdomen, probably what is now known as appendicitis; and after lingering three days he closed his eyes and bade farewell to those who stood about his bedside. His last spoken word was "Rebecca!" uttered as he stretched his arms upward as if to greet his beloved awaiting him on the other side.

And so, on the 26th of September, 1820, died the Washington of the West, as peacefully as a little child falling asleep in its mother's arms.

His venerable form, clad in one of his buckskin hunting suits, his snow-white hair brushed back from his forehead, was laid in the cherry-wood coffin and conveyed the following day to the Flanders Callaway home. Meanwhile news of the event had flown over the country, and on the day appointed for the funeral a vast concourse of his neighbors assembled to pay their last respects to the beloved dead. So great was the throng that the house could not contain a tenth-part of it, and the coffin was carried to the large barn, where the mourners filed by and dropped upon the silent face the last tears of love and devotion.

Appropriate remarks were made by Rev. James Craig, a son-in-law of General Nathan Boone, and by Rev. James Welch, who paid an eloquent tribute of love to his old friend.

Then the coffin was carried to the little cemetery on the hill and deposited in the grave close by the side of Rebecca. And so ended the long and honorable life of a great and good man.

Walking, walking,

Always walking,

Toward the West.

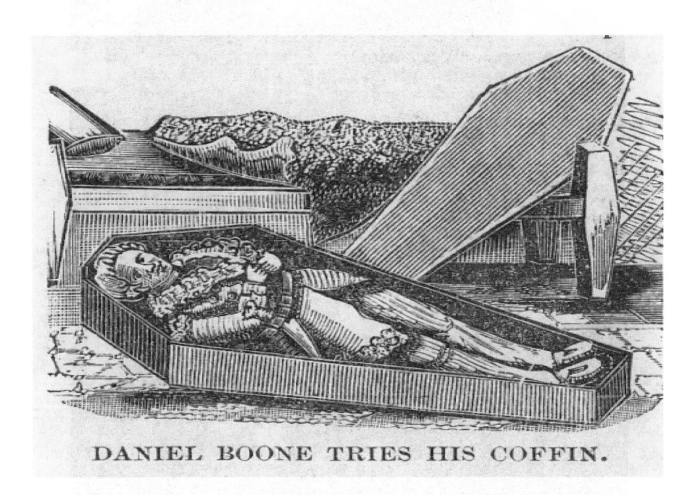

DANIEL BOONE TRIES HIS COFFIN.

Location of the Graves of Uncle Daniel and Aunt Rebecca.

The Daniel Boone House as it Appears at the Present Time.

The old pioneer died in the room to the right of the entrance on the first
floor.

Mss. p. 468
Present Appearance of the Rear of the Boone Mansion.

Circa 1903

On his last Hunting Trip.

Daniel Boone, from a sketch.

DANIEL BOONE

ELIJAH BRYAN.

Born May 5th, 1799. Age, 87 years, 5 months and 14 days. Photographed October 19th, 1886.

JAMES BRYAN.

Born July 29th, 1806 Age, 80 years and 15 days. Photographed October 19th, 1886.

GRACE BRYAN.

Born March 11th, 1807. Age, 79 years, 7 months and 9 days. Photographed October 19th, 1886.

L. E. MOORE.

Born July 24th, 1848. Daughter of James and Grace Bryan. Photographed October 19th, 1886.

HON. J. F. JONES
CALLAWAY CO.

MAJOR BAUGHMAN
THE
MONTGOMERY CO. HERMIT

MRS. SAM. MILLER
THE FIRST METHODIST
OF CALLAWAY CO.

COL. NATHAN BOONE

DANIEL BOONE

HON. IRVIN O. HOCKADAY
CALLAWAY CO.

LOUIS HOWELL.

FRANCIS SKINNER

MRS. REBECCA HEALD.

MRS. THOMAS HOWELL.

Grandfather's Double-Log Cabin, 130 Years Old and still standing.

Jonathon Bryan's

MSS. P. 56. 38

61

at time of Photographing

Grandmother shot the Indian by the side of the tree on right. The Boone stone house is one mile to the right, or east.

built about 1810

occupied as a home

Daniel Boone cabin built in 1795, and

Birth Place of W. S. Bryan Augusta, Mo